CONSPIRACY AND VIRTUE

Conspiracy and Virtue

Women, Writing, and Politics in
Seventeenth-Century England

SUSAN WISEMAN

OXFORD
UNIVERSITY PRESS

OXFORD

UNIVERSITY PRESS

Great Clarendon Street, Oxford ox2 6dp

Oxford University Press is a department of the University of Oxford.
It furthers the University's objective of excellence in research, scholarship,
and education by publishing worldwide in

Oxford New York

Auckland Cape Town Dar es Salaam Hong Kong Karachi
Kuala Lumpur Madrid Melbourne Mexico City Nairobi
New Delhi Shanghai Taipei Toronto

With offices in

Argentina Austria Brazil Chile Czech Republic France Greece
Guatemala Hungary Italy Japan Poland Portugal Singapore
South Korea Switzerland Thailand Turkey Ukraine Vietnam

Oxford is a registered trade mark of Oxford University Press
in the UK and in certain other countries

Published in the United States
by Oxford University Press Inc., New York

First published 2006

British Library Cataloguing in Publication Data

Data available

Library of Congress Cataloging in Publication Data

Data available

Typeset by SPI Publisher Services, Pondicherry, India
Printed in Great Britain
on acid-free paper by
Biddles Ltd., King's Lynn, Norfolk

ISBN 978-0-19-920512-7

10 9 8 7 6 5 4 3

for
Nicholas Wiseman and Tim Armstrong,
and remembering Ian Heavens

Acknowledgements

Work on this project was begun with the support of the Leverhulme Trust and completed with support from the Arts and Humanities Research Board. I am very grateful indeed for their help. I am particularly grateful to the staff at the British Library, particularly in the Rare Books Room. I am also grateful to the staff of the following libraries and archives: Bodleian; Chatsworth Archives; Kendal Record Office; Abbot Hall Art Gallery (thanks to Hannah Neal); Nottinghamshire Archives; Portland Collection, University of Nottingham; Friends' House; National Library of Wales, Aberystwyth; Beinecke; Dr Williams Library; Senate House Library; Birkbeck College (special thanks to Ken Mackley). I am grateful to Manchester University Press and Palgrave Macmillan who gave permission for the reproduction of small portions of material.

I am very grateful to the three readers at Oxford University Press for their detailed and thoughtful responses to my work and to David Carles, Sophie Goldsworthy, Andrew McNeillie, Tom Perridge, Elizabeth Robottom, Christine Rode, and Val Shelley for their help at the Press. Thanks to the following who read parts of this material: Tim Armstrong, Philippa Berry and Margaret Tudeau, Erica Fudge, Helen Hackett, Hilary Hinds, Ann Hughes, Fritz Levy, Peter Mack, Michelle O'Callaghan, Paul Salzman, Julie Sanders, Erica Sheen, Hilda Smith, Rachel Weil. For help of many kinds I am very grateful to Mary Baine Campbell, Bernard Capp, Erica Fudge (again), Anne Goldgar, Margaret Healy, Tom Healy, Kate Hodgkin, Ann Hughes (again), Kate Lilley, Patricia Pender, John Stokes, Alison Thorne, Suzanne Trill, Tim Wales. Thanks to David Norbrook for acting as a referee at two crucial stages. I am grateful to colleagues for discussion—Anthony Bale, Luisa Calè, Stephen Clucas, Sally Ledger, Alan Stewart, Althea Stewart—and to the early modernists: Judith Hudson, Ed Paleit, Lynne Robson, Sam Smith, Liz Stevenson, Thomasin Westcott, Margaret Wilkinson, Liz Wood. Unfortunately the mistakes remain my own. The understanding of Catherine Catrix, Lisa Penfold, and especially Tatiana Dias has helped greatly. Particular thanks to Anne Janowitz for moral and practical assistance over a long period, and for sleuthing in New York. Particular thanks, too, to Rebecca Beasley for she knows what. Much Less Acceptably also played a part. To Tim and Nicholas, who should not have had to put up with this for so long, the greatest thanks.

S.W.

May 2006

Contents

Illustrations

Illustrations 2, 4, 6, and 7 are reproduced by permission
of the British Library. Illustration 7 is from the Thomason Tracts.

Abbreviations

BL	British Library
CSPD	*Calendar of State Papers Domestic*
DNB	*Dictionary of National Biography* (2004)
EAL	*Early American Literature*
ELH	*English Literary History*
ELR	*English Literary Renaissance*
MLA	Modern Languages Association
NLS	National Library of Scotland
HJ	*The Historical Journal*
HLQ	*Huntington Library Quarterly*
HMC	Historical Manuscripts Commission
HMSO	Her Majesty's Stationery Office
JHI	*Journal of the History of Ideas*
PP	*Past and Present*
SEL	*Studies in English Literature*
ST	T. J. Howell, *Complete Collection of State Trials* (London, 1816)
TLS	*Times Literary Supplement*

A Note on Style

In quotation, except where notice is given, such as when j and v are modernized, or where other changes are indicated, the text follows the editions used. For pre-1700 texts place and date of publication only are given in references, except where the printer or bookseller or other information is significant. When the change of year in March versus January is significant it is indicated, but usually the year is taken to begin on 1 January. Reference numbers to tracts from the British Library Thomason collection (e.g. E. 717) have been given as appropriate.

Contentions

Political, (*Greek*) belonging to Policy, or the Government of the Commonwealth, which comprehends the Laws, Order and Conduct to be observed for the Support and Government of States and Societies.[1]

POLITICS, GENDER, AND WRITING IN SEVENTEENTH-CENTURY ENGLAND

Sappho, Eloisa, Mrs Macaulay, the Empress of Russia, Madame d'Eon, etc. These, and many more, may be reckoned exceptions; and, are not all heroes, as well as heroines, exceptions to general rules? I wish to see women neither heroines nor brutes; but reasonable creatures.[2]

Sir William Vavasour's drawing his forces by my house by the King's command, I dare not, I cannot, I must not, believe it, since it has pleased our most gracious King to make many solemn promises that he would maintain the laws and liberties of this kingdom. I cannot then think he would give a command to take away anything from his loyal subjects, and much less to take away my house. If Sir William Vavasour will do so I must endeavour to keep what is mine as well as I can, in which I have the law of nature, of reason, and of the land on my side, and you none to take it from me.[3]

---

[1] *The New World of Words* (London, 1691). The same definition is in Edward Phillips's *The New World of English Words* (London, 1658). John Florio, *Queen Anna's New World of Words* (London, 1611), p. 388, offers 'Politia, *policie, politike or civill governance of a Towne or Commonwealth*'.

[2] Mary Wollstonecraft, *Vindication of the Rights of Woman* (London, 1792), in *Works of Mary Wollstonecraft*, ed. Janet Todd (London: William Pickering, 1989), V, 146 n.

[3] Brilliana Harley to Henry Lingen, 26 July 1643, *Calendar of the Manuscripts of the Marquis of Bath Preserved at Longleat, Wiltshire* (London: HMC, 1904), LVIII, 8.

A comparison of these two passages tells us it is time to look again at women's relationship to politics in the early modern period. The first is by Mary Wollstonecraft, writing in 1792, the second by Brilliana Harley, writing in 1643 when she was defending her castle against the forces of Charles I. Although both passages concern women's relationship to a political world, proximity illuminates their differences. Both passages respond to women's theoretical exclusion from the sphere of political action, but they do so in very different ways. Wollstonecraft appeals to women as a category; there is a contrasting absence of sex as a ground of appeal in Harley's polemic. Where Wollstonecraft argues for women's inclusion in the public arena on the basis of their sex, Harley asserts laws, liberties, and property. Reason appears in each: for Wollstonecraft it is a human characteristic which women can come to share; for Harley it is a law. Harley implies that she can be considered a 'subject'; her political claims are grounded in law, liberty, subjecthood, property, nature, reason, land—not in being a woman. Contrastingly, Wollstonecraft's claims are for 'women'. Given that Harley's claim to act politically is *not* based overtly on her status as a woman, the conceptual underpinning of her words invites investigation. What kind of relationships did seventeenth-century women have to the political sphere and how did women and men think and write about them?

This study uses literary and other written evidence to analyse women's relationships to politics in seventeenth-century England. It takes as its starting place some of the specific characteristics, revealed by even such a brief comparison as that above, of seventeenth-century and later, more modern, texts. What happens when we begin to consider seventeenth-century women's relationship to the political sphere from which they were theoretically excluded? In sum, it becomes clear that the idea that women were excluded from the political sphere, far from meaning that women and politics had no link, rather shaped the ways in which that connection was registered in writing. Analysis of the languages which did relate women and politics makes clear that commentary on politics, on the one hand, and claims now recognizable as feminist, on the other, were neither synonymous nor, necessarily, interwoven. Examination of the canon of political theory (narrowly defined) and its formation in modern times suggests that this material alone is unlikely to adequately disclose women's relationships to politics. Therefore, each of the ensuing chapters assesses an aspect of the way women and the political realm relate to one another; each chapter addresses the way that the exclusion of women from the political arena produces a figurative, oblique, complex, politics. Methodological and conceptual questions attend analysis of writing which articulates the complex, unstable, and implicitly politicized situations of women. The first issue is the selection of material for study—which period, which texts, which contexts tell us about this topic? But the issue of approach is of equal importance. At times strikingly familiar but also strange, the early modern world is paradoxically close and distant. Any emphasis on recovery must coexist with reflection on the methods and difficulties of that task.[4]

Let us take the question of period first. Consideration of the ways in which we can find women's relationships to politics in early modern texts, and the forms that those relationships take, bring to the fore issues about temporality and periodicity to which I will return below. However, in thinking about gender and politics in seventeenth-century England it can be helpful to keep in mind a broad distinction between the linguistic, symbolic, and imagistic resources available to imagine the political realm and political action—what might be called the political imaginary—in modern and early modern times. That broad contrast, defining the temporal scope of the study, also allows us to begin to see the specifics of the way early modern imaginative writing shapes women's relationship to politics. While there are, clearly, changes in writing about women and politics in the mid- to late seventeenth century, this is not a study of decline or improvement. This project's argument concerns women's relationship to politics at a particular time; it neither involves a long enough timescale nor deals with the kind of material which offers information on improvement or decline.[5] The kind of discursive and ideological shifts examined in this study reveal

---

[4] See Danielle Clarke, *The Politics of Early Modern Women's Writing* (London: Longman, 2001), pp. 1–15. For an overstated but bracing critique of feminist scholarship as hagiographic see Jonathan Goldberg, *Desiring Women Writing* (Stanford: Stanford University Press, 1997).

[5] On periodicity and progress in women's history see Amanda Vickery, *The Gentleman's Daughter: Women's Lives in Georgian England* (New Haven: Yale University Press, 1998), pp. 1–10; A. J. Vickery, 'Golden Age to Separate Spheres: A Review of the Categories and Chronology of English Women's History', *HJ* 36, No. 2 (1993), pp. 383–414.

ways of knowing, and of imagining, rather than improvement or
deterioration in the lot of women.

Nor, indeed, does the material encountered here invite us to return to
the prolonged and irresoluble debate about whether royalism or radicalism was better for women, though they were different. The concern
here is, rather, women's relationship to the political sphere at a specific
time. The study covers the period from 1620 to 1688, attending pre-
eminently to the period of and after the Civil War. During this period
many, perhaps most, men and women paid attention to politics; the
conceptual issues raised by war affected most writers. Concomitantly,
intense political motivation brought to the fore writers of relatively
diverse status; the bottom of the social order canvassed in this study is
represented by a labouring woman, a seamstress who obviously also had
connections with the book trade. Lengthy writings from those of the
lowest social status may come to light, but below a certain level of
prosperity hardship inevitably militates against textual production. At
the same time as political upheaval created political readers and writers,
surviving texts and debates indicate that gender was not peripheral but
instead central to political thinking and writing. While gender is, as we
shall see, important at particular points in political theory, it was even
more consistently important in how politics was imagined and the
languages in which it was debated. Moreover, during this period
women made significant contributions to a range of discourses considered at the time to articulate political concerns—poetry, letters, memoir,
scandal, drama, utopia.

Two further, equally strong, reasons to study this period are its
historiographical centrality and its importance to narratives of political
and feminist theory. The seventeenth century has been crucial to the
canon of political theory as a time of epochal shift in two, linked,
teleological narratives of the emergence of modernity: first, the rise of
liberalism and contract theory, second, the story or stories, of the
changing relationship of the public and private spheres. The position
of women was significant within the texts used in each debate and, as
importantly, the significance of women and gender in mid-seventeenth-
century England has been the focus of many critical interventions by
contemporary social and political theorists. In so far as there is a debate
on women's relationship to the early modern political sphere it is to
be found, as we will see, in writings on contract theory (including

discussion of the public and private spheres) and in debate on the question of feminism in the early modern period.

In terms of the selection of material, there is at first sight a dearth of evidence of women's political action. After all women were in general assumed not to be involved in politics in seventeenth-century England, and that assumption was conceptually and ideologically significant for contemporaries, notwithstanding evident exceptions in the material world.[6] However, the question of what texts, situations, or writers reveal or suggest about women's relationship to politics brings a wealth of material into view, for women were inevitably, consistently, *in relation to* a political sphere from which they were also imagined as excluded. Very many early modern writings articulate, trope, or image that association. Exploration of the politicized subject from this vantage point suggests that there are many stories of women's relationship to politics that have not been told, and many stories which, in being told, have shed their politicized dimensions. To attend to such stories is not to invent heroines or to write saints' lives. The circulated writings of Elizabeth Jekyll and Mary Love, or the letters of Rachel Russell, or the familial politics linking Anne Bradstreet and the prophet Elizabeth Avery, have much to tell us about the connections of women to the political realm, and what those meant for men and women. Here I attend to those which, analysed from a literary perspective, illuminate political issues and languages. Collectively, these writings show women's relationships to politics articulated in the interstices of what then seemed to be private or public; in the importance of reason on the one hand and affect on the other; in the extensible meanings of virtue; in the power of genre; in modes of production and circulation; in the tense links between politics, religion, family, and the desire for order. Thus, rather than follow the example of scholarship which attends primarily to the coherent arguments of political theory and treatises, I explore many different kinds of writing. Besides well-known figures such as Aphra Behn, Anne Bradstreet,

---

[6] Hilda Smith, *All Men and Both Sexes: Gender, Politics, and the False Universal in England, 1640–1832* (University Park: Pennsylvania State University Press, 2002); Patricia Crawford and Sarah Mendelson, *Women in Early Modern England, 1550–1720* (Oxford: Oxford University Press, 1998); Alice Clark, *The Working Life of Women in the Seventeenth Century* (London, 1919; repr. London: Routledge, 1992); Barbara Harris, *English Aristocratic Women, 1450–1550* (Oxford: Oxford University Press, 2002); Amy Louise Erikson, *Women and Property in Early Modern England* (London: Routledge, 1993).

Margaret Cavendish, Queen Christina of Sweden, John Milton, and John Lilburne, the writings of figures such as John Bargrave, Elizabeth Poole, Lady Rachel Russell, and Sarah Wight are discussed. While this is not a study of religion, the centrality of religious thought and the interlacing of political and religious motivation logically require attention. For many of the writers studied here, even as they do at times explicitly struggle to separate the two, religion and politics continually impact upon one another. The Bible, after all, was often read as the foundational theocratic text, and religious belief provided justification for political actions.[7] In teasing out the political implications of Sarah Wight's experience of grace or, indeed, the ways in which Queen Christina of Sweden was perceived during the English Republic, religion is very important. However, the evidence indicates that although religion was undoubtedly a central concern for almost all the writers studied, politics and religion were not for them synonymous, nor was one subsumed by the other. Sarah Wight, for example, seems to have struggled fiercely to have her words understood as spiritual exegesis rather than political commentary. Yet she also seems to have been happy for the same spiritual words to be published in a highly politicized context. The importance of religion, therefore, is recognized in the scope of the study and in its architecture: The focus is substantially, though not exclusively, on writing which has affiliations to what can be broadly defined as Protestant ways of thinking about the politics of seventeenth-century England.

In canvassing a relatively broad spectrum of mainly, but not exclusively, Protestant writers and situating sectarians and royalists in relation to each other, this project complements work on women's place in the politicized languages of royalist and sectarian cultures.[8] Critics and historians have

---

[7] See e.g. Katharine Gillespie, *Domesticity and Dissent in the Seventeenth Century: English Women Writers and the Public Sphere* (Cambridge: Cambridge University Press, 2004), and Erica Longfellow, *Women and Religious Writing in Early Modern England* (Cambridge: Cambridge University Press, 2004).

[8] See Hero Chalmers, *Royalist Women Writers 1650–1689* (Oxford: Oxford University Press, 2004); Hilary Hinds, *God's Englishwomen: Seventeenth-Century Radical Sectarian Writing and Feminist Criticism* (Manchester: Manchester University Press, 1996); Elaine Hobby, *Virtue of Necessity* (London: Virago, 1988); Phyllis Mack, *Visionary Women: Ecstatic Prophecy in Seventeenth-Century England* (Berkeley and Los Angeles: University of California Press, 1994); on the later period see Carol Barash, *English Women's Poetry 1649–1714* (Oxford: Clarendon Press, 1996).

examined the ideological connections between royalism and feminism.[9] Others have interpreted the politics of sectarian women's writing, paying close attention to the nature of prophecy and women's speech and writing within the sects.[10] However, through the examination of a wide swath of Protestant thought, interrelationships as well as boundaries are revealed. Indeed, even where strongly 'internal' modes of thought and writing existed, as in the sects during the 1640s, these writings had connections to the wider world. To see, as I do, diverse writings as, at times, related, is not, however, to argue that the category of 'woman' overrode the categories of 'religion' or 'politics' for early modern writers. Nor is it to suggest that male writers of all religious or political views somehow banded together with the express purpose of excluding women from the political sphere. Rather, there are very clear interrelationships between polemical Protestant writings and the wider culture which received and responded to them, and ideological differences can coexist with generic similarities. Thus royalists and radicals attack, even imitate, one another's style. Pro-Stuart writers reconsider their past in the light of the events of the Restoration, as do nonconformists. The concentration on Protestant politics further allows us to trace some of the political impact of the counterpoint authors make of Protestantism, Catholicism, and classical philosophy. In sum, my overarching narrative and argument follow the thread of women's place and participation in the Protestant debates of the Civil War into the Restoration, yet it is also necessary to attempt to do justice to relationships across political divides.

At the same time, a concern to develop an analytical method suitable to the complex representations on view, rather than a desire to fit them into an overarching narrative of change or progress, shapes this study's choice of materials and moments. The exclusion of women from politics is imaginatively important in several ways. Practice varied but, at least in theory, women were often excluded from many forms of

[9] Barash, *English Women's Poetry, passim*; James Loxley, *Royalism and Poetry in the English Civil Wars* (Basingstoke: Macmillan, 1997); Timothy Raylor, *Cavaliers, Clubs, and Literary Culture* (Newark: University of Delaware Press, 1994); Hilda Smith, *Reason's Disciples* (Urbana: University of Illinois Press, 1982).

[10] Hinds, *God's Englishwomen*; Hobby, *Virtue of Necessity*; Mack, *Visionary Women*; Diane Watt, *Secretaries of God: Women Prophets in Late Medieval and Early Modern England* (Cambridge: D. S. Brewer, 1997).

government and politics in sixteenth- and seventeenth-century Europe. At the start of our period the influential translation of Jean Bodin's *Six Books of Commonweal* (1606) gives a flavour of the interdiction: 'I think it meet for them to be kept far off from all magistracies, places of command, judgements, public assemblies, and counsels.'[11] In *De Republica Anglorum* (1583) Thomas Smith had acknowledged that the ruler might be female but had dealt with women specifically in the sections on the growth of families into commonwealths and in a brief section on wives and marital contracts.[12] Famously, in the *Discourses* Machiavelli's discussion of women's relationship to politics concerns how they have brought about 'the downfall of states'.[13] As we shall see, seventeenth-century contract theorists and patriarchalists tackled women's relationship to the political sphere in greater detail, but what each group has in common is that it tends to fall back on the implicit assumption that female authority was circumscribed in being over children or based within the family.

In terms of legal theory, in T.E.'s *The Lawes Resolution of Womens Rights* (1632) Eve's sin was presented as accounting for women's lack of political voice:

Eve because she had helped to seduce her husband hath inflicted on her, an especiall bane. *In sorrow shalt thou bring forth thy children, thy desires shall be subject to thy husband, and he shall rule over thee.*

See here the reason of that which I touched before, that women have no voyse in Parliament, they make no Lawes, they consent to none, they abrogate none. All of them are understood either married or to be married and their desires or subject to their husband, I know no remedy though some women can shift it well enough.[14]

T.E.'s comment, that 'some women can shift it well enough', even as it is misogynistic, also seems to acknowledge a tension between theoretical statements and social relations. The clear statement of theory does not, for him, tell the whole story. In English law, famously, the relationship between father or husband and governor was dramatized by the fact that

---

[11] Jean Bodin, *Six Books of Commonweal*, trans. Richard Knolles (London, 1606).

[12] Thomas Smith, *De Republica Anglorum* (London, 1583; repr. Menston: Scolar Press, 1970), pp. 43, 101–6, 12–13.

[13] Niccolò Machiavelli, *The Discourses*, trans. Leslie J. Walker SJ, ed. Bernard Crick, rev. Brian Richardson (Harmondsworth: Penguin, 1979), pp. 477–8.

[14] T.E., *The Lawes Resolution of Womens Rights* (London, 1632), p. 6.

the murder of a husband was petty treason. Yet, significantly, the idea that women were, except in exceptional cases, excluded from the sphere of official politics and subject to a husband may have produced an opacity in consideration of them. Is a female grain rioter transgressing the law of government or family? When a woman writes of state matters and policy—as do Dorothy Sidney (the sister of the republican Algernon Sidney), Rachel Russell, Brilliana Harley—are they gossiping or entering into a public sphere where government can be criticized? Is a woman's printed petition on behalf of her husband or John Lilburne a political or a 'private' matter? Each question indicates the way women's theoretical exclusion provided the languages in which their political involvement was to be debated. Evidently, one of the shared contexts of all the writers discussed was the shaping of their discursive world by firmly held if contradictory ideas about women *per se* and women's relationship to politics.[15] Though relatively stable and certainly readily available, such precepts were in a dynamic, not a static, relationship to the cultures that produced them.[16]

Women's exclusion from the political sphere had, for the purposes of this present study, two effects. First, it meant that the category of women, though not an official political category, consistently influenced discourse on and of politics. Secondly, the idea of exclusion makes literary and cultural production a very rich source for the examination of political attitudes and understandings in both men and women: exclusion makes figural language, myth, narrative, and poetry crucial modes of political expression. Thus, in considering the relationship between women and politics in the early modern period, writing and cultural production more widely are of central importance. Such texts enable us to trace not only the 'facts' of women's interventions in political networks but the conceptualizations of women's relationships to politics at distinct social levels and from a range of views. Correspondingly, many kinds of writing illuminate the ways in which women's official exclusion from the political sphere seems to have taken effect in shaping their cultural interventions and their place in the political

[15] Pedagogic anthologies include such material: Kate Aughterson, *Renaissance Women: A Sourcebook* (London: Routledge, 1995); N. H. Keeble, *The Cultural Identity of Seventeenth Century Woman: A Reader* (London: Routledge, 1994).

[16] A helpful summary of sources of such ideas is Merry Weisner, *Women and Gender in Early Modern Europe* (Cambridge: Cambridge University Press, 2000), pp. 13–47.

imaginary. Theoretically without relation to politics except through the male, women's relationship to politics has a vivid figurative life in written and visual texts. Myth and fiction give shaping force to cultural conceptions generally, and in specific cases they can generate as well as register understandings of women's relationships to the political sphere.[17] To give a brief example, the resistance theorist Christopher Goodman attacks Mary Tudor as a 'wicked Iezebel: who for our sinnes, contrarie to nature and the manifest word of God, is suffred to raigne over us in Goddes furie'.[18] Typical in its use of analogy rather than argument to elucidate women's relation to politics, Goodman's splenetic use of example cannot efface the very female rule it condemns: the example of Jezebel acknowledges female rule even in the very act of refusing it.

My main question, then, is how we can map, or remap, the way in which women's relationship to politics was imagined and represented in early modern England. This question necessitates two approaches: a re-examination of many early modern texts discussing authority, honour, identity, gender, and political events in the early modern period; and a reconsideration of the analytical writings debating early modern women's relationships to politics which are dominant within literary and other disciplines. Most of this study will canvass the rhetorics of political relationship in early modern texts. The next section of this introduction, however, provides a more precise location of the study in the existing critical debates on women and politics.

CONTEXTS

This study's primary aim is to explore women's relationships to politics in some of the extensive seventeenth-century evidence. Three critical debates have influenced the way this relationship has been understood. The debates are as follows: discussion of the rise of feminism and its possible pre-history in seventeenth century writing (in literary criticism

---

[17] Margaret Whitford, *Luce Irigaray: Philosophy in the Feminine* (London: Routlege, 1991), p. 185.
[18] See Christopher Goodman, *How Superior Powers Ought To Be Obeyed* (Geneva, 1558), p. 9.

and in history); the discussion of contract theory (within the discipline of political science); the cross-disciplinary discussion derived from Habermas's work on the public sphere. The present study is situated in relation to these debates, draws on materials generated by them, but remains methodologically distinct from them.

The disciplines of literary criticism and history offer nuanced accounts of gender and its contradictions in seventeenth-century England. Within literary studies, particularly, this account is grounded in questions about gender and the Renaissance. When, in *The Civilisation of the Renaissance in Italy*, Jacob Burckhardt told his reader that amongst the elites Renaissance women and men 'stood on a footing of perfect equality' his comment seemed, almost, an aside.[19] Yet it has set the parameters of what has become a mighty debate on women, equality, and feminism. Did the Renaissance, and indeed the seventeenth century, see an improvement in the lot of women? How might that be measured?[20] Joan Kelly-Gadol's response to Burckhardt asks 'Did women have a Renaissance?', and she answers by contrasting 'the emancipation of women' with that of men. This comparison generates Kelly's brilliant insights concerning the gendered impact of social and cultural change which animate her foundational essay.[21] Yet, having taken its cue from Burckhardt, her argument is tied to the question of improvement or decline for women.[22] Much subsequent literary-critical writing on women's relationship to politics has taken up the question of

---

[19] Jacob Burckhardt, *The Civilisation of the Renaissance in Italy*, trans. S. G. C. Middlemore (Harmondsworth: Penguin, 1990), p. 250. Two fascinating studies responding to the question of women's relationship to great events and social structures are Constance Jordan, *Renaissance Feminism: Literary Texts and Political Models* (Ithaca: Cornell University Press, 1990); Weisner, *Women and Gender*.

[20] See Weisner, *Women and Gender*, pp. 1–7.

[21] Joan Kelly-Gadol, 'Did Women Have a Renaissance?' in her *Women, History and Theory* (Chicago: University of Chicago Press, 1984), pp. 19–50; repr. in *Feminism and Renaissance Studies*, ed. Lorna Hutson (Oxford: Oxford University Press, 1999), pp. 21–47: 21.

[22] Thus, while in the specific period of this study some, like Hilda Smith, see sectarian religion and republican politics as privileging men and excluding women, others, like Barbara Taylor, restate the importance of radical religion as part of a prehistory of feminism. Two illuminating studies taking opposite views: Smith, *All Men*; Barbara Taylor, *Mary Wollstonecraft and the Feminist Imagination* (Cambridge: Cambridge University Press, 2003), pp. 95–142.

the emergence of a feminist tradition, or 'pro-woman argument'.[23] From Isabella Whitney to Aemilia Lanyer and Judith Drake, it is certainly the case that early modern writings by women and some men shape criticisms of political and social structures which systematically privilege men.

Yet, as critics reading Katherine Philips, Lucy Hutchinson, Margaret Cavendish, Katherine Chidley, Elizabeth Poole, or Anna Trapnel are aware, at other moments, and in other texts, such writers focus on church government or political power. Women were to be obedient to their husbands but also to God. They were subordinate, yet ran households. Men and women offered arguments about women, but their engagements with political arguments did not always begin with or become arguments about women. Moreover, as indicated by Ann-Rosalind Jones's analysis of the ways in which women negotiate genres in order to make them productive for themselves, women's relationships to writing were complex. Women cannot helpfully be understood as simply excluded from kinds of writing, nor can their relationships to genre be understood simply in terms of appropriation or subversion without giving an excessively generalized account of men's and women's understandings of genre and rhetoric.[24]

Although in pursuing politics rather than feminism the aim of this study is distinct from historical and literary-critical work on the genealogy of feminism, such work forms a crucial context for it. However, evidently, to study the connections between political debates and gender *solely* through the question of feminism—or indeed, solely through writings by women—would narrow the field of material available. To study pro-women writing alone would put early modern texts in the service of a genealogy of feminism: the future of feminism, emerging from the early modern period, becomes the issue. As scholars recognize, in early modern England attitudes to gender were contradictory and complex.[25] Although some political writing does address the condition

---

[23] Jordan noted that to discuss feminism in the Renaissance is problematic, and offers 'pro-woman argument' as a cumbersome but more accurate substitute (*Renaissance Feminism*, p. 2). See e.g. Anna Maria van Schurman, *Whether a Christian Woman Should Be Educated*, ed. and trans. Joyce L. Irwin (Chicago: University of Chicago Press, 1998).

[24] Ann-Rosalind Jones, *The Currency of Eros: Women's Love Lyric in Europe, 1540–1620* (Bloomington: Indiana University Press, 1990).

[25] Patricia Crawford, ' "The Poorest She": Women and Citizenship in Early Modern England', in *The Putney Debates*, ed. Michael Mendle (Cambridge: Cambridge University Press, 2001), pp. 197–218: 199 and *passim*; Smith, *All Men*, pp. 73, 86–107; Laura

of women specifically, a broader approach is to ask, with Hilda Smith, what politics meant for early modern women and—reciprocally—what they meant for politics.[26] Thus, the present study begins by asking: how was women's relationship to the political sphere imagined and expressed by men and women writing in seventeenth-century England? The second debate which impinges on this study is that concerning the relationship between the public and private spheres. I turn to Jürgen Habermas's discussion of the public sphere in modernity, not to situate the emergence of a literary public sphere earlier or later than he suggests, nor to apply his model, but to indicate the nature of this study's relationship to Habermasian thinking. It might seem axiomatic that to write about the political is to write about the public, but once we begin to consider women's relationship to politics in terms of manu-script writing, images, examples, the division of public versus private proposed by Habermas has some perceptible limitations. Although *The Structural Transformation of the Public Sphere* is 'an historically saturated discourse of society', Habermas engages with history in the interests of an analysis of the emergence of modernity which he views as an 'unfinished project'.[27] In his argument the seventeenth century features as a turning point. Habermas selected the Glorious Revolution (1688) as the moment at which the public sphere, as he understands it, emerges in Europe. For Habermas, 'The bourgeois public sphere may be con-ceived above all as the sphere of private people come together as a public', and within it 'The medium of political confrontation was peculiar and without historical precedent: people's public use of their reason.'[28] Responses to Habermas have engaged with ways in which his historically narrated model might be used to analyse the early modern period. Several writers on the English revolution, most notably David Norbrook and David Zaret, have asked about the

Gowing, *Domestic Dangers: Women, Words and Sex in Early Modern London* (Oxford: Clarendon Press, 1996); Lois G. Schwoerer, 'Women's Public Political Voice in England, 1640–1740', in *Women Writers and the Early Modern British Political Tradition*, ed. Hilda Smith (Cambridge: Cambridge University Press, 1998), pp. 56–74.

[26] *Women Writers*, ed. Smith, p. 2.

[27] Joan Landes, 'The Public and the Private Sphere: A Reconsideration', in *Feminists Read Habermas*, ed. Johanna Meehan (London: Routledge, 1995), pp. 91–112: 93; Jürgen Habermas, *The Structural Transformation of the Public Sphere*, trans. Thomas Burger with Frederick Lawrence (Cambridge: Polity Press, 1989), p. 3.

[28] *Structural Transformation*, p. 27.

political nature of exchanges in the public sphere.[29] Feminist writers, particularly those discussing the French Revolution, have debated the potential existence of counter- or multiple public spheres and women's use of critical reason.[30] Thus, writers have sought to reintroduce a concern with politics to Habermas's model, to raise the question of gender in relation to it, and to discuss its historicist potential as a description of epochal shifts. To what extent can Habermas's narrative be reworked to contribute to an historicist study of gender and politics?

Significantly, behind Habermas's bourgeois public sphere we can trace the split between private and public found in Greek philosophy. Habermas indicates that in delineating the public sphere in modernity he is returning to concepts of Greek origin. In the division between *oikos* and *polis* male householders move freely into the *polis*, the sphere of public action. The term *polis* reminds us of that term and sphere which Habermas reconfigures as the public—the political. Habermas is in part responding to Hannah Arendt's commentary on the private and the public, and a return to her writing reminds us that he has chosen the term public over the term political. Arendt, less optimistic about modernity than Habermas, locates the public realm as the political and understands modernity as characterized by the substitution of the realm of the social for that of the political.[31] Arendt distinguishes 'a private and a public sphere of life' in which 'the household and the political realms ... have existed as distinct, separate entities at least since the rise of the ancient city-state'.[32] She notes that 'the privative trait of privacy', whereby 'a man who lived only a private life ... was not fully human', was central to the classical concept of the private.[33]

---

[29] David Norbrook, *Writing the English Republic: Poetry, Rhetoric and Politics 1627–1660* (Cambridge: Cambridge University Press,1998), pp. 12–14; David Zaret, *Origins of Democratic Culture: Printing, Petitions and the Public Sphere in Early-Modern England* (Princeton: Princeton University Press, 2000), pp. 3–17 and *passim*; Joad Raymond, *Pamphlets and Pamphleteering in Early Modern Britain* (Cambridge: Cambridge University Press, 2002).

[30] Joan Landes, 'The Public and Private Sphere', in *Feminism: The Public and the Private*, ed. Joan Landes (Oxford: Oxford University Press, 1998); Marie Fleming, 'Women and the "Public Use of Reason"', in *Feminists Read Habermas*, ed. Meehan, pp. 117–36.

[31] Selya Benhabib, 'Models of Public Space: Hannah Arendt, the Liberal Tradition, and Jürgen Habermas' (1992), repr. in *Feminism*, ed. Landes, pp. 65–99: 72.

[32] Hannah Arendt, *The Human Condition* (Chicago: University of Chicago Press, 1958), p. 28.

[33] Ibid., p. 38.

For Arendt, public action was founded on the 'destruction of all organized units resting on kinship'.[34] For Habermas, participation in the bourgeois public sphere rests on a property qualification but, after admission to this sphere, the individual participates in an agonistic community of discussion whose ideals (if not practice) involve the abrogation of hierarchy based on wealth and status. The split between *oikos* and *polis* (fundamental to Arendt's conception of the political and Habermas's understanding of the public) exists in order to enable the masculine political agent. However, the sharp split between *oikos* and *polis*, so important for Arendt and Habermas, does not readily map on to seventeenth-century English society, where even public office itself was intimately tied to familial and social bonds.[35] In effect, the clarity of the split between public and private in this tradition of political thought disrupts its potential to describe or analyse the spheres of early modern England. The concepts of *oikos* and *polis* were only part of the seventeenth-century political equation. As we will see in the discussion of Bulstrode Whitelocke, though republican thought was bound up with the idea of public good, there was certainly no decisive split between familial and public.[36] This was true in different ways for men and women, but the sexes shared the ready imagistic thought which linked the two.

However, importantly, the work of Habermas with Christopher Hill's distinct linking of the early modern period to rational modernity (now accompanied by the work of their respondents and critics) has greatly enlarged our ability to understand the significance of the public dialogues, not just the printed material, produced in seventeenth-century England and differently in Wales, Scotland, and Ireland. It is evident that a great upheaval in public debate, and in what

---

[34] Ibid., p. 24. On Arendt's problematic discounting of slavery see Benhabib, 'Models'.

[35] For Arendt, one effect of the dissolution of the political into the social in modernity is that, as modern subjects, we have a serious inability to grasp the decisive split between *polis* and *oikos* implicit throughout classical thought for 'in the modern world, the two realms indeed constantly flow into each other like waves on the never-resting stream of the life process itself'. Arendt, *The Human Condition*, p. 33.

[36] For a nuanced discussion of the complex relationship of private and public in 18th-century culture, and a perceptive account of the critical discussion of the place of women in 'public culture', see Harriet Guest, *Small Change: Women, Learning, Patriotism, 1750–1810* (Chicago: University of Chicago Press, 2000), pp. 1–15.

was debated, took place during the 1640s and 1650s. And the debates of this period do seem to have been crucial in founding a self-reflexivity concerning debate and dialogue—something which could facilitate thinking in Habermasian terms about a public sphere.[37] Women's petitions, for instance, though a generically limited form, do demonstrate their involvement in the political sphere of print, even as the texts themselves make ambiguous claims with regard to the nature of women's rights of address.[38] Some more discursively, as well as circumstantially, complex texts discussed here—such as Elizabeth Poole's publications—were definitely part of a public, political debate which can in part be understood in Habermas's terms of private individuals debating state and public affairs. For much of the material analysed here, though, the terms offered by Habermas would be reductive. Although in seventeenth-century England print and transformations in print culture—including the appearance of printed and commoditized news, pamphlets, and petitions—made public opinion a substantial factor in political life, that transformation did not mean that manuscript writing was always or inevitably to be considered private. For example, the circulated manuscript compilation of Elizabeth Jekyll's pleas and prayers, which clearly had political ends, cuts across Habermas's understanding of both the public and the use of *reason*. Reason and affect, public and familial, print and manuscript, religion and secular argument combine in constituting women's relationship to politics.

In sum, Habermas's model is not simply applicable to women's relationship to politics in seventeenth-century England; the boundaries between private and public were much more mobile and shifting than Habermas suggests, and they were often marked clearly only at a moment of perceived transgression (we might think of Elizabeth Avery being condemned while Anne Bradstreet is commended for different forms of public, political, intervention). While women might at times be politically powerful, and they certainly did make public, printed,

---

[37] Writing on political languages in the Civil War includes Norbrook, *Writing the English Republic*; Elizabeth Skerpan, *The Rhetoric of Politics in the English Revolution* (Columbia: University of Missouri Press, 1992); Nigel Smith, *Literature and Revolution in England, 1640–1660* (New Haven: Yale University Press, 1994).

[38] The foundational article remains Patricia Higgins, 'The Reactions of Women, with Special Reference to Women Petitioners', in *Politics, Religion and the English Civil War*, ed. Brian Manning (London: Edward Arnold, 1973), pp. 178–222.

interventions in political debate, such actions were in complicated relationships to family, household, religion, and politics. The deep grounding of women's claims to political intervention in thought concerning family and property is not often or readily expressed in arguments derived from *oikos* and *polis*, particularly if those are, as their meaning properly demands, narrowly defined. The theoretical exclusion of women from the political can be seen as mapping closely but certainly not identically on to splits between private and public. In the very force of pathos, even in the refusal to speak politically (in the case of Wight), or in the assumption of political voice on the basis of family and property (in Brilliana Harley's case), women might not be exactly participants in a public sphere. Yet in their texts we register a use of resources which impacts on, and enters, the public sphere in complex ways—and which can also be seen as providing a source of *political*, if not publicly political, identity and self-understanding. Thus, 'politics' and 'public' are not quite synonymous; the term 'politics' (rather than necessarily 'the public' or 'the public sphere') consistently shapes my response to evidence. Habermas's idea of a public sphere which emerged, crystallized, at a certain point; his sense of shifting relationships to land; his sense that the market in general changes society as it grows more important—these ideas are important as set against evidence and the questions, more closely canvassed here, of women's relationship to the political. While at times this study draws upon Habermas's idea of the public sphere it does not use it as a framework for investigation.

Consideration of the relationship between public and private brings us to the third major debate over women and politics: the arguments over the role of contract theory. While the grounding modern conspectus of the foundations of modern political thought understands this to have nothing to do with women in literal or discursive terms, feminist political theorists have thoroughly investigated the way in which liberal political theory, contract theory, has made the world for men and women.[39] The terrain of the discussion is the emergence of possessive

[39] The study offers 'an outline account of late medieval and early modern political thought'. Quentin Skinner, *The Foundations of Modern Political Thought*, 2 vols. (Cambridge: Cambridge University Press, 1978), I, ix. See also the essays in *Political Discourse in Early Modern Britain,* ed. Quentin Skinner and Nicholas Phillipson (Cambridge: Cambridge University Press, 1993).

individualism—the idea that an individual has rights over him (or her) self and can, accordingly, make contracts. In this debate, early modern contract theorists see civil society as constituted 'by the (ostensibly) universal bonds of contract not the particular, natural bonds of kinship and fatherhood'.[40] Contrastingly, patriarchal thinking is characterized by recourse to 'the family' as the 'most basic' of 'social units' and a source of imagery.[41] Political theorists configure the emergence of contract theory as a dialectical process generated by a narrowly defined canon of seventeenth-century texts and authors. In this narrative, Thomas Hobbes's theory of contractual power in *Leviathan* is countered by Sir Robert Filmer's insistence on patriarchal rule derived from Adam in *Patriarcha*. This is in turn countered by John Locke's emphasis on contract in *Two Treatises of Civil Government*.

When we turn to the texts involved we find relations between men and women at the foundations of the authors' understandings of commonwealth. Hobbes is important to feminist political theorists as having understood women as equal to men in the state of nature. While Hobbes is aware that 'in the logical beginning' equality of the sexes pertains, yet he also knows that 'historically, paternal right and the subjection of wives was the established custom'.[42] Hobbes, therefore, leaves unanswered, partially answered, or illogically answered (according to how scholars interpret his words) the question of why women submit to men and therefore the question of why politics is the realm of men. There has also been much discussion of his ambiguous account of the relationship between marriage and the state.[43] Contrastingly, Sir Robert Filmer's arguments offer a radical development of patriarchal thought by identifying political and paternal rule; the two are bound together in a

---

[40] Carole Pateman, *The Sexual Contract* (Cambridge: Polity Press, 1988), p. 3.

[41] G. J. Schochet, *The Authoritarian Family and Political Thought in Seventeenth-Century England* (London: Blackwell, 1975; repr. New Brunswick, N.J.: Transaction, 1988), p. xiii.

[42] Susan Moller Okin, *Women in Western Political Thought* (Princeton: Princeton University Press, 1979), pp. 197–9; Carole Pateman, ' "God Hath Ordained to Man a Helper": Hobbes, Patriarchy and Conjugal Right', in *Feminist Interpretations and Political Theory*, ed. Mary Lyndon Shanley and Carole Pateman (Cambridge: Polity Press, 1991), pp. 53–73: 66.

[43] A fascinating discussion is offered in Victoria Kahn ' "The Duty to Love": Passion and Obligation in Early Modern Political Theory', in *Rhetoric and Law in Early Modern Europe*, ed. Victoria Kahn and Lorna Hutson (New Haven: Yale University Press, 2001), pp. 243–68: 258.

narrative of power derived from Adam. Replying to Hobbes's characterization of the state of nature in *Leviathan*, Filmer asserts Adam's primacy
not only as ruling 'over the woman and the children' but 'over the whole
earth'.[44] On the right of kings Filmer is unequivocal. He writes, 'There
is, and always shall be continued to the end of the world, a natural right
of a supreme father over every multitude'—and for him this continues to
be the case even when true rule has been usurped.[45] In John Locke's *Two
Treatises*, too, gender relations are important in the discussion of power.
In the *First Treatise* Locke replies to Filmer's assertion that Adam's title to
sovereignty comes 'by the subjection of Eve'. Locke concludes that God's
words to Eve, 'and thy desire shall be to thy Husband, and he shall rule
over thee' (Genesis 3: 16) imply no grant of kingship. Rather, the words
bind Eve to

no other Subjection than what every Wife owes her Husband, and then if this be
the Originall Grant of Government and the Foundation of Monarchical Power,
there will be as many Monarchs as there are Husbands. If therefore these words
give any power to Adam, it can only be a Conjugal Power, not Political, the
Power that every Husband hath to order the things of private Concernment in
his Family, as Proprietor of the Goods and Land there, and to have his Will take
place before that of his wife in all things of their common Concernment; but
not a Political Power of Life and Death over her, much less over any body else.[46]

Locke emphatically desires to separate power in conjugal relations from
the power of monarchs.[47] Evidently, relations between the sexes are

---

[44] Sir Robert Filmer, 'The Originall of Government', in *Patriarcha and Other Writings*, ed. Johann P. Sommerville (Cambridge: Cambridge University Press, 1991), p. 187.
[45] Filmer, *Patriarcha*, p. 11.
[46] John Locke, *The First Treatise*, in *Two Treatises of Government*, ed. Peter Laslett
(Cambridge: Cambridge University Press, 1960), p. 192.
[47] Melissa A. Butler, 'Early Liberal Roots of Feminism: John Locke and the Attack
on Patriarchy', in *Feminist Interpretations*, ed. Shanley and Pateman, pp. 74–94. Butler
argues that in this account men have power over women but by earthly not divine means.
Even so, she argues that Locke's understanding of contractual rule at points is hard to
distinguish from the 'natural' power of fathers because, ostensibly consenting, children
recognize the power of the father as lawmaker (ibid., p. 87). Diana Coole, however, notes
that, with regard to the family, Locke modifies both Hobbes's sense that 'preservation
rather than generation' yielded power and Filmer's insistence that the father has absolute
power not only over the woman (a given) but over offspring up to the point of their death.
Diana Coole, *Women in Political Theory* (Brighton: Harvester, 1988), pp. 88–9; Thomas
Hobbes, *Leviathan*, ed. Richard Tuck (Cambridge: Cambridge University Press, 1991).

crucial to the theories and figural language of Hobbes, Filmer, and Locke. However, motivation is vital—that Filmer understood his interventions as a defence of the rights of the Stuarts was crucial in precipitating Locke's attacks on him in the *Two Treatises*. Moreover, other influential thinkers are excluded from the canon; as a republican John Milton, for example, sought to distinguish power in the household from the monarch's role in the state. Also excluded from the debate are many significant writers on society and politics who use less sharply or oppositionally defined patriarchal or contractual modes of thought. However, whether the grounding of authority in patriarchal or fraternal ideology (or monarchical or republican theory) can be construed as better for women is a vexed question.[48]

The seventeenth-century material in this debate has been used selectively and in a specific way. Feminist political theorists have returned to the narrative of contract because, as Carole Pateman puts it, 'The most famous and influential story of modern times is found in the writings of the social contract theorists. The story... tells how a new civil society and a new form of political right is created through an original contract.'[49] Contract theory—understood as the idea that no one, no man, can be subject to another without his consent—is traced by political theorists from an *origin* in the seventeenth century to, for example, John Rawls's theory of justice.[50] Accordingly, feminist political theorists have made a wide range of arguments concerning the implications of contract theory for women.[51] Arguing that contract theorists leave unchanged

---

[48] Norbrook concludes with an allusion to the real emergence of this debate in 'later liberal theory' where the state/household split is, theoretically, effected and the household is naturalized as not open to negotiation or connected to the political sphere (*Writing the English Republic*, pp. 483–4). See Smith, *All Men*, pp. 109–33.

[49] Pateman, *The Sexual Contract*, p. 1.

[50] This account, which situates the 'origins' of contract theory in the 17th century, can be found in a wide range of contrasting texts, textbooks, and anthologies, e.g. *Social Contract Theory*, ed. Michael Lessnoff (Oxford: Blackwell, 1990); Patrick Riley, *Will and Political Legitimacy* (Cambridge, Mass.: Harvard University Press, 1982).

[51] See Moira Gatens, 'Corporeal Representation in/and the Body Politic', in *Cartographies*, ed. Rosalyn Diprose and Robyn Ferrell (London: Allen & Unwin, 1991), pp. 79–87; Coole, *Women in Political Theory, passim*; Okin, *Women in Western Political Thought*. As Mary Lyndon Shanley and Carole Pateman, in *Feminist Interpretations*, p. 1, rightly argue, feminist reinterpretations of the canon of political theory 'have revolutionary implications' for the understanding of 'such central categories as citizenship, equality, freedom, justice, the public, the private and democracy'—in modernity. 'In mainstream political theory, the public sphere is assumed to be capable of being understood on its own,

'conjugal right', Carole Pateman tracks the emergence of the 'domestic' as a sphere imagined or assumed by contract theorists to be outside a discourse of rights.[52] For Pateman contracting individuals are men; as contract comes to dominate the political world men ensure their status by further subordinating women and children. The radical potential of contract remains unrealized and contract theory produces the non-contractual domestic prison-house. The early modern debate on contract, for her, initiates the scandal of modernity in consigning women to the domestic space and cutting that off, conceptually, from political thought. She sees the history of consent theory as consisting of 'attempts by theorists to suppress the radical and subversive implications of their own arguments'.[53]

Pateman's incisive and pathbreaking assessment of conjugality under contract, her account of contract theory's consigning of women to a non-contractual domesticity, is widely used and debated. Pateman's work offers a crucially important account of one strand in the emergence of modernity. However, when we consider early modern writings in their specific contexts there are other issues, too, to take into account, such as context and reception. For example, as Mary Lyndon Shanley notes in her discussion of marriage, contract theory gradually came to permeate that thinking—for although all legitimate forms of rule were ordained by God, while 'contractarian ideas first developed in analyses of the proper basis of authority, they *gradually* began to appear in discussions of other human associations as well'.[54] Shanley gives the example of the 'conceptualization of the marriage contract in the course of the seventeenth century'. Shanley's important argument that 'contract

---

as if it existed *sui generis*, independently of private sexual relations and domestic life. The structure of relations between the sexes is ignored and sexual relations stand as the paradigm of all that is private or non-political.'

[52] Pateman, '"God Hath Ordained"', p. 59.

[53] Carole Pateman, *The Disorder of Women: Democracy, Feminism and Political Theory* (Cambridge: Polity Press, 1989), p. 71; see also pp. 71–89. Pateman also illuminatingly writes, 'nothing of significance for democracy is seen in the patriarchal opposition between the "public" (economy/state) and the "private" (domestic, conjugal and intimate life), an opposition which is both presupposed and repressed by democratic theorists' (ibid., p. 5).

[54] Mary Lyndon Shanley, 'Marriage Contract and Social Contract in Seventeenth Century English Political Thought', in *The Family in Political Thought*, ed. Jean Bethke Elshtain (Brighton: Harvester, 1982), pp. 80–95.

thinking' affected domestic as well as other forms of political discourse is significant, for example, to the way we might read Milton's *Doctrine and Discipline of Divorce*. As she indicates, however, contract theory did not immediately inhabit all forms of social thinking. Thus, rather than use the seventeenth-century contract debate solely as the starting place of a story of modernity, it is possible, as does Victoria Kahn, to return to contract theory 'in the making'. Kahn examines the way language and contract entwine to create a kind of political subject.[55] Yet, contract was 'in the making' for a long time and was far from a clear, sole, or self-evident language of politics.

It is the nature of their orientation towards modernity, and the way they chose to see the seventeenth century in relation to that, which links these three major debates on women and politics and which, to an extent, distinguishes each from the present study. Each, in a different way, looks to the mid-seventeenth century as a watershed: their interest in the texts of this period is in the way they reveal the emergent problematics of modernity. The present study, too, inevitably concerns itself with relationships between seventeenth-century England and modernity and, accordingly, it draws on work emerging from the three debates analysed here. However, rather than focus on modernity as a realization of the potentials of seventeenth-century crises, modernity is significant for the present study in two ways. First, in responding to the evidence of the material the ensuing discussion tries to keep in mind that modernity is a path amongst others not taken. Second, as much as it figures as an end point or naturalized development, modernity in this study supplies the role of contrast: it illuminates some of the differences as well as similarities or contiguities of past and present.

Thinking and writing on the relationship of women and politics in the early modern period cannot be considered an offshoot of the contract debate, though it has connections to it. Throughout, the motivating interest of seventeenth-century contract theorists for feminist political theorists is the fact that the struggle between contract theory and patriarchalism precipitated debates in the modern, rather than the early modern, world. Contrastingly, the writings discussed in this study

⁵⁵ Victoria Kahn, *Wayward Contracts: The Crisis of Political Obligation in England, 1640–1740* (Princeton: Princeton University Press, 2004), pp. 1–2; Kahn, '"The Duty to Love"'.

mobilize cultural resources in the interests of particular political agendas rather than discussing political theory. In researching the relationships of women to politics the present study asks how politics is registered and shaped in a broad swath of kinds of writing. As John Dunn argues astutely about the problematic relationship of political theory to 'political activity', politics 'is not a clearly demarcated or self-identifying segment of the history of nature, but a huge, diffuse and very hazily located space of human action, experience and interpretation. The human attempt to understand politics . . . has no uncontentiously given core.'[56]

The models of nineteenth- and twentieth-century politics, as well as literary culture, have been critically deployed to create some anachronistic assumptions about early modern culture and politics.[57] Like this study, the debates I have been tracing are themselves founded on ways of thinking produced by the modern political sphere. In modernity—from the nineteenth-century franchise debates, through second-wave feminism, and in current debates about multiple public spheres—political change is bound up with discussions about women's political claims, and particularly claims articulated by women speaking 'as women' with all the contradictory emphasis on and refusal of femininity that implies.[58] Wollstonecraft's use of analogies between women and male slaves both demands for women equal terms with men and develops the cause of women as a specific case and group. One of the defining characteristics of modernity is the incorporation of women *as women* into the political sphere: this was not, my research suggests, exactly part of the intellectual or social formation familiar in seventeenth-century England. The early modern divisions of the world, both similar to and different from our own, can seem opaque or even unformed. Obviously enough, being modern has costs, benefits, and blind spots when it

[56] John Dunn, *The History of Political Theory and Other Essays* (Cambridge: Cambridge University Press, 1996), pp. 11–38: 26.

[57] Margaret J. M. Ezell, *Writing Women's Literary History* (Baltimore: Johns Hopkins University Press, 1993), pp. 34–5, 41.

[58] For these issues see *Feminism*, ed. Landes; *Feminists Theorize the Political*, ed. Judith Butler and Joan Wallach Scott (London: Routledge, 1992). Denise Riley, '*Am I That Name?': Feminism and the Category of 'Women' in History* (Basingstoke: Macmillan, 1988), is the most illuminating discussion of the contradictory emphasis on and refusal of femininity produced by feminism. Riley develops her account of identity and 'the great categories of being as they stiffen or sag' (p. 3) in *The Words of Selves* (Stanford: Stanford University Press, 2000), especially pp. 1–21.

comes to understanding the political imaginary inhabited by early modern people. However, this project attempts to attend to the rhetorics which open women to politics, and politics to women, in seventeenth-century England, and to the images and stories of women's relationship to politics. It is to the ways in which these can be traced that I now turn.

METHODS

If, as I am arguing, women's relationship to politics can be traced in a wide range of literary and cultural locations, how can those articulations be interpreted? Sharing with men the available ways of thinking about the political world, women comment on the world as it appears to them and use the interpretative categories ready at hand. In a society where gender is not a founding category of argument, but rather an issue which is important but recognized *contingently*, which patterns of thought and writing *did* significantly put women and politics together, how can they be traced, and is it possible to place their eclipse with any precision? Gender was not for them, as it is for us, a crucial taxonomic term covering various aspects of social and cultural life. Women were, inevitably, understood in relation to other categories which are themselves shifting. 'Women' was not consistently a foundational category *within* the political sphere but, rather, writing on and representations of 'woman' make visible the political aspects of gender relations.[59]

Early modern people had much to say about women and gender, expressing opinions on divers topics—queens, whores, heroines, the family, households, and divorce. However, as Rachel Weil puts it, they might 'not see these issues as being connected' or, indeed, more closely connected to other items or issues.[60] The regular, indeed customary, use of gender in signifying—and debating—power relations in the early modern period makes it a rich tool for the investigation of political writing. The category 'women' was the object of intense questioning

[59] Riley, *'Am I That Name?'*, pp. 1–2.
[60] Rachel Weil, *Political Passions: Gender, the Family and Political Argument in England 1680–1714* (Manchester: Manchester University Press, 1999), pp. 3–4.

and assumptions concerning women were circulated actively in discussions.[61] However, 'women' were circumstantially related to political issues rather than being, as later, the ground of claims to political intervention. Thus, the exclusion of women from the political sphere was immensely influential in shaping the language and conceptualization of women's relationship to politics. Simultaneously, gender is, as Joan Scott suggests, a powerful tool of historical analysis, not one used by contemporaries.[62]

In her study of early modern elites Barbara Harris argues convincingly that 'the interpenetration of private and public concerns', as when women argued their husbands' petitions, 'opened politics to women'. That this configuration was long-lived is suggested by politically inflected social history such as Richard Cust's important discussion of honour.[63] Although the idea that 'private' virtue underwrites women's activities, including interventions in the public sphere, is an assumption recurring in and connecting early modern and later forms of thought, the categories of private and public are unstable—rendered visible, even brought into being, in instances of perceived transgression rather than in the more stable dicta of conduct literature.[64] At times, certainly, we find private virtue used to underwrite political intervention. Indeed, categories associated with 'privacy' explicitly imagine women as subject to authority even as they isolate them from the exercise of that property. The early modern woman, under her husband's rule as he is under God's (or as Eve is subject to Adam), is highly visible as a subject bound to be obedient, and a huge quantity of political imagery and ideas draws on the implied relationship of the political system and the household.[65] As

---

[61] See Harriette Andreadis, *Sappho in Early Modern England: Female Same-Sex Erotics 1550–1714* (Chicago: University of Chicago Press, 2001); Valerie Traub, *The Renaissance of Lesbianism in Early Modern England* (Cambridge: Cambridge University Press, 2002).

[62] Joan Wallach Scott, 'Gender: a Useful Category of Historical Analysis', in *Feminism and History*, ed. Wallach Scott (Oxford: Oxford University Press, 1996), pp. 152–80.

[63] Barbara Harris, 'Women and Politics in Early Tudor England', *HJ* 33, No. 2 (1990), pp. 259–81; Richard Cust, 'Honour and Politics in Early Stuart England', *PP* 149 (1995), pp. 57–149. I am grateful to Margaret Wilkinson for discussion of honour.

[64] Alan Bray and Michael Rey, 'The Body of the Friend: Continuity and Change in Masculine Friendship in the Seventeenth Century', in *English Masculinities 1600–1800*, ed. Michele Cohen and Tim Hitchcock (London: Longman, 1999), pp. 65–84: 65. As has been argued, conduct literature may well at present be over-used as a source of assumptions about public and private. See the helpful summary in Alison Wall, *Power and Protest in England 1525–1640* (London: Arnold, 2000), pp. 81–95.

[65] See Jordan, *Renaissance Feminism*, pp. 308–9.

well as supplying a rich imagistic vocabulary, patriarchal ideas of government *generate* rather than forestall attention to the position of women within the household and, by analogy, the political sphere. However, no stable rule consistently divided private from public. Rather, the ideologies and iconographies of women 'opened' on to politics as circumstances dictated, in ways that could at times be used by women as well as in misogynist discourse. Early modern discourses on femininity combined a relatively stable iconography of femininity with less stable ideologies of gender.[66] As Ann Hughes has argued, it is necessary both to examine the parts women played in politics and to begin to trace shifts in the relationship between politics and gender.[67] What follows addresses as complementary questions what women were writing and thinking and the discursive importance of gender.

Obviously, status and position (geographical as well as social) are significant in shaping, even determining, women's relationship to politics. In the case of queens—Elizabeth I, Mary Tudor, Mary Queen of Scots—political theory and gender intersect most vividly. Calvin, replying to John Knox's inflammatory queries about the government of Scotland, advocated acceptance of even a female ruler of the wrong religious persuasion; for Calvin, it was not allowable to forcibly resist an idolatrous ruler, and women rulers were to be accepted as divine punishment.[68] Arbella Stuart had a life in which sexuality and politics became indistinguishably interwoven, while her aunt, the Countess of Shrewsbury, was a highly active political intriguer. These contrasting examples indicate wholly distinct ways in which elite women related to

---

[66] Or to put it another way, as Gordon J. Schochet emphasizes, politics, as a symbolic language, is bound to the social forms it grows out of and comments on but is not an unmediated representation of them. Schochet's insistence on a 'non-isomorphic' relationship between symbol and social patterns, on the difficulty of determining both the causality and moment of conceptual change, offers a corrective to teleological accounts of the growth of contract. See his introduction to the 1988 edn. of *The Authoritarian Family*, pp. xxiii, xxii.

[67] Ann Hughes, *Women, Men and Politics in the English Civil War* (Keele: Keele University Press, 1998), pp. 3–4.

[68] Jean Calvin, 'Letter to Sir William Cecil from Geneva sometime after January 29, 1559', in *Zurich Letters 1558–1602* (Cambridge: Parker Society, 1857), p. 745. On queens specifically see Harris 'Women and Politics'; Paula Louise Scalingi, 'The Scepter and the Distaff: the Question of Female Sovereignty, 1516–1607', *The Historian* 14 (1978), pp. 59–75.

1. Raised work adaptation of *Eikon Basilike* (T 117). Reproduced by permission of the Victoria and Albert Museum

the political world: if Stuart's politics was situational, Shrewsbury's was emulatory, *arriviste*, active. Thus, family, status, position are used with ease as counters in political debate by women associated with Protestant and parliamentarian critique in the 1640s (Brilliana Harley, Anne Bradstreet) or with republicanism (Lucy Hutchinson), as much as by others characterized as royalist (Margaret Cavendish). But they were not the only resources available. These naturalized social markers were not the isolated or only aspect of women's political commentary. In the letters of the Harleys or, indeed, in the visualizing of Stuart renewal shown in the raised-work image of Charles I (Figure 1), we can see that it is not simply the case that politics is absorbed as if from outside into 'women's networks', or that women's letters, unlike men's, were not understood as political discourse (as might be thought of the letters of Dorothy Sidney).

Far from women's political writings and imaginings existing solely at the level of relationships which can be understood as preceding political consciousness, political language and ideas are articulated in a range of places. During the period studied here the political positions held by those of non-aristocratic, middling, status become visible, in part because of the nature of the print culture during the Civil War. The relationship to politics of women of even lower social status becomes intermittently visible in the records of petitions and protests. The Civil War period provides plentiful examples of women involved in political and religious disputes. Sarah Wight, Elizabeth Poole, Katherine Chidley, Anna Trapnel, and Mary Cary are amongst the best known, and these women were not members of the ruling elite. Like the better-known Lucy Hutchinson, Elizabeth Jekyll, wife of the City merchant John Jekyll and the mother of the divine John Jekyll, kept a commonplace book in which she kept records and comments on political events. However, as I suggested earlier, the focus on written and substantially quasi-literary sources, while it provides a corpus of material for investigation, excludes the evanescent evidence of other forms of coerced testimony. When Margaret Henshall calls her husband a 'roundhead' the language of insult blends with that of politics, and only the circumstances could disclose the relationship—whether close or tenuous—between the two. Similarly, when in 1657 Katherine Whitehead *alias* Linsey, widow, is ordered to appear at the next Middlesex Sessions to answer 'for her uncivill carriage in going to bed to Collonell Sexby when she kept him in his sicknesse', the nature of the relationship and of her politics (if any) remains enigmatic.[69] Although Laura Gowing's work on the powers which shaped women's lives, and which they struggled to control, suggests that there is likely to be politics in the legal archives, the literary and largely voluntarily penned writing canvassed here means that in this study such points of view are glimpsed rather than visible.[70]

None of the women mentioned above, except perhaps the queens, could be considered to be involved in politics by birth, yet it would be perverse to consider their writings, speeches, and activities as unrelated to both historical conjunctures of politics and the theories of how the political sphere should operate that were dominant during their lifetimes. The logic of the argument that women's exclusion from the political realm shapes their relation to it has also determined this study's

---

[69] *Middlesex Sessions Rolls*, 5 Dec. 1657, p. 226.
[70] Laura Gowing, *Common Bodies: Women, Touch and Power in Seventeenth-Century England* (New Haven: Yale University Press, 2003).

inclusion of a wide selection of both authors and genres. Women often discussed in relation to politics (such as Anna Trapnel, Margaret Cavendish, Aphra Behn) are situated alongside others whose writings have not been seen as revealing much of significance about women's relation to politics (such as Sarah Wight, Anne Halkett), yet such texts and their transmission clearly reveal as much, though different, material about the ways in which women were in relationship to politics as, for instance, political assertion and opinion. By the same token, I do not necessarily privilege genres which resemble modern political genres. For instance, petitions were explicit attempts to influence the political process and participate in the power of publication to shape public opinion, and they leave us textual evidence of political positions and publicity.[71] Accordingly, petitions, as evident forms of political intervention, have been the focus of much discussion. Yet critical concentration on them in part registers the generic recognizability of the petition to a modern reader rather than their equally significant specificity as speech acts.

In looking at the evidence for early modern women's relationship to politics we are offered deceptively familiar images and iconography. However, these images and icons were configured differently in the seventeenth century than they are for us. Seventeenth-century English writers discuss women and women's relationship to politics—explicitly and implicitly—but use taxonomies significantly different from the categories of women and gender as they came into being in Enlightenment feminism. It is, I would suggest, possible to trace languages which initiate, describe, trope, and narrate women's relationship to politics. However, scholarship has been relatively slow to take up this question of how to think about early modern women's relationship to politics. The literary and cultural sphere—writings on religion, marriage, government by men and women—is, I am arguing, where we can trace these issues, in genres from the letter to the long poem, in published and unpublished material.

---

[71] Zaret, *Origins of Democratic Culture*, pp. 216–65. Zaret works with a Habermasian model, making explicit its trajectory towards liberalism and situating the emergence of the idea of public opinion as implicitly part of the legislative process very early—in the mid-17th century. See e.g. on *An Agreement of the People*, 'we are on the brink of a formal platform for a liberal-democratic model of the political order' (*Origins*, p. 265).

Although organized in a rough chronology, the chapters of this study are arranged according to the aspects of women and politics which they explore. There are eight chapters, each of which looks at women's relationship to politics from a different viewpoint; these chapters are grouped in pairs, arranged according to the nature of the material discussed. Rather than, for example, following nonconformist or royalist writing through the century the study takes as its focus what seem to be moments and kinds of writing which reveal something about women's relationships to politics: it aims to provide not a narrative of a particular group but a discontinuous study which allows us to see a range of politicized vocabularies and issues. Thus the first two chapters explore the ways in which we can see women and politics put together by contemporaries. Each of these chapters analyses how, why, and when forms of language have political resonance. Two subsequent chapters investigate the way in which religion, gender, and politics were put in relationship to each other in the 1640s. The questions of women's interventions in literary forms and of how gender was represented are explored in chapters on poetry and on the ways in which Queen Christina of Sweden was discussed in the 1650s. Two chapters explore and discuss emotional language and claims to legitimacy in Tory and nonconformist writing after the Restoration. I begin, then, by enquiring into the relationship between rhetorical strategies, women, and politics; the next chapter explores the role of the example.

PART I

POLITICAL RHETORICS

1

Rhetoric

It seemed a very pleasant object, to see so many Semproniaes (all the chiefe Court Ladies filling the Galleries at the [Earl of Strafford's] Tryall) with penne, inke, and paper in their hands, noting the passages, and discoursing upon the grounds of Law and State.

(Thomas May, *The History of the Parliament* (1647), Bk. I, p. 92)

D.D.D

To the pretious name and honour of Dorothy Selby,
The relict of Sir William Selby, Knt
The only daughter and heir of Charles Bonham, Esq.

She was a Dorcas
Whose curious Needle turn'd the abused Stage
Of this leud world into the Golden Age,
Whose Pen of Steele and silken inck enroll'd
The Acts of Jonah in Records of Gold.
Whose arte disclos'd the Plot which, had it taken,
Rome had tryumph'd and Britain's walls had shaken;
In heart a Lydia and in Tongue a Hanna,
In Zeale a Ruth, in wedlock a Susanna;
Prudently, simply, providentially Wary,
To th' world a Martha and to Heaven a Mary

(Epitaph for Dorothy Selby, Ightam Church, Kent[1])

If, as I am suggesting, the literary and cultural sphere is likely to disclose women's relationship to politics in seventeenth-century England, what evidence is there, and how can it be interpreted? The introduction

---

[1] Selby died 15 March 1641. See Sophie Jane Holroyd, 'Embroidered Rhetoric: the Social, Religious and Political Functions of Elite Women's Needlework, *c*.1560–1630', Diss., University of Warwick, 2002.

suggested that women's theoretical exclusion from the political sphere generated not silence but highly developed linguistic and often figurative responses. This and the subsequent chapter investigate how, why, and when language had political resonance. Aiming to look afresh at the question of political languages and reading, this chapter analyses women's involvement in politics by examining the use of the example in seventeenth-century texts.[2] It concentrates on exemplarity because of its pervasive presence in early modern writing, because of the tensions it sometimes generated for readers, and because of the way it shows gender at work in the interpretative acts of readers and writers. Furthermore, example was one of Aristotle's basic tools of rhetoric and played a key role in Protestant exegesis. Examples are male and female and are used by writers of both sexes. The centrality of examples in seventeenth-century England is indicated by the range of locations in which readers encountered them. As well as forming part of longer texts they were abstracted in compendia such as Thomas Heywood's *The Exemplary Lives and Memorable Acts of Nine the Most Worthy Women of the World*—which mixes biblical, classical and recent female worthies and heroines (Figure 2). They were embodied in the hangings at Hardwick (Figure 3). Exemplary thinking was habitual, too, in commemoration—in epitaphs, funeral sermons, and in commemorative volumes like John Batchiler's memorial to his relative, Susanna Perwich, pearl of 'the Ladies University' in Hackney.[3] Dorothy Selby's epitaph, quoted above, demonstrates the pervasive but not necessarily simple role of exemplarity in measuring the virtue of early modern women and men. The biblical figures to whom Selby is likened are both primary and secondary in our understanding of her qualities—they are models for women, and so primary. But as we read they also precede and echo the poem's main object—Dorothy Selby—who both follows and in some ways ambiguously seems to exceed them. Even in an epitaph the processes invoked by exemplarity can be complex.

[2] See John D. Lyons, *Exemplum: The Rhetoric of Example in Early Modern France and Italy* (Princeton: Princeton University Press, 1989), pp. 3–8.

[3] Thomas Heywood, *The Exemplary Lives and Memorable Acts of Nine the Most Worthy Women of the World* (London, 1640); John Batchiler, *The Virgins Pattern: in the Exemplary Life and lamented Death of Susanna Perwich, Daughter of Mr. Robert Perwich* (London, 1661), p. 125; Ian Maclean, *Woman Triumphant: Feminism in French Literature 1610–1652* (Oxford: Oxford University Press, 1977).

2. 'Esther', from Thomas Heywood, *The Exemplary Lives and Memorable Acts of Nine the Most Worthy Women of the World* (London, 1640), p. 44

3. 'Lucrecia', embroidery from 'The Virtues', Hardwick Hall. Reproduced by permission of the National Trust

In this chapter material is drawn mainly from the mid-century, roughly 1639–60, and I explore classical and biblical examples before looking at instances of exemplary reading. A survey would demand attention to a practically endless list—Cleopatra, Christ, Deborah, Ruth, Cornelia are only the start. The pervasiveness of example makes it necessary to narrow the focus. Accordingly, the chapter explores three particular cases which, with others, recur in my study—Arria, Lucretia, and Esther—and it analyses example as part of the gendered dynamics of political language in seventeenth-century England.

EXEMPLARITY AND POLITICS: ARRIA, LUCRETIA, ESTHER

The end of so admirable a vertue was this. Her husband *Paetus* wanting the courage to doe himselfe to death, unto which the Emperor's cruelty reserved him; one day, having first employed discourses and exhortations, shee tooke a Dagger that her husband wore, and holding it outright in her hand, for the period of her exhortation: Doe thus *Paetus* (said she) and at that instant, stabbing her selfe mortally to the heart, and presently pulling the dagger out againe she reached the same unto her husband, and so yielded up the ghost, uttering this noble, generous and immortall speech, *Paete non dolet*, she had not the leasure to pronounce other than these three wordes, in substance materiall and worthy her selfe, *Holde*, Paetus, *it hath done me no hurt*.[4]

What can the history of an example tell us? In 'Three Good Women' Montaigne juxtaposes three exemplary classical wives, one low-born and the other two 'noble and rich'.[5] Arria, the wife of Cecinna Paetus, is one of these. Her words encouraging him to die circulated as an example of classical virtue in early modern England.

Arria's suicide can be registered as virtuous within a stoic frame. However, even as it claims the function of a moral exemplar this instance is complicated and ambiguous; Arria's suicide is an implicit criticism of her husband's cowardice: only her example forces him to do

---

[4] Michel de Montaigne, *Essays*, trans. John Florio, 3 vols. (1603; repr. London: Dent, 1910), II, 477. See Sarah Pomeroy, *Goddesses, Whores, Wives, and Slaves* (London: Robert Hale, 1975), pp. 149–89.

[5] Montaigne, *Essays*, II, 476.

the honourable thing. Thus, this particular example works also by putting women in relation to politics and political philosophy. It makes the connection through praise of suicide and, so, of Stoicism; Montaigne is following up an earlier discussion of history and Stoic philosophy.[6] Montaigne uses this moment in his essay to turn from the questions of marriage to the virtues underpinning a good life and so again to the terrain of judgement. English readers would have found Arria in Montaigne's essays, some English reworkings, and in two main Latin texts. John Florio's translation of the essays was published in 1603, and further editions appeared in England in 1613 and 1632. Pliny the younger told the story in a way which made the political cowardice of Paetus a by-blow, arguing that other virtues in Arria's life were more important than her suicide. Martial's epigram on the topic was much translated and always, it seems, with close and even fetishistic attention to her words of reprimand. Tacitus too, telling the story of Arria's daughter the wife of Thraseas, a victim of Nero, who is persuaded to live on for the sake of her daughter, reminded readers of the mother.[7]

For contemporary readers, if the Stoic quality of Arria's virtue facilitated her appeal, her self-violence was also potentially attractive. The tension between passivity and action in her behaviour also maps readily on to the idealized model of martyrdom, a form of death both acknowledged and denied as political. Arria can be used as part of a critique of tyranny. Accordingly, Arria, though not of course used as frequently as the death of Socrates, has an exemplary existence in seventeenth- and even eighteenth-century English writing—and one which consistently focuses the reader's attention on female political virtue. For example, Montaigne's essay is recycled by Thomas Heywood.[8] Two further uses of Arria, very different from each other, clarify her role in linking female behaviour and politics. First, we find her late in Charles I's personal rule

---

[6] Michel de Montaigne, 'Of Bookes', in *The Complete Essays*, ed. M. A. Screech (Harmondsworth: Penguin, 1993), p. 843; Timothy Hampton, *Writing From History: the Rhetoric of Exemplarity in Renaissance Literature* (Ithaca: Cornell University Press, 1990), p. 174.

[7] Plinius Caecius Secundus, 'To Nepos', in *Pliny: Letters*, trans. William Melmoth, rev. W. M. L. Hutchinson (London: Heinemann, 1915), I, pp. 247–51. See *The Epigrams of Martial*, trans. Walter C. A. Ker (London: Heinemann, 1919), I, 30; *The Epigrams of Martial* (London: George Bell, 1875), pp. 30–1. See e.g. *The Annals and History of Cornelius Tacitus Made English By Several Hands*, 3 vols. (London: Matthew Gillyflower, 1698).

[8] See e.g. Thomas Heywood, *The Generall History of Women* (London, 1657), p. 221.

in a volume dedicated to Dorothy Sidney. Addressed by the poet Edmund Waller as Sacharissa, sister to Algernon Sidney and in later life an ironic political commentator. Dorothy Sidney is described as 'the first and last of these Stories'.[9] Arria's last speech is here extended to offer a Stoic example to the late 1630s. '[K]now', this Arria tells Paetus, 'that ere two days expire' he will be 'beheaded by a base hangman, offered up a tame sacrifice to insated tyranny. Awake the Roman in thee.' She asks Paetus, 'what canst thou hope for from a Tyrant abjur'd by all the Vertues[?]'.[10] The Stuarts may be implicated here. In the 1760s Arria appears again in Catharine Macaulay's republican *History of England*, particularly of the English Civil Wars and their aftermath. Macaulay writes of Arria with reference to a period of faction when patriotism needed to be distinguished from conspiracy, the Rye House plot. Macaulay describes the life of Rachel Russell, the widow of Lord Russell, executed for his part in plotting against the King:

A series of her letters to doctor Fitzwilliams, a clergyman, are very affecting descriptions of the contest between a passionate grief and the principle of pious resignation; and the uninterrupted sorrows of a long life, prove that it was the sense of religion, the duties of a mother, and the promise which she had made Lord Russell in the hour of parting, that she would preserve her life for the sake of his children, which alone prevented her from following the example of the Roman Arria, in that act of conjugal heroism for which this illustrious woman is so justly celebrated.[11]

Effecting an exemplary association despite the fact that as a Christian Rachel Russell lived on rather than emulating Arria's 'justly celebrated' suicide, Macaulay proposes Russell as a modern heroine whose virtue equals and even trumps that of her Roman precursor. Macaulay's use of an exemplary Roman matron suggests two things. First, it illustrates political and stylistic allegiance to classical modes, and so to the reading patterns associated with example. Secondly, Macaulay is calling upon a history of uses of this particular example to signal feminized political virtue, in this case inflected by the eighteenth-century emphasis on the

---

[9] George Rivers, *The Heroinae* (London, 1639), A3ᵛ.
[10] Ibid., pp. 13, 14.
[11] Catharine Macaulay, *History of England* (London: C. Dilly, 1781), VII, 446.

knowledge of the heart. Uses of Arria over a period of two centuries are linked by their shared reliance on the rich, identificatory, and self-canvassing practices of early modern reading. Macaulay's version is partially explained by her commitment to republican history, but by the same token it indicates the uneven way in which cultures of reading and interpretation change.[12] Not as famous as the life of Cato or the negative example of Catiline, the example of Arria was nevertheless current.

A contrastingly multivalent example is that of Lucretia, who is often associated with the examples of Tarquin and Brutus in stories of the founding of the Roman republic. One of the 'hinges on which the history of Rome turns', Lucretia's story of virtue and republic certainly puts women and politics in the same frame.[13] We might expect Lucretia to be a clear figure for republicanism, but in fact she stands in a complex relationship to political action and female virtue. If Arria's impotence is transformed to power by Stoic suicide, Lucretia's suicide holds a place as one of the most oppositely interpreted of classical self-murders.[14] Indeed, instability is crucial to Lucretia's status as an example. Moreover, given that even the earliest known telling of the story is a *re*telling, those using Lucretia came to her with a consciousness that the example had a history. Amalgamating material from earlier myths, the historian Livy tells the story thus.[15] A group of men drinking in the quarters of Sextus Tarquinius discuss their wives. Boasting that his is the most virtuous, Collatinus interrupts the debate to urge them to surprise their wives. Galloping to Rome, the men find all their wives engaged in the pursuit of luxury. Collatine's wife, Lucretia, alone is hard at work spinning. Seeing Lucretia, Tarquin becomes enflamed by lust and returns after dinner to burst into her bedroom. Even when he threatens to kill her, Lucretia refuses him. However, crucially:

---

[12] See Philip Hicks, 'Catharine Macaulay's Civil War: Gender, History, and Republicanism in Georgian Britain', *Journal of British Studies*, 41, No. 2 (2002), pp. 170–98.

[13] Pierre Bayle, cited in Ian Donaldson, *The Rapes of Lucretia* (Oxford: Clarendon Press, 1982), p. 8.

[14] Ibid., *passim*.

[15] Livy, *The Early History of Rome*, trans. Aubrey de Selincourt (1960; repr. Harmondsworth: Penguin, 2002), pp. 100–3; Bettina Matthes, *The Rape of Lucretia and the Founding of Republics* (University Park: Pennsylvania State University Press, 2000), pp. 23–50.

'If death will not move you,' Sextus cried, 'dishonour shall. I will kill you first, then cut the throat of a slave and lay his naked body by your side . . .' Even the most resolute chastity could not have stood against this dreadful threat.

Lucretia yields. Sextus enjoys her, and rides away, proud of his success.[16] The next day Lucretia calls together her father, husband, and Brutus. She tells the story and demands revenge. Her suicide, she asserts, will be testimony to her innocence, and she plunges a dagger into her heart. Brutus pulls out the dagger and urges the men to drive the Tarquins from Rome. So the republic came to be founded. And later Brutus, in defence of republican Rome, sought the death of his own sons.

As this brief retelling shows, the narrative has much potential for shifts of emphasis and interpretation. Lucretia could be understood as resisting or as consenting. From St Augustine's attack on her virtue ('if she is adulterous why is she praised? If chaste, why was she put to death?') to Rousseau's complex reworking of the issues in his *Nouvelle Héloïse*, the story of Lucretia has held an ambiguous place in political philosophy and related discourses: is she to be rightly characterized as virtuous or as desiring?[17] Thus, in the *Discourses* Machiavelli wrote, 'we read in Livy's history that the outrage done to Lucretia deprived the Tarquins of their rule', yet his own representation of the adulteress Lucrezia in *La Mandragola* depicts her as keen to have sex with another in order that she and her husband can have children—'I'm sweating with excitement', she tells us.[18] As Melissa M. Matthes argues, the sexualized significance of the story and the questions it raises about political action, women, and the public good are at the heart of each retelling.[19]

Written and visual interpretations of Lucretia permeate English sixteenth- and seventeenth-century culture and particularly political

---

[16] Livy, *Early History of Rome*, p. 101.
[17] Augustine, *The City of* God, trans. Henry Bettenson, ed. David Knowles (Harmondsworth: Penguin, 1972), pp. 29, 30, quoted in Donaldson, *Lucretia*, p. 29. See also pp. 28–39, and, on Rousseau, pp. 84–6.
[18] Niccolò Machiavelli, *The Discourses*, trans. Leslie J. Walker SJ, ed. Bernard Crick, rev. Brian Richardson (Harmondsworth: Penguin, 1979), p. 477; *La Mandragola*, scene 10 in *Machiavelli*, trans., and ed. Peter Bondella and Mark Musa (Harmondsworth: Penguin, 1979), p. 459.
[19] Matthes, *The Rape of Lucretia*, pp. 3–7.

meditations, and these often show the example's productive and ambiguous status. In the earlier period we find the Hardwick needle-work image (Figure 3). Mary D. Garrard thinks that one or two paintings of Tarquin and Lucretia, at least one by Artemesia Gentileschi, were in Charles I's collections.[20] Thomas Heywood's *The Rape of Lucrece* was acted at the Red Bull in Clerkenwell in 1608, 1630, and 1638. Shakespeare's poem on the subject was repeatedly reprinted. Its central section foregrounds the melancholy nature of Lucrece's suffering in an explicitly political, though not republican, context when Lucrece uses a narrative representation of Troy to articulate her problem. Lucrece turns to an image, 'a piece | Of skillful painting, made for Priam's Troy', using the image to figure her situation to herself, tracking simultaneously the painter's art in making 'a dry drop' seem 'a weeping tear'.[21] The image is used to build up a classical typology linking sexual betrayal and political crisis and using the image, explicitly, to figure meditation on the link between the crisis in 'crest'—honour, family, the domestic—and the political world played out in the tale of Priam and the rape of Lucrece—both, as poem and readers know, psychic crises which prefigure psychic and political transformation. The rape of Lucrece is here used to link the affective and political.

When we ask what happened to Lucretia in the mid-century crisis the answer is ambiguous. When Shakespeare's *Lucrece* was republished (under the Protectorate in 1655) with John Quarles's *The Banishment of Tarquin: or, the Reward of Lust* the frontispiece alone perhaps registers the reshaping of the story for a changed world (Figure 4). Hanging over the scene the head of Shakespeare instantiates the aesthetic primacy of the text. Lucretia, in classical garb by classical pillar, commits suicide. She is being approached by someone, possibly Brutus. Maybe the frontispiece turns attention to the suicide of Lucrece as a prequel to political change, but certainly not with a republican political imperative.

---

[20] See Santina M. Levey, *An Elizabethan Inheritance: The Hardwick Hall Textiles* (London: National Trust, 1998). Mary D. Garrard, *Artemesia Gentileschi: The Image of the Female Hero in Baroque Art* (Princeton: Princeton University Press, 1989), pp. 110, 201, 514. Compare Francis Haskell, 'Charles I's Collection of Pictures', in *The Late King's Goods*, ed. Arthur MacGregor (London: Alistair McAlpine; Oxford: Oxford University Press, 1989), pp. 203–31: 211.
[21] William Shakespeare, *The Poems*, ed. F. T. Prince (1969; repr. London and New York: Routledge, 1992), ll. 1366–7, 1375.

4. Shakespeare's *Lucrece* with John Quarles's *The Banishment of Tarquin: or, the Reward of Lust* (1655), frontispiece

Obviously, the vocabulary of republicans like John Milton and Algernon Sidney is marked by this story.[22] In the pro-republican newspaper *Mercurius Politicus*, as the battle of Worcester approached, Marchmont Nedham would trace the progress of Charles Stuart, as 'young Tarquin'. Praising the 'sweet . . . Air of a *Commonwealth*' in which men can 'breath freely, and be lively', he issues a warning: 'But oh—! *Young Tarquin* is a coming with a world of *Majesty* and *Vermin*; and there's not a Royalist in *England* but dreams of an *Office* (Sir *Reverence*) to be at least *Groom of the Stool* (if the *Kirk* do not rob him) or *Lord Chamberlain* among the *Ladies*, if his nose be not put out of joynt by Some hot-metalled *Laird*, or *nine peny Scotchman*.'[23] Evidently, 'Tarquin' was well enough known for Nedham to assume popular recognition. An author of a rather different political opinion, Margaret Cavendish conjures up Lucretia in a salon scene as a subject of a debate about history and the virtue of wives amongst visiting ladies: was she right to kill herself? The ladies, disputing, become so deeply involved that a passionate quarrel ensues: in this scene history, virtue, and Lucretia are the subjects of female mediation and discussion.[24] At the Restoration, Susan J. Owen comments, Nathaniel Lee's retelling of the tale of Tarquin's rape in *Lucius Junius Brutus* 'carried extra force' because the story had long been used against the Stuarts.[25] Aphra Behn's 'The Fair Jilt' and *Love Letters Between a Nobleman and his Sister* are two of many Restoration texts which draw on Lucretia's ambiguous status.

Even a brief tour like this shows that Lucretia and her stories were debated everywhere in the Civil War and Restoration. Far from being solely an exemplary virgin for republican writers, the evidence suggests that Lucretia remained an ambiguous, volatile, and popular example.

---

[22] See e.g. John Milton, *Of Prelatical Episcopacy* (1641), in *Complete Prose Works of John Milton*, ed. Don M. Wolfe, vol. I (New Haven: Yale University Press; Oxford: Oxford University Press; Geoffrey Cumberlege, 1953), pp. 618–52: 640; *A Second Defence of the English People*, in *Complete Prose*, ed. Don M. Wolfe, vol. IV(i) (New Haven: Yale University Press, 1966), pp. 538–686: 682; *Quam Diu*, in *Complete Prose*, ed. J. Max Patrick, trans. Paul W. Blackford, vol. V(ii) (New Haven: Yale University Press, 1971), pp. 489–95: 495. Algernon Sidney, *Court Maxims*, ed. Hans W. Blom, Eco Haitsma Mulier, and Ronald Janse (Cambridge: Cambridge University Press, 1996), p. 29.

[23] *Mercurius Politicus*, No. 5, Thursday, 4 July–Thursday, 11 July 1650.

[24] Margaret Cavendish, *CCXI Sociable Letters* (London, 1664), letter LIV, pp. 108–11.

[25] Susan J. Owen, *Restoration Theatre and Crisis* (Oxford: Oxford University Press, 1996), p. 176.

Indeed, the story's appeal, its piquancy, lay in its contradictoriness. Writers and readers were pushed to resolve or retain the questions Lucretia posed. Did her story offer an understanding of female virtue which extended women's capacities from sexual chastity to political planning, or did the narrator need to take a view on her sexual culpability? It is the contexts of writing and interpretation which shape what these figures exemplify in each instance. It would be a rash commentator who discounted the familiarity of this example and story in the early modern period: most uses of Lucretia are knowingly interpretations. If, as Ian Donaldson argues, it is possible to split some of the interpretations into sexual and define others as political, these versions are aware of each other; in seventeenth-century England philosophical, political, and erotic interpretations of Lucretia were intertwined.[26] While in later chapters we will find writers trying to use Lucretia's example for their own purposes, here we can note the sustained ambiguity which formed the background to such appropriations.

What of biblical examples? Arria offers an enduring classical example which was relatively stable in its interpretation, and in Lucretia's volatile status we see the rational and the affective, the sexual and the political combining in the understanding of women's connection to the political realm. Esther is a biblical example whose significance was debated by contemporaries. Her story can be summarized as follows. Replacing the naughty wife Vashti who would not come when she was called, Esther is chosen from amongst the palace virgins to be the wife of King Ahasuerus. Esther has been brought up with Mordecai. Mordecai sat at the gates of the palace and Haman, who found favour with the King, cannot bear that, where all men bow to him, Mordecai will not. Moreover, Haman decides to destroy the Jews. Mordecai tells Esther to be a 'supplicant' to the King for the Jews. So, notwithstanding that the King only sees those he calls for, she goes before Ahasuerus. Ahasuerus asks, 'What is thy petition?' and Esther invites him and Haman to a banquet the next day. Haman's relatives build a high gallows for the unbearable Mordecai. However, when Haman comes before the King, Ahasuerus has been reading the chronicles of his reign. In it he finds that Mordecai has told of a plot against the King and he decides to reward Mordecai. Haman appearing before him at that moment, he asks

---

[26] Donaldson, *Lucretia*, pp. 8–12.

Haman what is a good reward for the servant of a king? Thinking
Ahasuerus plans to reward him, Haman states the reward and ends up
taking a horse and fine apparel to Mordecai. After this he goes to the
banquet, at which the King again asks Esther her petition. Esther explains
Haman's plan against the Jews. Haman is hung from the high gallows he
intended for Mordecai and—this is the foundation of the feast of Purim—
Ahasuerus appoints a day on which the Jews can take revenge on those who
plot against them. A story of female transgressive supplication forgiven, a
story of invited and successful petitioning, a story of a reversal of fortune:
the story of Esther might also be seen as a story of feminine counsel to a
misdirected governor and, of course, a double revenge.

Like all examples, Esther was an early modern author's flexible friend.
Often used as an example of evil counsel and loyalty to a community,
Esther also figured the courage of the reformed church. Significantly,
'Ester Sowernam's' essay in the Jacobean controversy over the nature of
women was entitled *Ester hath hang'd Haman*. In 1640, with Deborah
and Judith, Esther was one of Heywood's exemplary Jewish women,
though she is presented ambiguously (Figure 2). In France the complexity of her story was acknowledged when she became the subject of
one of Racine's religious tragedies.[27] Rebecca Bailey has noted her
significance for the Roman Catholic Henrietta Maria and her circle.
However, Esther acquired particular and deepened significances during
the mid-century crisis, becoming virtually a patron saint of Civil War
women's petitions.[28] Probably the most discussed political genre in
which women participated in the Civil War, petitions are often both
powerful and formulaic. In them we see an example, Esther, at the heart
of intense political debates; she puts before us the complex question of
the collective, public, political dimension of women's political demands.
On 4 February 1642 *A True Copie of the Petition of the Gentlewomen and
Tradesmens-wives, in and about the City of London* was delivered to the

[27] Peter Merlin, *A Most Plaine and profitable Exposition of the Booke of Ester, delivered
in 26. Sermons* (London, 1599), p. 548. Esther Sowernam, *Ester hath hang'd Haman: or
An Answer to a lewd Pamphlet, entituled, The Arraignment of Women* (London, 1617);
Heywood, *Exemplary Lives*, p. 44.
[28] See Patricia Higgins, 'The Reactions of Women, with Special Reference to Women
Petitioners', in *Politics, Religion and the English Civil War*, ed. Brian Manning (London:
Edward Arnold, 1973), pp. 178–222. On Catholicism see Rebecca Bailey's forthcoming
monograph provisionally entitled *Staging the Old Faith: Roman Catholicism and the
Theatre of Caroline England*.

Commons.[29] The petition was delivered by Mrs Anne Stagg, '*a Gentle-woman and Brewers Wife, and many others with her of like rank and quality*' and the Commons '*sent them an answer by Mr PYM*' who '*came to the Commons doore*': 'We intreat you to repaire to your Houses, and turne your Petition which you have delivered here, into Prayers at home for us.' Less favourably, a newsbook focused on the status and sex of the petitioners, calling them as 'two or three hundred Oyster wives, and other dirty and tattered sluts', and it described the riot which followed the petition's delivery.[30] Acknowledging that petitioning might seem 'strange, and unbeseeming our sex', they assert 'the right and interest we have in the common and publique cause of the Church, it will, as we conceive (under correction) be found a duty commanded and required'.[31] 'Neither', we read:

are we left without examples in Scripture, for when the state of the Church, in the time of King *Ahasuerus* was by the bloody enemies thereof sought to be utterly destroyed, we find tha[t] *Ester* the Queen and her Mayds fasted and prayed, and that *Ester* petitioned to the King in behalf of the Church; and though she enterprised this duty with the hazard of her own life, being contrary to the Law to appear before the King before she was sent for, yet her love to the Church carried her thorow all difficulties, to the performance of that duty.[32]

The story of 'the Queen and her Mayds' legitimizes women petitioning rulers. The interest in the public good claimed by women here, however, is both religious in foundation and stops short of a claim to citizenship (Esther's royal status elides that question). Twelve years later, in 1653, women petitioners sought the reversal of the 'most unrighteous Act against Mr *Lilburne*'.[33] Close to Lilburne's own rhetoric, these petition-ers are 'much sadded to see our undoubted Right of Petitioning with-held', having failed to have their petition received by Parliament. 'Your Honours' they say 'may please to call to mind':

the unjust and unrighteous Acts made by King *Ahasuerus* in the case of *Mordecai* and the Jews; yet *Esther* that righteous woman being encouraged by the justness of

[29] *A True Copie of the Petition of the Gentlewomen and Tradesmens-wives, in and about the City of London* (London: R.O. & G.D. for John Bull, 1641(2)), E.134 (17). Also printed as *A True Copy...* (London: J. Wright, 1642); Higgins, 'Reactions', pp. 187–8.
[30] *True Copie*, p. 6 (A4ᵛ) mispag., *Certaine Informations*, no. 30, E.65 (8).
[31] Ibid., p. 6.
[32] Ibid., pp. 6–6 mispag. (A4ᵛ).
[33] *Unto every individual member of Parliament* (London, 1653).

the Cause (as we at this time are through the justness of Mr. *Lilburn*'s Cause, and the common Cause of the whole Nation) did adventure her life to petition against so unrighteous Acts obtained by *Haman* the Jews enemy.

Although this addresses MPs, through being printed the petition also claims a wider audience. Petitioners anticipate that the Commons will not be 'worse unto us, then the Heathen King was to *Esther*, who did not onely hear her Petition, but reversed that decree or Act gone forth against the Jewes, and did severely punish the obtainer thereof'.

Petitions using the story of Esther as an example both hint at and retreat from claims to women having political rights. The story of Esther permits a subtle assertion of political will, at times made under the banner of virtuous submission and at others an assertion of right. Petitioning was a specific and sometimes idealized part of the imagined resources of communication between ruled and rulers. In a certain sense, petition so conceived bypasses the civil sphere altogether by uniting subject and ruler. So the 'right of petitioning' calls up an ideal image of relations between ruler and subjects. Yet, evidently, the assertion of a right to such direct and ideal communication emerges as part of a claim that the subject is deprived of rights. Women's petitions, then, are both critical and obedient; they both claim and eschew rights, both assert and deny that women are political subjects. If political history misses much of women's relationship to politics because of the institutions it examines, then the petition as a form brings groups otherwise not considered in relation to politics into the historian's frame of reference.[34] Yet it may also be the case that group actions have been readily available for feminist analysis, apparently reflecting back to us some of the specifically modern methods of single-issue politics and direct action.

Civil War petitioning existed in a complex and contradictory social matrix.[35] By the 1640s it had a long and diverse history and its forms included the manuscript pleas of individuals (women had long petitioned for the release or return of menfolk from prison or the

[34] Patricia Crawford, ' "The Poorest She": Women and Citizenship in Early Modern England', in *The Putney Debates*, ed. Michael Mendle (Cambridge: Cambridge University Press, 2001), pp. 197–218: 198.

[35] See Mihoko Suzuki, *Subordinate Subjects: Gender, the Political Nation, and Literary Form in England, 1588–1688* (Aldershot: Ashgate, 2003), pp. 132–64, esp. 145–59; Anne Marie McEntee, ' "The [Un]Civill Sisterhood of Oranges and Lemons": Female Petitions and Demonstrations', in *Pamphlet Wars*, ed. James Holstun (London: Frank Cass, 1992), pp. 92–111.

galleys) and printed interventions. The 1640s, then, brought not so much new forms as new circumstances to the petitions and other genres of supplication. To petition as an attempt to influence formal politics is an assertion, if not always an articulated claim, of what a modern reader would call citizenship. At the same time, as Patricia Crawford helpfully reminds us, there was no debate about women's franchise in the period under discussion.[36] Petitions did attract attention.[37] The potential of Esther's story to assert both a claiming of rights and a kind of obedience is important, perhaps even the key to its popularity with petitioners. When we ask whether women's petitions are demands for citizenship or feminine supplications, we can see that Esther helps them to make productive the ambiguous position of the petitioner.[38] For the reasons explored here, then, the petition is an important but ambiguous clue to women's relationship to politics in the mid-century; it is a genre whose formulaic and repetitious incarnations can make it seem, sometimes, perhaps, misleadingly, a privileged key to understanding the place of women in the political sphere.

Arria, Lucretia, and Esther are important but, in different ways, ambiguous figures in the mid-century struggle over authority. To understand their role and those of others we need to turn from examples to the *idea* of the example.

THEORIES OF THE EXAMPLE

How can we theorize a little more specifically the role of the example? Machiavelli's dictum that 'All the things happening in the world, in all times, have their own parallels in the classical period' shows the importance of classical example but tells nothing of its use. In seventeenth-century England readers could find a wide range of commentaries on the use of example. George Puttenham, discussing 'historicall Poesie', canvasses the role of the example for vernacular readers:

[36] Crawford, '"The Poorest She"', p. 199; Keith Thomas, 'Women and the Civil War Sects', *PP* 13 (Apr. 1958), pp. 42–62.

[37] Letter from Sir John Scudamore to Brilliana Harley, *Calendar of the Manuscripts of the Marquis of Bath Preserved at Longleat, Wiltshire* (London: HMC, 1904), I, 8–33: 16–17.

[38] Compare Lucy Hutchinson, *On the Principles of Christian Religion* 'addressed to her daughter' (London: Longman, 1817), p. 121.

There is nothing in man of all the potential parts of his mind (reason and will except) more noble or more necessary to the active life then memory: because it maketh most to a sound judgement and perfect worldly wisedom, examining and comparing the times past with the present, and by them both considering the time to come, concludeth with a stedfast resolution, what is the best course to be taken in all his actions and advices in this world: it came upon this reason, experience to be so highly commended in all consultations of importance, and preferred before any learning or science, and yet experience is no more than a masse of memories assembled, that is, such trials as man hath made in time before. Right so no kinde of argument in all the Oratorie craft, doth better perswade and more universally satisfie then example, which is but the representation of old memories, and like successes happened in times past.[39]

If Puttenham offers example as a stable part of a shared pattern of memory, Montaigne's account found it contrastingly unreliable. Asserting that 'Example is an uncertain looking glass, all-embracing, turning all ways', he turns our attention to the power of reading and interpretation to make and remake what might seem to be the same example.[40] The stability Puttenham implies and Montaigne's crisis of signification represent two poles of theoretical consideration of the example; the writing and reading dynamics of exemplarity take place between them. In terms of actual texts, readers followed paths through texts as indicated by paratextual material, and textual and marginal prompts. Indexes, for instance, gave lists of biblical exempla used with page numbers, as in Henry Jessey and Sarah Wight's *The exceeding Riches of Grace* (1647). The apparatus reminds us of what the rhetoric books tell us of the use of example, and the repeated use of particular examples alerts us to their potentially over-determined, if not stable, significance.

However, that Arria consistently serves to put women in relation to politics tells us little about how each example was interpreted. Deep reading need not imply stability. How should we imagine mid-century readers of examples? Examples require the reader to negotiate between taking the proper name as an incantation or using the name to unlock a retelling of the life—but the experience of that choice, a particular

[39] George Puttenham, *The Arte of English Poesie*, ed. Gladys Doidge Willcock and Alice Walker (1936; repr. Cambridge: Cambridge University Press, 1970), p. 39. See Peter Mack, *Elizabethan Rhetoric: Theory and Practice* (Cambridge: Cambridge University Press, 2002), p. 91.

[40] Montaigne, *Essays*, III, 13.

reader's reaction at a specific time, is emotional and identificatory as well as reasoned. When should the reader stop reading into an example? An example gives the reader a task which halts the narrative flow and potentially connotatively exceeds the bounds of argument. What Elizabeth Cowie argues in the context of images can be helpful here: readers will be moved by examples in unexpected, perhaps undesired, ways. The 'truth' of an example is in the complex identification of the interpreter and 'identification does not involve a simple matching of self' and subject, but rather an experience of the example which blends reasoned and emotional responses.[41] Arria's life as an example is comparatively stable in the details that are picked out for our attention, but even so interpretations would have had hazards. Can Rachel Russell's husband, executed for his part in the Rye House plot, charitably be described as Paetus? What is a reader's emotional and reasoned reaction to suicide? As much as being a 'clearing' (as it was designated in medieval writing) or clarification, the example can be a complicating addition, something which 'adds itself, it is a surplus' to explanation.[42] Its evocation of a parallel narrative must call our attention to the way it is an artful, but also at times a dangerous, supplement.[43] In the mid-seventeenth century, example, not always used sophisticatedly, seems to have been a trusted tool of persuasion at all levels of discussion.

Although in studies of the topic the seventeenth century is often characterized as a time when exemplarity became synonymous with mere authority, it might be more accurate to say that the seventeenth century had its own debates on exemplarity.[44] Part of the significance of examples for readers concerned use and applicability. Thomas Hobbes and John Locke both warned against the extension of meanings by the use of metaphors and historical examples (Hobbes finds himself using them nonetheless).[45] Yet examples continued to be important in the

---

[41] Elizabeth Cowie, *Representing the Woman* (Basingstoke: Macmillan, 1997), pp. 1–14: 5.

[42] Jacques Derrida, *Of Grammatology*, trans. Gayatri Chakravorty Spivak (Baltimore: Johns Hopkins University Press, 1977), p. 144.

[43] Hampton, *Writing from History*, p. 19.

[44] See also François Rigolet, 'The Renaissance Crisis of Exemplarity', *JHI* 59, No. 4 (1998), pp. 557–63: 558; Michel Jeanneret, 'The Vagaries of Exemplarity: Distortion or Dismissal?', *JHI* 59, No. 4 (1998), pp. 565–79: 578.

[45] See Thomas Hobbes, *Leviathan*, ed. Richard Tuck (Cambridge: Cambridge University Press, 1991), ch. 4, 'Of Speech', esp. metaphors (p. 31); John Locke, *Essay*

business of interpretation well into the Restoration and in some cases long beyond; the habit of exemplary reading in its complex rather than citational forms was a long-lived mode of interpretation. Exemplarity remained a building block of interpretation, supplying a framework for reading which, though often acknowledged as having complex implications, also seems to have been used as though it was simple. Indeed, we find Catharine Macaulay using the Stoic example of Arria in the mideighteenth century.

Recent discussions of the early modern example have seen it as inviting readers to make connections between textual worlds and their own. Simultaneously, it is recognized as implying a problematic of reading. As Timothy Hampton comments, exemplarity:

shifts the problem of imitation, much discussed by recent critics as a cornerstone of *writing* in the Renaissance, to the level of *reading*. The exemplary figure in a Renaissance text can be seen as a marked sign that bears the moral and historical authority of antiquity and engages the reader in a dialogue with the past—a dialogue to be played out . . . on the stage of public action.[46]

Hampton emphasizes that the example signals not so much clarification as the complexity of interpretation. Readers using examples, though, were not always those participating in the humanistic shift from exemplary reading to the 'public action' described by Hampton, for while some readers saw themselves as actors in the world there were also many others, including women, who do not, but who did read, interpret, and emulate.[47] Many discussions of the rhetoric of exemplarity restrict themselves to a narrow time frame, a narrow corpus of texts, and the experience of elite male readers; the gendered reading of examples has received limited attention.

Rather than being 'merely' ornament, the examples in an early modern text gave the reader a route, but one which, by the seventeenth

Concerning Human Understanding, ed. Peter H. Nidditch (Oxford: Clarendon Press, 1975), III, x, 'Of the Abuse of Words', pp. 490–508: 508. See also discussion in Gordon J. Schochet, *The Authoritarian Family and Political Attitudes in Seventeenth Century England* (1975; repr. New Brunswick, N.J.: Transaction, 1988), p. xxv.

[46] Hampton, *Writing from History*, p. 5.

[47] See Kevin Sharpe, *Reading Revolutions: The Politics of Reading in Early Modern England* (New Haven: Yale University Press), pp. 27–89; Anthony Grafton and Lisa Jardine, ' "Studied for Action": How Gabriel Harvey Read his Livy', *PP* 129 (1990), pp. 30–78.

century at least, not only was uncertain but might be experienced as such. In the context of the religious and political fervour of the mid-century readers had an apprehension of the importance of experience, and so of the applicability of an example. To some, at certain moments, it even seemed that the present might excel the classical past and produce a new age of examples, even miracles. While such thinking led to the Quaker James Nayler entering Bristol on a donkey in duplication of Christ's entry into Jerusalem, it also led other readers to interpret examples in nuanced and self-conscious ways. One distinction between biblical and classical examples is their relationship to time. While in strict typology the events of the Old Testament prefigure Christ's life, the early modern reader of biblical examples approached the central story of the life of Christ from the other end of the timeline. As we find in some of the texts we come to, this is complicated by the writer's and reader's own relationship to the times prophesied in the Bible: is this the time when maidens dream dreams? Who are the women who dream? To think through examples, particularly in the mid-century period, meant to think about one's own world; the examples which put women into communication with politics and vice versa both registered that world and, by forming patterns of reading and understanding, to an extent shaped it.

It is possible, as this chapter does, to examine examples as we find them in these texts. But the really telling parts of the history of exemplarity—the circumstances and particulars of reading and writing—leave fewer traces. Women's reading of example was conjunctural—and specific, often over-determined; locations were important in women's opportunities to read. Domestic instruction (as recorded by Lady Margaret Hoby and Lady Anne Clifford) took place within the household; it supplies one reiterative and didactic scene of exemplary reading and writing. Ministers instructed in reading and note-taking. 'Reading', for upper gentry and elite women, seems to have included solitary reading and being read to—by men and by waiting women. The walls of the prayer closet enclosed intense identificatory experiences of scriptural reading, yet at the same time the bedroom might become the situation of collective interpretation as men and women witnessed a woman, physically weak, made strong by grace. As Richard Rambuss puts it, '[s]cripture [becomes]—a virtual language machine for producing self-reflexive expression and understanding'; to read an example in such circumstances is also to explore one's self—and, as Rambuss also implies, if this understanding of reading hardly produces an autonomous self, neither can interpretation and self-interpretation be seen as wholly hegemonic.[48] These may have been the locations where some of May's 'Semproniaes', Sara Wight and Brilliana Harley, came to know interpretation and see its wider applications.

READING AND DOING: EDWARDS AND CHIDLEY, ATTOWAY AND MILTON

To find exemplarity at work we need to see interpretative exchanges, and I will examine two instances. In 1646 the Presbyterian hereisographer Thomas Edwards abused Katherine Chidley as a 'brazen-faced audacious old women resembled unto Jael'.[49] Behind this simple (if nasty) insult there is an enigmatic history. In 1641 Chidley had prefaced her attack on Edwards, her *Justification of the Independent Churches*, with a quotation from Judges 4: 21: 'Then Jael, Heber's wife took a nail out of the tent, and took a hammer in her hand, and went softly unto him, and smote the nail into his temples and fastened it to the ground, (for he was fast asleep and weary) and so he died.'[50] We cannot know whether Edwards is recalling his earlier tangle with Chidley. What we can see at work is the importance and instability of example, its ability to link apparently unlike situations and discourses. Concomitantly, we see its tendency to exceed requirements. When Chidley prefaces her text with Jael's deed it seems to describe female heroism, albeit of a kind so extreme as to be troubling. Edwards uses the same figure to emphasize unfeminine, hard, bold, and rebellious qualities. But what makes this possible is that Chidley's own use of Jael is problematically ferocious—it is hard to stabilize Jael as an unproblematic figure for female virtue.[51]

---

[48] Richard Rambuss, *Closet Devotions* (Durham: Duke University Press, 1998), p. 115.

[49] Thomas Edwards, *Gangraena* (1st edn. London, 1646; repr. Exeter: Rota, 1977), pt. III, p. 170. On Edwards see Ann Hughes, *Gangraena and the Struggle for the English Revolution* (Oxford: Oxford University Press, 2004), pp. 64–5, 113–14, 175, 193, 244–5, 273–5.

[50] Katherine Chidley, *Justification of the Independent Churches* (London, 1641), title page.

[51] See Hilary Hinds, *God's Englishwomen* (Manchester: Manchester University Press, 1996), p. 71.

Example could open politicized discourses to women, but circumstances made examples inconsistent and subject to interpretation.

The instance of Mistris Attoway suggests cultural awareness of the importance of example and interpretation as simultaneously crucial and dangerous in putting women in relation to politics. It allows us also to consider women as readers of examples. We turn once more to Thomas Edwards in his anatomy of the sects, *Gangraena*:

> There are two Gentlemen of the Inns of Court, civill and well disposed men, who out of novelty went to her the women preach, and after Mistris *Attoway* the Lacewoman had finished her exercise, these two Gentlemen had some discourse with her, and among other passages she spake to them of Master *Miltons* Doctrine of Divorce, and asked them what they thought of it, saying, it was a point to be considered of; and that she for her part would look more into it, for she had an unsanctified husband, that did not walk in the way of *Sion* nor speak the language of *Canaan*; and how accordingly she hath practised it in running away with another womans husband, is now sufficiently known to Mr. *Goodwin* and Mr. *Saltmarsh*, and is one of the lies like all the rest in Mr. *Edwards Gangraena*.[52]

Mistris Attoway, for Edwards, is an example of the problematic power of reading in combination with female concupiscence. Although she is reading a text which explores social issues of familial rather than overtly governmental power, as her actions indicate, Milton's text had substantial political implications. Mistris Attoway interprets according to example with—for Edwards—catastrophic consequences.

What this example gives us is not a woman reading political theory but a woman canvassing a text which, in its insistence on marriage as a revocable contract, inevitably raises the question of who can dissolve that contract. In Milton's tracts of 1643–4 this argument became associated with the issue of the licensing of books and so with the

---

[52] Mistris Attoway is mentioned in Edwards, *Gangraena*, pt. I, pp. 84–5, pt. II, pp. 10–11, pt. III, pp. 26–7 (see Exeter, 1977 edn.; see also 1st edn. (1646) plus appendix, pp. 120–3). This quotes letters by Attaway and Jenney justifying running away together in Miltonic terms. William Jenney writes to his wife: 'I thought good write unto you these few lines to tell you that because you have been to me rather a disturber of my body and soule, then to be a meet help for me . . . And for looking for me to come to you againe, I shall never come to you againe any more. I shall send unto you no more concerning any thing. If you had been a kind woman unto me I should never have parted with you' (p. 123). Milton's *Doctrine and Discipline of Divorce* is mentioned in *Gangraena* on pp. 34 and 154 (marginal note), and pt. II, pp. 10–11.

question of public debate.[53] Famously, Milton sees the absence of appropriate 'conversation' as 'a daily trouble and paine of losse in some degree like that which Reprobates feel' and so 'unprofitable and dangerous to the Common-wealth, when the household estate, out of which must flourish forth the vigor and spirit of all publick enterprizes, is so ill contented and procur'd at home, and cannot be supported'.[54] The function of the household here, and in the later *Judgement of Martin Bucer*, is to facilitate the man's ability to act in the public world.

For Edwards, Mistris Attoway was an example of the way female reading and interpretation outside the structures of the national church endangered state and family. Even so, his telling of it is evidence of the deep engagement with political issues and practices fostered by the exemplary methods of reading. Certainly this story shows example as a resource in building a politicized identity. Mistris Attoway reminds us that, if we are thinking about women's relationship to the political sphere both as we might find it revealed in women's texts and as we find it imagined in the texts of men, there are places to begin other than the teleological narrative of the foundations of modern political thought; other texts besides canonical political theory played key roles in shaping women's relationship to politics. Whether or not Mistris Attoway lived and breathed, her ambiguous role in *Gangraena* is to show a woman making a gendered and politicized textual interpretation. Moreover, the nature of the text interpreted, as well as the characterization of the interpretation, helps us to think about women's relationship to politics in (but also out of) the gathered churches. *The Doctrine and Discipline of Divorce*, on which Mistris Attoway generally models her conduct, addresses issues of rule from the oblique direction of theorizaton of the family and biblical and classical interpretation. *Doctrine and Discipline* has implications for the *polis*, but begins with

---

[53] See the 2nd edn. of *The Doctrine and Discipline* (1643, 1644); *The Judgement of Martin Bucer* (1644); *Tetrachordon* (1645); *Colasterion* (1645). In the 'Post-script' to *Martin Bucer* (July 1644), apparently fearing that his tract would not be licensed, Milton began to make the arguments that he would follow up in *Areopagitica* in November of that year. In this 'Post-script' he asserts that his work, containing only as much as texts written under Catholic censorship should at 'a time of free speaking, free writing, not find a permission to the Presse' would be shocking. John Milton, *Complete Prose Works*, ed. Ernest Sirluck, vol. II (New Haven: Yale University Press; Oxford: Oxford University Press, 1959), pp. 416–79: 478.

[54] *Doctrine*, in *Complete Prose*, II, 217–356: 247.

the household. We find women as political writers and readers interpreting such texts about the 'family' but with wider implications. The recorded or imagined instance of Attoway's reading suggests strongly that, as I have been suggesting, examples were construed not in a simplistic didactic way but as a language for examining the relations between the political, domestic, and sacred domains.

To revisit my questions, what evidence is likely to reveal women's relationship to politics in seventeenth-century England? Which methods are helpful in interpreting this evidence? The evidence assessed here suggests that both the use of exemplarity (including, here, the biblical example and type) and particular examples were part of the textual features which made such connections. It is clear that women are not assigned a singular position in exemplarity—we need not, for example, think of exemplary women locked always into positions of mediation between men (though this was sometimes the case), but as diverse in their implications; the purposes of examples are contingent. Nevertheless, consideration of examples does reveal a repertoire which signalled to a reader that politics was being discussed. A reader encountering Arria, Lucretia, and Esther would anticipate the emergence of a political point, and the same can be said of Jael, Judith, Medea, and Antigone. Eve is a special case. The presence of such figures indicates that women were useful in thinking about politics; it shows that men and women used female, as well as male, examples to make political points; and—as in the case of 'Mistris Attoway'—we can see the ambiguous potential of women reading exemplarily. The evidence suggests, too, that examples were potentially unpredictable, certainly complex. They inflect the treatment of women's relationship to politics in subtle, but not wholly predictable, ways. Readers—and other writers—can deliberately or accidentally 'misread' them.

More generally, exemplarity directs our attention to the interpretative chain of reading whereby scenes or figures are taken from a text, then used by another reader, then perhaps reused. A reader always meets an example in the form of a *re*interpretation. The example is a sign which is an addition, a surplus to explanation in covering a void and implies, as Montaigne reminds us, its own making and unmaking by the reader.[55] A text using (interpreting) examples and a reader reading—both are part

[55] Derrida, *On Grammatology*, p. 144.

of often powerful dynamics of identification and disidentification.[56] While virtue is crucial to the process of reading it does not necessarily, simply, reside in the example. Examples permit the coexistence of what elsewhere appear as contradictions. If exemplarity invites a reader to use reason it also provokes empathy, and identification. Exemplarity is intertextual, pulling into a text meanings from elsewhere. In the writing of a text the same example can be positively or negatively inflected. Writers and readers, too, needed to make decisions about whether or not to agree to an example's force as illustrative and ideal.[57] Exemplary reading reminds us that early modern readers grouped things differently, read differently. Forceful as it was for contemporaries, perhaps because of its very familiarity, exemplarity is not much explored by historians of political theory.

In the coming chapters we will encounter many examples and readers. We can now approach them with a sense of the reading patterns associated with example. We can say that examples were crucial in putting women in relation to politics. But, when writing of women, what can we mean by 'politics'? Forming a methodological pair with this one, the next chapter looks more closely at what politics might be; examining particular cases, it asks how we can consider writings, particularly those by women, to be 'political'.

---

[56] See Suzanne Trill, 'The Erotics of the Gaze in Æmilia Lanyer', in *Women and Culture at the Courts of the Stuart Queens*, ed. Claire McManus (Basingstoke: Macmillan, 2003), pp. 103–21.

[57] Jeanneret, 'The Vagaries of Exemplarity'.

2

Test Cases: Brilliana Harley
and Anne Clifford

If, in theory, the absence of women was part of what guaranteed the
sanctity of the political sphere in early modern England, how can we
conceptualize the relationship of women to that sphere? One line of
enquiry, pursued in the last chapter, is to analyse the gendered rhetoric
texts employ in order to better understand the interpretative possibilities
available to writers and readers. A complementary approach, used here,
is the examination of the reading and writings of particular women and
their circumstances. Accordingly, this chapter discusses two writers who
have not usually been considered in the same frame as politics, Brilliana
Harley and Anne Clifford. They, and the language they use, are test
cases for this study in two ways. First, when we ask what are the
relationships between their writing and politics we find, in different
ways, that each corpus is deeply immersed in political concerns. Second,
however, the ways in which their writings register political concerns
require that we expand and refine what we mean by politics. The
reception and transmission of these women's texts tell us about changes
in the understanding of politics and of women's relationship to it. In
Harley's case we need to look at the border between politics and religion
and consider the status of property in the making of political claims;
Clifford requires us to recall that to claim land and inheritance constitutes a form of political identity. Both writers trouble modern interpretations of the border between 'private' and 'public', and both remind
us that, although this study focuses mainly on the mid- to late seventeenth century, many of the ideas drawn on during that period have
roots in the debates and events of the early years of the century, or even
earlier, in legal, religious, and political thinking of the sixteenth century.
Each writer encounters and opposes authorities stronger than herself

and in doing so they draw on conceptions and languages of political subjectivity which, while they share some contours, are also radically different. As test cases, then, these writers invite us to understand that women were deeply enmeshed in political ideas, and to begin to reformulate what we think of as political.

PRIVATE, PUBLIC, 'PURITAN', POLITICAL: BRILLIANA HARLEY'S LETTERS

Let us begin with an example. On 25 October 1638 Brilliana Harley wrote from Brampton Bryan, close to Wales, to her son Edward at Oxford:

Good Need- I hope these lines will finde you well at Oxford. I longe to reseave the ashurance of your coming well to your journyes end. We have had faire weather sence you went, and I hope it was so with you, which made it more pleasing to me. You are now in a place of more varietyes then when you were at home; therefore take heede it take not up your thoughts so much as to neglect that constant sarvis you owe to your God. When I lived abroode, I tasted something of those willes: therefore I may the more experimentally give you warning. Remember me to your tutor, in home I hope you will finde dayly more and more cause to love and respect. I thanke God my coolde is something better then when you left me. I pray God blles you, and give you of those saveing grasess which will make you happy heare and for ever heareafter.

> Your most affectinat mother,
> Brilliana Harley[1]

Most of Brilliana Harley's edited letters are to her son Edward or Ned. Here we see her written negotiation of their separation when he went to university. That he is in Oxford, a place of infinitely more variety than Brampton, divides mother and son. Yet, Harley asserts, she herself knew the wiles of that world when she was 'abroode' and can warn him against it with knowledge. He is far away indeed, but Oxford and the Welsh borders are still close enough that they might share weather. And, with

---

[1] Brilliana Harley to Edward Harley, 25 Oct. 1638, Letter IX in *Letters of the Lady Brilliana Harley*, ed. Thomas Taylor Lewis (London: Camden Society, 1854), p. 7. Unless otherwise stated, letters are to this recipient. In referring to Harley's writings in general, printed editions are used.

luck, Ned's tutor will induct him into the service of God as his parents would wish. This first letter attempts to compass the literal, psychic, and social distance of Brampton from Oxford as well as Ned's emergence as a young adult. There are none of the references to material things and comforts—eggs, watches, pies—that have at times been taken as characterizing Harley's correspondence; rather, we see clearly her concern with godly life, and the world.[2] However, although Jacqueline Eales's important and detailed study has meticulously located Brilliana Harley as an active participant in the Puritan and political context of her family she is still understood by many readers as suffering the impact of the Civil War rather than developing a political analysis. For these readers, Harley's letters disclose a private world of affection and anxiety—pies and prayers.[3] Harley did remain in Brampton Bryan while her husband, Sir Robert Harley, sat in the House of Commons in London. However, while Harley's letters indeed demonstrate the affective bonds of a seventeenth-century family, they also consistently analyse changing political events. In examining Harley as a writer with a critical religious agenda, and who became a political commentator and interlocutor, what follows offers a necessarily detailed account of intersection of local, neighbourly, kin, but also national issues as they mark Harley's letters.

On 17 November 1638, for example, Harley reminds Ned that Christ 'toold his decipels that theare must be wars and rumers of wars . . . greate trubells and wars must be, both to purg his church of ipocrits, and that his enemies at the last may be utterly distroyed'. She writes of 'The Quene mother', so 'transported with joy, as they say, at the sight of the quene, that shee was in a trance'. Worth telling, too, is that Brilliana had heard 'theare was a cardenalls cape brought to the Custom Howes, valued at a high rate, but none would owne it'.[4] Drawing this section of the letter to a close, she tells Ned that to 'requete your intelligence', or reimburse him for sending her information, she

  [2] See Letter XII, 17 Nov. 1638 (ibid., pp. 9–11); Letter XL, 10 May 1639 (ibid., pp. 51–3).

  [3] Crucial for study of the Harleys is Jacqueline Eales, *Puritans and Roundheads: The Harleys of Brampton Bryan and the Outbreak of the English Civil War* (Cambridge: Cambridge University Press, 1990).

  [4] Letter XII, 17 Nov. 1638 (*Letters*, p. 10).

lets him 'know what I heare'. This letter, like many others, reveals Edward and his mother swapping 'intelligence' with some intensity. In 1638 'hot' Protestants like Brilliana and Ned Harley were hungry for political change.[5] Under Charles I's personal rule and as the Civil War began, many, such as the diarists Ralph Knyvett and Ralph Josselin, recorded their eagerness to understand and perhaps influence events.[6]

Most of what Brilliana Harley wrote was letters. As a genre the letter was used for several distinct kinds of writing, sometimes public and sometimes private. Both as a writing practice and as a testing ground for ties of friendship and allegiance, the letter in the official and 'domestic' forms was crucial to the making of social and literary-political culture in Stuart and Civil War England. The main means of both domestic communication and of news-carrying throughout the first half of the seventeenth century, the letter was a form simultaneously public and private. Extending into verse epistle at one border and list of enclosures at the other, it could be aesthetically crafted or quotidian. The same letter would carry matters political and commonplace. Writing of women's use of letters, James Daybell notes the flexibility of the genre and the different purposes for which they were employed. Harley's letters, driven by purpose, were formal and informal and they illuminatingly register the growing tensions generated by the impending war.[7] Harley's letters give us a great quantity of detail about the shaping of one particular woman's relationship to national and local politics, and about her actions. Offering an excellent corpus in which to trace the gendering of political authority in family, kinship, and neighbourly relationships

---

[5] On hot Protestants, see Peter Lake with Michael Questier, *The Antchrist's Lewd Hat: Protestants, Papists and Players in Post-Reformation in England* (New Haven: Yale University Press, 2002), pp. xiv–xvi and *passim*.

[6] Thomas Knyvett, *The Knyvett Letters (1620–1644)*, ed. Bertram Schofield (London: Constable, 1949); *The Diary of Ralph Josselin, 1616–1683*, ed. Alan Macfarlane (London: Oxford University Press for the British Academy, 1976).

[7] *Early Modern Women's Letter-Writing, 1450–1700*, ed. James Daybell (Basingstoke: Palgrave, 2001), pp. 2–3. Regarding the political significance of women's letters see *The Letters of Lady Arbella Stuart*, ed. Sarah Jayne Steen (New York: Oxford University Press, 1994); *Elizabeth Cary Lady Falkland: Life and Letters*, ed. Heather Wolfe, Renaissance Texts from Manuscript 4 (Cambridge: RTM, 2001), *passim*. See also *Letter-Writing in Renaissance England*, ed. Alan Stewart and Heather Wolfe, Folger Shakespeare Library (Washington, D.C.: University of Washington Press, 2004).

as well as in the household, Harley's letters also reveal the political implications of religious positions.

Some of what Harley brings to her letter-writing has roots in the Puritanism of the early part of the century, and that will be discussed later. First, however, I want to examine the networks of local and familial relationship suggested in Harley's letters, and investigate the ways in which hot Protestantism supplied Harley with a Civil War politics. What can the detailed materials of Harley's everyday engagements tell us about her political identity, her connection to politics? Brilliana Harley sends letters to Edward (or Ned) at Oxford in 1638, and her correspondence follows him to London in 1640, continuing to her death in 1643. During this time, as Parliament and King were increasingly at loggerheads, the Harleys' religious and political position was known, perhaps infamous, in Herefordshire. Thus, while Harley expresses to Ned her belief in Parliament's political and religious case, her letters simultaneously register the complicating factors of her daily life. Within the discourses of love, reciprocity, and dependence that the high gentry and nobility of Herefordshire used to articulate their local and national interrelationships we can see emerging and hardening differences. Although distinctions probably seem clearer with hindsight than they were for those experiencing them, from 1641 we can trace an increasing tension, marked by the way Harley describes flashpoints for conflict—an election, the departure of a loved relative to join the king at York, a fair, a church service.

Relations with neighbours were slow to unravel. While relations with the Scudamore family, with whom there had always been religious differences, were gradually tested to the point of fracture, relations with another neighbour, Sir William Croft, remained complex. Earlier Sir William Croft seems to have shared Sir Robert Harley's unwillingness to submit to the methods of Charles I's personal rule; Crofts and Harleys seem to have enjoyed a warm connection. However, on 25 March 1641 Brilliana reports:

Sr William Croft is much against the parlament, and utters his minde freely: he was much displeased that they would petition the Parlament: he toold Mr Gower he was a moufer of sedistion; and my cosen Tomkins was very hoot with him: they say the parlament dous theare owne biusness, and not the cuntryes. I shall long to heare from you. . . . On munday before Easter, Mr Kirll and some other gentellmen intend to seet forward with the petition, which I hope will be well taken.[8]

By midsummer of the next year the Herefordshire gentry were drafting position statements.[9] Brilliana writes to Sir Robert with a report of a visit from Sir William Croft (described by Jacqueline Eales as an active commissioner for the King). Croft attempted to bridge political differences by distinguishing public and private connections: although 'his private affection' to Harley remained the same, 'in the way of the public he would favour none'.[10]

Similar tensions affect kinship relations. Harley writes to Edward of her sister Lady Frances Pelham, in Lincolnshire (her nephew—another Edward—joined him at Oxford). Frances left a manuscript spiritual record, 'Expressions of Faith', containing advice, poetry, and meditations and dedicated to her 'dearly beloved Children'.[11] Although Frances Pelham seems to have shared many of her sister's views, her husband, Sir William Pelham, did not. After Frances's death in 1641 Harley's comment that her children 'want theare mother' probably had political as well as familial implications, but relations with Sir William and other Pelhams continued to be cordial: Brilliana Harley sends a buck to her 'cosen Pelham', and records news from the family.[12] In May 1642 the widowed Sir William Pelham wrote to her 'out of Linconscheere', and Harley relays the news to Edward:

I see my brother Pelham is not of my minde. I thinke now, my deare sister was taken away that she might not see that which would have grefed her harte.

Sr William Pelham rwites me word he has given up his liftenantcy and his gooing to Yorke, to the king, being his sarvant, as he rwites me word, as so bound by his oath.[13]

Harley's attitude indicates the profound interpenetration of practical and political considerations. Civil war loomed, and Pelham's letter, recognizing the power of political differences, stands as a kind of farewell.

[8] Letter CVI, 25 Mar. 1641 (*Letters*, p. 121).

[9] See e.g. ibid., pp. 223–4.

[10] Quoted in Eales, *Puritans and Roundheads*, p. 159: see n. 17.

[11] Portland Collection, Nottingham University, PwV89 'Expressions of Faith', fo. 1ᵛ.

[12] Letter CXVII, 21 May 1641 (*Letters*, p. 130); Letter XLV, 4 July 1639 (ibid., pp. 59–60); Letter C, 15 Feb. 1640/1 (ibid., pp. 113–14). See Eales, *Puritans and Roundheads*, p. 35.

[13] Letter CLIV, 17 May 1642 (*Letters*, p. 161).

Yet, it would appear that the very letter which signified an absolute political parting of the ways spoke of a desire to maintain precisely those kin relationships disrupted by political divisions. As Harley conveys its meaning to Ned, Pelham's letter leaves kinship ties broken but also affirmed. And as we shall see, in practice, Harley's ties with Pelham continued. At the same time as Pelham's political disagreement with the Harleys became clear, another incident may register the Harleys' political isolation even as it speaks to us of the management of local competition. In May 1642 Brilliana Harley tried to have her son made a burgess. She used intermediaries to canvass the possibilities with care and found that Lord Scudamore's son was standing. On 3 June she wrote that 'I sent to Heariford to let them know that...I did not further desire it for you,...and desired if my lords sonne did not stand, that then they would give you theare vosies, which they then promised they would, and tooke my thankes very well.'[14] As Michael J. Braddick notes, the legitimacy of social and implicitly political values was tested through the mechanisms of office-holding.[15] Here we see Harley active in such local politics, albeit by proxy, but apparently losing influence; Harley's strategy of avoiding open conflict may evade open defeat. It also avoids making explicit the importance of politics in local connections.

Even in late 1642, although Harley's opinions were well known, a huge supporting network held in place quotidian ties.[16] It is not until June 1642 that Harley tells her son, 'I acknowledg I doo not thinke meself safe wheare I am.'[17] Indeed, it shows, perhaps, how slowly and incompletely ties of association dissolved that on 25 June 1642, when Brilliana Harley was already considering how to get hold of shot to defend property and principles, she writes to Ned offended at a slight by Croft: 'Sir William Croft came to see me: he never asked how your father did; spoke slightly, and stayed but a littele.' Croft had come 'from my lord Harbert', who was raising levies for the King, and he too, Harley surmised, was making preparations for war: 'I heare that he has commanded the beackon new furnisched, and nwe piche put into it. I have

---

[14] Letter CLX, 3 June 1642 (ibid., p. 166). The issue runs from 20 May 1642 (Letter CLVI, ibid., pp. 163–4) to 3 June.
[15] Michael J. Braddick, *State Formation in Early Modern England c.1550–1700* (Cambridge: Cambridge University Press, 2000), pp. 68–90.
[16] Eales, *Puritans and Roundheads*, p. 159.
[17] Letter CLXI, 4 June 1642 (*Letters*, pp. 166–7).

sent to inquire affter it; if it be so I will send your father word.'[18] Harley's
final comment illuminates the paradox of friendship in war: 'I never hard
of a man so changed as they say Sr William Croft is. He gave me a slight
visit.' She continues, 'I have sent up the pistolls your father sent for, by
the carrier.'[19] Harley's resentment coexists with her war preparations:
where is friendship, where enmity in local politics?

Fascinated as Harley was by reports of parliamentary debates, local
circumstances were what governed her safety. The summer months
before Charles I finally raised his standard are marked by a sequence
of incidents which made Harley fearful. Rank notwithstanding, where
Harley lived politics was expressed in the reversal of neighbourliness and
found expression in festival aggression as well as in official forms. She
witnessed the transformation of local rituals as they became animated by
religious and political symbolism and emotions. Two incidents, one at a
nearby fair, the other at church, indicate the way festivity became a form
of protest. On 4 June 1642 Harley wrote:

At Loudlow they seet up a May pole, and a thinge like a head upon it, and so
they did at Croft, and gathered a greate many about it, and shot at it in deristion
of roundheads. At Loudlow they abused Mr Bauges sonne very much, and are
so insolent that they durst not leave theare howes to come to the fast.
I acknowledg I doo not thinke meself safe wheare I am. I loos the comfort of
your fathers company, and I am in but littell safety, but that my trust is in God;
and what is doun in your fathers estate pleasess him not, so that I wisch meselfe,
with all my hart, at Loundoun, and then your father might be a wittnes of what
is spent; but if your father thinke it beest for me to be in the country, I am very
well pleased with what he shall thinke beest.[20]

Maypoles, besides signifying 'traditional' festivity, signalled the
intensification of competition between those who sponsored godly
reformation and others who, with various views, from Laudianism
to festive aggression, took up other positions. Maypoles put the
conflict on the ground. Famously, in *New English Canaan* (1632)
Thomas Morton wittily recorded a maypole set up at Pasonagessit
near Plymouth, New England, to name the place Mary or Merry
Mount. To emphasize the obvious sexual innuendo it was dressed
with a saucy message which 'being enigmatically composed, pusselled

---

[18] Letter CLXVII, 25 June 1642 (ibid., p. 173).   [19] Ibid.
[20] Letter CLXI, 4 June 1642 (ibid., pp. 166–7).

the Separatists'.[21] In Harley's vicinity, at Ludlow and Croft, the animosity towards roundheads was sufficiently intense to suggest that symbolic violence might presage literal attacks. Although she presents herself as an obedient wife she makes it clear that she is worse than isolated in the local royalist culture; clearly, her own political views were known. We can trace political differences emerging with increasing explicitness in Harley's local and social relationships. At the faultlines it is, as here, acknowledged that religious and political differences at times override neighbourly reciprocity.

Two weeks after the maypole incident she writes, 'Since your father thinkes Hearefordsheare as safe as any other country, I will thinke so too', yet she wishes she could be in London. The same letter recounts further disruption:[22]

This day Mr Davis came from Heareford, wheare he went to preach, by the intreaty of some in the town, and this befell him; when he had ended his prayer before the sermon, which he was short in, becaus he was loth to tire them, 2 men went out of the church and cryed 'pray God blles the kinge; this man dous not pray for the kinge;' upon which, before he read his text, he toold them that m[isters] had that liberty, to pray before or after the sermon for the church and state; for all that, they went to the bells and range, and a great many went into the church-yard and cryed 'roundheads,' and some said, 'let us cast stones at him!' and he could not looke out of doors nor Mr Lane but they cryed 'roundhead.' In the afternoon they would not let him preach; so he went to the cathedral. Thos that had any goodness weare much trubbled and weepe much.

These actions and words, even as they express political and religious difference, are also part of the local, informal, economy of bullying and punishment. As David Underdown and Ann Hughes make clear, we can expect to find such divisions expressed, as here, in the form of religious and cultural differentiation rather than in the abstract language of political theory.[23] As Hughes writes, 'a recognition of ... political conflict

[21] Thomas Morton, *New English Canaan* (London, 1632), in *Tracts and Other Papers Relating Principally to the Origin, Settlement and Progress of the Colonies in North America* (Washington, 1838), II, 1–125.

[22] Letter CLXV, 20 June 1642 (*Letters*, pp. 170–1).

[23] David Underdown, *Somerset in the Civil War and Interregnum* (Newton Abbott: David & Charles, 1973), pp. 11–30 and *passim*; Ann Hughes, 'Local History and the Origins of the Civil War', in *Conflict in Early Stuart England*, ed. Richard Cust and Ann Hughes (Harlow: Longman, 1989), pp. 224–53.

within counties' can coexist with the recognition of the nature of 'local patterns of allegiance' and, I would add, the languages expressing these.[24] Civil War allegiances are bound to local issues, but, as Harley's words make evident, that does not mean that men and women see local *rather* than national issues as important. At least in Harley's Hereford-shire at the outbreak of war the language of local reciprocity vividly represented national political tension and estrangement.

One vocabulary which helps us to understand Harley's circumstances is that of gift exchange: Marcel Mauss and those who follow him repeatedly stress that gift economies have some (though far from all) of the characteristics of a political system and perform *some* of the same functions. Thus, Mauss interpreted gift exchange as 'a form of political contract'. Neighbourly reciprocity can be understood as partaking of some of the characteristics of the larger political system, echoing, changing, and addressing formal political concerns. Insisting on the gift's role as *preceding* the state, Marshall Sahlins reminds his reader of Hobbes's comment that: 'the nature of Warre, consisteth not in actual fighting' (or not in that alone) 'but in the known disposition thereto, during all the time there is no assurance to the contrary'.[25] Rather than think of a gift economy as chronologically preceding a state, it is helpful to consider Harley's letters as disclosing the simultaneous, and increas-ingly contradictory, operations of reciprocity and state.[26] A second point is also useful: Sahlins reminds us that gift exchange and reciprocity indicate that war and enmity are being held at bay; gifts deflect aggres-sion and reintegrate troubling emotions into communal practices. The connections of national and local politics are visible, as is the way the breakdown of reciprocity allows the aggressive expression of competi-tiveness of several kinds. Although there was some part of loyal rela-tionships that participants seem to have felt was reserved from overtly political connections, the execution and rituals of such relationships symbolized political tensions. Brilliana Harley used religious convic-tions to make sense of events around her. On 19 July 1642, a month before Charles raised his standard at Nottingham, Harley wrote to her

[24] Hughes, 'Local History', p. 232; see also p. 249.
[25] Marshall Sahlins, *Stone Age Economics* (Chicago: Aldine Atherton, 1972), pp. 172, 169.
[26] See Braddick, *State Formation*, pp. 1–8, 48–54, 59–61, 68–90, 298–300, 309–15.

son Edward, 'neare the Parlament Howes'. Gesturing towards the story of Esther she wrote, 'I thanke God I am not afraide. It is the Lords caus that we have stood for':

> He will now sheawe the men of the world that it is hard fighting against heaven. And for our comforts, I thinke never any laide plots to route out all Gods chilldren at once, but that the Lord did sheawe Himselfe mighty in saveing His sarvants and confounding His enimyes, as he did to Pharowe, when he thought to have destroyed all Israell, and so Haman.[27]

As we see, though geographically remote Harley energetically bound herself to now politicized religious conceptions. Her letters suggest that religious ideas and convictions supplied a theoretical framework which governed her actions. They also led her to take up explicitly political positions.

A brief excavation of the earlier writings of the Puritan Brilliana Conway and her future husband Robert Harley suggest that the foundations for Robert Harley's support for the Parliament in 1642, and for Brilliana Harley's political action and writing when her house was besieged by royalists, were laid in the 1620s. In 1621, just before Brilliana became his third wife, a marriage which cemented his place in nation and county, Sir Robert Harley wrote an account or meditation, called the 'character' of a 'P' for Puritan.[28] As Jacqueline Eales notes, Harley is relatively unusual, though not unique, in identifying with the often satirical term 'Puritan'. In taking up the positive rather than the satiric potential of the Theoprastian character, Harley may have been influenced by the 1621 compendium volume of Joseph Halls's *Characters of Virtues and Vices*.[29] From the definition of a 'P' as 'he that desiers to practise what others profess' Harley moves directly to questions of rule:

> He is the best Instructor of a Prince & the best Counsellor to a King, the one he will teach first to know god that he may in time be the worthyr to beare his

[27] Letter CLXXVII, 19 July 1642 (*Letters*, pp. 180–1).

[28] BL Loan 29/27 bundle 6. Quotations from Jacqueline Eales, 'Sir Robert Harley, K.B. (1579–1656) and the "Character" of a Puritan', *British Library Journal*, 14 (1989), pp. 134–57. On Lucy Hutchinson and 'puritan', see Reid Barbour, *English Epicures and Stoics* (Amherst: University of Massachusetts Press, 1998), pp. 266–8.

[29] See Paul Salzman, *Literary Culture in Jacobean England: Reading 1621* (Basingstoke: Palgrave, 2003), pp. 167–70; Patrick Collinson, *The Puritan Character: Polemics and Polarities in Early Seventeenth-Century English Culture* (Los Angeles: William Andrews Clark Memorial Library, 1989), pp. 15–23.

greate name. The other he will ever perswade that gods worde, the p[er]fect rule of good governme[nt], is best for hym, on whome he hath sett his owne name, ~~for his name~~ w[hi]ch makes hym Hono[u]red ~~feared~~ but his word makes hym wise.

He Honours & obeyes his sup[er]iors as children should thyr parents in the Lorde, no for feare but fo[r] science[30] sake & as the civill magistrate beres the name of god so he esteemes him next to god *ordine et autoritate*.

A few lines serve to take the reader to the Puritan as ideal counsellor and thence to the key question of obedience to the higher powers. Comparison with familial authority frames the subject's relationship to the 'civill magistrate' as love rather than coercion; the magistrate is next only after God in the subject's duty of obedience. The analysis rapidly transfers godly virtue from inward discipline to an outward sphere of organization and influence guaranteed by acute self-searching. It moves on to a critical analysis of church government. Discussing the way in which a Puritan is regarded, Harley writes that he 'wonders why He is stilled a man of disorder when he is so willinge to obey all law com[m]ands'. Yet, like so many of the discussions of obedience canvassed in this study (most obviously the cases of Poole, Wight, Jekyll, and Love), the very words in which Harley expresses the Puritan's commitment to civil authority call attention to the potential for disobedience to the secular power contained in the promise of obedience to God's law. That the ruler to whom obedience is owed is a good ruler in the Puritan frame is made explicit in the epigraph 'the twelfth year he began to purge Judah and Jerusalem', removing 'the carved images, and the molten images'. Patrick Collinson has insisted that the term 'Puritan' generates contextual rather than absolute meanings. Robert Harley's embracing of the term is revealing about his views in 1621, offering hints concerning a godly formulation of true obedience.[31] For Robert Harley, a godly ruler rejects the icon, is active in the spiritual

---

[30] Eales, 'Sir Robert Harley', notes that this may mean conscience, self-knowledge.

[31] Collinson, *The Puritan Character*, p. 17; Peter Lake, *Anglicans and Puritans? Presbyterianism and English Conformist Thought from Whitgift to Hooker* (London: Allen & Unwin, 1988); Anthony Milton, *Catholic and Reformed: The Roman and Protestant Churches in English Protestant Thought, 1600–1640* (Cambridge: Cambridge University Press, 1995), pp. 4, 8, 65, 68–9. On the term's later history Raphael Samuel, 'The Discovery of Puritanism, 1820–1914: A Preliminary Sketch', in *Revival and Religion Since 1700*, ed. Jane Garnett and Colin Matthew (London: Hambledon Press, 1993), pp. 206, 201–47.

welfare of his subjects, purges the kingdom. For him, religious decisions could be the foundation of civil, political, action: the civil magistrate is obeyed *after* God.[32] In 1639 Robert Harley himself destroyed a painting showing 'the great God of haven [and] earth'; from spring 1643 he actively chaired the committee dedicated to demolishing superstitious monuments. As Jacqueline Eales remarks, Harley's preoccupations (including his attack on church icons and his concern to promote a preaching ministry) connect Civil War concerns with those of the earliest Reformation.[33] Harley's values were shared by many in Parliament, but Herefordshire was different.

So much for Robert Harley. Some distance away, in Warwickshire in 1622, Brilliana Conway was meditating on conscience:

The name of conscience teaches that it is a joynt knowledg where with God is joynd with us
Some say it is a very siting in our harts with a pen setting down our good and bad Acttions
Conciens is a faculti of the mind taking and understanding taking notis of all our thoughts words and acttions.

Following William Perkins she concludes, 'Conciens is a part of the understanding where by a man knows what he thinks What he desiers, and what he willes and also in what manner he knoweth thinketh, or willeth, either good or evill . . . Our concience bears witness not for a day but for ever'.[34] The commonplace book shows her sense of the interpenetration of writing, knowledge, godliness, and duty. Such views hint that Brilliana shared with her future husband the assumption that obedience to a political power depended on the judgement of conscience. Both Robert Harley and his future wife are drawing on the powerful analysis of godly government produced by the Reformation Church. Sir Robert Harley's connections to Elizabethan Puritanism were particularly to Presbyterianism, and among his possessions he had the preamble to the will of Humphry Fenn, one of the movement's main survivors.[35] Both Robert and Brilliana left material which linked them to the

[32] See e.g. Eales, *Puritans and Roundheads*, p. 40.
[33] Eales, 'Sir Robert Harley', pp. 137–40.
[34] Brilliana Harley, commonplace book, Portland Collection, University of Nottingham, PL F1/4/1, fo. 84[r].
[35] Eales, 'Sir Robert Harley', p. 144.

Presbyterian strain of Puritanism. However, there is a powerful critique implied in both Brilliana and Robert's vision of an ordered government. Moreover, it is likely that they were also aware of the very strong statements of the opposition between conscience and the civil powers which could be found Puritan writings on resistance.

In 1579, taking his cue from the ousting of Mary Queen of Scots, George Buchanan had written:

> government is created as a people vest authority, by a contract, in a ruler or rulers. Since no man is perfect, rulers are not trusted with absolute power... [the] people safeguard their interests by defining, in the laws, the scope and limits of the powers of their government.

For kings to be bound by law was 'no limitation' of 'power, dignity or liberty', and a ruler who 'attacks the liberties and institutions of his own country is to be counted as a public enemy'.[36] Genevan exiles returning to London expressed similar views. Christopher Goodman noted that those 'bewitched with Satan's false illusions' are 'not able to put difference betwyxte obedience & disobedience'. For Goodman, the role of counsel was 'to brydle the affections' of rulers.[37] John Knox, too, had been central in the reorientation of Calvinism from a position which supported obedience to the ruling powers to an espousal of resistance: Knox's distinction between a prince acting according to God's ordinance and *ultra vires* opened up a space between the Pauline injunction to obey the powers decreed by God and the actions of, for example, an ungodly prince or one acting contrary to God's law.[38] As the Civil War began Buchanan's anti-tyrannical sentiments had renewed force. Their resurgence can be seen, for example, in Anna Hume's publication of a new, unexpurgatedly and controversially Buchananite, edition of her father's

[36] George Buchanan, *De Jure Regni Apud Scotos; The Powers of the Crown in Scotland*, trans. Charles Arrowood (Austin: University of Texas Press, 1949), p. 10. See also Roger A. Mason and Martin S. Smith, *A Dialogue on the Law of Kingship among the Scots* (Aldershot: Ashgate, 2004), pp. xv–lxiii.

[37] Christopher Goodman, *How Superior Powers Ought To Be Obeyed of their Subjects* (Geneva, 1558), pp. 9, 34. See James E. Phillips, 'George Buchanan and the Sidney Circle', *HLQ* 12 (1948), pp. 23–56.

[38] John Knox, *On Rebellion*, ed. Roger A. Mason (Cambridge: Cambridge University Press, 1994), pp. xviii–xix, 95, 191–2. On female rule: 'The First Blast of the Trumpet against the Monstrous Regiment of Women', in *On Rebellion*, pp. 13–14. See also J. W. Allen, *A History of Political Thought in the Sixteenth Century* (London: Methuen, 1957), pp. 103–17.

History of the Houses of Douglas and Angus in 1644 with its 'discourses which authorize Rebellion'.[39]

Brilliana Harley does not explicitly ground her actions in the writings of Knox, Goodman, or Buchanan. However, she does write of her actions in terms which seem aware of these arguments and which, certainly, justify her resistance to a ruler in terms of law. In the last texts we have from her pen, to which I now turn, we can see national politics and an awareness of abstract political arguments about obedience, loyalty, and property in her local context. In 1643 war came to Brampton Bryan. And when the war came to Harley it was her neighbours who brought it. Writing in relation to the material discussed earlier, in which gifts are understood as keeping enmity at bay, Jacques Derrida describes an enemy as 'reliable to the point of treachery; and thereby familiar'. It seems that Harley's relationships with her opponents were never so consolingly reliable or consistent.[40]

As early as 14 February 1643 she wrote to Ned that a 'counsell of ware' had been debating the best way to take her Brampton Bryan house. Those with her 'are still threatened and injured'; 'none beare part with me but Mr Jams, who has shown himselfe very honest; none will looke towards Brompton, but such as truely fears God'. Her spies have told her that the new plan is:

> they will starve me out of my howes; they have taken away all your fathers rents, and they say they will drive away the cattell, and then I shall have nothing to live upon; for all theare ame is to enfors me to let thos men I have goo, that then they might seas upon my howes and cute our throughts by a feaww rooges, and then say, they knew not whoo did it; for so they say, they knewe not whoo draeve away the 6 coolts, but Mr Coningsby keepes them, though I have write to him for them. They have used all means to leave me no man in my howes . . .

She concludes that they 'tell me, that I shall be safe but I have no caus to trust them'.[41] Isolated, unvisited, friendless, she receives 'intelligence' of royalist

[39] William Drummond, in George P. Johnston, 'The First Edition of Hume of Godscroft's History', *Publications of the Edinburgh Bibliographical Society*, 4, pt. 1 (1900), pp. 149–72: 156. For Anna Hume's cancelled dedication see pp. 152–3, 172. *David Hume of Godscroft's The History of the House of Douglas*, ed. David Reid, 2 vols. (Edinburgh: Scottish Text Society, 1996), I, xiii.

[40] Jacques Derrida, *Politics of Friendship*, trans. George Collins (1994; London: Verso, 1997), p. 83.

[41] Letter CLXXXV, 14 Feb. 1643 (*Letters*, pp. 188–9).

plans. Her besiegers' political concerns seem to have been mixed with interests concerning property and gender. However, the siege provoked Harley to a contrastingly clear (and of course, being openly exchanged between emissaries, public) articulation of the foundations of her Puritan and parliamentary politics. We find these in her responses to royalist commanders and Charles I himself, as she defended her castle against royalist forces.

The feared siege began on 26 July 1643, the day after Prince Rupert took Bristol. Three royalists (Henry Lingen, Sir William Pye, William Smallman) informed Brilliana Harley that the forces of Sir William Vavasour, drawn up before her castle, were resolved to reduce it.[42] As we saw in the introduction, Harley responded by insisting, 'I must endeavour to keep what is mine as well as I can, in which I have the law of nature, of reason, and of the land on my side, and you none to take it from me.'[43] The simultaneously symbolic and literal meanings of property evoked here exemplify the shifting registers of the siege discussions. Early in the siege, on 31 July, Harley sent Sir William Vavasour a letter running over all the grounds of her defence. Her servants bear arms only 'for mine and their defence, a thing warranted by the laws of the land'. She is unwilling to yield that her house may become a garrison and she herself be 'a prisoner in my own house'. Should she so yield:

I should speak myself guilty; and thus more much I say, my dear husband hath entrusted me with his house and children, and therefore I cannot dispose of his house but according to his pleasure, and I do not know it is his pleasure that I should entertain soldiers in his house; and surely Sir, I never will voluntarily betray the trust my husband reposeth in me. I have hitherto believed very well of you, and that I may do so, I will not—if I can help it—try how your soldiers will deal with me; and I trust the Lord my God will deliver me and mine out of all my enemies hands; but if it hath pleased the Lord to appoint that your cruelties and wrongs to me and mine, and some of the inhabitants of this town, must help to fill up the measure of all the cruelties now used against those that desire to keep faith in a good conscience, I shall not be displeased; for when the measure of cruelties is full, the day of deliverance will soon appear to the Church of God which is now afflicted.[44]

---

[42] Eales, *Puritans and Roundheads*, pp. 149–77.

[43] Brilliana Harley to Henry Lingen, 26 July 1643, *Calendar of the Manuscripts of the Marquis of Bath Preserved at Longleat, Wiltshire* (London: HMC, 1904), I, 8. On natural law see e.g. R. S. White, *Natural Law in English Renaissance Literature* (Cambridge: Cambridge University Press, 1996), pp. 3, 4.

[44] *Calendar*, I, 12–13.

In the course of this letter she mentions the law of property and then her owed obedience to her husband in whose trust she maintains children and property. His commands take precedence. This in turn gives way to her claim that her sufferings, should she suffer at his hands, will serve to make up those apportioned to the saints before their day of deliverance comes. Given the foundations of her actions in religious beliefs, it is notable that Harley's invocation of her God at this point is the only such direct address made to the religious valences of these political conflicts. Framed in terms of her potential suffering, her text nevertheless makes clear *why* she defends her house as, for an instant, she expresses to those opposing her the sentiments so often shared with Ned—both her conviction of rightness and her sense of the suffering of the righteous. Religion forms the bedrock of action, and it is joined, crucially, by the literal and symbolic stakes of *property* in licensing 'defence'. The need to explain, perhaps explain away, the fact of her political and military action makes Harley's defence, though clear, complex. The words Harley selects to justify her actions speak quite vividly about her ideas concerning obedience to the *lawful* actions of the magistrate. They also disclose an understanding of property and of the wife's role as a head of household in the absence of her husband, and offer a positive account of women's political action grounded in these. It almost seems that in Harley's writing physical attack on property precipitates or even *enables*, rather than follows, a triumph of the vocabulary of religion and national politics as dominant languages. Certainly, in what turned out to be her final expression of political views, nation and propriety eclipse the vocabulary of reciprocity. It seems that at the point of siege Harley's motivations issue in clear, politicized, language. Even at this point, though, Harley asks to send a message to her royalist relation, Pelham, with whom earlier we saw her parting political company while maintaining some kind of kin tie.

Harley's careful articulation of women's political action as justified by her family and property contrasts sharply with the ways in which her besiegers put together gender and politics. Her writings during the siege unite theoretical and present concerns; her proceedings suggest a war which was both grounded in deep, enduring, conflicts and suddenly manifest, present. On 21 August 1643, at the height of the siege, Charles I wrote to Brilliana Harley that 'in respect of your sex and condition' he is anxious about instructing Sir John Scudamore regarding 'forcing or firing' the castle. Capitulation would earn 'free pardon', but further resistance would mean 'ruin and destruction'.[45] Charles's formulaic letter contrasts with a vivid exchange between Harley and Sir John Scudamore two days later on 23 August. Harley asks to 'send you [Sir John Scudamore] my petition to our most gracious king'; she receives an explosive reply.[46] Scudamore tells her that her brother-in-law, Pelham, is far off in Lincoln with the King's forces who have lately reduced it. He tells her of the King's triumph everywhere. And in a postscript he continues his attempt to lower her morale, simultaneously giving his analysis of women's part in the Civil War:

Were your ladyship informed how absolute the King is both in the north and west, and how much his party increaseth in Kent, Surrey and other counties about London...you would perhaps judge the defending of London itself three months will be a very difficult business....These and many other particulars I should have acquainted your ladyship with, had I been admitted to your presence. The suburbs against the city in arms; the women against the House of Commons in multitudes; the train bands of London against the women who cry out for their slain and imprisoned husbands; divers women killed by the soldiers on this tumult; Mr Pym beaten by the women and with much difficulty escaped their fury by water.

Starting as an attempt to intimidate its addressee by contrasting the king's progress with the rout of his enemies, this evocation of the chaos of London politics in late summer 1643 takes on a life of its own. While modern commentators habitually compare Brilliana Harley to the royalist Lady Bankes who also ran a siege, her contemporaries compared her with the royalist Lady Aubigny.[47] Politically closer to Harley, in the 1639 campaign in Scotland pistol-carrying Scotswomen, 'dangerous Amazons', were commented on.[48] So the question of women and military action was under consideration.[49] Scudamore, however, turns

[45] *Calendar*, I, p. 14.   [46] Ibid., pp. 16–17.

[47] Ibid., pp. 8–33; Eales, *Puritans and Roundheads*, p. 163.

[48] From Sir Henry Herbert, June 1639, in *Epistolary Curiosities*, ed. Rebecca Warner (London: Richard Cruttwell, 1818), pp. 20–7, esp. 22–3.

[49] See Patricia Higgins 'The Reactions of Women, with Special Reference to Women Petitioners', in *Politics, Religion and the English Civil War*, ed. Brian Manning (London: Edward Arnold, 1973), pp. 178–222. On royalist woman besieged, see Ernest Broxap, *The Great Civil War in Lancashire*, 2nd edn. (Manchester: Manchester University Press, 1974). For a helpful discussion of similar issues see Katherine A. Walker, 'The Military

to the peace petitions of 1643, women's part in the defence of London, and the push for peace. Contrasting the powerlessness of the widowed women of the trained bands with those calling for peace and beating Pym, Scudamore both acknowledges the importance of women in the symbolic actions of the Civil War and puts Harley in the company of women of generally lower status. Harley's attempt to describe publicly her cause and grounds is given negative associations while, confusedly, women's pro-Stuart stirring up of opinion is positive. Crucially, while Scudamore wishes to terrorize Harley with other defeats, he is repeatedly drawn to acknowledge the roles of other women, strangely like Harley's, in political protests. Protest is valued in relation to the political cause rather than the sex of the protestor, but Scudamore also repeatedly instances women protestors.

Harley's siege letters can perhaps be seen as a culmination of her thought on the subjects of religion, law, and property and offer clear grounds for her behaviour. But if we find her articulating a clear position, we also find those she addressed violently and contradictorily engaging with women as political agents. The dialogue between Scudamore and Harley shows both women's participation in politics at the start of the Civil War period and the pressure that activity put on familiar assumptions about gender and politics, public and private. These ideas had been under pressure before, but the wars showed up the faultlines in attitudes to women's relationships to political action and some of the ties—including marriage, property, and public good—used to legitimate the blurring of public and private roles.

What happened next? By September 1643 Brilliana Harley had died of illness in Brampton Bryan. She was buried 'within the castle'.[50] Sir Robert Harley took the solemn League and Covenant. This path led to him being among those responsible for the removal of the Book of Common Prayer and the setting up of the Directory of Worship.[51] He was briefly imprisoned during Pride's Purge. Refusing to take the Engagement, he and his sons entered political limbo in the 1650s, unable to return to their estates.[52] Sir Edward Harley, though, went

Activities of Charlotte De La Tremouille, Countess of Derby, during the Civil War and Interregnum', *Northern History,* 28, No.1 (2001), pp. 47–64.

[50] Captain Priamus Davies, 'An Account of the Sieges of Brampton Castle and the Massacre of Hopton Castle', *Calendar,* I, 22–33.

[51] Eales, 'Sir Robert Harley', p. 147.   [52] Ibid., p. 148.

on to have a career in the Commons under Charles II, whom he greeted at Dover.[53] However, another event offers a significant echo to Brilliana Harley's political interventions. On the last day of Charles I's trial, a woman understood to be Anne Fairfax (Lady Vere's daughter, Brilliana's cousin) the wife of Cromwell's general, and a Presbyterian, was in the court to hear the King 'answer to a Charge of Treason, and other high Crimes, exhibited against him in the name of the people of England'. Hearing the charge she 'interrupted the Court, (saying, not half the People,) but she was soon silenced'.[54] While supporting Charles, the very language of her protest, calling upon the people of England, attests to the importance (if also vagueness) of the people as the basis of authority. In the context of the Harley networks, Anne Fairfax's protest can be understood more readily as speaking of the privileging of conscience over mere human laws than as feminine transgression.

We cannot know what Brilliana Harley would have thought of Parliament and Charles I by 1649. But her writings do illuminate a sequence of issues to which this study will return, issues which dominate women's relationship to politics and its history and historiography in the Civil War period. One topic that recurs throughout the study of the sects is the questioning of the power of the civil magistrate facilitated by several different forms of Protestantism. More immediately, it is clear from Harley's writings that within the discourses that have been understood as removing women from politics—family, household, kinship—that very relationship can be traced. As Jacqueline Eales reminds us, Harley was an exemplary wife: the organizing principles of that were precisely what underpinned her actions and words.[55] The clarity with which we can see the compatibility of Harley's self-presentation and self-understanding as an obedient wife with her activities is not, as such, surprising. Yet, the actions and words to which her principles and obedience led her make her a foundational case in my discussion of politics, for we can see very clearly in the nature of this

[53] In March 1651 Edward Harley wrote to his brother Thomas, contrasting the 'sweet country aire' and the city with its 'beasts more savage as we meet every day'. *Letters*, p. 216.

[54] *A Continuation of the Narrative Being the Last and final days Proceedings of the High Court of Justice*, 29 Jan. 1648, p. 4; Eales, *Puritans and Roundheads*, p. 4.

[55] Jacqueline Eales, 'Patriarchy, Puritanism and Politics: The Letters of Lady Brilliana Harley (1598–1643)', in *Early Modern Women's Letter Writing*, ed. Daybell, pp. 143–58.

obedience the powerful ties which connected women to politics. Harley, and other women, were brought into contact with politics through materials often seen as parts of the barrier to such involvement— through the household, through religious faith and opinion, through marital obedience, and through local and kinship ties. Present political actions drew on a long memory of Protestant thought. Though Harley is not of the same social status as the much earlier elite women described by Barbara Harris, her writings disclose the predictable importance of many of the same ties. Harris sees 'the exclusion of aristocratic women from formal political power and office' as 'natural' and 'virtually un-questioned' yet, as she argues, kinship networks incessantly involved women in political manoeuvring, though this might not be understood as such, as they attempted to enhance family fortunes.[56] Harley's case indicates that we need to think of these networks of relations as having ideological aspects recognized by participants and ones which, in the early 1640s, become evidently determining even as the habits and ties of kinship remain in place. Harley's writings give us a war in which ties involve both politics and networks: the situation was, it seems, partly naturalized and partly understood as a tangle by participants. Thus, the moment of religious and political choice *recurs* rather than being isol-able as the moment of war. In Harley's constant reference back to her husband in London it is clear that her politicized experience of her world is affected by the changes in the role of Parliament. Her writing during the siege not only shows the way her identity as dutiful wife was brought to justify conduct based on abstract principles bound to the defence of property, but was also a response to the presence of Parlia-ment as part of a formation of an apparatus of state and government which she saw herself in relation to.

Harley's words offer an example of the importance of wifely obedience, household, kinship, property, locality, and religion in the writings of early modern women. These texts also suggest the ways women were put in relation to politics, and saw themselves in relation to it, as religious and political issues divided local and national groups. The picture Harley's letters give, this chapter argues, raises fundamental issues about the nature of women's relationship to politics—as writers and addressees, as

[56] Barbara J. Harris, *English Aristocratic Women 1450–1550* (Oxford: Oxford University Press, 2002), pp. 17, 26, 175, and *passim*.

believers, as holders of property, and as inhabitants of particular places and relationships—in the early to mid-seventeenth century.

WRITING LAND AND LINEAGE: ANNE CLIFFORD

Brilliana Harley staked a substantial claim on her relation to property. To what extent did involvement in land, and so law, open the political realm to women? Although the cultural places of land and lineage are understood as highly politicized, texts by women on such topics are often interpreted as 'private' instead of part of social and political culture. Lady Anne Clifford, daughter of George, Earl of Cumberland, and ultimately heir to his huge northern estates, is a test case in the relationship between lineage and political involvement, and, for reasons I will come to, a limit case for the present study.

Anne Clifford puts before us the continuing importance of the claim to land as a claim to a political place. Her obsession with land and with the inscription of ownership and lineage is evident in her diaries but as significantly present in the monuments and buildings she commissioned (such as the monument to Edmund Spenser, the monument which marked the last spot where she saw her mother at their parting in 1616, her almshouses), and particularly in the Great Picture, her biographical and genealogical triptych. Yet she is not usually understood as using political languages but as offering a subject for the exploration of elite female identity.[57] However, the assumption that the personal and private is dominant in Clifford's texts, an assumption held by a recent editor, anachronistically binds a varied body of texts to a modern conception of private life.[58] Moreover, the early diary, on which such a picture of Clifford substantially rests, cannot be productively assessed in complete isolation from other things Clifford commissioned, built and signed—texts and artefacts which consistently invite us to question the separation of private and public that concentration on the personal implies. Indeed, the strategies these texts use to interweave familial

[57] Alice T. Friedman, 'Constructing an Identity in Prose, Plaster and Paint: Lady Anne Clifford as Writer and Patron of the Arts', in *Albion's Classicism: The Visual Arts in Britain, 1550–1660*, ed. Lucy Gent (New Haven: Yale University Press, 1995), pp. 359–76, esp. 359, 361.

[58] *The Diaries of Lady Anne Clifford*, ed. D. J. H. Clifford (Stroud: Alan Sutton, 1992), p. xii.

happenings and politics suggest that they address a readership which is imagined with increasing fullness and precision through Clifford's writing life. Clifford's very neglect of some public events, particularly pronounced towards the end of her life, suggests not that she had no views on government or the wider world, but that we should look elsewhere for the interpretative narratives she used.[59]

Almost all Clifford's textual and cultural work produced from 1605 to her death in 1676 responded to one crucial fact: her father's will deprived her of her right by entail to inherit his lands. Initially with her mother's help, Clifford went to law. The legal details are not my subject here. However, Katherine Acheson's invaluable research tells us that Clifford's case was based on the 'interpretation of laws and practices regarding the inheritability of baronies by female issue'.[60] Clifford's case rested on the status of an entail of lands on heirs male or female (the case brought by Clifford's mother in 1606) and on tenure (the 'physical possession of estates') which was heard in the Court of Wards in April 1608.[61] Further suits were heard in the Court of Common Pleas (1615), and before the Council of the North (1616), and James I gave judgment in favour of the Earl of Cumberland's designated heir, his brother Francis Clifford, in 1617. When Francis died in 1628 Clifford renewed her suit.[62] She produced several types of writing (diary, chronicles and 'annual summaries', and the 'Life of Me'), each highly systematic in their return to her status as heir.[63] Such texts, as many writers on Clifford recognize, manifest 'sustained public opposition to . . . property settlements'.[64]

The early 'diary' describes her struggles with James I and VI, the death of her mother, and the to- and-fro strife of her first marriage. The reader, even if that reader was perhaps initially imagined only as Clifford herself, is invited to decode Clifford's relationship to court politics through textual

---

[59] See e.g. *The Diary of Lady Anne Clifford*, ed. V. Sackville-West (London: Heinemann, 1923), p. xliv; see also Paul Salzman's helpful discussion in: 'Revenants: Vita Sackville-West's Evocation of Anne Clifford and Aphra Behn' (forthcoming). I am grateful to Dr Salzman for sharing this work with me.

[60] *The Diary of Lady Anne Clifford 1616–1619*, ed. Katherine O. Acheson (New York: Garland, 1995), p. 3.

[61] Ibid., pp. 3–5.   [62] Ibid., pp. 2–3.   [63] Ibid., p. 14.

[64] *Diaries*, ed. Clifford, p. xii. See Barbara K. Lewalski, *Writing Women in Jacobean England* (Cambridge, Mass.: Harvard University Press, 1993), pp. 125–53: 125; Margaret J. M. Ezell, *Writing Women's Literary History* (Baltimore: Johns Hopkins University Press, 1993), pp. 34–5, 41.

juxtapositions. For much of the 1610s Clifford was sequestered at Knole at the behest of her husband, who opposed her claim. The great tracts of land were fought for in battles over personal movement and space, focusing on Clifford's chamber to which she was often confined, or self-confined. Her husband was 'much abroad' while 'I stayed in the Countrey', her mood determined not by life around her but 'as I had news from London' about the case. The tension between local life, the lawsuit, and events in the wider world are articulated in her use of marginal notes.[65] Her stubbornness produced a situation where, after an interview with her husband's relatives and the Archbishop of Canterbury, when 'Much persuasion was used by him and all the company, sometimes terrifying me & sometimes flattering me', she was permitted to consult her mother.[66]

In March 1616 Clifford visited her mother. As she was doing so she seems to have recorded happenings in court and in London (the wider world, but also a corollary for Clifford's own experiences) in marginal notes: 'Upon the 24th my Lady Somerset was sent by water from Blackfriars as Prisoner to the Tower.'[67] Francis Howard, Countess of Somerset, the wife of the king's favourite Robert Carr, was soon to be infamous as the poisoner of Sir Thomas Overbury. Here, however, she provides an analogue for Clifford's own ill-treatment by James. In May Clifford takes up the story, recording that 'my Lady Somerset arraigned and condemned at Westminster hall where she confessed her fault and asked the King's Mercy, & was much pitied by all beholders'. Like Howard, Clifford suffers public opprobrium and is to be pitied. Clifford notes:

Upon the 24th, being Friday, between the hours of 6 and 9 at night died my dear Mother at Brougham, in the same Chamber where my father was born, 13 years and 2 months after the death of Queen Elizabeth and ten years and 7 months after the death of my father. I being 26 years and five months, and the Child 2 years wanting a month.[68]

The text uses coincidence, repetition, and juxtaposition to lend depth and significance to events as the reader moves between national and familial narratives. Even this early diary—which is the lynchpin of

---

[65] *Diaries*, ed. Clifford, pp. 33, 28.   [66] Ibid., p. 29.
[67] Ibid., p. 30, n. 8.   [68] Ibid., p. 35, n. 16.

critical accounts of Clifford as a private writer isolated from the wider world—offers strong evidence that Clifford sees herself, and invites her reader to see her, in the highly politicized contexts of the law and the contrast between the Elizabethan and Jacobean courts. Even in this period Clifford was attempting to influence that wider public, even political, world. In 1620, just after the first diary breaks off, she set up a monument to Edmund Spenser in Westminster Abbey.[69] The monument's memorialization of the Elizabethan past might be interpreted as a criticism of James.[70] Certainly, it is a politicized statement which, through an aesthetic stance, announced Spenser's greatness, that of his deceased patron, and that of the patron's daughter—Clifford. Although apparently at polar extremes of 'private' versus 'public' statements, diary and monument both assert the demands of inherited political status. In their implicitly pejorative contrast of good Elizabethan past with Jacobean present, both, in different modes, blend familial and politicized issues.[71] The apparently open fragments of the 1616 diary thus draw the reader into a world in which events reverberate in relation to the lawsuit, the court, and aristocratic virtue and status. The Spenser monument announced Clifford's aesthetic, but also lineal, claims to the world.

Twenty-three years after the Spenser monument was set up, because of a sequence of deaths, Clifford did inherit her lands. The end of the war (at Charles I's execution) is marked by her escape from London and her 'place of refuge', the house of her parliamentarian second husband, the boorish Earl of Pembroke. If deprivation was the spur to Clifford's textual production, the oft-reiterated moment of restitution is central to her later writing and images. On Clifford's return to her Skipton estate

---

[69] George C. Williamson, *Lady Anne Clifford* (Kendal: Titus Wilson & Son, 1922), p. 63. See Walter Lewis Spiers, 'The Note-Book and Account Book of Nicholas Stone', *Walpole Society Proceedings*, 7, ed. A. J. Finberg (1919), p. 54 (plate 14b). The statue was restored in marble in 1778. On 28 January Clifford records Moll Neville reading her copy of Spenser's *Faerie Queene* (*Diaries*, ed. Clifford, pp. 47–9), which was dedicated to Anne Clifford's father, as was his *Four Hymns* to her mother. See George C. Williamson, *George, Third Earl of Cumberland* (Cambridge: Cambridge University Press, 1920), a4ʳ; Richard Helgerson, *Forms of Nationhood* (Chicago: University of Chicago Press, 1992), p. 131; Michelle O'Callaghan, *The 'Shepheards Nation': Jacobean Spenserians and Early Stuart Political Culture, 1612–1625* (Oxford: Oxford University Press, 2000), pp. 1–3, 10–11, 112–13.

[70] See Helgerson, *Forms of Nationhood*, p. 133. The date of the edition shown in the Great Picture (1578, 1600, or 1607) is discussed in Williamson, *Clifford*, p. 341 n. 6.

[71] Susan Stewart, *On Longing* (Durham, N.C.: Duke University Press, 1993), p. x.

she reminded herself and others, 'I was never till now in any part of yt Castle since I was 9 or 10 weeks old'.[72] Restored, Clifford refined and consolidated the complex stories of the early diaries. Land, buildings, and writing all come to signify her redeemed estate as she re-encodes the past. In reasserting the issue of tenure so important in her law case, Clifford's insistence on her re-entry as a life-defining event makes a point about lineage, and the fruits of time. Forty-four years since her disinheritance by her father, and six months after Charles I's execution, she at last arrives in Skipton castle, her birthplace.[73] The movement towards the climactic moment dominates the writing of the 1650s.[74] Clifford's weaving together of places, events, and genealogy convey to the reader that providence has restored her to her right.

The dynamic between loss and compensation appears vividly, in visual and verbal form, in the Great Picture painted in London probably in the 1640s soon after her inheritance was confirmed (Figure 5). The politics of Clifford's retreat is illuminated by the totemic placing of relatives, and, in two panels, of books. The chorographic and chronicle impulses simultaneously attempt to repair an imagined rupture of appropriate relations between self and land, present and past, and aim, by asserting the full presence of the present subject in relation to land and chronicle, to transcend that problem. This image is of a mixed mode, partly portraiture, partly genealogical, partly biographical, commemorative, and memorial. In its status as a narrative of Clifford's life and genealogical proof of her entitlement the painting, as Richard Wendorf suggests, calls attention to the 'fundamental relation... between portraiture and documentation'.[75]

The Great Picture is Clifford's pre-eminent statement on restoration and retreat. It speaks of her social and physical location in visual language that asserts her national importance but also requires fairly

---

[72] BL MS Harl. 6177, fo. 67^{r-v}. This is a transcription of an earlier manuscript. See *Diaries*, ed. Clifford, p. 100.

[73] BL MS Harl. 6177, fo. 67^v.

[74] The repetition and temporal shaping that mark Clifford's writing are to an extent obscured by D. J. H. Clifford's narrativization of her life. The 'diaries' seem to have been written up retrospectively from notes. Welding them into a 'life' also involves obscuring, for example, the presence of part of the actual 'memoriall' in the third Book of Record begun in 1649, in which the memorial of 'my owne life' (fo. 226) follows two and a half substantial volumes on lineage, including copies of documents, coloured pedigrees, etc.

[75] Richard Wendorf, *The Elements of Life* (Oxford: Clarendon Press, 1990), p. 9.

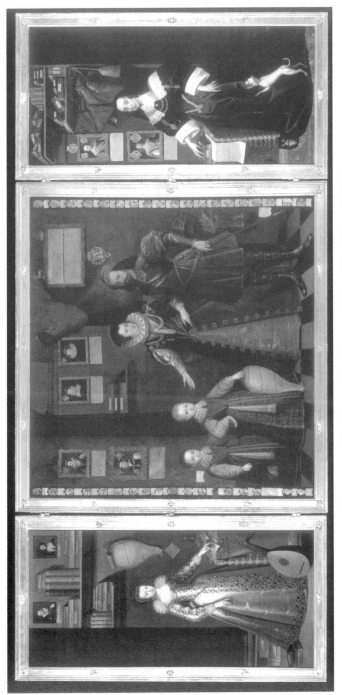

5. 'The Great Picture', commissioned by Anne Clifford. Reproduced by permission of the Abbott Hall Museum

complicated reading processes. The image unites the genealogical and spatial, even chorographic, desire to make the land speak of her owner-ship and place, demanding distinct and layered modes of interpretation all of which serve to situate Clifford at the heart of land (Westmorland), family (heir) and, therefore, as a political agent—sheriff. As a triptych the image combines the narrative and spatial strategies of Clifford's textualization of her world. It represents the times of loss and restoration as chambers furnished with items of significance, including portraits, books, animals, armour, and inscriptions. The viewer is required to combine spatial and temporal interpretation, and to move between a representational image and narrative, captioning and genealogy. The triptych's interpretative focus is on the period of Clifford's family, her intellectual and political formation, and the present. The central panel, perhaps by Jan Van Belcamp, is augmented by heraldry and writing.[76] The Elizabethan moment of the central image shows a political and familial stability which exists both to be disrupted (in the reign of James) and to be fulfilled (in Clifford herself and her relation to her genealogy). Thus, the image is both complex and simple; it repeats the pattern of Clifford's written and built texts in using the moment of her inheritance as the point of closure. The painting proposes two or more histories that permit that end. At least two starting places are offered: the opening of Clifford's life as suggested by the central panel copied from images made a month after her conception, and the moment, memor-ialized in the first panel, at which she was deprived of her right. The evident control of the patron in the composition, issuing in volumes of detail, does provide a third moment of departure for the viewer. Each starting place is out of sequence and separate, yet makes no sense except in relation to the others, undoing and complementing them in Clifford's progress towards her final plenitude.

Each chamber represents a significant moment in Clifford's life, yet the painting cannot be precisely read from left to right. The central panel presents in a chamber the earliest events in the image—before Anne's birth. It contains eight differently sized portraits, including Anne's brothers Sir Robert Clifford and Francis Lord Clifford (who

---

[76] Belcamp was a copyist and keeper of Charles I's pictures. Francis Haskell, 'Charles I's Collection of Pictures', in *The Late King's Goods*, ed. Arthur MacGregor (London: Alistair McAlpine; Oxford: Oxford University Press, 1989), p. 226.

died in 1589 and 1591 respectively), next to them her mother (central to this panel and therefore to the whole composition), and next to her Clifford's father, the will-maker. We are told these were copied from images painted in London in June 1589, just after Anne was conceived.[77] The point of the panel, clearly, is that Anne is expected. The four other portraits in the panel indicate Clifford's chosen connections. These are images of Clifford's aunts: Anne, Countess of Warwick and Elizabeth, Countess of Bath were maternal aunts, from the side of the family not usually strongest in the making of political alliances. Here Clifford (as in her early narrative of Elizabeth I's funeral) keeps the viewer's and reader's attention on maternal networks of kinship connected to the Elizabethan court. Connections to Clifford are emphasized.[78] Even as Clifford claims lineage in support of her case, first for legal redress and later to endorse the fullness of her enfranchisement, it is inflected by her situation. Thus the central panel foregrounds masculine power, lineage, and control. Yet, apparently mere background, the images of the aunts and the inscriptions foregrounding female agency, longevity, and courtly virtue set up a dynamic, dependent on the viewer's knowledge of the fates of Anne's brothers and subsequent events, whereby feminine inheritance challenges and outlasts masculine, as is suggested by the gestures both parents are making towards the two male heirs.

Clifford's very survival enabled her to select and shape the narrative. The left-hand panel shows Clifford at 15, at the moment of her father's death. Anxieties and deprivations are present in the picture, but, as in the later writing, here figured as overcome by full inheritance—as the relationship between this image and that of the older Clifford makes clear. The presence of Anne on the left of the image signals the start of a second story, not the one of her lineage and inheritance, but of the loss and recovery of her lands. The inscriptions tell us,

When shee was 15 yeares and 9 months old, her father died in Savoy Hous, London, the 30 of Oct: 1605: And presently after hir Moother comensed great suits in Law for hir sayd only daughters right to the Baro: of Clifford,

---

[77] On the death of Clifford's brothers, see Williamson, *Clifford*, pp. 335, 493.

[78] *Diaries*, ed. Clifford, pp. 21–7. For details on female kin see Williamson, *Clifford*, pp. 491–2 and *passim*. On kinship see also Christine Kalpische-Zuber, *Women, Family and Ritual in Renaissance Italy*, trans. Lydia Cochrane (Chicago: University of Chicago Press, 1985), pp. 75–85.

Westmoreland and Vesey, and for the Sheriſwick of that County, and for
Skipton Castle, and ye antient lands belonging to it, whearin the Countess
shewed much wisdome and resolucion.

The inscription goes on to chart the death of Margaret Russell, Clifford's
widowhood, and her remarriage.[79] The inscription of the final panel
takes up the narrative of her life after the death of the Duke of Dorset,
detailing her marriage to Pembroke. It closes with the death of Henry
Clifford, Francis Clifford's son, the fact that even though he died in
1643 the 'misery of the then Civell warrs kept her from having profits of
those lands for a good while after'.[80]

Evidently the triptych requires that we hold word and image in a
dynamic relation while making absolutely explicit that the point of the
narrative is that the final panel is reached—in which, after the expectation
in the central panel and the deprivation implicit in the left-hand panel,
Clifford is a full and completed subject. Once again the text invites the
reader to tease out the relationship between the details given. The titles
and placing of the books enable the reader—as with the Knole diary—to
weave Clifford's claims into a commentary on public and political issues.
What emerges is an articulate politics of retreat and endurance, mediated
by an emphasis on place, entitlement, and family. The books in Clifford's
images suggest that her estate in Westmorland was its own polity, a
princedom set up within, and in response to, first republican and then
restored Stuart politics. The books, as much as the genealogies, assert
Clifford's ambitions, making the link between virtue and Stoic self-discipline and the architecturally and chorographically articulated claim to a
kind of princehood.[81] History, chorography, and the imagining of the self
are represented by the poetical and historical writings of her tutor, Samuel
Daniel, William Camden's *Britannia*, the *Manuell* of Epictetus, Boethius's
Consolations of Philosophy, and Montaigne's *Essays.*[82]

The third panel, showing Clifford at the moment of composition, is
turned towards the image of her younger self, addressed across the image
of the Cumberland family. Of central importance to both these figures is

---

[79] Williamson, *Clifford*, pp. 494–5.   [80] Ibid., p. 507.

[81] The central panel contains the Bible, Thomas Lodge's translation of Seneca, a
manuscript book 'of Alkumiste Exstractions of Distillations and excellent medicines',
which might have been assembled by her mother, and 'The Psalmes of David' in the
countess's left hand. Williamson, *Clifford*, pp. 498–9.

[82] See *The Whole Workes of Samuel Daniel Esquire in Poetrie* (London, 1623), p. 73.

William Camden's *Britannia*, which Clifford's tutor might have read to her. If we open *Britannia* we find it describes the locations of Clifford's power, lost and regained. The early editions contain maps, including one of Westmorland, with Latin etymologies and discourses on the places of Clifford's inheritance—Skipton, Appleby, Brougham— all of which turn out to have significant British or Roman pasts. Noting the Cliffords' acquisition of this 'very proper and a strong Castle', Camden likens Skipton, 'in the middest' of 'craggy stones, hanging rocks', to '*Latium* in Italie'.[83] Thus *Britannia* illuminates Clifford's pedigree, gives a desirable historical narrative to her lands, and situates those lands in relation to the whole of the nation. The stoic self-discipline of the books in the first image has been transformed into a tripartite claim to possession and virtue grounded in lineage, place, and nation.

The final image of Clifford implies her highly public, landholder's virtues. The books in the third panel—tumbled on the shelf above and behind Anne—are evidently her present resources. These books suggest the overlayering of 'public' and 'private', personal and political, in their combination of, for example, George Strode's *The Anatomie of Mortality* and Henry Wotton's *Elements of Architecture*. The selection of Wotton's text, integrating the classical and homely, suggests the assertive localism implicit in the politics of Clifford's retreat. The second part of Wotton's book begins:

Every Mans proper *Mansion* House and *Home*, being the Theater of his *Hospitality*, the *Seate* of *Selfe-fruition*, the *Comfortablest part* of his owne *Life*, the *Noblest* of his Sonnes *Inheritance*, a kinde of private *Princedome*; Nay, to the *Possessors* thereof, an *Epitomie* of the whole *World*...[84]

Clifford's building programme, like her repeated self-representation, was at the heart of her creation of a northern princedom.[85] Wotton's architecture made available European configurations of social space and,

---

[83] William Camden, *Britannia* (London, 1586), p. 694. Of Appleby he contrastingly comments, 'were it not that by reason of antiquity it had deserved to be counted the chiefe towene of the shire' it would be 'little better than a village' (p. 761). Brougham is significant for 'huge stones in forme of Pyramides ... which may seeme to have beene pitched and erected for to continue the memoriall of some act there atchieved' (p. 762).

[84] Sir Henry Wotton, *The Elements of Architecture* (London, 1624).

[85] See Katharine Hodgkin, 'The Diary of Lady Anne Clifford: A Study of Class and Gender in the Seventeenth Century', *History Workshop*, 19 (1985), pp. 148–61: 155.

displayed here, suggests that Clifford's project was conceived in terms of the building of a principality. These choices demonstrate her insistence on family, lineage, and place as implying a conception of political and national status. They underpin an assertion of retreat with an implicit evaluation of renewed Stuart rule.

The books in the Great Picture show us the materials which Clifford used to build a dual subjecthood: an inner life ordered by her fortuitously restored status as 'heir' and an external life as a northern Renaissance prince. They indicate her resources in structuring a recapitulation of the story of deprivation and inheritance as a textual and spatial narrative of power restored. That she selected Wotton on architecture, Montaigne on the self, Daniel on poetry and history and Camden's chorography to stand for her concerns indicates her sense of the wider implications of her localist interventions linking land to the nation. To write a 'memorial' of 'mee', to repair a castle, build, sign, and organize an almshouse, regulate one's lands, and assert control of one's tenantry is, as the presence of these books demonstrates, to be sharply aware of contemporary discourses of antiquarianism as they impinge on understandings of law (in terms of precedent), place, and nation.[86]

The books in the Great Picture make biographical claims for Clifford as they situate her and the things and writings she has produced in relation to space, time, and status. As Mihoko Suzuki tells us, in the Great Picture she gets to reshape history and space around her, turning the meaning of historical events towards her own life.[87] Yet—perhaps because of its very impulse to include all connections and meanings— the image is a more open text than any other finished text that Clifford produced, for all that it appears to be a final and definitive statement. The books act as markers of knowledge and status but also indicate the web of discourses that organized late Stuart perceptions of the estate and countryside. Drawing as they do on Italian models hybridized with more English understandings of the pastoral virtues associated with the House, the discourses permeated Clifford's thinking on her place in

---

[86] Legal books are missing, though, of course the great Books of Record are full of legal precedent and proof. Ironically, one of the spiritual preparations for death in the final image, George Strode's manual for dying, *The Anatomie of Mortalitie* (London, 1618), was written by a lawyer. See A3ʳ.

[87] Mihoko Suzuki, 'Anne Clifford and the Gendering of History', *Clio*, 30, No. 2 (2001), pp. 195–229: 211.

the estates of Westmorland. It would be simultaneously inadequate and excessive to say that she conceived of Westmorland on the model of the Palladian estate or that she understood herself as recreating Renaissance Italy amongst the lakes and moors. As Vita Sackville-West notes, she did spend years, 'lording it over the north', governing 'from the midst of a little court of her own'.[88] She did, it seems, see her land as a kind of princedom built from the resources of a library, memory, buildings, and genealogy. But she also needed to have those claims recognized, and that may be why the story or stories imaged in the Great Picture are oriented towards both an inward audience of family (who need to know and accept Clifford's narrative) and the outer world—at least those who came into her castle.

It is precisely Clifford's status as an unusual, elite woman which illuminates so vividly the politicized implications of diaries, images, monuments. To claim land is to claim a political place, and Clifford occupied, potentially, a position usually reserved for the masculine elite. As Samuel Daniel's poem to her stresses, she was one that 'such a faire advantage have | Both by your birth and happy pow'rs'.[89] Clifford's elite status and later wealth, the very circumstances that enabled her to produce her texts, make her far from representative, but the discourses she used—legal, familial, lineal—extended throughout Stuart and Civil War society, tying feminine identity to the political sphere.[90] Anne Clifford's focus on property illuminates conceptions of self as tied to a network including the local and the national. Her texts suggest the political implications underlying both retreat—*otium*—and the claim on land. To assert legal ownership of land was to make one kind of claim to centrality. To go off and live on it was to make another gesture towards the Stuart court.

Clifford reminds us that lineage and family were political discourses throughout the period we are looking at. Her texts remind us of the quotidian and symbolic importance of inheritance to early modern society, a power on which the political theory of Sir Robert Filmer draws. Inviting us to expand the kind of languages that we see as

---

[88] *Diary*, ed. Sackville-West, pp. xxxviii, xxxiv, xlv.

[89] 'To the Ladie Anne Clifford', in *The Whole Workes of Samuel Daniel*, pp. 71–3.

[90] Amy Louise Erickson, *Women and Property in Early Modern England* (London: Routledge, 1993), p. 4. Erickson notes that the concentration on the elite transfer of property is problematic in generalizing with regard to family relations.

potentially political, Clifford's textual assertions also prompt us to
recall that, to a contemporary, the politics of genealogy was readily
understood. Clifford's texts are the only assertions of political place
based solely on inheritance that this study deals with; they offer a
salutary reminder of the enduring power of a land-based politics, of
the power of the elite, and of the endurance of an elite as opposed to a
public sphere. Clifford addresses the public who pass across her land.
She is acutely aware of the value of publicizing her lineage. And her
productions, though in manuscript and written on buildings, are to an
early modern reader as evidently political as the printed petition.

However, if all the women I examined in this study shared Clifford's
attitudes, she would have been living in a more stable society than was the
case. For there are some important senses of politics with which Clifford
is only limitedly concerned. Her engagement with the political world is
familial and might accurately be described as self-interested, even pri-
vatizing. Her engagement with the Overbury scandal, for instance,
involves assimilating it to her own position—she draws it into her own
narrative. The genealogical elaboration of the Great Picture, too, expands the meaning of the family to fill every inch of space. Clifford
characteristically moves away from national politics towards a local life;
in her writing and thinking the house, household, and estate are made,
inscribed, as worlds within the big world. Clifford can be seen in reaction
to the power of both the Stuart and Civil War states. That is not to say
that local and familial politics is unimportant—far from it. There is no
doubt that she has relationships, too, to the national political world: both
deliberate, considered, relations and those made by the accidents of birth
and life history. While Clifford's appropriative textualizing makes lineage
into an assertive politics, this is qualified by the reactive formation of her
political engagement. Her valuation of lineage brings into focus the
politicized nature of familial claims. Yet when we attend to these relationships it also becomes evident that, importantly, some women had
other significant kinds of relationships to politics. The contours of an
idea of politics are disclosed by Clifford's distinction between national
and lineal, yet her apprehension of national issues is characterized by
insistence on family and land. Because Clifford's actions commit her to
a developed assertion of the politics of lineage, her example makes us
see some of the other things that the other subjects of this study share.
Many are interested in, not simply forced to engage with, national issues

(variously defined, and not excluding local questions); they have a sense of public good; some have a sense of the specificity of women's relationship to politics, and all are reflexive about the pleasures and perils of a role in political or religio-political controversy.

What, then, does this study of the texts of Brilliana Harley and Anne Clifford disclose about women's relationships to politics in seventeenth-century England? First, their rhetorics and the points they are concerned to make are very different—as we might expect, given that women's political commitments, engagements, and vocabularies must have been very diverse. Harley and Clifford are writers, but also interpreters of texts, and particular acts of interpretation are subject to powerful forces and bound to circumstances.[91] The materials they produce, however, indicate that women's relationship to the political sphere is not simply one of exclusion but evidently complex, imagistic, textual. Each writer deploys the materials on which authority is founded—law, religion, family, property. Each corpus reminds us of the diversity of vocabularies in which politics was discussed in the seventeenth century. Each case reminds us that the borders between public and private were not clear, indeed in each case the building of a politicized or directly political claim on family and property indicates that the vocabulary of private and public is a relatively blunt tool for discussing the relationship between gender and politics. Equally forcefully, each case reminds us of the early modern foundations of political involvement. When recognizing an emphasis on property as a 'law', or the claim of inheritance to influence the political world we are prompted to remember the differences between the basis of a modern and an early modern political world. The law, protecting property, is a political tool; as D. W. Hanson remarked, 'legal ideas are not and cannot be radically removed from political ideas and interests'.[92] Both writers prompt us to trace the understandings of seventeenth-century thinking on politics back to

[91] See Roger Chartier, 'Texts, Forms, and Interpretations', in id., *On the Edge of the Cliff: History, Language, and Practices* (Baltimore: Johns Hopkins University Press, 1997), pp. 81–9.

[92] D. W. Hanson, *From Kingdom to Commonwealth: The Development of Civic Consciousness in English Political Thought* (Cambridge, Mass.: Harvard University Press, 1970), p. vii; see also pp. 1–17.

earlier contexts—to the Reformation, to a medieval statute, to a long-standing kinship or neighbourly network.

Brilliana Harley evidently regarded her authority as derived from her husband's status and property; we can see that this framework facilitated rather than precluding intervention in the very political sphere reserved for men. Reading Clifford's celebration of her vast sequestered inheritance in the cataclysmic year 1649, and looking at the genealogically obsessed Great Picture from the 1640s, when Harley was writing frantically to London for news, we must for a moment reconsider the dominant political struggles with which the rest of my project is primarily engaged. There are, it seems distinct forms of politics operating; these sometimes touch, sometimes bypass, the world this study explores. Brilliana Harley shares more concerns with the other subjects of this study. She puts before us questions which recur: how are we to think about action and writing based on scripture—can we make a split between politics and religion? What is the relationship between local and other political forms and powers? On what foundation, if any, can women assert the public good? In sum, Clifford and Harley invite us to reconsider the nature and bases of women's involvement in politics and to expand what we see as political. In looking at the relationship of these two women to politics we can begin to rethink both the position of early modern women and the categories of politics. The chapters which follow build on this section's discussions of the rhetorics connecting seventeenth-century women to politics to explore the way in which gender, religion, and politics interact in the sectarian politics of the 1640s.

II

RELIGION AND POLITICS

3

The Political Work of a Spiritual Text: Sarah Wight, Henry Jessey, and *The exceeding Riches of Grace*

> What is the language using us for?
> It uses us all and in its dark
> Of dark actions selections differ.
>
> (W. S. Graham, *Implements in their Places*)

WOMEN AND MEN, POLITICS AND RELIGION: THE SECTS

May 24. 1647. *Mris* SARAH WIGHT, being then still very weak in body, (and keeping bed since *April* 6.) said thus to the *Relator: I would others might hear how gracious the Lord hath dealt with me,* the chiefest of sinners, that none might DESPAIR and murmure, *as I have done*... [1]

So, in the midst of the political turmoil of 1647, when the sectarian congregations were under severe pressure, Sarah Wight authorized the publication of her experiences. This and the following chapter investigate the political implications of women's involvement in sectarian writing in the later years of the 1640s. The material discussed in these chapters—printed writings as opposed to the manuscripts considered in the preceding chapter—carries the discussion of women's relationship to politics

---

[1] *The exceeding Riches of Grace Advanced By the Spirit of Grace, in an Empty Nothing Creature,* 'published' by Henry Jesse[y] (London: Matthew Simmons for Henry Overton and Hannah Allen, 1647), a8^r.

into the explicitly public terrain of religious and political controversy. Each of the paired chapters explores women's relationship to politics from the point of view of their participation in public debate, assessing the place of their texts, responses to their texts, and factors forming political and textual identities in the heated drama of the later 1640s. Examining primarily the writings associated with Sarah Wight and Elizabeth Poole, the chapters trace the debate within the gathered churches about the nature and extent of worldly versus spiritual authority. This debate intensified after the second Civil War, and polarized at the regicide.

Taking up the events and publication associated with an adolescent's experience of grace, this chapter investigates women's relationship to spiritual and political discourses in the context of the disputes amongst the army, Independents, Presbyterians, and Levellers in the late 1640s. In the search for a true path the very terms 'Independent' and 'Presbyterian' were disputed. *The exceeding Riches of Grace* makes public Sarah Wight's experience, even as she is confined to her chamber. The events described— Wight's spiritual experiences, conferences, interrogations—lasted over the spring and summer of 1647 when Wight's chamber became the location of visiting, counsel, discussion, and, perhaps, a kind of pilgrimage. Events caught up the members of the gathered churches of London, Bristol, and Wales and their associates in the army, but also drew in men and women of a very different religious and political complexion from the text's 'relator', Henry Jessey: those who visited Wight included some at the heart of power. What was published as *The exceeding Riches* claims in part to record speech. Even as Sarah Wight uttered her words Henry Jessey was recording them, giving them precise biblical location, and preparing them for publication. Taking the experience of one woman—an empty vessel— as an exemplary drama of faith, *The exceeding Riches* unfolds the question of the nature of testimony, the meaning of grace for the Christian, and the nature of spiritual versus political claims and hierarchies.[2] It invites us, therefore, to consider the political work a specifically spiritual discourse can undertake in the world; the relationship between text and body in ecstatic experience in Civil War London; the way in which gender shaped political and spiritual claims.

---

[2] See Patrick Collinson, *The Religion of Protestants: The Church in English Society 1559–1625* (Oxford: Oxford University Press, 1982), pp. 129–30; Anna Trapnel, *The Cry of a Stone*, ed. Hilary Hinds, Medieval and Renaissance Texts and Studies 220 (Tempe: Arizona Center for Medieval and Renaissance Studies, 2000), pp. xiii–xiv.

Bringing together, if not entirely uniting, speech and text, standing as a record of ceremony and ministry but also turning these events towards politics, *The exceeding Riches* is an example of the way religious experience, method, and writing were sometimes the ground of the power struggle amongst Independents, Presbyterians, and Levellers at the end of the second civil war. The text's divisions—into the 'causes' of publication, a central section based on the spoken words of Sarah Wight, and a section on 'uses'—at least in theory distinguish between Wight's 'Testimony' and Jessey's interpretation as 'an eare-witnesse'.[3] However, questions of agency and authorship are only partly resoluble; ambiguity in these matters coexists with an intense concern with self-authentication and truth. Yet it is partly because of the uncertainties about whose will is at work, who might be considered author of the text (as, it seems, Wight considered herself), that *The exceeding Riches* becomes a rich source for investigation of the relationship between religious and political claims. Temporal and authorial discontinuities allow us to probe the ways in which Wight and Jessey treat the political potential of Wight's experience of grace.

Although largely ignored in histories of the Civil War, *The exceeding Riches* has been discussed by writers considering the self. It has been read as a text in the Puritan tradition of *ars moriendi*, and its uses of physical suffering to signify the speaker's conflicted, liminal, position between 'this world and the next' have been interrogated, as have its implications for understanding of feminine prophecy and inedia. The transformation of values as private bedchamber becomes (public?) audience room has been canvassed.[4] While the question of the self is not absent here, the main focus of what follows is on the politics of 1647, and the

---

[3] *Riches*, A2^r, 'Uses' pp. 153–9, a1^r.

[4] Barbara Ritter-Dailey, 'The Visitation of Sarah Wight: Holy Carnival and the Revolution of the Saints in Civil War London', *Church History*, 55 (1986), pp. 439–11; Diane Purkiss, 'Producing the Voice, Consuming the Body: Women Prophets of the Seventeenth Century', in *Women, Writing, History 1640–1740*, ed. Isobel Grundy and Susan Wiseman (London: Batsford, 1992), pp. 139–58: 144–50; Hilary Hinds, *God's Englishwomen: Seventeenth-Century Radical Sectarian Writing and Feminist Criticism* (Manchester: Manchester University Press, 1996), pp. 43–4; Diane Watt, *Secretaries of God: Women Prophets in Late Medieval and Early Modern England* (Cambridge: D. S. Brewer, 1997), pp. 61, 127; Katharine Gillespie, *Domesticity and Dissent in the Seventeenth Century: English Women Writers and the Public Sphere* (Cambridge: Cambridge University Press, 2004), p. 185.

relationship between the political and the spiritual within and without the text.[5] For, with links to the conversion narrative and offering a highly pointed analysis of Christian as opposed to worldly obedience, *The exceeding Riches of Grace* seems likely to have spoken to its first readers both spiritually and politically. The ensuing discussion of this text has three objectives: to assess some of the ways in which 'grace' might be claimed as an operatively political issue working in the world, to canvass the relationship between religious and political discourses, and to continue consideration of the textual strategies which put women in relation to politics.

The 1647 edition of the text is marked by the urgency of prophecy at a time of oppression. Wight begins her experiences at a moment when 'All the Independent party are exceedingly sunk in spirit' under the assault of the Presbyterians in Commons, London, and army.[6] As Elizabeth Avery wrote, connecting Babylon and Parliament's violence to the saints: 'remember *March* and *April Anno.Dom.* 1647'.[7] Times were bad.

TEMPTATION, GRACE, AND OBEDIENCE: READING *THE EXCEEDING RICHES*

The beginning of her more violent Temptations was thus: Her superior bid her doe a small thing, judging it meet and lawfull: Shee did it, doubtingly, fearing it was unlawfull: and as shee did it, a great Trembling in her hands and body fell upon her: being condemned in her selfe. About a moneth after, returning home, having been abroad, shee had lost her hood, and knew shee had lost it. Her Mother asked her, for her hood. Shee suddenly answered, My Grand-mother hath it. Her heart condemned her instantly, and trembled againe exceedingly.

---

[5] On politics, Carola Scott-Luckens helpfully sees the text's desire to promote unity within the congregations: 'Propaganda or Marks of Grace? The Impact of the Reported Ordeals of Sarah Wight in Revolutionary London, 1647–52', *Women's Writing*, 9, No. 2 (2002), pp. 215–32: 225. Ritter-Dailey sees the text as a 'petition' for 'reconciliation'. See 'The Visitation of Sarah Wight', pp. 439–11.

[6] Bodl. MS Clarendon, vol. 29, fo. 193, Letter of Intelligence April 15/25, quoted in Mark A. Kishlansky, *The Rise of the New Model Army* (Cambridge: Cambridge University Press, 1979), p. 161.

[7] Elizabeth Avery, *Scripture-Prophesies Opened* (London: Giles Calvert, 1647), p. 15. Collected by Thomason, 8 November.

And these were the first chiefe occasions of her deep despaire: And upon this, shee had cast into her Conscience, that *shee was both a Thiefe, and a lyar*, and was terrified ever since, that shee was shut out of Heaven, and must be damn'd, damn'd.[8]

These incidents, although they are proposed as the seeds of the 12-year-old Sarah Wight's despair from which blossomed the wonderful workings of God's grace, are for much of the text invisible, buried. They disappear after this brief reference, only surfacing again explicitly in the last pages, where Jessey sets out the 'uses' of Wight's words and story. We do not have them in Wight's own words. Yet they introduce us not simply to the narrative source of Wight's experience but also to one of the central issues of the text about which both Wight and Jessey have much to say—obedience.

Partaking of some the enigmatic quality of a fairy- or folk-tale, these details evoke a life where the subject's ability to take action is determined by internal and external coercion. The account dramatizes the world of the child and the servant, a world dominated by the power of superiors, and where it is perilous both to act and to do nothing. In the rest of the text, the cause here described has an impact similar to that of the pea on the princess: it causes a huge, transforming, response. However, where a modern psychoanalytic reading might see the melancholy of wounded narcissism, Wight and Jessey's text understands sin punished by conscience (and not necessarily disproportionately) within the dynamics of despair and grace, obedience and disobedience. When, on 6 April 1647, Wight began to experience or accept God's grace she found a vocabulary of self-forgiveness in which to speak of a highly charged, partly eroticized, 'full', relationship with God. The language she finds also attacks the misappropriation of human power. Grace—free grace—enables her to find a way to make her sins, like those of the Magdalene, an advantage in prompting God's forgiveness and allowing her to 'find' grace. At this point conscience is apprehended in its true aspect and Wight's judgement is realigned to reverse her earlier misconception of who was sinner and sinned against, who obedient and disobedient: seen clearly, Wight's sin becomes obeying a mere superior against her conscience.

---

[8] *Riches*, p. 7.

Conscience, obedience, religious toleration, and the nature and extent of the power of the civil magistrate were, for the gathered churches, in a complex relationship. From the start of the Civil War the sectaries had asserted their desire as fact: within the precarious alliance of forces which had fought against the King their position had been that a true civil magistrate had nothing to fear from them: their interests were spiritual. However, they also argued that the civil magistrate had no true power to coerce religious belief. This was a point included as the 'reserve of religion' in the Leveller *Agreement of the People* and was to prove a major sticking point in the constitutional wrangles of November and December 1648 as the Rump prepared to try the King. For the gathered churches in 1647 obedience ostensibly remained, as in the 1559 Book of Common Prayer children's catechism—'to love, honour, and succour my father and mother. To honour and obey the king and his ministers. To submit myself to all my governors, teachers, spiritual pastors and masters. To order myself lowly and reverently to all my betters.'[9] Yet such hierarchical ties were undeniably undermined by debate on the civil magistrate's power of coercion in religion. By the crisis of the second civil war, the religious and political alliance between those who, like Sir Robert Harley, took the Solemn League and Covenant and their more religiously radical allies in the first war was intensely felt. In 1647 nobody knew the outcome of the divisions that were beginning to emerge after the Civil War. The paradoxical and ambiguous nature of the divisions lent itself readily to a dramatization of the power of grace. It was always to be remembered that God's word overrode civic reverence. Grace, to use contemporary terms, though it would not come to all, was sufficient for all. In such circumstances the possession of grace conferred power which was spiritual and *therefore* had authority in the world. The command to obey conscience is not grounded in heterodox theology, but a part of Calvinism given heavy emphasis within the gathered churches. Nevertheless, in Wight's case, the extraordinary implications for local, household, and wider civic and governmental hierarchical relationships are explored. To these wider

---

[9] *The Book of Common Prayer 1559*, ed. John E. Booty (Washington, D.C.: Folger Shakespeare Library, 1976), p. 286. On catechisms see *Political Ideas of the English Civil Wars*, ed. Andrew Sharpe (London: Longman, 1983), pp. 26–9; Susan Amussen, *An Ordered Society: Gender and Class in Early Modern England* (Oxford: Blackwell, 1988), p. 36.

implications, and how Wight and Jessey understand gender as relating to them, I will return.

The exceeding Riches puts before us the harsh sufferings caused by Wight's disobedience to conscience. Despairing, 'shee could believe nothing but Hell and Wrath to be her Portion' and was tempted to believe 'that there was no heaven, nor hell, but in our Conscience: and that shee was *damn'd already, being an unbeleever*'. Jessey, and later Wight, both detail the self-violence to which she was tempted—'shee oft attempted wickedly to destroy her selfe, as by drowning, strangling, stabbing, seeking to beat out her braines, wretchedly bruising, and wounding her self'.[10] Thus we hear, much later, how:

> there being a window to the House-tiles, shee crept out, (to do like *Judas*, to cast herself down to dissolve herselfe,) and in the dark shee *saw* there a fire, and *Satan* as a *roaring Lyon* in it: yet still being perswaded through his delusion there was no other hell, but that she felt in her conscience, shee went within a quarter of a yard of the edge … [11]

Having failed to jump, she sits by the chimney and beats her brains against it. Later Jessey tells us of another apparently suicidal attempt when it 'was put in her mind to goe thence that night to the *Dog-house*, (shee had heard of) in *Moorfields*, there to offer her selfe to the Dogs, to eate her up, that her Mother might never heare of her more'.[12] Here a heady mixture of apparently vengeful and self-loathing impulses takes a form which seems to play on the eucharist. Certainly, the forms of Wight's deathly imaginings suggest the part played by theatre, parody, and church symbolism in the experience of despair.[13]

All this changed on 6 April when, while the gathered churches felt themselves oppressed by carnal leaders, the 15-year-old Sarah Wight began to experience God's grace.[14] However, the status of her prophecy—in the sense of exegesis and shared experience—was potentially compromised by exactly the qualities of weakness and femininity which made her an example of God's strength. The ways in which her body manifested the triumph of grace troubled observers, as Wight's physical condition seemed to become worse rather than better. Though claiming

---

[10] *Riches*, pp. 7–8.　　[11] Ibid., pp. 127–8; see also A3ᵛ.
[12] Ibid., pp. 128–30.
[13] See also Hannah Allen, *Satan his Methods and Malice Baffled* (London, 1683).
[14] *Riches*, p. 15.

to be filled with assurance of grace she was confined to her bed, sometimes deaf and blind and, most significantly, she did not eat. For sustenance she only drank a little water or sometimes beer. These actions, alarmingly similar to her earlier suicidal temptations, put her body, and so her sex and age, at the centre of a drama of grace with significant spiritual and political implications. Did such symptoms reinforce Wight's 'Testimony' to God's grace? The question of whether her physical condition authenticated or undermined the authority of her words may have been a strong prompt to Jessey to supply the reader with interpretative frameworks.[15] Is she to be considered a prophet? What was her relationship to the political situation of 1647 in which the army and Independents were increasingly desperate? At the same time as focusing attention on Wight's voice and physical condition, the text prompts us at every turn to consider the place of grace in the Bible. The words, if not the biblical citations, are presented to the reader as in a strong sense 'hers'.

Jessey's emphasis on the significance and truth of Wight's experience involves him in twin editorial strategies: he sets before us what he claims are her words and, around these, he sets up interpretative frameworks. Indeed, he supplies such extensive justificatory and explanatory material that it forms a parallel text. Orienting the reader by grounding Wight socially and spiritually, Jessey prints a letter from her brother at All Souls and biographical material disclosing her widowed mother's crisis and her relatively high status. Simultaneously, 'A Table of the Places of holy Scripture, that in this Book are opened, illustrated, and applied' invites a reader to take the word first, not the event, and read the examples as illustrating grace as suggested by scriptural quotations. A list of significant visitors shows Wight's imbrication in the political as well as the religious events of that summer, as do introductions by Jessey and John Saltmarsh.[16] For Jessey, making up a text for the printer, issues of key importance are grace, the nature of the vision or prophecy and its general and particular relationship to the world of 1647, and order and obedience. However, the interpretations Jessey invites the reader to make are disrupted by changing events and, in consequence, we can to some extent trace the interpretative frameworks he proposed for the events from April to autumn.

---

[15] *Riches*, a7^{r-v}.   [16] Ibid., A2^r–a8^v.

At first, Wight's refusal of food and altered consciousness seem to have been assimilated to an interpretation of her as experiencing grace on her deathbed; Jessey compares Wight to the recently published account of another woman's good death, *Mistress Drake Revived*. Joan Drake, after doubting for all her adult life, as she is dying begins '*talking of the best things perpetually night and day*' with sudden outpourings of joy. They send 'post to *London* for two Physitians, hoping by their advice to have made her rest: but all in vaine, *No physick could cure her but heavenly physick*'.[17] Drake's ecstatically good death is especially significant in a culture where, as Ralph Houlbrooke notes, without ritual or sacramental shaping, death brought an 'agony of uncertainty about God's judgement'. To be taken up with praises of the Lord at such a terrifying and truth-provoking moment is in itself a substantial authentication of grace: if death was the supreme test of faith who would have the presence of mind and temerity to fake ecstasy when truly about to meet their maker? A good death, as Houlbrouke observes, was turned outwards towards witnesses who were to be encouraged and comforted. He mentions, too, the serious consideration given to the experiences of figures whose unstable relation to full reason made them both potentially more sinful and readier vessels of God's word.[18] There was good reason for Jessey to have anticipated that Wight's experiences would fit this reassuring pattern, particularly given her extreme physical symptoms.

While Jessey initially understood Wight's behaviour and eloquence as an experience of grace at the point of death, from the start the phenomena before him raised other questions, too. What was the status of religious melancholy—specifically, where was the gateway between physiological and spiritual experience? Considering this, Jessey compares Wight's account of being 'strongly carried' in a temptation and drawn out of it by an incident with a cup to an experience of Mrs Honeywood.

[17] John Hart, *Trodden Down Strength, by the God of Strength, or, Mrs Drake Revived* (London, 1647), pp. 135, 160.

[18] Ralph Houlbrooke, *Death, Religion and the Family in England 1480–1750* (Oxford: Oxford University Press, 1998), pp. 147, 154–70; id., 'The Puritan Death-Bed, c.1560–1660', in *The Culture of English Puritanism, 1560–1700*, ed. Christopher Durston and Jacqueline Eales (Basingstoke: Macmillan, 1996), pp. 122–44: 141. See also Philippe Ariès, *In the Hour of Our Death*, trans. Helen Weaver (1977; London: Allen Lane, 1981), pp. 95–201.

This pious and hypochondrial Elizabethan gentlewoman had been treated by divines, physicians, and others at the border of healer and prophet.[19] Honeywood's story was available in Simon Foxe's memoir of Foxe in the 1641 edition of *Acts and Monuments*—a text which it seems Jessey kept by him.[20] Jessey himself is said to have participated in miraculous healing. Also amongst the interpretative tools Jessey uses is a tactful interest in physic. He also attends questioningly to the nature and status of Wight's fasting, her body (especially blindness and sight), and her likely death.[21]

Wight did not die. However, by the time it emerged at midsummer that she would live, Jessey had sent sheets to the printers—the time of the event and of the text were tangled up. Explanations besides that of deathbed grace had to be found. Indeed, the longer the event continued the greater the need for convincing explanation. Similarly, the longer Wight lived and the more she spoke, the greater the need for careful editorial form. Thus, while Wight's most sustained analyst, Barbara Ritter-Dailey, rightly emphasizes Wight's 'impending death', the narrative shape of a good death is less than half the story; it is precisely the narrative form that Jessey, and perhaps Wight herself, were forced to overwrite.[22] The discourse of the deathbed was retained in the text in this and later editions; cohabiting with other interpretations it continues to perform significant narrative and spiritual tasks.

Jessey explicitly describes his attempt to interpret events; in 'To the Christian Reader', dated 16 July 1647, Jessey refers to having stored up material before 27 April and to being pressed by friends to disseminate it. On 27 April, he tells us, 'The *Earthly Vessel* of conveyance being then most likely to return to earth, within a few daies', he prefixed the letter, and, it seems, sent off some material to the press. However, Wight lived on though 'as weak as before' and 'unable to eat at all for *eleven weeks*

---

[19] *Riches*, pp. 11–12. See Alexandra Walsham, ' "Frantick Hacket": Prophecy, Sorcery, Insanity, and the Elizabethan Puritan Movement', *HJ* 41, No. 1 (1998), pp. 27–66: 42.

[20] Thomas Freeman, ' "The Good Ministrye of Godlye and Vertuouse Women": the Elizabethan Martyrologists and the Female Supporters of the Marian Martyrs', *Journal of British Studies*, 9 (2000), pp. 8–34: 19–20.

[21] Jesse[y] attended 'a great meeting of many Sectaries ... for the restoring of an old blind woman to her sight, by anointing her with oyl in the name of the Lord': Thomas Edwards, *The Third Part of Gangraena* (London, 1646 edn.), p. 19.

[22] *Riches*, A3ᵛ–A4ʳ; Ritter-Dailey, 'The Visitation of Sarah Wight', pp. 444, 446, 452.

together'. And although the material was at the press 'in the mean while, one day after another was occasion of *enlarging* it, by *conferences* &c. and of *her still drawing nearer death*, in outward appearance, till June 11'; a good part of the material was printed before 11 June and 25 June—'*the daies of the Lords wonderful raising up of her body by faith*'.[23] From the reader's point of view, then, layered interpretative discourses thread their way through, and surround, *reportage*. These items seem to have been added to the text at different times.[24] Even as Jessey attempted to fix events in print, their trajectory and meaning were changing. Wight and Jessey agreed that her experiences were of grace. So, amongst the introductory supporting documents, Jessey cites Nathaniel Holmes's tract, *Gods Gracious Thoughts Towards Great Sinners*.[25] Printed by Matthew Simmonds, with whom Jessey had close connections, and collected by Thomason in 1647, this text addresses God's willing promise of 'free mercy' to sinners—it emphasizes the potential of grace, participating in the debate over free grace by giving biblical citation and exegesis to confirm its availability. Significantly, a reader could, if they chose, use the 'Table' of Jessey and Wight's text to the same purpose. As I will show, Holmes and Jessey both saw true obedience to God as having implications for worldly hierarchy.

Grace is a crucial tool in the interpretation of Wight's experiences in *The exceeding Riches*; it bridged Wight's and Jessey's concerns, and its prime importance is emphasized in a prefatory letter by John Saltmarsh. An army chaplain at the epicentre of political and sectarian activity, Saltmarsh had written on free grace and on Independency. In *Smoke in the Temple* (1646) he had defined Independency as a 'church called by the Word and Spirit into consent or covenant'—and governed by 'brethren'. Calling for unity amongst those Protestants outside the national church, he upheld ordinances (the 'legal' aspect of faith) but insisted that they were not 'above or beside the *Law-giver*'.[26] In the same treatise he supported liberty of printing and debate within the church:

---

[23] *Riches*, A6^{r-v}.

[24] Ritter-Dailey, 'The Visitation of Sarah Wight', p. 442.

[25] Nathaniel Holmes, *Gods Gracious Thoughts Towards Great Sinners* (London: Matthew Simmonds, 1647).

[26] John Saltmarsh, *Smoke in the Temple*, 'second edition corrected' (London: Ruth Raworth for Giles Calvert, 1646), A4^{r}.

Christ governs by the people *ministerially*, not over the people *authoritatively* only; and the people being once in his *Church*-way, lose their *old* capacity for a *new*, and are raised up from people, to Brethren, to Churches. ... The *interest* of the people in *Christs Kingdom* is not onely an *interest* of *compliancy*, and *obedience*, and *submission*; but of consultation, of *debating*, *counselling*, *proph-esying*, *voting*, &c. and let us *stand fast in that liberty wherewith* Christ *hath made us free*.[27]

Saltmarsh advocated toleration, downplayed 'legal' things (such as absorbed those advocating a national church, or Presbyterians more generally), emphasized prophecy, and thought that grace might redeem even the worst of sinners.

Wight, emerging from within the gathered church, illustrated much of Saltmarsh's thesis. Bound into her legal—outward, unregenerate—situation Wight had been on the brink of suicide, but grace had brought her redemption. The circulation of believers around her and her services to others positively exemplified the operations of a church founded on an equality of gathered saints rather than outward hierarchy. It was precisely these qualities which Saltmarsh felt that the army grandees had lost after they ceased to attend to the rank and file, and in 1648, in a letter published by his wife after his death, he accused Fairfax and Cromwell of stopping 'the breathings of God in meane private Christians'.[28] For Saltmarsh, good government—religious and civil—began with the ideas and voices of the godly; Wight was, for Saltmarsh, one of these. Saltmarsh's words, addressing the covenant of grace, also told the reader of a position in the world:

I finde in this *Spirituall Treatise* of yours, two things very *experimentall*; the *one* is her *legall*, and the *other* her more *Gospel* condition: In the *first*, shee is in *bondage*, in *blackness*, and *darkness*, and *tempest*; in much *distresse*, and *shadow* of *death*, her life *drawing nigh unto hell*: and afflicted with all his waves, (*Psal.* 88.3.7) In her *Gospel* state, I find God *shewing wonders* to the *dead*, making the *dead* to rise and praise him ... (Psal. 118. 10, 11, 12.) ...[29]

Advocating publication 'to the *Saints*', Saltmarsh sees that Wight's experiences show the dangers of obeying the world—including church government—and the advantages of true spiritual obedience.

---

[27] John Saltmarsh, *Free Grace* (London, 1645); id., *Smoke in the Temple*, pp. 61–2.
[28] John Saltmarsh, *Englands Friend Raised from the Grave* (London: 1648), A2^r.
[29] *Riches*, a2^{r-v}.

For Saltmarsh and Jessey grace was a longed-for and reassuring experience of God's promise of plenitude and forgiveness. As importantly, in the period after the Civil War the role of grace in the collective experiences of the gathered churches provided an explanation for the rejection of church structures. On the interpretation of grace was founded a claim to theological truth and religious experience powerful enough to challenge both a national church and a secular magistracy—or, in practice, the Presbyterian hegemony. In 1647 to emphasize the term 'free grace' was to be connected with a version of Calvinist theology and so a religious grouping.[30] Free grace was of huge significance to those around Wight: Walter Cradock, who visited her and vouched for her maid, often quoted ' "Ye are not under the law but under grace" (Rom. vi, 14)' against the encroachment of legalism into Christian life.[31] To be under a new covenant of grace rather than law was essential to a religious Independency. What it might mean to claim grace, and most particularly the question of the relationship between 'free grace' and 'legal' or worldly structures, puzzled many others besides Wight. Though the claim to 'free' grace was not limited to Calvinism it created one of several practical boundaries within it, hiving off those who emphasized God's grace from, amongst others, those who emphasized church discipline. The history of holy dying into which Jessey had planned to fit Wight was perhaps the least controversial branch of the history of grace in Anglophone Protestantism. On the other hand, Anne Hutchinson's accusation that New England ministers emphasized secondary evidence of grace—in effect preaching a covenant of works—had been at the heart of major controversies in Boston only a decade or so earlier.[32] Grace and controversy went hand in hand.

---

[30] John von Rhor writes of the covenant of grace: 'To speak of the nature of the covenant of grace in Puritan thought is to speak actually of its two natures. Puritan theology was not a rational whole, but was drawn by its own inner impulses into two directions, those generated by the experiential and voluntaristic concerns of Gospel piety and those precipitated by the inherited dogmatic demand for the doctrine of predestination. Evangel and election bequeathed to Puritan theology a double agenda, and the idea of the covenant became, at least in some measure, the point of connection, if not of reconciliation. So the one covenant has two qualities: it is, on the one hand, the instrument of God's sovereign rule in all that pertains to salvation.' John von Rohr, *The Covenant of Grace in Puritan Thought* (Atlanta: Scholars Press, 1986), p. 56.

[31] Geoffrey Nuttall, *The Welsh Saints 1640–1660* (Cardiff: University of Wales Press, 1957), pp. 30–4: 31.

[32] See Amy Schrager Lang, *Prophetic Woman: Anne Hutchinson and the Problem of Dissent in the Literature of New England* (Berkeley: University of California Press, 1987),

What does Wight's 'own' language, or what is presented as such in *The exceeding Riches*, suggest about her interpretation of her experiences? Wight's words are presented in 'records' of two kinds of 'conferences'. In one Wight counsels individuals and groups which include 'many strangers' but are always—in the text at any rate—women. In the second kind Jessey reports interrogations testing the significance of Wight's vision and vocation.[33] Obedience and disobedience, which the reader knows to have played a key part in Wight's own spiritual trajectory, loom large in these conferences. Thus, Sarah reminds a 'gentlewoman' of God's power and distances her preaching from any connection with works, asking: '*Did Christ dye for the obedient, or for the disobedient? Christ died for the disobedient and rebellious, that they might partake of his obedience.*' Wight later also reminds the woman not to think of her own 'unthankfull, undutiful' behaviour, but of '*what is in Christ for you*'.[34] Obedience to God is not a simple matter, and Wight's conversations repeatedly turn to the struggle against despair; she emphasizes explicitly that Christ looks after even those who 'refused *to be comforted*'.[35] Evidently Wight's ability to act as a physician of souls rests on her having been tested by despair and having experienced grace. In the conferences 'despair' and 'comforts' resonate with the question of liberation from forms of bondage.[36] God liberates the willing recipient of grace, and grace is consistently understood as true obedience to faith— an obedience which transcends temporal duty.

Detailed assessment of one 'conference', not necessarily typical, shows the way in which Wight's language uses the Bible to dramatize, at times eroticize, experiences of liberation through grace. We read, '*Another maid* that was not born in *England*, being *in affliction*, both in soul and body, came to her; telling her of her sad *Temptations*.' Jessey, coincidentally reminding us of his role in the text, tells us that the maid's words 'were better understood by Mris Sarah than the writer: and sometimes were guessed at, from the *Answers* given to her'.[37] These factors suggest that this maid is a visitor listed as '*Dinah* the Black', an identification made more likely by the language Wight uses to make some of the points about redemption, bondage, and liberty:[38]

pp. 1–71; Emery Battis, *Saints and Sectaries: Anne Hutchinson and the Antinomian Controversy* (Chapel Hill: University of North Carolina Press, 1962).

[33] See e.g. *Riches*, pp. 50, 54, 65 (groups), and 61, 74, 76 (afflicted women).
[34] Ibid., pp. 74, 76.   [35] Ibid., p. 104.   [36] See e.g. ibid., p. 44.
[37] Ibid., pp. 122, 123.   [38] Ibid., A1ᵛ.

Maid. I am a filthy wretched sinner.

Mris Sarah. *Who was a sinner like me? Who was worse then* Mary Magdalen, *then* Peter, *then* Paul? *Yet they obtained mercy. Are you tempted against your selfe?*

Maid. I am oft tempted against my life.

Mris Sarah. *Why, what causeth it?*

Maid. Sometimes this, because I am not as others are: I do not look so, as others doe.

Mris *Sarah. When Christ comes and manifests himself to the soul, it is black in it selfe, and uncomely: but He is fair and ruddy, and he cloaths the soule with his comeliness that * he puts on it, and makes it comely therein: and in him the soule is all faire, and there is ᵃ no spot or wrinkle, nor any such thing in his account; because he hath clensed it by his bloud, from all sin. Its* Rom.5.8.10 *not you that do it but Christ that will do it*

[*Ezek. 16.6.10;* ᵃ Cant. 4.7; Rom. 5.8.10.]

As she addresses the maid's concerns with difference and 'filth', Wight's usual advice to have faith in God's goodness and to acknowledge his power is translated into a vocabulary of colour. While the problem with the maid's body might not be that of colour at all—she describes herself as 'a dry barren ground' for grace, and Jessey says that she is troubled in both spirit and body—Wight's response certainly foregrounds darkness as a foundation on which God can work. The maid's self-description as 'filthy', implying both physical excrement and darkness, elicits from Wight an explicit identification with the Magdalene as well as Peter and Paul. The cross-gender identifications illuminate the way Civil War thinkers, like other Protestant exegetes, used many forms of biblical exemplarity.[39] The presence of such identifications, though, needs to be seen in the context of this particular text's simultaneous emphasis on the body—specifically Wight's body—and biblical language.

How does Wight use the Bible? The physicality of the Magdalene's desire, like the physicality of other religious desire, was troubling to Calvin and later Protestants. Debora Shuger makes a helpful distinction between modes of writing in which erotic desire is consistently genital and other forms. Particularly in the later seventeenth century she finds desire and eroticism tied ever more closely to desire expressed as sexual,

---

[39] On identification and poetry see Richard Rambuss, 'Pleasure and Devotion: The Body of Jesus and Seventeenth Century Religious Lyric', in *Queering the Renaissance*, ed. Jonathan Goldberg (Durham, N.C.: Duke University Press, 1994), pp. 253–79.

explicitly genital.[40] Unlike genitally oriented erotic writing, physicality and eroticism in early modern spiritual discourse can be diffuse. In this instance, identification with the example of the Magdalene allows the text to be suffused with desire for liberation from the burden of sin; desire is diffuse, grounded in the experience of grace rather than the body. In *The exceeding Riches*, identification, physicality, and desire provide a vocabulary which evokes a longing for freedom. Wight's dramatization of her own and Dinah's relationship with God, using both the Magdalene and a description of Christ (as in the Song of Songs, the desired beloved), renders the experience of bondage and liberation in eroticized terms.

Prophecy, as it occurs in *The exceeding Riches*, has a specific claim on the language of exemplarity distinct from the poetic, on the one hand, and the dissolved self of visionary prophecy on the other.[41] Wight's 'recorded' words suggest the discursive specificity of religious identification; they cannot simply be assimilated to poetry using the idea of the Magdalene, nor, like Trapnel's texts, are they prognostic prophecy.[42] Like the Magdalene, Wight has experienced despair and God's grace—she is like her exemplar in sin, suffering, and in physical longing. The very circumstances of the 1640s both prompted exegetic and prophetic speech and writing and shaped the forms these took. Submission to Christ can resolve doubt, as did the appearance of Christ to his followers, and the experience of this greater obedience is expressed here in terms of divine sustenance and liberation. Wight exploits and enlarges the idea of spiritual bondage relieved so that it becomes the Christian's central experience.

In Wight's writing the physicality of the body (for Dinah in despair, 'filthy'; for Wight in ecstasy, fed by God) is licensed by the diffuse rather

[40] Debora Kuller Shuger, *The Renaissance Bible: Scholarship, Sacrifice, and Subjectivity* (Berkeley: University of California Press, 1994), pp. 167–91.

[41] On 1620s Puritanism, and women's prophecy 'subtly eroding patriarchal dominance' in the 1620s, see David R. Como, 'Women, Prophecy, and Authority in Early Stuart Puritanism', *HLQ* 61, No. 2 (2000), pp. 203–22.

[42] While, obviously, prophetic and poetic address might be used together, contemporaries were aware of differences and distinctions. The figure of the *vates*, the poet-prophet, is not to the fore in such Civil War exegetical prophecies. Compare Sharon Achinstein, 'Romance of the Spirit: Female Sexuality and Religious Desire in Early Modern England', *ELH* 69 (2002), pp. 413–38: 416–17.

than genital location of desire. And so in this interview the coming of the bridegroom, the making darkness fair and lovely, and the liberation from slavery can be three simultaneous ways of describing Wight's and Dinah's experiences:

Did he bear and carry the Israelites [Job 19: 30], *that had been bond-slaves in* Aegypt, *through the Wildernes, into* Canaan, *(notwithstanding all their sins and provocations, and hardnes of heart,) and will not he bear you, and carry you, out of your selfe, into himselfe, though you be a bondslave to sin and Satan? He works, anone shall let him* ...

The connections between the subject's experiences and its biblical analogues are not allegorical: they are both literal ('*He works, anone shall let him*') and have an implicit relationship to obedience and disobedience—to worldly power relations (the Israelites liberated). Situating Wight as part of a cultural encounter amongst Americans, the Irish, and Africans, which provided resources for the emergence of a 'revolutionary Atlantic', Peter Linebaugh and Marcus Rediker see 'the deliverance from internal and external bondage as simultaneous' in Wight's words.[43] Yet the connection between inner and outer is left for the reader to make rather than enforced. Wight's words to the maid mix colour and slavery, drawing on the Song of Solomon as well as Job, but that biblical language is turned towards the *spiritual* state of the maid—readers can infer implications from her external condition. Wight's words implicitly acknowledge the power of worldly bondage and suffering and promise release in grace. Submission to Christ has implications for social structures at one remove, but that remove, crucially, has to be made by the reader, and the connecting step is not supplied in Wight's words. What does it tell us about Wight's shaping of the relationship between the spiritual and the political that she does not make explicit the connection to the external world?

Seeking to interpret Wight's experiences for the world, more qualified visitors interrogate Wight. Some turn to the darker possible interpretations of her state; their questions imply that she might perhaps be possessed, or (more prosaically) still in the grip of her earlier 'temptations', mentally ill, not eating because preserved by the devil rather

---

[43] Peter Linebaugh and Marcus Rediker, *The Many-Headed Hydra: The Hidden History of the Revolutionary Atlantic* (London: Verso, 2000), pp. 88–9.

than God. If the examinations recorded by Jessey are rigorous, those
interviewing her nevertheless seem careful, aware of the world's reaction
and carefully distinguished from the reported scoffings of sceptics.
Present himself as participant and recorder, Jessey recounts perhaps
the most extended of these interrogations, by Dr Coxe and others on
Monday, 31 May. Wight's questioner may have been Thomas Coxe, an
army physician. The nature of Coxe's party may be testimony to the
wide range of people who were intrigued by Wight, who included the
wife of Lord Francis Willoughby of Parham. Lord Willoughby was a
Presbyterian member of the Upper House. He became Speaker of the
Lords after the impeachment of two Independents and was impeached
himself after the army entered London. Willoughby's wife's funeral
sermon testifies to her sympathy for sectaries and her discrimination
in religious affairs.[44]

Coxe's questions test Wight's status as a recipient of God's grace. In
his first question Dr Coxe reminds Wight of the interpretations of those
hostile to her: 'Some say of your *Comfort*, that it is a *Delusion*: some say
it is not. *Q*. How do you *know* tis no *Delusion*?' In response Wight offers
her cure, talking of her terrors and temptations and her faith that
nothing could allay them but God. But she asserts the priority of her
experience—'*You cannot know what my comforts are except you knew
what my* terrors *were.*' Coxe's rejoinder is to ask how she knows 'this
working in you, is the *Spirit* of God?' to which she replies '*Where the*
Spirit *of God is, there is libertie: he sets the soule at liberty, that was in*
bondage; *for I was in* bondage.' She continues, '*he set me at* liberty; *that I
am not* under the Law, *but* under Grace'.[45] In response to the question
'*Whether have you SIN in you?*'—designed to test her for Anabaptist
leanings or heterodox claims to sinlessness—Jessey records Wight's
promotion of her agenda throughout the text—that all can be saved
by God's free grace: 'Yes' she has sin but as 'a thorne in the flesh (as *Paul*
had,) *to* humble *me: but not to* condemne *me*.'[46]

Once she has passed these tests her questioner turns to the problematic status of her body, pressing her to explain why she is physically
'weaker with your joyes, than you were with your Terrors?' Wight replies

---

[44] *Riches*, pp. 113–22; *DNB*; Revd William Firth, *A Saints Monument* (London,
1662) (see e.g. pp. 390–6 on Parham's religion).
[45] *Riches*, p. 113.   [46] Ibid., p. 115.

that '*in my Terrors, when I abus'd my body; but I never felt it, till now. I beat my head oft against the wall; and took my flesh in my teeth: and the more and ofter I did it, the lesse I felt it.*' It is now that God '*hath brought me to my selfe, now I feel it*'.[47] Addressing her most suspicious physical symptom Coxe asks her the one question to which she does not have a fully reassuring reply: 'Why do you not eat?' and whether she doesn't 'refuse the creatures out of Temptation?'. Wight's reply is that she is not tempted—'*I would eat, if I could: my stomack was then fild with terror that I could not eat; and now with joy. If I could, I would take the Creatures; but for the present I cannot.*'[48] Her reply on this occasion, as on others, fudges the fact that her inedia is constant from her terrors to the present; she does not claim that she is fasting but implicitly acknowledges her need to eat and to prove her humanity by appropriate consumption of flesh.

On 20 April Jessey writes:

The *Relator* having heard shee now had not eaten any thing at all for twenty-foure dayes or more, and drunk nothing in all this time since *April* 6. but only faire water, neither that, but two or three little cups together, once in two or three dayes. He desired her, if she could, to eat, to preserve life: for when the Lord saith, *Thou shalt not kill*: he implies the Affirmative, *Thou shalt use all good meanes to preserve life*.[49]

Rather than understanding her as fasting—something on which he had a considered opinion when he died, apparently leaving a discussion of it among his papers—Jessey reports himself as suggesting to Wight that inedia can be seen as a suicidal impulse, and one which threatens to undermine the credibility of her visions as the product of true grace.[50] The potential of inedia to be understood, as here, as suicidal temptation deepens Diane Purkiss's view that it both replicates feminine relations to food and also turns that relation to the speaker's advantage. Wight may use inedia to resist the commands of her brother and mother but she is also repeatedly forced to acknowledge its problematic, possibly sinful, status.[51] Wight's inedia, then, must also, simultaneously, be seen as she and contemporaries saw it, as an ambiguous, not conclusive, token of

---

[47] Ibid., pp. 115–16.   [48] Ibid., p. 116.   [49] Ibid., p. 38.
[50] Henry Jessey, *Miscellanea Sacra* (London, 1665), pp. 1–12.
[51] Purkiss, 'Producing the Voice', p. 145.

her changed state. Earlier examples of diabolically inspired starvation include that of the 14-year-old Mary Glover, where physicians and those favouring supernatural explanations confronted one another at a trial for witchcraft: the stakes in the interpretation of bodily symptoms were high.[52] Wight is constrained by God not to eat, and, possibly, particularly not to eat meat. She is (she says) fed well by him in a way which is of course invisible to those around her: '*I have Jesus Christ, I have enough: he feeds me with delights—He not onely hath drops; but he flows in of himselfe.*'[53] Erotic and eucharistic, Wight's words counter her interrogators with claims of God's coercion; Christ forcibly shapes her inner life. Accordingly her replies express both willingness to take up the appropriate theological position ('*I would take the Creatures*') but she waits; '*if hee see it best for his glory, and my good, I wait for a power from him for this*'.[54] Because of its key status as sinful or holy, in the representation of inedia we can trace some of the coercive forces at work in the text and perhaps the events.

Addressed on outward manifestations, Wight presents the grounds on which her spiritual health might be judged as the realm of her *inner* experience—experience of which her body as well as her words is an index, the very ground on which her identity as a speaker is founded. We can perhaps trace here the movement from compulsions understood as external (both her 'superiors' and the suicidal temptations) to an internal compulsion—both to speak her faith and to refuse food. Maybe we can trace in Wight's response a psychic but also worldly need to produce herself as a coherent and defended spiritual subject. Asking about the psychic form power takes, Judith Butler reminds us of the way power that 'at first' seems external can assume 'a psychic form that constitutes the subject's self-identity'.[55] However, external coercion (from God) expressed in her refusal to eat threatens the legitimacy of her spiritual authority even as she uses it to claim authenticity. Given the conflicting imperatives it is not surprising that when questioned about food Wight seems a less deft verbal negotiator of her experiential authenticity—at these moments we can catch sight of

[52] *Witchcraft and Hysteria in Elizabethan London: Edward Jorden and the Mary Glover Case*, ed. Michael MacDonald (London: Tavistock/Routledge, 1991).

[53] Ibid., pp. 56–7.

[54] Ibid., p. 16.

[55] Judith Butler, *The Psychic Life of Power: Theories in Subjection* (Stanford, Calif.: Stanford University Press, 1997), pp. 1–4: 3.

the imperatives governing her position. The fraught spiritual status of food refusal makes plain what is at stake in her questioning and in the surveillance to which she is subject: we see in her struggle to give a winning answer the ghost of a definitively wrong answer, and its cost.

If Wight's discourse on her body offers a rich sense of her awareness of the spiritual and worldly politics of her position, so too does her treatment of the explicitly political questions raised by a closeness of her speech to specifically prognosticatory prophecy. Coxe's last question forces the issue:

Last *Qu. May* 31. was; Whether is any thing revealed to you, how it shall goe with the Church of God?
Ans. *I know, and verily believe, it shall goe well with those that fear the Lord.*
Qu. How mean you, in spirituall, or in outward things?
Ans. *Specially in spirituall, I mean: and so far as it is for their good, in outward things, God will dispose of them* [More was said to a like *Question* before, but it is not printed.][56]

Well might Coxe enquire after the fortunes of God's people. In March, when Wight was still troubled with her terrors, the power of the City and Presbyterians was being used against the Independents. On 17 March Presbyterians in the City petitioned for Charles I to take the Covenant and the army to be disbanded. The campaign against the army in the Commons and Lords intensified through Wight's spring of grace. On the very day Coxe was interrogating Wight, about a mile away in Cromwell's house in Drury Lane, Cornet Joyce was at a secret meeting which was to lead to him seizing the King for the army and, in doing so, seize the political advantage from the Presbyterians.[57] For observers, Wight's experience of grace must have seemed to have a relation to the sufferings of the saints.

Coxe's question, as she indicates, is designed to lead her from inward to outward things—from the spiritual wellbeing of the 'Church of God' to its worldly success. Noting the brevity of her answer as printed, Jessey implies that she answered more fully elsewhere.[58] However, it seems clear that Wight deflects the invitation to canvass the future of the

---

[56] *Riches*, p. 121.
[57] S. R. Gardiner, *History of the Great Civil War* (London, 1889; repr. Gloucestershire: Windrush Press, 1987, 1991), III, 221, 266.
[58] See also *Riches*, p. 88.

saints. Her formulation of their fortune '*so far as it is for their good, in outward things, God will dispose of them*'—surely a carefully reticent response to the opportunity to make political prophecy—is backed up by a reminder of God's disposal of the outer world to the benefit of the spirit. The text's 'record' of this incident suggests much about Wight's view of the vexed connection between spiritual and political arenas. Indeed, the division Wight attempts to make between spiritual and 'outward' things was one that the Independents repeatedly sought to make productive for themselves—the question of the need for *godly* magistracy and the issue of obedience to the given powers was repeatedly canvassed. But how politicized potentials were realized (or not) when the words were interpreted—first by Jessey and then by his readers—is, as we shall see, a different matter.

By the time the text was published Wight's experiences had been resolved, not by death but into ministry. Weak, Wight '*found not such contentedness to live, as shee desired, but rather longing to be dissolved*'.[59] Yet at this point she finds it her duty to 'arise', and to live.[60] Just as God had raised up her soul, 'now he perswaded her, that he will raise up *her body also*: that she might be a *Witness* of the Grace of God, to *minister* to others, what he had *administered* unto her'. Comparing herself to Paul, she also begins to think of biblical instances of '*ministering to others*'. The final stages of Wight's transformation to ministry again model identification, signalled in citation and quotation as well as ascribed to Wight herself. Thus, she recalls 'Luke 8.end; where *Christ* said *Maid, arise*'.[61] She eats, attends a ceremony of thanksgiving, and after hearing John Simpson preach at Allhallows, 'her heart was drawn out to go to two women, that were in deep despaire'.[62] Indeed, though not well, Wight lived on into the Restoration to attend to other ecstatic deaths: when, on 12 January 1665, Anne Overton was dying Sarah Wight sent a message.[63] Thus, Wight refused to predict or to explicitly comment on politics but was, ultimately, able to use the experience of grace as the initiation of a mission to those who were despairing.

---

[59] See also *Riches*, p. 132.   [60] Ibid., p. 134.   [61] Ibid., pp. 135–7.
[62] Ibid., pp. 138–43, 147, 148, 150.
[63] Robert Overton, 'Gospel Observations', Princeton University Library, fo. 89. Ann Overton expressed her dying wish to be buried 'as neare ye olde prophet Mr Jesse, as could be' (fo. 90).

While Wight's care not to predict the future might have disappointed Coxe and Jessey, it may well have served to protect her from the great penalties which might follow from the explicit derivation of political implications. Any authority Wight claimed inhered simply in her experience of grace—that is to say, her claim to experience the strength of God's power was partly bound up with her weakness as an 'empty nothing creature'. As we can see, she was already sharply aware of the worldly penalties following even that claim—penalties which included, of course, mockery and accusations that she '*was madde*' or '*counter-feited*' which Coxe himself mentioned, or the assertion brought back to her that she was claiming to be wiser than Solomon. Wight, unlike Jessey, seems to be careful to eschew any explicit utterance of political prophecy or turning of her words to the present. She seeks to claim her physical sufferings as an authenticating ground of her experience, yet this, too, is consistently questioned by interrogators. The texts show that Wight has had to engage, consistently, with the way her spiritual state seemed to observers, as indeed to sceptics, 'not a "state of mind"' or soul, 'but rather a state of the body'.[64] There was also the risk of serious harassment, trial, and imprisonment such as Trapnel suffered, and used to powerful effect in her writing.[65] The way in which, in other circumstances, Anne Hutchinson negotiated with her New England interrogators, and what she suffered, reminds us that the stakes of the claim to spiritual authority were high.[66] And punishment or reward were experienced in this world.

The central section of the text, with its claims to voice Wight's words, repays such close attention because it shows her negotiation of the different potentials of the languages of grace and her attempts to control a volatile language which, at every turn, seems likely to use her, and to drag her into dangerous, secular politics. Rather, Wight's language offers a literalism and a careful circumscribing of the claims which she is making on the basis of her experience; she frames her words in ways which both defend her experience and explicitly refuse to generalize or

---

[64] Pierre Bourdieu, quoted in Sarah Beckwith, *Christ's Body: Identity, Culture and Society in Late Medieval Writings* (London: Routledge, 1993), p. 45.

[65] *Riches*, pp. 116–17; see also p. 125.

[66] *The Antinomian Controversy*, ed. David D. Hall (Durham, N.C.: Duke University Press, 1990); Michael Dittmore, 'A Prophetesse in Her Own Country', *William & Mary Quarterly*, 3rd ser., 57, No. 2 (2000), pp. 349–92.

speculate on its basis. This very attention to the border between the political and the spiritual gives us rich material for tracing a woman's apprehension of her relationship to politics and of the distinction between that and Jessey's understanding of it. Evidence, including his comparison of Anna Trapnel and Sarah Wight, suggests that the difference between political and spiritual prophecy was important and troubling to Henry Jessey. And it was Jessey who wrote the material that frames *The exceeding Riches* for its readers.

Henry Jessey wrote the final part of the text, its 'Uses'; these proposed 'uses' further clarify the political dimensions of spiritual experience.[67] The issues of age, sex, and undeservingness which mark Wight's vocabulary with a constant awareness of the dangers of transgression are among the qualities which make her a good example for Jessey. However, his aims differ from hers. He returns the reader to the causes of Wight's despair discussed at the opening of this chapter—her minor disobedience to a superior and ensuing sense of sin—and extrapolates from this to explore issues of godly versus worldly obedience. The text's 'uses', then include, first, to see God's work, second, to help Christians not to judge those who speak harshly of themselves, and:

3 *Use*. To be a *Caution*, and as *a Warning-Piece* both to all *Superiours* and *Inferiours*. 1. To all *Superiours*; whether *Husbands, Parents, Masters*, or any *Officers* in *State* or *Church*, to beware of *urging any*, by any meanes, *to doe*, speak, subscribe, *or act any thing against their Conscience, or with a doubting Conscience*.

2 *Branch*. The like *Caution* it may be also, *to all Inferiours, to wives, to children, to servants, flock*, and *subjects*: against fearing *man*, that shall *dye*, more than the *living God*: and obeying man, rather then God, by doing, speaking, or acting of any thing, to please men, that the word of conscience shew, to be displeasing to God. Least for your so doing, your terrors and punishment, may be as great, or greater than those of this handmaid, for the like offence: Yea *least God teare you in pieces, and there be none to deliver you*, Psal.50.22. and least both you and your Commander repent, when it is too late.[68]

It would be hard to mistake this message: disobey and God might '*teare you in pieces*'. The dangers of obedience to man are vividly emphasized

---

[67] *Riches*, p. 151. Jessey may be modelling the text on Hart, *Drake Revived*'s 'Uses', pp. 168–9.
[68] *Riches*, p. 153.

and are placed absolutely explicitly in relation to the orthodox power relations of early modern England—the image of order which, in some senses, was an agreed ideal. As we will see, there was a specific, if partly concealed, contemporary resonance in Jessey's interpretation of conscience as absolutely overriding the earthly powers. More immediately, Jessey's insistence that true obedience is the lesson to be learned, although it of course has far-reaching social implications, simultaneously appears as an emphatic statement of a relatively orthodox aspect of Protestantism. Wight herself can be seen as addressing social relations from within a discourse of spiritual experience. While asserting the liberating power of grace for those suffering from despair and a bad conscience, she resists attempts to make her supply prophecies concerning the political world, towards which her audience and later readers clearly saw her speech as tending. Jessey, a man and a minister, takes Wight's experiences and shows their uses in the world.

Jessey's illustrations of the danger of misplaced obedience are, significantly enough, of two young people. One, rather like Wight, is a maid, who was deliberately given work to do on a Lord's day evening (her parents fear she is becoming too 'precise'). She does it against her conscience and, Jessey ends ominously, 'I never could heare that shee got any comfort.'[69] The second, with whom Jessey sympathizes from experience, is '*a young Gentleman*, being a scholler, of whose deep despairing of ever being saved' because of having submitted to the '*Oathes and Subscriptions imposed by the Governours in the University*' even though '*he had his Conscience warning him; yet thus doubtingly, or against his Conscience, he yielded to the Ordinances of his Superiors*'.[70] Jessey's conclusion demonstrates that he saw the text as addressing current affairs. These examples

may suffice for a *warning to Heads and Governors in Universities, and Corporations*; and to all *Magistrates, Officers, Masters, Husbands, and Parents, all Superiours* whatsoever, to beware of *laying on heavy burdens, by Oaths, Subscriptions, or Commands*.[71]

For Jessey at least, this choice of examples suggests that people in their teens were to be considered as in the process of becoming adult—ultimately Sarah Wight cannot be considered a child, exactly, but rather

---

[69] Ibid., pp. 153–4.   [70] Ibid., p. 154.   [71] Ibid., p. 155.

a maid on the very brink of adulthood. While Wight can certainly be seen as, in Dorothy Ludlow's terms, a 'God-intoxicated adolescent', that does not, as these examples indicate, mean that her words and behaviour were without political significance: it is evident that Wight herself understood that her 'exclusively spiritual' discourse was part of a volatile political situation.[72]

Where Wight guards the implicit nature of her words' political force, Jessey politicizes them in prefatory material, and above all in a final section on 'uses'. While it is not possible to know whether he had Wight's agreement, it is clear that she allowed her experiences and words to be used as an example—and this final section shows most clearly what Jessey thought that meant. Jessey saw Wight's words in a political context.[73] Wight's own sense of authorship, exemplarity, and ministry evidenced in this text and in later editions also suggests that it would be problematic to see Jessey as intervening to wrest the text far from her own understandings of it. It seems that she understood that spiritual language could evoke one response, political language another. Wight's words suggest a continued concern with obedience to God alone as crucial to a spiritual state; this is where she and Jessey appear to be united in their understanding of the meanings of her experience of grace. Thus, the text suggests that if Wight and Jessey had distinct understandings of her experience, these interlocked: each understood grace as a force which could work to change the world. If it was problematic for Wight to claim directly political authority, for Jessey, Wight's status as a young woman oppressed by her superiors who found true spiritual obedience gives her example its spiritual *and* political punch. Just as Wight puts her own undeservingness to work as spiritual capital, her age, her sex, and her close brush with death make her a discursively powerful example for Jessey. Wight's responses indicate that it is in her very avoidance of political pronouncements that we can see her own attempt to shape her relationship to the political situation, yet she also regarded the published, politicized, text as hers. More generally, the claim of the primacy of spiritual experience was one

[72] Dorothy P. Ludlow, 'Shaking Patriarchy's Foundations: Sectarian Women in England, 1641–1700', in *Triumph Over Silence: Women in Protestant History*, ed. Richard L. Greaves (Westport, Conn.: Greenwood Press, 1985), pp. 93–124, esp. pp. 102–3.
[73] See also Gillespie, *Domesticity and Dissent*, p. 183.

which did political work for the gathered churches in 1647. Wight's words as they appear in this text offer a clear case, I would suggest, of women's exclusion from the political sphere shaping their relation to that sphere in complex ways.

As Wight's case suggests, seventeenth-century religion and politics are productively researched at the points where we can trace both men's and women's involvement; this is the case with the Civil War congregations. Patrick Collinson's description of fevered 'affairs, spiritual affairs' expresses some of the intensity of congregational relations.[74] This close study of one text has probed the faultlines of spiritual and political claims, gender, textual control. Wight was not the sole author—or even the author—of 'her' text, and while Ritter-Dailey and Ludlow are clearly right to emphasize the range of political and religious opinions held by those who visited her (and who are named, and so to an extent co-opted by the text), it is also the case that, in the text published with her permission, we can see the political significances of her experiences being shaped to a particular view of the crisis of 1647. Yet, while Jessey evidently is a gatekeeper, organizing the meanings of her words by analogue and interpretation, he was also her minister and part of her elective fellowship in a gathered church. Just as this is not a case of a woman's body being interpreted by a man's words (though there are elements of that), neither is it a clear cut case of a child's apolitical visions being politicized by their editor. Not a clear case of woman as symptom man as interpreter, Jessey and Wight shared relationships with the London churches. The effects of events in the summer of 1647 for those churches are key factors in reading the text. In order to have some sense of the world addressed by Jessey and Wight's textual shaping of the events, and the political implications it held, we need to look in two directions—towards the history of the gathered churches, and to the politics of 1647 and the part these churches played in that. And it is, as we have seen, Jessey, rather than Wight, who puts the text to work in the overtly political sphere.

---

[74] See Patrick Collinson, '"Not Sexual in the Ordinary Sense": Women, Men and Religious Transactions', in *Elizabethan Essays* (London: Hambledon Press, 1994), pp. 119–50: 132.

THE WORLD OF THE TEXT: 1647, HENRY JESSEY,
AND WOMEN IN THE GATHERED CHURCHES

It remains to try to clarify the likely political and religious situation of a potential reader of Wight and Jessey's text. To respond to this question we need to explore the gathered churches in 1647 and the roles of women and men in them. There were good reasons why the saints might feel that Wight's case suggested their own—suffering, as they were, under the supremacy achieved by the Presbyterian Denzil Holles in Commons and Lords.[75] Throughout the spring of 1647 the Presbyterians had dominated Parliament and the City, and there they ruled, and overruled, the saints. The army had been petitioning for arrears, and in March 1647 the Commons and Lords had begun to canvass the possibility of disbanding it.[76] As the summer ripened, the Presbyterian plan of army disbandment proved their downfall. The army's seizing of the King was decisive, and as summer ended an uneasy alliance of Independents and army was gaining power.

Active in these events, Henry Jessey was also pivotal in marketing *The exceeding Riches* and, as we shall see, wrote other materials polemically expressing the position of the saints in 1647. Jessey's own story illuminates, first, the history of the gathered churches and, second, the relationship to printed controversy of women from within those churches by the later 1640s. After a false start in the national church, Jessey had begun his career as chaplain at Assington in Suffolk, where he was friend and neighbour to the Winthrop family, with whom he maintained contact after their departure for New England.[77] Jessey almost went to New England but instead he came to London in the summer of 1637 and then became pastor of the Jacob church.[78] The history of this church is one key to the audience and context of Jessey and Wight's words in the summer of 1647. Returning from exile in Middleburg in 1616, Henry Jacob had set up a church with a quite specific rubric:

[75] Kishlansky, *The Rise of the New Model Army*, p. 161.
[76] Gardiner, *History*, III, 221–8.
[77] Murray Tolmie, *Triumph of the Saints: The Separate Churches of London 1616–1649* (Cambridge: Cambridge University Press, 1977), p. 18.
[78] Ibid., pp. 7–49.

church government was to be exercised with the consent of the people (this justified the elective joining of a church) but Jacob did not make those he gathered choose between parish membership and his church—members could legitimately maintain both. His church was a rival to the parish churches, but it was only semi-separated from them and so—crucially for its future role—not isolated but in continual communication with members who were also involved in various parishes; intercommunion with the parishes was even encouraged.[79] From the start, of course, many members were themselves separatists and—for a range of theological reasons which the rubric of the Jacob church, notably, did not require them to make specific—took no parish communion. The third pastor of this church, Henry Jessey, like his predecessors a minister, fostered its latitudinarian, even liberal, attitude. He helped to found a congregational church in Llanvaches, South Wales; in 1640 he oversaw a division of the church, with Praise-God Barbone meeting with his half in Fleet Street while Jessey lived close by in the liberty of the Tower.[80] A scion of the Jacob church will reappear in the next chapter when we follow William Kiffin, a member of Samuel Eaton's strictly separatist church which split off in 1633.[81] By 1647, then, Jessey was deeply involved in struggles between old allies—Presbyterians, Levellers, and separatists.

In this context, Jessey ensured that Wight's words would come to their first readers larded with authenticating names of visitors.[82] The provenance and arrangement of these witnesses and interlocutors is informative. First, Jessey orchestrated the prefatory and other material by an inner circle—John Saltmarsh, Walter Cradock (from the Llanvaches church, Cradock had been appointed preacher at All Hallows-the-Great), John Simpson (whom Wight heard preach on 30 June towards the end of her period of prophecy).[83] Listed Independents and gathered ministers included Hugh Peter, the Welsh Boehmist Morgan Lloyd, John Browne

---

[79] Ibid., pp. 9–11.   [80] Ibid., pp. 18–19.   [81] Ibid., p. 22.

[82] Several prominent visitors are traceable. See Ritter-Daily, 'The Visitation of Sarah Wight', *passim*.

[83] *Riches*, a1ʳ; See John Simpson, *The Perfection of Justification maintained against the Pharisee* (London: M. Simmonds, 1648), pp. 67–8. While Wight may not have heard Simpson preach on free grace on 30 June, the topic is a major theme of his massive volume of sermons (1648). See also Dewey D. Wallace, Jr., *Puritans and Predestination: Grace in English Protestant Theology 1525–1695* (Chapel Hill: University of North Carolina Press, 1982), p. 119; von Rohr, *Covenant of Grace*, p. 53.

(the associate of Vavasour Powell), and Daniel Lloyd. There may have been members of the Broadmede congregation of Bristol.[84] Leveller connections are there: 'Mris Wilson' was from the 'Nags-head', a scene of Leveller meetings in 1648.[85] Besides Dinah the Black, we find the printer Hannah Allen and the prophet Anna (or Hannah) Trapnel. Other women, radicals and, as we shall see, patrons, link Wight to the Presbyterian heart of power; the reader is reminded that Wight's message was heard beyond the gathered churches. Isabella Mayerne, the Dutch wife of the Huguenot physician, seems to have been a friend of Jessey.[86] Lady Clotworthy, wife of Sir John Clotworthy, had long worshipped outside the established Church. Lord Lisle, Sir John Clotworthy, Nathaniel Fiennes were all members of the influential Derby House Committee, which was key in determining policy and army matters under Denzil Holles.[87] As we see, many female visitors who are signalled as sponsoring the text had access to powerful men. Wight's visitors were, Jessey tells us triumphantly, 'sufficient to witnesse what they have seen, or heard, and beleeve'.[88]

The printed list of witnesses tells us of quantity, but not relationships within the gathered congregations. As Murray Tolmie notes, by the eve of Civil War separatism and baptism, particularly the two questions of re-baptism and the baptism of believers (i.e. the complete abandonment of paedobaptism), had complicated the relationships amongst the Jacob church and the six churches that had grown from it.[89] Jessey's ministry maintained the outgoing tradition of the Jacob church: he continued intercommunion and was open to the new religious manifestations of the 1640s. Indeed, as we will see in his considerations of Anna Trapnel, 1647 might have been a significant year in testing, and changing, the boundaries of what he himself considered possible in his time. It may be that for Jessey, in 1647, building the New Jerusalem was becoming

[84] *The Welsh Saints*, pp. 20, 39, 37 n. On Morgan Llwyd and Boehme see Nigel Smith, *Perfection Proclaimed: Language and Literature in English Radical Religion 1640–166* (Oxford: Clarendon Press, 1988), p. 186.

[85] On Levellers at the Nag's Head see Ritter-Dailey, 'The Visitation of Sarah Wight', p. 453; Pauline Gregg, *Free-Born John: A Biography of John Lilburne* (1961; repr. London: Dent, 1986), p. 229.

[86] Henry Jessey, *Of the Conversion of Five Thousand and Nine Hundred East-Indians* (London: John Hammond, 1650), A4ʳ.

[87] Kishlansky, *The Rise of the New Model Army*, pp. 161–4.

[88] *Riches*, pp. 9, 10.   [89] Tolmie, *Triumph*, pp. 25–7.

a possibility in a new way (see Figure 6).[90] We know that Jessey had significant relations with some of the most visible women writing in the sects. Jessey's attention to women throughout his writings is an enigmatic, but suggestive, map of associations in what Ann Hughes rightly calls the 'flux, overlap and confusion' which coexisted with some more formal structures in the gathered churches.[91]

Jessey's connections demand to be explored at greater length than is possible here. Textual evidence associates him, and others, with women of the gathered churches. Thus, John Simpson, to whom Sarah Wight appealed to prevent her suicide, converted Anna Trapnel in the early 1640s.[92] Trapnel knew Jessey as early as 1647. There is some evidence to allow speculation that Jessey might, just possibly, be the Relator of Trapnel's later prophecy at Whitehall, *The Cry of a Stone*.[93] Mary Cary's *The New Jerusalem* (1651) was dedicated to Elizabeth Cromwell, Bridget Ireton, and Margaret Rolle (wife of the eminent judge), and had recommendations from Henry Jessey, Hugh Peters, and Christopher Feake.[94] Sarah Wight's letter of 1656 was dedicated by 'R.B.' to Bridget Ireton in her second marriage—as Lady Fleetwod.[95] Another explicit connection to the Jacob church antedates the 1640s. Anne Hutchinson seems to have taken against Jessey's predecessor as minister of the Jacob Church, John Lathrop, when she encountered him on the boat for New England

---

[90] Henry Jessey, *A Description and Explanation of 268 Places in Jerusalem* (London, 1654).

[91] Ann Hughes, *Gangraena and the Struggle for the English Revolution* (Oxford: Oxford University Press, 2004), p. 177. On the use of sources for this period by Tolmie and Kishlansky see ibid., pp. 169–87.

[92] 'A Postscript' to *The exceeding Riches of Grace Advanced* (London, 1648), pp. 159–60.

[93] Internal evidence is deeply unreliable and may more likely indicate self-conscious modelling. That is still of interest. The similarities are: dating practices and terms; use of the term 'Relator' as in Wight; the fact she refers to Jessey; the use of citation.

[94] Mary Cary (Rande), *The Little Horns Doom & Downfall* with *A New and More Exact Mappe or Description of New Jerusalem's Glory* (London, 1651), A3ʳ–a7ᵛ, and also her *Excellencie of the Spirit* (London, 1645), and *A Word in Season to the Kingdom of England* (London: Giles Calvert, 1647). See also the fifth monarchist tract, *The Resurrection of the Witnesses* (Mar. 1648), and see David Loewenstein, 'Scriptural Exegesis, Female Prophecy, and Radical Politics in Mary Cary', *SEL* 46, No. 1 (2006), pp. 133–53.

[95] Sarah Wight, *A Wonderful Pleasant and Profitable Letter Written by Mris SARAH WIGHT, To a Friend, EXPRESSING The joy is to be had in God IN Great, Deep, Long, and Sore Afflictions occasioned by the Death of her Brother, the Troubles of her Mother; but especially the workings of God in her own heart*. Published for the Use of the Afflicted (London, 1656). Dedicated to the Lady Fleetwood by R.B.

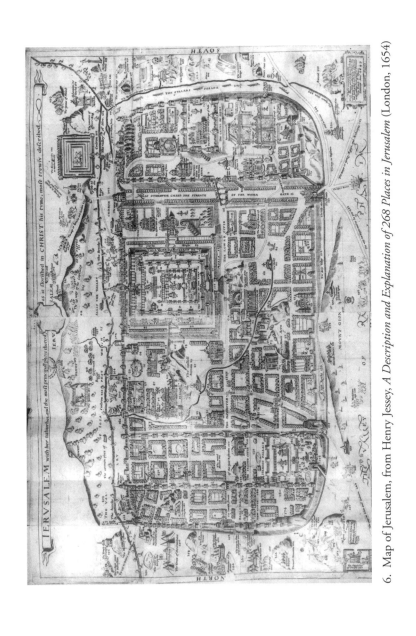

6. Map of Jerusalem, from Henry Jessey, *A Description and Explanation of 268 Places in Jerusalem* (London, 1654)

in 1634. Their disagreement may have followed a controversy about re-baptism and intercommunion which had emerged during his pastorship.[96] That other New Englander, Hugh Peters, had knowledge of both Hutchinson and Wight.[97] So, women in the churches were writers of polemic and dedicatees, perhaps patrons. But their views differed. Let us turn to the part of women and some aspects of the relations of ministers and congregations by examining three women writing and speaking within the gathered churches: Katherine Chidley, Mary Cary, and Anna Trapnel were key in writing or speaking of the particular nature of the saints for a wider audience. In different ways, too, each one illuminates connections between women and politics.

Katherine Chidley emerged from the Duppa church. One of the most significant and vital scions of the Jacob church which split off before the Civil War, this gathered church was 'ferociously separatist' and sponsored a lay pastor.[98] In dialogue with the heresiographer and defender of a national church, Thomas Edwards, Chidley (whom we met in Chapter 1) became one of the earliest, most precise, and articulate defenders of the gathered churches. Chidley's *Justification of the Independent Churches* (1641) asks 'Whether it be lawfull for such, who are informed of the evils of the Church of *England*, to Separate from it?' She answers—on the same grounds that Milton later began to justify divorce—that the Church of England's government by 'Canon Lawes (the Discipline of Antichrist)' made it no church.[99] Separation was mandatory, not optional. Chidley drew on Revelation to give an idealized description of relations amongst the Independent churches: 'there were seven Churches in *Asia*, and these seven Churches were compared to seven golden Candlestickes [Rev. 1: 20] and every Candlesticke stood by it selfe, and held forth her own light'.[100] For Chidley, the secular and religious fields are separate: just as 'the Magistrates of

---

[96] 'Examination of Mrs. Anne Hutchinson', in *The Antinomian Controversy*, ed. Hall, p. 322.

[97] See ibid., e.g. pp. 313–14, 318.

[98] Tolmie, *Triumph*, p. 21; *Tub-preachers overturn'd* (London, 1647).

[99] Katherine Chidley, *Justification of the Independent Churches* (London, 1641), *2ʳ; Thomas Edwards, *Reasons against the Independant Government of Particular Congregations as also against the Toleration of such Churches to be erected in this Kingdome* (London, 1641).

[100] Chidley, *Justification*, p. 19; see also Hinds, *God's Englishwomen*, p. 95.

Coventry cannot execute their office in *Shrewsbury*'.[101] *Good Counsell, to the Petitioners for Presbyterian Government*, probably by Chidley, carefully distinguishes 'Parliament' and 'persecution' by divines.[102]

As a writer, Chidley can use drama to her own ends. She offers Edwards a forum to test the case in public debate:

And now (Mr *Edwards*) for conclusion of the whole I doe here affirme, that if upon sight of this Booke, you shall conceive that I have either misconstrued your words, or accused you without ground (necessarily drawn from your own speeches) or that I have mistaken the sence of any Scripture, that I have quoted in this Booke or that I have not answered you directly to the point (by any oversight) Then chuse you sixe men (or more if you please) and I will chuse as many, and if you will we will agree on a Moderator; and trie it out in a faire discourse & peradventure save you a labour from publishing your large Tractates which you say you intend to put out in Print against the whole way of Separation . . .

If she is overcome, she reminds him, 'your conquest will not be great, for I am a poore worme, and unmeete to deale with you'.[103] The highly visible form of public debate to which Chidley refers to here sometimes, though altered in the process, did find its way into print.[104] Chidley, apparently offering to participate, proposes the verbal equivalent of representative combat—a role seen as demanding unusual courage even of men.[105] Extreme but also rhetorically adroit, Chidley works to keep Edwards inescapably in the wrong.[106] And she continued to torment Edwards about his 'large Tractates'.[107]

---

[101] Chidley, *Justification*, p. 11. In the *Justification*, her earliest and most complete defence of Independency, Chidley seems to have been one of the earliest respondents to Thomas Edwards's attack on separation, *Reasons against the Independant Government of Particular Congregations*. See also *Justification*, 4ᵛ.

[102] K.C. [(?)Katherine Chidley], *Good Counsell, to the Petitioners for Presbyterian Government, That they may declare their Faith before they build their Church* ((?)London, (?)1647).

[103] Chidley, *Justification*, pp. 80–1.

[104] See Ann Hughes, 'The Pulpit Guarded: Confrontations Between Orthodox and Radicals in Revolutionary England', in *John Bunyan and his England*, ed. Ann Laurence, W. R. Owens, and Stuart Sim (London: Hambledon Press, 1990), pp. 31–50.

[105] Ibid.

[106] For Chidley's 'audacious' behaviour see also Thomas Edwards, *Gangraena* (1646 edn.), pt. III, p. 170, and the discussion in Ch. 1 above.

[107] Chidley, *A New-Yeares Gift to Mr Edwards*, p. 2.

Chidley's attack on the authority of the established Church was, as Ian Gentles argues motivated by religious views.[108] But it did not leave secular authority intact. Her controversy with Edwards ran from 1641 to his publication of *Gangraena* (1646), and she uses polemic and satire to challenge his arguments for a national church. Chidley is interested in the secular magistrate's attitude to the churches; like many texts generated by the gathered churches in the 1640s she demands that readers acknowledge the foundational importance of religious freedom—only on that ground of a true relation to Scripture and exegesis can a new life be founded. The social and political order has implications for the all-important business of true—and therefore separated—worship.

The exceeding Riches of Grace is not like Chidley's animadverting argument, but Wight and Chidley evidently share a desire to witness the views of the saints to a wider public. Jessey's and the Duppa congregations were connected, and Jessey might well have connected them personally. When Wight wanted water to wash her eyes 'desiring shee might now *see* her mother also, and that shee might *heare* her mother speak', Mrs Dupper, 'her neighbour in *Lawrence Pountney*-lane, held open her eyes and *shee* saw and knew her mother'—and immediately her ears, too, were opened and she heard her mother's forgiveness.[109] It is more than likely that this Mistress Dupper who held open Wight's eyes was a relative of the preacher of Chidley's church satirized in *Tub-preachers overturn'd* (1647) as a cow-keeper, and earlier defended by Chidley as a 'well-meaning' Christian preferable to a 'will-meaning' Priest.[110]

By 1647, however, it seems possible that some things also set apart the two women and their churches. Ian Gentles tells us that in 1645 Samuel Chidley, Katherine's son, was involved in conferences and disputations on the possibility of worship in Anglican churches: he seems to have defeated John Goodwin in pulpit debate. However, Samuel also tangled with John Saltmarsh and Dr Nathaniel Holmes, as well as Hanserd Knollys (who may have baptized Jessey in 1645).[111] In 1647 Samuel participated in drafting *The Agreement of the People*.

---

[108] Ian Gentles, 'London Levellers in the English Revolution', *Journal of Ecclesiastical History*, 29 (3 July 1978), pp. 281–300: 284.

[109] *Riches*, p. 25.

[110] Chidley, *Justification*, p. 23; *Riches*, p. 25, see also p. 10.

[111] Gentles, 'London Levellers', pp. 289–90.

It seems likely that Chidley herself was a Leveller petitioner. However, information about Samuel does not give us his mother's views, just as the fact that Katharine Chidley was a member of a sister church does not tell how close this made her to Jessey's congregation. Certainly, there are connections, and Chidley and Wight do seem to have shared a friend.[112] As Hughes notes, a major source of evidence, Thomas Edwards's *Gangraena*, tends to focus on individuals and on specific congregations.[113] Besides individuals, though, the writings and what we can tell of the participation of Wight and Chidley also suggest the vital role which lay prophecy and debate, and women's part in them, threatened—or promised—to play in later 1647 and after.

About Mary Cary little is known, but Jessey did recommend her tract *The New Jerusalem* (1651) and it was dedicated to women who had visited Wight in 1647. We also know that on 23 June 1647, a week after Wight rose from her bed and as newsbooks reported Parliament's agreeing to the army's demand that they impeach eleven MPs, Thomason collected *A Word in Season to the Kingdom of England*, printed by Giles Calvert and written by one 'M.Cary'. The place of lay prophecy—in the sense of exegesis, teaching and 'dreams'—is one of Cary's topics and, for her, it is integral to the reconfiguring of the state. Arguing that God, having 'wrought ... great deliverances' for England, may now 'expect that England should bring forth answerable fruit', Cary dramatically divides her readers into the 'positive' and 'negative' parts—helpers and hinderers of the work of Christ.[114] Cary's characterization of the work of Christ here, and more markedly in later writings, combines an implied societal programme engaging with national public good and, as she here hints, a chiliastic sense of the world's imminent transformation. Her message to all ('from the King that sits upon the Throne, to him that sits upon the Dunghill; ... Parliament, and Synod, Citie and Country') is intended to show 'from the Scriptures', 'those paths which (a nation walking in them) will be the readiest way, and shortest cut, to a happy and flourishing estate'.[115] Chiding rulers to be wise, and 'beare the sword' only 'for the punishment of evill doers', Cary

---

[112] On Sarah Jones see Phyllis Mack, *Visionary Women: Ecstatic Prophecy in Seventeenth-Century England* (Berkeley: University of California Press, 1992), p. 98.

[113] Hughes, *Gangraena*, pp. 173–5; see also pp. 107, 113–15.

[114] Mary Cary, *A Word in Season to the Kingdom of England* (London: Giles Calvert, 1647), A2ᵛ.

[115] Ibid.

complains that 'drunkards, whore-mongers, adulterers, and swearers' are to be found 'in the streets, and in every corner of the City', sinning with 'a face of brass'. Rulers must 'let Jesus Christ raign over you ... incroach not in the least degree upon his prerogatives, who as King must only raign in the consciences of his people'.[116]

Cary repeatedly defends free prophecy within the gathered churches, arguing that 'as the wind bloweth where it listeth, though we see it not, so doth the spirit':

God did not tie up the spirit of Prophesie in Law, neither to the Priests and Levites, nor the Prophets, nor the sons of the Prophets; but gave of their spirit to *Amos* a Heards-man, and to others: much less hath he tied up the Spirit of Prophesying now in the Gospel, unto such and such degrees of humane learning...

Do not you enact any law against any Saints exercising the gifts of the spirit, that are to be given to them in Preaching or prophesying: because the Lord hath promised in the latter dayes, to power out his spirit more abundantly upon all flesh, & your sons, and your daughters shall prophesie: your old men shall dream dreams ...[117]

The reference to Joel 2: 28 might be general, but she continues, 'and the time of the accomplishing of this promise more fully, is neer at hand: for the total overthrow of Antichrist and his finall ruin shall suddenly be'. Finally, she addresses explicitly the relationship between prophecy and ministry: God 'makes no distinction in the exercise of this gift of the spirit, between an Officer of the Church and another; for he makes it to appear that any Member of the Church may exercise this gift, though none may execute the office of an Elder, but such as are ordained' by 'Presbytrie'. Discussing a relationship which is exactly that between Jessey and Wight, Cary's text situates it in the politics of 1647—as she sees it, the governors are seeking to suppress the saints while plain sin walks boldly in the streets. The vision Cary presents here invites comparison with Wight's words. Cary explicitly invokes of the potential of this world to be, in these latter days, transfigured and made anew. Cary's millenarian social programme was to be laid out in *Twelve Humble Proposals* addressed to the Barebones Parliament in 1653. In 1648 her *The Resurrection of the Witnesses* characterized the army as

---

[116] Ibid., A4^r.   [117] Ibid., p. 5

taking a first step towards a millennium which was imagined in dense detail in *A New and More Exact Mappe or Description of New Jerusalem's Glory*.[118] In *A Word in Season* (1647) Cary does not emphasize the way the world can reveal the truth of the Bible and vice versa, though this 'recognition of affinity' (as Hilary Hinds puts it) between spiritual and temporal realms dominates her later and explicitly fifth monarchist writing.[119] However, Cary's insistence on a near future in which world and scripture will become one in the 'latter days' shapes a text in which the rule of God, urgently needed in the present, has immediate implications for the social and political world.

The millenarian inflection of Cary's 1647 writings returns us to Jessey's ministry and his relationship with Anna Trapnel. As we know, Trapnel visited Wight. From 1646 Jessey and others (including the later fifth monarchist Christopher Feake) joined in keeping up a lecture twice a week at All-Hallows, Hannah Trapnel's church in 1650. One clue about the relationship between prophecy and the world appears towards the end of *The exceeding Riches* when Jessey introduces Trapnel's prophecies of 1647:

About the same time of *June* beforesaid, the *Relator* heard of one *H.T.* that then had great enjoyments of God, and could not take in a crumme or sip of the creature, for full *six dayes* together, yet being in bodily health. It being believed by many good people, the *Relator* desired to speak with the *party*, who is of *approved godliness*; and did; and was certified thereby of the truth thereof, *viz.* from *Jun.9.* the end, till the beginning of *Jun.* 16. 1647. And that both in that time, and before, *the Lord had given in severall discoveries of things to come*. Some particulars whereof were then related, (*viz. Jun.*19) It seemed strange to him. Yet he durst not then reject it, being related in a tender modest manner, *exalting God* therein.

That this was an important moment, perhaps a turning point, in the way in which lay prophecy in the gathered churches, politics, and visions were connected is also suggested by Trapnel herself. Looking back at the same event in the biographical section of *The Cry of a Stone*, she recalls a nine day fast, her highly politicized vision of 'the army coming in Southwark-way, marching through the city with a great deal of silence and quietness' (as occurred on 8 August), and that she was

---

[118] Mary Cary, *The Little Horns Doom and Downfall* with *A New and More Exact Mappe or Description of New Jerusalem's Glory* (London, 1651).
[119] Hinds, *God's Englishwomen*, p. 139.

'judged by divers friends to be under a temptation, as H.J. and Jo.S., to be under a temptation for not eating'.[120] This looks like Jessey and Simpson.

The censure Trapnel recalls is differently presented by Jessey in *The exceeding Riches* as a process which ends with him changing his attitude. Recalling that 'its *no* where said in *Scripture*, that Prophecy, or Miracles, or Knowledge are ceased', he notes also that Fox had cited '*Prophecies* of late times, revealed to *John Hus*, to *Martin Luther*, yea, and to *himselfe*.'[121] While Jessey's suspicions of inedia have already been discussed, his shifting attitudes towards questions about prophecy and politics are also revealing. Jessey's pairing of Trapnel and Wight suggests that he simultaneously desired and feared the emergence of an explicitly political prophetic voice. Trapnel is a prophet who is doing exactly what Wight refused to do in having political visions, or seeing them as explicitly political. Always open to new experience (to the extent that in 1659 someone described him as 'a very pious man, peacably disposed, & full of charity, marvellous facile and easily drawne in to countenance any thing that hath a face of goodnesse'), by midsummer 1647 Jessey had many reasons to identify the interests of the army with those of the gathered churches.[122] To prophesy the arrival of the army in London—complete with the apparently accurate prediction of the stealthy tread of the soldiers through the midnight streets of Southwark—was, by June 1647, to predict exactly what the Independents desired. While the Presbyterians had ruled in City and Parliament in the spring and summer of 1647, so much so that it seemed that they would be able to push through their plans to disband the army and permanently change the balance of power within the forces that opposed Charles in 1641, by the late summer the army was not only awakened to its danger but present on the outskirts of London, advancing and retreating according to Parliament's response to its demands.[123]

---

[120] Trapnel, *The Cry of a Stone*, p. 8.

[121] *Riches*, pp. 139–40.

[122] *Calendar of the Correspondence of Richard Baxter*, ed. N. H. Keeble and Geoffrey Nuttall, 2 vols. (Oxford: Clarendon Press, 1991), I, 417. Letter 615, from William Allen Sr. (controversialist and retracted separatist who welcomed the Restoration) to Baxter, describes Jessey thus.

[123] Kishlansky, *The Rise of the New Model Army*, pp. 139, 161.

Chidley seemed to contemporaries 'audacious'. Phyllis Mack describes Cary as the most radical of female prophets.[124] Anna Trapnel, in the 1650s, was to be a powerful and frightening political voice. These three, active within the gathered churches in 1647, participated in formulating the ministry, theology (to an extent) and—above all—political implications of the position of the churches.[125] Additionally, these writings from the gathered churches (and perhaps *The exceeding Riches* shows this most clearly) may offer us some insights into the way in which government in the churches shaped writing and speech. While the *theological* controversies were by custom largely though not exclusively the property of ministers (Chidley and Cary both write on such matters), gathered members had a substantial sphere of debate open to them. This sphere was guaranteed by recourse to the prophetic books of the Bible, to the statement of Joel on dreams and prophecies, and to the traditions of Protestant exegesis and prophecy. Perhaps, the contribution of women in and out of the gathered churches to the controversies of 1647 supplies evidence of a civilian correlative to the radicalization of the army. Certainly, the religiously formed and grounded political commentary of non-elite women in this year indicates something of the way in which spiritual and political crisis was experienced and expressed through several social strata.

Moreover, the nature of women's writings from within the gathered churches suggests relationships between female members of their congregations and ministers in which social, spiritual, and political issues were negotiated. While—evidently—ministers like Saltmarsh, Simpson, and Jessey retained major control of the theological debate, the spiritual

---

[124] Mack, *Visionary Women*, p. 117.

[125] It seems likely that, for example, Mary Pope would have known of these writers. Arguing for the return of Charles I, Pope's *A Treatise of Magistracy* spoke from a position distinct from the ambiguous Independents' position on obedience. A member of Thomas Coleman's church, Mary Pope asserted that, unlike the Presbyterians, the Independents had not made clear their views on magistracy—'*I could not tell what their minds were, unlesse it be now lately made out*'—but she took it that they, with Presbyterians, '*held forth that the Magistrate was not the chiefe Officer in the Church jure divino, or that he had at all any Office therein, by way of government*'. Mary Pope, *A Treatise of Magistracy, Shewing, the Magistrate hath beene, and for ever is to be the chiefe Officer in the Church, out of the Church, and over the Church*, (London, 1647), C3^r. See also Nigel Smith, *Literature and Revolution in England, 1640–1660* (New Haven: Yale University Press, 1994), p. 125. See also Jeremy Taylor, 'No Doctrine that destroyes Government is to be endured', in *A Discourse of the Liberty of Prophesying* (London, 1647), pp. 246–8.

experiences of the congregation had powerful social and political force. We can recall Saltmarsh's description of ministry—'*debating, counselling, prophesying, voting, &*'. As Thomas Edwards had seen, ministers of the gathered churches were precipitated into an intense relationship with those they gathered. Edwards was a hostile witness. Even so, when he hears a report that a woman had been 'one of Mr. *Iacies* Church; but she is fallen off from that Church (as many others have)' we can glimpse the substantial sphere of discussion opened up to the gathered—and so to the female gathered—in the seven churches of London.[126] Part of the congregation's power was, as we find repeatedly, the power to leave or re-form. The intense relationship between minister and member that we see in *The exceeding Riches*, and which is implied in the introductions to the texts of Cary and Trapnel if not Chidley (whose church, of course, differed from the others in using lay ministry), invites consideration of the 'politics' of the internal workings of the gathered churches. As Hilary Hinds's observation that women were integral to the life of the sects recognizes, successful ministry required a dynamic relationship with the congregation.[127] Intense relationships between women and ministers had characterized such separate churches since the Reformation. Whether the 1640s brought new prominence to women's existing roles in these churches, whether these roles were new, or whether they were given new forms and meanings in printed controversy is hard to tell. However, the quantity and nature of printed material issuing from women in the congregations of these churches both indicates the spiritual claims made in their relations with ministers and offers a context for women's contributions, sometimes controversial, to political debates. It is hardly surprising that in the shifting world of the gathered churches relationships should be densely, complicatedly, intertwined. The nature of those connections suggests the way in which, in these circles, women's spiritual interventions had an impact on the political world. We can see women involved—with men—in church membership and government, in writing conversion narratives, and in determining the implications of the experiences of grace, ministry and teaching, political prophecy.[128]

---

[126] Edwards, *Gangraena* (1646 edn.), p. 89.
[127] Trapnel, *The Cry of a Stone*, p. xxx.
[128] Bernard Capp, *The Fifth Monarchy Men* (London: Faber & Faber, 1972), p. 82; Owen C. Watkins, *The Puritan Experience* (London: Routledge & Kegan Paul, 1972),

We have examined the context in which *The exceeding Riches* was published. But what did it contribute to the political situation of the saints in 1647? Another text helps us to see it a little more clearly. In 1651 a *Declaration* was published by the ministers of the gathered churches. Amongst the signatories was Henry Jessey.[129] Those signing the *Declaration*, something like a manifesto for their position, claimed authorship of an earlier text—from 1647. In 1647—the year under discussion here—Matthew Simmonds had printed *A Declaration By Congregationall Societies in, and about the City of LONDON; as those commonly called Anabaptists, as others. In way of Vindication of themselves*.[130] This clarifies the position of the congregations, at least as their ministers saw it. The points of justification were liberty, magistracy, propriety, and (perhaps recalling the case of Mrs Attoway)—polygamy. The tract returns the reader to the toleration debate, arguing that, though the gathered churches have been represented as 'advocates of all licentious liberty, disorder and confusion', they 'desire not any liberty for any, but in order to the good of all'.[131] Contemporaries should aim, like them, to:

preserve the Civill power within its due and proper bounds, distinct, and unconfounded with that power which is quite of another nature; we are exclaimed against by some (who have the boldness to affirme, or the weaknesse to believe) as if we were enemies to all Magistracy and Government, or as if we intended to throw down those hedges that are set about mens estates, and to lay

e.g. pp. 18–36 and *passim*; Patricia Caldwell, *The Puritan Conversion Narrative: The Beginnings of American Expression* (Cambridge: Cambridge University Press, 1983); on church government see Karen L. Edwards, '*Susannas Apologie* and the Politics of Privity', *Literature and History*, 3rd ser., 6, No. 1 (1997), pp. 1–6.

[129] *A Declaration of divers Elders and Brethren of Congregationall Societies, in and about the City of LONDON* (London, 1651).

[130] *A Declaration By Congregationall Societies in, and about the City of LONDON; as those commonly called* Anabaptists, *as others. In way of Vindication of themselves.* TOUCHING 1. Liberty 2. Magistracy. 3. Propriety 4. Polygamie (London: M. Simmons for Henry Overton, 1647). Tolmie comments: 'The extent of Baptist participation in the 1647 *Declaration* would have come as a shock to the Levellers had it been known' (*Triumph*, pp. 170–1). John K. Graham also discusses the tension in the use of and claims associated with the terms 'Independent' and 'Presbyterian' in 'Searches for the New Jerusalem', in *Religion, Resistance, and Civil War. Proceedings of the Folger Institute Center for the History of British Political Thought*, ed. Gordon J. Schochet (Washington: Folger Shakespeare Library, 1990), III, 31–51: 48, 50.

[131] *A Declaration By Congregationall Societies*, pp. 4–5.

both the one and the other common: Though the truth is, wee have been, and resolve to bee as faithfull assertors, and zealous maintainers, to our power, both of Magistracy, and government, and of the Liberty of mens persons, and propriety of their estates (to speake without vanity) as any other men whosoever.[132]

Despite a final declaration that 'Magistracy and government in generall is *The Ordinance of God*' and that they do not seek to overthrow it, it is clear that, as in Jessey's orientation of *The exceeding Riches of Grace*, the authority of conscience exceeds that of the civil magistrate. They also argue, in ways that seem to mesh with the Leveller demands, that men holding civic office should not be subject to religious coercion such as the demand to take the Covenant.[133] However, these saints are not Levellers: their belief is in a religious elite grounded on a covenant of grace rather than works. While hostility to a national church underlies their discussion of the apostolic teachings and of the magistrate (and this is reinforced very clearly in the 1651 declaration), they are explicitly hostile to those who seek to 'throw down those hedges' which bound property. They want the world remade by grace, not through secular commonality. Albeit anonymously, this tract drew a clear demarcation between the gathered churches and the Levellers, and emphasis on the covenant of grace was crucial in defining their attitude to the civil power. As Tolmie argues, in 1647 the gathered churches were keen to distinguish themselves from another group with whom then and now they were linked in contingently close but spiritually tense, uneasy, alliance—the Levellers.[134] Sectaries and Levellers had quite distinct aims. By the next year, as we will see in Chapter 4, some Levellers felt that the gathered churches had betrayed them. The 1647 *Declaration* seems to be an early indication of their position.

The anonymous *Declaration* and *The exceeding Riches* illuminate one another in suggesting a more specific religio-political matrix than has hitherto been found for the prophetic text. *The exceeding Riches*, like the *Declaration*, sponsored by Jessey and the gathered churches in later 1647, shows the desires of the gathered churches, or at least their ministers. Seen in conjunction with the claims of the *Declaration*, the publication of Wight's experiences of grace, the careful use of witness testimony, seems as much or more an assertion of primacy than a bid for

---

[132] Ibid., p. 7.   [133] Ibid., p. 8.   [134] Tolmie, *Triumph*, pp. 171–2.

unity. Besides its spiritual work and work clarifying the understanding of the implications of grace for social and political hierarchy, *The exceeding Riches of Grace* seems to have been designed to clarify the place of the gathered churches in the power struggle. The emphasis on free grace for the gathered churches would also, potentially, have a counter-secular effect of drawing authority back into the spiritual realm and reminding its readers, in a different way from the *Declaration*, that worldly authority rightly belonged to the possessors of grace. After all, the most sustained religious impetus of Wight's conferences was that grace fulfils the promise of the law. The *Declaration* implies that Presbyterians and Levellers could—should—stand aside in favour of the saints.

To return to the questions raised at the start of this discussion, what were the political implications of the writings of women in the gathered churches? It is both intuitively compelling and historically not wholly accurate to polarize the dual aspects of Puritanism as implying, on the one hand, antinomian indiscipline and, on the other, 'magistracy and ministry joining together in a war on sin'.[135] The (only partially ascertainable) events of *The exceeding Riches*, and its publication itself show us the tensions within the tendency that some contemporaries saw as antinomian and the conflicts within the pull towards worldly authority. Tensions between the claim to spiritual authority and the realization of its implications in self-consciously politicized terms mark *The exceeding Riches* throughout, and map unevenly onto the positions taken by the text's 'speakers'. While it would be wrong to see the text as presenting Jessey's claim to magistracy, his words nevertheless turn the reader's attention towards the world. The claims of grace and free grace, associated with antinomianism and here expressed in the context of the London gathered churches, do stake out authority in the world—in politics—on the basis of experimental faith.

The exceeding Riches of Grace joined battle in the immediate and intensifying debate over the role of divine grace and predestination in

---

[135] David R. Como, 'The Kingdom of Christ, the Kingdom of England, the Kingdom of Traske: John Traske and the Persistence of Radical Puritanism in Early Stuart England', in *Protestant Identities: Religion, Society, and Self-Fashioning in Post-Reformation England*, ed. Muriel C. McClendon, Joseph P. Ward, and Michael MacDonald (Stanford, Calif.: Stanford University Press, 1999), pp. 63–82: 63.

salvation. The political debates were as intense and in October 1647 the Putney debates began. At the same time, the Westminister Assembly was debating the renewal of the national church. However, it was its spiritual power which made Wight and Jessey's text endure.[136] It was far from a 'little unknown book', as Wight later described it.[137] *The exceeding Riches* had an afterlife and, apparently, readership. After the 1647 edition the Short-Title Catalogue lists 'editions' in 1648, 1652, 1658, and 1666. The edition of 1652, smoother than that of 1647 and at pains to emphasize that Wight does not 'deny the ordinances', was itself reprinted in 1761, and there were further editions in 1790 and 1798: it seems to have had an active life as a conversion narrative and as eighteenth- and nineteenth-century nonconformist reading.[138] It was recommended as a guide to melancholy by Timothy Rogers in 1691.[139] Compared to Trapnel's *Cry of a Stone*, whose two editions were both printed in 1654, *The exceeding Riches of Grace* looks like a text very fully integrated into continuing religious debate and remembered at moments of crisis.[140] It seems likely that the qualities that made this text endure are specifically those which gave it significant status as an example of free grace in the politicized debates about the nature of religious experience in 1647: it is a text which, repeatedly, reminds the reader that God's grace is found within by remembering his power. This message of grace made the text suitable

[136] Wallace, *Puritans and Predestination*, p. 112; see also pp. 112–22.

[137] *A Wonderful Pleasant and Profitable Letter Written by Mris SARAH WIGHT, To a Friend*, EXPRESSING The joy is to be had in God IN Great, Deep, Long, and Sore Afflictions occasioned by the Death of her Brother, the Troubles of her Mother; but especially the workings of God in her own heart. Published for the Use of the Afflicted (London, 1656), p. 24.

[138] *The exceeding Riches of Grace Advanced* (London: Henry Cripps, Lodowick Lloyd, Livewell Chapman, 1652), +4ᵛ. See e.g. *Jesus Christ, the Same Yesterday, To-day, and For ever: or, the Riches of his Grace displayed In the Conversion of Mrs Sarah Wight* (1761, no publisher). In *The Exceeding Riches of Grace* ((?)1790) J. A. Knight's 'Advertisement' addresses the much-shortened text to 'the acceptance of the poor and afflicted ones of Christ's stock'. Joseph Ivimey, the historian of dissent, wrote a 'Recommendation' to *The Exceeding Riches of Grace, and the Care of Divine Providence; Exemplified in the Conversion and Subsequent History of Benjamin Lawson* (London: printed for John Lawson, 1826). This is an autobiographical account of 'an afflicted youth, deprived of his Speech by Scrofula' which seems to be self-consciously using the same title. Through Timothy Rogers's treatise, *A Discourse on Trouble of Mind* (London, 1691; repr. 1706, 1808, 1825), Wight's text was recommended by the editor of *Trodden Down Strength* (London, 1782), p. 3. John Saltmarsh's works had a similar trajectory.

[139] Rogers, *Discourse*, pp. xxiii, 428.

[140] See Scott-Luckens, 'Propaganda or Marks of Grace?', pp. 227–8.

reading for those in religious despair, but it was the very same quality that, for readers in 1647, and particularly for the editor Henry Jessey, had pointed relevance to the moment's theological debates and political events.

Perhaps more obviously than the sole-authored texts by women, *The exceeding Riches of Grace* suggests that there was an intense politics in the relationship between ministers and prophets; this is part of what marks the text. The 1647 edition shows Jessey and Wight, while meeting over the implications of godly rather than worldly obedience, considering and claiming different remits for the politics of grace. We see here a woman managing, or attempting to manage, spiritual language which, at every turn, tows her towards political claims. The context and collaborations of *The exceeding Riches* suggest some aspects of the roles of women in the gathered churches in terms of the power of the gathered, particularly women. So, distinctly, do the writings of Katherine Chidley, Anna Trapnel, and Mary Cary. The case of Trapnel, in a different way from Wight, also suggests the political force of spiritual experience in the later 1640s. If we see in *The exceeding Riches* Wight developing a ministry while policing a border between religion and politics, once in print we see her words in the context of the saints' struggle for political, not only spiritual, dominance. To obey God, to obtain grace and to rule as a spiritual elite are, for the ministers of the gathered churches, harmonious goals. As we shall see, though, for the men and women of the gathered congregations, in 1648–9 an obedience to God's will and providence came to mark out a very specific political path.

4

Regicide, Pamphlets, and Political Language: The Case of Elizabeth Poole

> ... Thus Eve her night
> Related, and thus Adam answered sad.
> Best image of myself and dearer half,
> The trouble of thy thoughts this night in sleep
> Affects me equally; nor can I like
> This uncouth dream, of evil sprung, I fear;
>
> (*Paradise Lost* V, 93–8)

As Maurice Bloch reminds us, if the category of politics is not either to dissolve into culture or harden into ceremonial, it is necessary to study 'the reality of social intercourse'—'people speaking to each other'—but also to analyse and theorize such events.[1] In the light of Bloch's comment, this chapter asks what happened to the political and spiritual languages of women in the sects at the regicide, through an exploration of the published texts of Elizabeth Poole. The chapter continues my discussion of the political implications of printed texts emerging from the sectarian struggles of the 1640s, tracing the political languages and positions of sectaries responding to the regicide. The regicide—even before it happened—produced a coercive requirement for explanation and, at the same time, put huge pressure on the explanatory languages available.[2] In examining Elizabeth Poole's place in the controversies, this chapter addresses the complexity of women's relationship to the figural languages and print debate which emerged in response to that event.

---

[1] *Political Language and Oratory in Traditional Society*, ed. Maurice Bloch (London: Academic Press, 1975), p. 2.

[2] See Hilda L. Smith, *All Men and Both Sexes: Gender, Politics, and the False Universal in England 1640–1832* (University Park: Pennsylvania State University Press, 2002), p. 110.

Just before Charles I's trial, Poole spoke before the greatest power in the land, the General Council of the army, and later she published material concerning the basis of rule at the regicide. However, she has received sustained attention from only a handful of scholars.[3] It remains the case that most discussions mentioning Poole ask which members of the General Council sponsored that appearance.[4] Who, historians ask, was pulling her strings? While the candidates proposed are well known—Cromwell himself, Henry Ireton, Nathaniel Rich, and Thomas Harrison—the issue inevitably remains shadowy and unresolved. This discussion focuses instead on Poole's contacts with other figures and, particularly, the role of her pamphlets in the debate after the regicide. In this story of Poole prominence is given to the radical publishers Giles and Elizabeth Calvert, the Baptist minister John Pendarves and his wife Thomasine, her minister William Kiffin and *his* old associate, John Lilburne.[5] Details—friends, meetings, dates of publication—are important, if ambiguous, aids in tracing Poole's part in the debate about

[3] Marcus Nevitt and Phyllis Mack provide incisive accounts of Poole's political and familial vocabulary and her relationship to obedience; Manfred Brod has followed Poole to her home town of Abingdon. See Marcus Nevitt, 'Elizabeth Poole Writes the Regicide', *Women's Writing*, 9, No. 2 (2002), pp. 233–48; Phyllis Mack, *Visionary Women: Ecstatic Prophecy in Seventeenth-Century England* (Berkeley: University of California Press, 1992), pp. 78–9 and *passim*; Manfred Brod, 'Dissent and Dissenters in Early Modern Berkshire', Diss., Oxford, 2002. See also Hilary Hinds, *God's Englishwomen* (Manchester: Manchester University Press, 1996), pp. 27, 156; Elaine Hobby, *Virtue of Necessity* (London: Virago, 1988), pp. 29–30, 211; Diane Purkiss, *Literature, Gender and Politics During the English Civil War* (Cambridge: Cambridge University Press, 2005), pp. 52–3; Suzanne Trill, 'Religion and the Construction of Femininity', in *Women and Literature in Britain 1500–1700*, ed. Helen Wilcox (Cambridge: Cambridge University Press, 1996), pp. 30–55: 43–4; Rachel Trubowitz, 'Female Preachers and Male Wives: Gender and Authority in Civil War England', in *Pamphlet Wars: Prose in the English Revolution*, ed. James Holstun (London: Frank Cass, 1992), pp. 112–33; Diane Watt, *Secretaries of God: Women Prophets in Late Medieval and Early Modern England* (Cambridge: D. S. Brewer, 1997), pp. 127–9; and Joad Raymond, *Pamphlets and Pamphleteering in Early Modern Britain* (Cambridge: Cambridge University Press, 2003), pp. 276–322.

[4] This question has been variously answered. Brod is sceptical of the view that Ireton sponsored it (a view put forward by Firth); Ian Gentles suggests that Rich did; a 1651 Presbyterian account has her as run by Cromwell; Brod tentatively but plausibly enough proposes Thomas Harrison: 'Politics and Prophecy in Seventeenth-Century England: The Case of Elizabeth Poole', *Church History*, 55 (1986), pp. 395–412: 403–5. See also Ian Gentles, *The New Model Army* (Oxford: Oxford University Press, 1992), p. 301; *A Briefe Narration of the Mysteries of State carried on by the Spanish Faction in England, since the Reign of Queen Elizabeth to this day* (The Hague, 1651); and Nevitt, 'Elizabeth Poole', p. 233.

[5] *CSPD* (1667–8), pp. 363, 369, 373.

regicide and her religious and political alliances. This chapter asks the twin questions of who bound Elizabeth Poole to politics, and what were the implications of her spoken, written, and published interventions.

DECEMBER 1648: WORDS BEFORE THE ARMY COUNCIL

All the Kings of the Nations, even they all sleep in glory, every one in his own house: but thou art cast forth as an abominable branch, like the raiement of those that are slaine, and thrust through with a Sword, which goe downe to the stones of the Pit, and a carkasse trodden under foot: Thou shalt not be joined with them in the grave because thou hast destroyed thine owne Land, and slaine thy people.[6]

This was the text on which Hugh Peters preached at St James's on the Sunday before King Charles's execution. His enthusiasm for the King's death led some to say that it was Peters, wearing a wig and false beard, who 'at one blow severed his head from his body'.[7] The blow that took Charles's head from his body transformed English politics, but it also expressed changes that had already happened. English writers were responding to the possibility of regicide for some time before the event. By the time of the trial many, like Hugh Peters, embraced the providential argument for killing Charles. In 1648, although they had for much of the 1640s been committed to political change coming as a consequence of spiritual change, 'the saints swerved aside, tempted by Providence'—and providence helped them to try, convict, and execute Charles.[8] It was the emerging unity of purpose between the congregational ministers and the army grandees, finally destabilizing the uneasy coalition of forces ranged against the king, which propelled Elizabeth Poole into action before the trial, and into print soon after.

On 17 December Peters had preached at Whitehall to a large audience, declaring that 'any persons' who came forward to the army 'should

[6] Isaiah 14: 18–20; this taken from Elizabeth Poole, *An Alarum of Warre* (London, 1649), sig. C1ʳ. See C. V. Wedgwood, *The Trial of Charles I* (London: Collins, 1964), p. 166.

[7] Wedgwood, *The Trial*, p. 184; 'John Rushworth's Account', in *The Trial of Charles I*, ed. Roger Lockyer (London: Folio Society, 1957), p. 137.

[8] Murray Tolmie, *Triumph of the Saints: The Separate Churches of London 1616–1649* (Cambridge: Cambridge University Press, 1977), p. 190.

find the Eares of the General, and the Officers open, to hear them . . . or receive any Propositions'.[9] It is possible that Poole was responding to the offer. In any case, two weeks after it, on 29 December 1648, one Elizabeth Poole of Abingdon was indeed called before the General Council of the army.[10] It was three weeks after the army purged Parliament of members who might act against their God-given mission—but what, exactly, was that mission? Did providence now dictate that the King should be tried and executed, or would execution compromise the saints and army? These were the questions facing the army. Poole did see the army as partly acting out God's will, declaring 'the presence of God in the army', but for her God's mandate stopped short of capital punishment. As Poole saw it, 'the businesse was committed to their trust, butt there was a great snare before them'. She later published these views in her 'vision'.[11]

On 5 January, the day before the Commons passed the ordinance setting up the High Court of Justice to try Charles, Poole returned to the General Council to say more and hand in a 'paper'. As William Clarke, secretary to the Council, recorded it:

(Gives in a paper.)
Col. Deane: I must desire to aske one question: whether you were commanded by the spiritt of God to deliver itt unto us in this manner?
Woman: I believe I had a command from God for itt.
Col. Deane. To deliver this paper in this forme?
Woman. To deliver in this paper or otherwise a message.[12]

After debate about her paper, Poole was called back in and questioned about its visionary, revelatory, status. Was hers an argument from reason or a vision to be communicated by touching their hearts? She responded, 'I saw noe vision, nor noe Angell, nor heard noe voice, but my spirit being

---

[9] *A Declaration, Collected out of the Journals of . . . Parliament*, 13–20 Dec. 1648, p. 20, quoted in Raymond Stearns, *The Strenuous Puritan: Hugh Peters 1598–1660* (Urbana: University of Illinois Press, 1954), pp. 329–30.

[10] Poole was not alone in addressing the officers. On 24 Jan. 1648/9 Thomason records Mary Pope, *Behold, Here Is a Word or, an Answer to the Late Remonstrance of the Army. And likewise, An Answer to a Book, cal'd the Foundation of the Peoples Freedomes; Presented to the Generall Counsell of Officers With A Message to all Covenant-breakers, whom God hates* (London, 1649).

[11] C. H. Firth, *The Clarke Papers*, 2 vols. (London, 1891, 1894; repr. London: Royal Historical Society, 1992), II, 150, 151.

[12] Ibid., p. 165.

drawne out about those things, I was in itt': Poole has, she suggests, seen the divine order rather than had an hallucination.[13] She again warned the Council that despite 'manifold temptations' they must not 'betray' their 'trusts'. They must not give away their power as might be implied in *The Agreement of the People*.[14] She repeated her message that, while they might try Charles and bring him to judgment, they should not execute him; as her first pamphlet says 'Bring him to his trial that he may be convicted in his conscience, but touch not his person.'[15] After questioning, Poole was dismissed. Whereas on 29 December Poole's words were received warmly, her second appearance went badly. As we know, in the weeks that followed, the army took the path she advised against; the Council began to set up the High Court of Justice to try Charles, and objections were left behind.

Clarke's record, as well as Poole's pamphlets, tell us about Poole's appearances.[16] Yet their implications remain enigmatic, her views being apparently unaligned with any substantial interest group. There is, though, one contemporary description which claims to understand Poole's political position and associates:

Whilst these things were debating, in came one of the Champions of *Israel*, attended by a *handmaid*, or *John Lilburne* and one of his *Hartfordshire* doxies. These two pretended severall *Revelations*; but *John* came in the poore way of a *Petition*, to enter the names of divers *Brethren* dissenting from many *heads* of their *party-colour'd Agreement*. But his *Girle* shee was in the spirit of a *Lyon*, and said she came *Ambassador* from the *Lord of hosts*; wherefore she had present *opportunity* given to vent the flames of *Zeale*, for feare she should throw *hand-Grenadoes*, bounce like a *pot-gun*, depart in wrath, and shake the dust off her *petty coates* against the *Councell*. Shee told the *Grandees* of their *Sinnes*, and the *Levellers* of their *Transgressions*; after which the *Brethren Ordered* her *Thankes*, and were it not too large I would have printed her *Sermon*. It might have served

13 Ibid., p. 168. See Mack, *Visionary Women*, pp. 68–86.
14 Firth, *Clarke Papers*, II, 163.
15 *A Vision: Wherein is manifested the disease and cure of the Kingdome being the summe of what was delivered to the Generall Council of the Army Decemb. 29 1648 Together with a true Copie of what was delivered in writing (the fifth of this present January) to the said Generall Conncel, of Divine pleasure concerning the King in reference to his being brought to Triall, what they are therein to do, and what not, both concerning his Office and Person* (London: 1648/9) (E.537 (24)); collected by Thomason 9 Jan. 1649, p. 6. See David Underdown, *Pride's Purge: Politics in the Puritan Revolution* (London: George Allen & Unwin, 1971), p. 173.
16 Brod, 'Politics', pp. 395–412.

handsomely to have shewne the *private Quarrells* and *deadly feuds*, which run in their *Divisions,* and petty *sub-Divisions* of *Faction*.[17]

So runs an account of Poole's first speech to the Council, given in the newsbook *Mercurius Pragmaticus.* When Clarke's notes indicate that John Lilburne, too, was at the General Council on the morning of the 29 December, should we connect his appearance with Poole's? As *Pragmaticus* and his readers knew, Lilburne had been in struggle with the army over the *Agreement of the People.* He and the Levellers wanted to establish a constitution with religion reserved from the magistrate, entirely in control of the individual; not something the providentialist 'saints' in the army relished. Their understanding of the godly differed from that of the Levellers. When the Council was preparing to try the King it was simultaneously, if in the event fruitlessly, considering *The Agreement of the People.*[18] So much for Lilburne's position. In late December Lilburne, like Poole, begged the Council to 'let no craft or policie of man hold you in suspence till new troubles arise'.[19] Poole, though, seems to have advised the Council against the *Agreement.* How, then, can we position Poole in the '*sub-Divisions*' and 'factions' of the moment? Some—incomplete—answers are supplied by her pamphlets.

MAY 1649: THE PAMPHLETS

'Behold I will lay your skirts upon your face, so that all that passe by may behold your nakednesse.'[20] So Poole's pamphlet threatens army and saints in the spring of 1649; God's loving messenger had become the

[17] *Mercurius Pragmaticus,* Tuesday, 26 Dec. 1648–Tuesday, 9 Jan. 1649, Fff 3ʳ.

[18] Frustrated by the lack of progress, on 10 Dec. 1648 Lilburne published the version of the *Agreement* which he believed had been agreed—*The Foundation of Freedom.* On 22 Dec. the officers debated the 'reserve' of religious freedom. On 26 Dec., after debate of the sixth reserve the Council adjourned until Friday at about 10 o'clock.

[19] John Lilburne, *A Plea for Common-Right and Freedom to his Excellency, the Lord General Fairfax, and the Commission-Officers of the Army* (London, 1648), Dated '*Decemb.* 28. 1648', p. 6; dated 29 Dec. by Thomason, p. 6. See Pauline Gregg, *Free-Born John: A Biography of John Lilburne* (1961; repr. London: Dent, 1986), p. 256.

[20] Poole, *A PROPHESIE Touching the Death of King Charles. Shewing many Reasons against the Taking away his life. Together With an Alarum to the Army* (London: J.H., 1649), p. 17. See *An Alarum* below. I am very grateful to Professor Anne Janowitz for her transcription of the New York Public Library edition of *An Alarum.*

army's polemical adversary. The spring following Charles's execution on 30 January brought a furore of pamphleteering, and Poole was among the authors. Like Poole's, many of the pamphlets were printed and sold in the City of London. Giles and Elizabeth Calvert, as we have seen, served a diet of radical material in their shop at the Black Spread Eagle at the west end of St Paul's, and other radical publishers clustered around Popes Head Alley. The polemical pamphlets of this first spring after regicide are characterized by speed of response rather than clarity of argument. Each pugnacious attack was rapidly answered by a riposte itself busy with detail and personal accusation. Pamphlets hot off the press clamoured for the attention of readers. Elizabeth Poole's texts, printed for this market, disclose her perspective on the regicide, army, and saints. And for reasons drawn out below, we need to re-evaluate the place Poole's pamphlets occupied in this paper storm.

Five months after Poole's first appearance at the General Council, on 17 May 1649, the bookseller George Thomason was out collecting pamphlets. Very likely he bought them where the printer tells us they were sold in 'Popes-head Alley and Cornhill'.[21] Acquiring what he presumably thought were both of Poole's pamphlets, Thomason in fact bought one pamphlet and a second which was partly a duplicate. We know this because the two pamphlets did in fact appear separately. They were also—presumably later—sold bound together as *A PROPHESIE Touching the Death of King Charles. Shewing many Reasons against the Taking away his life. Together With an Alarum to the Army.* This dual pamphlet is marketed as an address to the regicide and what has happened since. Indeed, Poole explicitly recalls Hugh Peter's sermon on Isaiah which so gleefully prognosticated that Charles would be 'a carkasse trodden under foot'. On its title page *A Prophesie* carried the verses from Isaiah 14, reminding readers of how Hugh Peters used it—as 'his Text chosen to Preach before the King, a little before he was BEHEADED'.[22] Thus, the pamphlets are framed as responding to Peters and so, by extension, to the coalition of saints and army. We also know that although the binding of *A Prophesie* suggests that for sense the reader needs to read Poole's 'vision' first, in fact it was *published* second and

[21] Maureen Bell, 'Hannah Allen and the Development of a Puritan Publishing Business, 1646–51', *Publishing History*, 26 (1989), pp. 5–66: 7.

[22] See *An Alarum of War* (London, 1649) (E.555 (23)) and *An Alarum of War* emended by Thomason to read *An[other] Alarum of War* (London, 1649) (E.555 (24)); *A Prophesie Touching the Death of King Charles* (London: J.H., 1649).

carries 'Errata to Alarum'. *An Alarum* was published first though, of course, as it appeared the 'Vision' might have been circulating in manuscript or even in a different print version. Certainly, *An Alarum* addresses a public that knew about Poole's appearance and the ensuing fracas. Thus, the ordering, packaging, and repackaging of the pamphlets suggests that Poole's writings, *pace* her critics, did indeed have an audience in spring 1649.[23]

Poole's published 'Vision' tells us that it responds to the army's position in late 1648. The army's *Remonstrance*, read in the Commons on 20 November, in a different way from Peter's bloodthirsty sermon promulgated the 'sovereignty of the people' and of providence. As David Underdown puts it, the *Remonstrance* showed the Commons that their power was at an end: providence and *salus populi* were combined in the army's bid for power.[24] By late December the Commons had been purged rather than, as planned, dissolved, and the Army Council increasingly felt itself bound to providence alone.[25] Addressing the crisis, Poole uses the metaphor of the body:

I was for many daies made a sad mourner for her; the pangs of a travelling woman was upon me, and the pangs of death oft-times panging mee, being a member in her body, of whose dying fate I was made purely sensible. And after many daies mourning, a vision was set before me, to shew her cure, and the manner of it, by this similitude: A man who is a member of the Army, having sometimes much bewailed her state, saying *He could gladly be a sacrifice for her*, and was set before mee, presenting the body of the Army, and on the other hand, a *woman crooked, sick, weak & Imperfect in body*; to present unto me, the weak and imperfect state of the Kingdom: I having the gift of faith upon me for her cure, was thus to appeal to the person, on the other hand, That he should improve his faithfulnesse to the Kingdom, by using diligence for the cure of this woman, as I by the gift of faith on me should direct him.[26]

As Poole's use indicates, the metaphor of embodiment was not solely royalist in its purchase.[27] In this 'vision' of a man (the army) and a

---

[23] Brod, 'Dissent', p. 173.   [24] Underdown, *Pride's Purge*, pp. 124–6.

[25] Ibid., p. 132.

[26] Poole, 'The summe of what was delivered to the Councel of War, Decemb. 29. 1648', in *A Vision*, p. 1. Also in Thomason: *An Alarum of Warre* (London, 1649), dated 17 May by Thomason, E.555 (23); not in An[other] *Alarum of Warre* (London, 1649), E.555 (24).

[27] See John Sanderson, *'But the People's Creatures': The Philosophical Basis of the English Civil War* (Manchester: Manchester University Press, 1989), on Hobbes pp. 90–6.

crooked woman (the land), like the women petitioners discussed earlier, Poole claims an interest in political outcomes. By presenting herself a 'member' in the woman's body, Poole invokes the idea of incorporation—membership—but also relies on the naturalized status of the metaphor of the body politic. We do, though, need to consider what the metaphor's significance was for her and why she might have used it.

She tells officers that 'there is but one step between you and restauration, the which whosoever taketh not warily shall stumble'; they must 'act', but—the refrain of those who feared the army's power—without worldly care for their own 'lives, liberties, freedoms'. Poole then prints what seems to be another message addressed to the Council:[28]

the King is your Father and husband, which you were and are to obey in the Lord, & no other way, for when he forgot his Subordination to divine Faithhood and headship, thinking he had begotten you a generation to his own pleasure, and taking you a wife to his own lusts, thereby is the yoake taken from your necks . . .

You have all that you have and are, and also in Subordination you owe him all that you have and are, and although he would not be your Father and husband, Subordinate, but absolute, yet know that you are for the Lords sake to honour his person. For he is the Father and husband of your bodyes, as unto men, and therefore your right cannot be without him[.][29]

The argument here is vexed. The army is to 'feare not to act the part of *Abigail*', remembering that, just as Abigail 'lifted not her hand against her husband to take his life, no more doe yee against yours'. Developing and changing her image, Poole writes, 'You never heard a wife might put away her husband, as he is the head of her body.'[30] Poole's language makes the reader consider relations between King and army. Thus, re-sexing the army as female, she offers a connection between contractual thinking and divine subordination. During the Civil War patriarchal thinking was primarily though not, as Poole's own use shows, exclusively, royalist; Poole uses the familiar patriarchal chain of authority. The message, like the vision, presents itself to Poole in mingled languages of contract and patriarchalism. Poole's language relies on the resonance of each image more than on an obvious structure of argument. And the force of the language is to invoke the King's authority as

[28] Poole, 'The summe of what was delivered to the Councel of War', in *Vision*, pp. 2, 4.
[29] Ibid., p. 6 (mispag.).   [30] Ibid., p. 5 (mispag.).

sacred. For Poole, the king's deep transgression required punishment; the army needed to secure his 'person', but not to execute him.

Having sacralized, but also problematized, paternal authority (the army, having 'inherited' the kingly power, 'stand as in the awful presence of the most high Father'), Poole also reactivates the marital image.[31] The King is the army's 'father and husband'. That the designation of sex and familial relationships is not wholly consistent or logical is authorized by the fact that each example proves the same major point: action can be taken when kings transgress, but that action has limits which, for Poole, are divine. The examples all indicate that the operation of civil society may be contractual but, *in the last instance*, social relationships are divinely decreed and God's representatives (kings and fathers) possess certain elements of divine authority. Within this framework, man and wife, king and country, are each relationships in which God's rule overrides contract.

G. J. Schochet argues that in the seventeenth century the possibility of a differentiation between family and society was emerging:

It is ... true that the patriarchal-familial conception had become the chief view of political origins by this time. ... this doctrine at least implied ... an understanding of the movement from family to state that determined political attitudes in ways which were initially unappreciated. Basic to all this was a failure to distinguish between the political and social realms of human experience—an unavoidable failure that reflected an ability to distinguish, in twentieth-century terms, between state and society.

Schochet convincingly suggests that the 'sudden appearance of patriarchal theories in seventeenth-century England' should be understood 'as a direct result of the early development of this new differentiation'. He sees this incipient differentiation as 'a direct challenge to European culture's own self-image'.[32] Certainly, Poole's metaphors seem to bear out this argument and belong to the moment of mixed apprehension he discusses: they strongly emphasize the 'fundamental interconnectedness' of concepts of politics and familial order upon which they drew, while registering a crisis in the bonds.[33] For Poole, the connections are also

[31] Poole, 'The summe of what was delivered to the Councel of War', in *Vision*, p. 3.

[32] Gordon J. Schochet, *The Authoritarian Family and Political Attitudes in Seventeenth Century England* (London: Blackwell, 1975; repr. New Brunswick: Transaction, 1988), p. 55.

[33] Ann Hughes, *Women, Men and Politics in the English Civil War* (Keele: Keele University Press, 1998), p. 6.

mystical. It is hardly surprising that the extreme circumstances of 1648 and 1649 should make threatened ideas of relationship between ruler and ruled appear in a vision, as if, far from being contractual and human, such relations were hedged about by divine limitations. Where the contract between King and people operates properly, Poole's vision implies, divine power is latent; it is the transgression of hierarchy which exposes more fundamental truths. Thus, at the point of crisis, a *corpus mysticum*, a state held together by love and divinely sanctioned bonds, becomes visible to Poole.

If the 'vision' revisits the regicide, the *Alarum* takes on events since, telling us about Poole's own experience and opinions in spring 1649. In 1649 the divine law Poole invoked seemed to lack earthly power.[34] Nevertheless, her true godliness contrasts with the worldly 'necessity' of Charles's killers. She mocks 'your carkassees, or the body of your confederacy' and spurious 'wisedomes, councels, devotions, humiliations, and religious consultations'.[35] A clear and polemical explanation of Poole's position as it was in spring 1649, the *Alarum* glosses and explains the words of the vision—addressing the material late modern critics have found enigmatic. 'When I told you the Kingly power was fallen into your hands', she explains, 'it was manifested by your earnest pursuit (in profession) after righteousness, judgement, truth, equitie' until 'nothing would satisfie you but the blood of the King, a man with whom you were in Covenant'.[36] Returning to the figure of marriage, she asserts that, while it is true that 'a just woman must deliver up her husband to the just claim of the Law', yet she will not 'rejoice over him to see his fall'.[37] Poole makes a point of revisiting Hugh Peter's sermon on Isaiah 4: 18–20. Quoting it in full, she concludes by giving Charles's response:

Thou hast destroyed thine own Land, and slaine thy people: the seed of the wicked shall not be renowned for ever. Prepare a slaughter for his Children, for the iniquities of their Fathers, let them not rise up nor possesse the Land, nor fill the face of the world with enemies. I have deserved this saith he (for he said I suffer justly, though by an unjust sentence).[38]

---

[34] On *corpus mysticum* see Ernst H. Kantorowicz, *The King's Two Bodies: A Study in Medieval Political Theology* (Princeton: Princeton University Press, 1957), pp. 232–72; Smith, *All Men*, e.g. p. 115.

[35] Poole, *An Alarum of Warre* (NYPL copy); also *An[other] Alarum*, p. 2.

[36] Ibid., p. 3.   [37] Ibid., p. 7.   [38] Ibid., p. 11.

Though far from a royalist, Poole invites sympathy for Charles I by presenting him as accepting his punishment. The army and the saints, on the other hand, must know, 'Behold! There is a worldly dark part in you which the Lord will destroy.' Indeed, as the 'children of him that ye have cut off', they are themselves the accursed children of Isaiah 14.

The *Alarum* opens with a claim on the public, '*Deare Reader, thou mayst marvell that I having so reproachfull a pursuit by them that are called Saints, when I was last at the generall Council, should hold up my head any more.*'[39] So Poole attacks and exposes the saints—her enemies, supporters of regicide, confederates of the army. As a human, Poole asserts that her accusers are as prone to error as she—'flesh in you brethren, judgeth flesh in me'. Apparently describing her own situation, she notes, 'Excommunication was ordained for the destruction of the flesh', and that 'drunke with the indignation of the Lord' she 'confessed all that was in my heart to you'.[40] However, the saints and army have betrayed their trust and exposed their godliness and faith as hypocrisy. The regicide leaves them skirts on face, their base motives exposed for all to see.

The pamphlets offer Poole's vision and its interpretation. For Poole the Commonwealth is both contractual and divinely regulated, both separately political and unified with the social. Poole's political vocabularies are only partially related to the texts of political theory from which the story of emerging contract theory have been built. For Poole, the claim to understand divine will is what mediates the speaker's relationship to the political sphere; the claim to interpret a vision builds into a claim to political influence. We can learn much about the possible positions available to women when we see Poole's printed words. But in order to understand their contextual implications we need a richer picture of her political associations. As Thomason was buying Poole's pamphlets, on 17 May, the last of the Leveller rebels who had hidden out at Burford was caught and killed in a wood near Wellingborough.[41] These events had taken place fairly close to Poole's home town of Abingdon. Two areas, then, invite further investigation: Poole's possible connections with Lilburne (now closely guarded in the Tower) and her associations around Abingdon.

---

[39] Poole, *An Alarum of Warre*, A2ʳ.

[40] Ibid., A2ᵛ.

[41] See the map in S. R. Gardiner, *History of the Commonwealth and Protectorate*, 4 vols. (1903; repr. Gloucestershire: Windrush Press, 1988), I, 51.

1645, 1653: THE '*SUB-DIVISIONS OF FACTION*'

If Poole was not, or not only, the puppet of the General Council, who was she and with whom was she associated? What do her relationships suggest about sectarian women and politics? To answer these questions we must focus in some detail on Poole's story. A key figure connecting the overlapping groups of Levellers and the Abingdon separatists was Poole's former minister turned condemner, William Kiffin. His existence reminds us that the regicide was not Poole's first brush with polemic. *A Briefe Remonstrance* (1645) traces a controversy over baptism between Poole's father Robert Poole, who seems to have been a supporter of a national church, and the minister who had already declared for believer's baptism and one of the major makers of Poole's story— William Kiffin. It seems that Elizabeth Poole had recently joined Kiffin's congregation, for Robert Poole accused him of 'seducing my Children and servants into your errours'.[42] Kiffin himself had converted in 1632, and by 1641 he was helping Lilburne with his pamphlets. Kiffin was a member of Samuel Eaton's church; he remained in it for some time when it was folded into Henry Jessey's congregation, even though he had become a Particular Baptist in 1642. His importance is indicated by his presence as a signatory to the London Particular Baptist *Confession of Faith* in October 1646.[43] Kiffin also seems to have had some thuggish associates, most notably Colonel Axtell, whose violent conduct towards a protesting woman at Charles I's trial—possibly Anne Fairfax— remained in many people's memories at the Restoration.[44] Baptist history, in which William Kiffin holds an important place, severely skews his memory by playing down his vigorous controversialism.[45] The serene benefactor described by Joseph Ivimey and B. R. White bears little resemblance to the pugnacious adversary who was at the heart of post-regicide fighting between saints and Levellers. To place

---

[42] William Kiffin, *A Briefe Remonstrance of the Reasons and Grounds of those People commonly Called Anabaptists, for their Seperation &c* (London, 1645), p. 3. Kiffin's counter-accusations suggest that Robert Poole was a Presbyterian, certainly, a supporter of a national church (pp. 6–7).

[43] Tolmie, *Triumph*, pp. 22, 27–9, 36–7, 45, 49, 54–7.

[44] *The Tryall and Condemnation of Col. Daniel Axtell* (London, 1660), A2^{r-v}.

[45] e.g. Joseph Ivimey, *The Life of Mr William Kiffin* (London: J. Messeder, 1833), p. 36.

him and Poole more clearly we must turn to the densely packed events and publications of spring 1649.

John Lilburne's relationship with Kiffin was of long duration. The regicide, however, brought a crisis in their association. Kiffin's vocal support for the army and endorsement of a providential justification of regicide set him at odds with Lilburne. When Pauline Gregg reminds us that Kiffin and Lilburne remained friends despite 'differences in religion' she might have added, 'and politics'.[46] Their friendship and alliance ruptured in the last months of 1648 and early 1649, at exactly the same time that Kiffin was pursuing Poole. The Levellers argued that the King could not be tried by the army (court-martialling a king was illegal, obviously enough) and the purged Rump had no authority to set up a court. Hence the pressure to embrace a legal constitution—*The Agreement of the People*. Kiffin was accused by Lilburne of betrayal in the early part of 1649.[47] The context was the political furore following the regicide which involved a frenzy of Leveller petitions by men and women. The dates of various pamphlets help to place Poole's pamphlets in the post-regicide acrimony and turmoil. On 26 February Lilburne had published *Englands New Chains Discovered*. *The Hunting of the Foxes*, possibly with Richard Overton and John Wildman, was published on 21 March. On Sunday, 24 March, Lilburne was reading a petition aloud to a crowd before Winchester House—the second part of *Englands New Chains Discovered*—which he presented to the Commons, still surrounded by a crowd, the same day. The Levellers had sent out agents with the pamphlet—to Berkshire and Hertfordshire amongst other places—to persuade people of the unlawfulness of the present power.[48] Perhaps among those agents were the 'Hertfordshire doxies' mentioned by *Pragmaticus*. On 26 March the Council sought to rebut *England's New Chains* part II, instructing John Milton to look into a reply. They took firmer action: on 28 March Lilburne, Thomas Prince, and—to Lilburne's surprise—William Walwyn were arrested.[49]

---

[46] Gregg, *Free-Born John*, p. 358; see also pp. 273, 311.

[47] See *A Declaration By Congregationall Societies in, and about the City of LONDON; as those commonly called* Anabaptists, *as others. In way of* Vindication *of themselves* (London: Printed by M. Simmons for Henry Overton in Popes Head Alley, 1647). Poole, *An[other] Alarum*, p. 8.

[48] Gregg, *Free-Born John*, p. 269.   [49] Ibid.

Kiffin's associate Daniel Axtell, whom we have already seen in action against the female protestor at Charles's trial, assisted in the arrest.[50]

William Walwyn, who had not participated in *Englands New Chains*, had it seems been writing *The Vanitie of the Present Churches, and Uncertainty of Their Preaching*, which appeared on about 12 March. Like Poole's pamphlets this was to be sold in Cornhill and Popes Head Alley. Walwyn attacks the current state of the gathered churches and their leaders, such as Kiffin. Scenting power, these fall away from ideals and produce 'nick-names and bitter invective reproaches' against any who question them. Walwyn satirizes the debates amongst and within the gathered churches, accusing ministers of being 'one while zealous for the baptizing of infants, another while for the baptizing of Beleevers only, and then again for no Baptisme at all for want of a true Ministry'.[51] These ministers, having 'as it were scumm'd the Parish Congregations' of the wealthy and zealous now 'dayly spet their venom privately and publickly, against any that either separate from them, or joyne not with them'.[52] 'Truth', Walwyn writes, is 'become the game of these birds of prey, these Ravens, Vultures, and Harpies'. Walwyn's view has changed considerably since he made common cause with Kiffin and others against Thomas Edwards. Seeing the deepening divisions between the gathered churches and the Levellers, Walwyn evidently feels betrayed and bitter. Kiffin, merchant-minister, is not mentioned by name, but he might well have been in Walwyn's mind.[53]

Lilburne was busy petitioning. Kiffin presented his own petition to Parliament on 2 April, provoking an immediate response from Lilburne, who expressed genuine or affected wonder that '*the Preachers in the Anabaptist Congregations*' are '*so mad at us foure, as this day to deliver so base a Petition*'. He even claims that the preachers have circulated one petition amongst their congregations and then delivered another:

---

[50] See Brod, 'Dissent', p. 407. On the Lilburne–Kiffin friendship see Gregg, *Free-Born John*, pp. 273, 311–12.

[51] William Walwyn, *Vanitie of the Present Churches* (1649), in *The Writings of William Walwyn*, ed. Jack R. McMichael and Barbara Taft (Athens: University of Georgia Press, 1989), p. 314.

[52] Ibid., p. 316.

[53] On making common cause against Edwards see *A Parable or Consultation of Physitians Upon Master Edwards* (London, 1646), pp. 247–62: 254.

they have delivered a lye and a falsehood, and are a pack of fauning daubing knaves
for so doing, but as I understand from one of M. Kiffins members, Kiffin himself did
ingenuously confesse upon the Lords day last, in his open Congregation, that he was
put upon the doing of what he did by some Parliament men, who he perceived were
willing and desirous to be rid of us four, so they might come off handsomely without
too much losse of credit to themselves:[54]

If Lilburne's and Walwyn's words seem harsh, Kiffin's reply in *Walwins*
Wiles (23 April), is worth considering. Exhorting the army to take
action against Lilburne and Walwyn, he extols it as *'such a transparent*
work of God in the world, that it dazels they eyes of all spectators'. God
takes 'Kings and Princes', *'giving them as dust to your sword'*.[55] Kiffin
augments the argument from providence with an attack on Walwyn's
Vanitie of the Present Churches:

but this whorish Dalilah perceiving your might by breaking her forces like Sampsons
coards, is trying her tricks to find out your strength, and the seat thereof, and well
perceiving that it lies in your hair *rested together in your* head *(we mean in your*
union with Christ, and each with other,) she hath applied her self in her several
Instruments, by her enticing words to cut you *from him, and then to* divide you
each from other, whose curious cunning in that unhappy work is here set forth in one
of her supposed faithful factors, Mr William Walwyn.[56]

Kiffin's attack on Walwyn as *'whorish Dalilah'* presents the actions
of those not signed up for providence as seduction. Kiffin's seductive,
re-sexed, Walwyn reminds us of the importance of the congregations
and supporters in this debate. Walwyn accuses the ministers of 'scum-
ming' the congregations; Lilburne claims the congregations are being
deceived. Strangely reminiscent of Elizabeth Poole's father in 1645, it is
now Kiffin who sees the congregations as seduced away from truth.
Poole, of course, was or had been a member of these churches.

With Lilburne in prison, petitioning which united his and the
Leveller cause began. On 23 April the women were to go to Westminster
Hall and seem to have been there from the 23rd to the 25th. The funeral
of Robert Lockyer brought out women to demonstrate with Levellers.
A further petition was acquired by Thomason on 5 May, and women,

[54] *The Picture of the Councel of State* (1649), Thomason date 11 April, p. 24
[55] William Kiffin, *Walwins Wiles* (1649), a1^{r-v}.
[56] Ibid., pp. 3–4.

'bold Amazons', were at the Commons on 7 May.[57] On 1 May Giles Calvert printed *an Agreement of the Free People of England.*[58] 10 May saw publication of William Kiffin's *Walwin's Wiles.* One week later Thomason collected Poole's pamphlets attacking the army and the saints. Poole, the *Agreement,* Walwyn, and Lilburne were addressing similar issues—and these topics were uppermost in people's minds. So, by the start of May, just before Thomason collected the misbound versions of two of Poole's offerings, the split was explicit and angry. Army and ministers opposed Levellers and soldier rebels. The congregations themselves seem to have been fought over.

What does this story of print furore tell us? The Leveller split with the congregations generated huge publicity on each side. The congregations seem to have been participants in events, their loyalty claimed by sides polarized by the regicide. We have seen that Lilburne had himself either attempted to drive a wedge between the congregations and their ministers, or expressed a pre-existing difference. So, the Poole–Kiffin controversy has a clear place in the general turmoil; in this print scrum readers aware of the dispute between Lilburne and Kiffin might well be interested in Poole's own experiences with Kiffin. And Poole's relationship with Kiffin echoes the way he turned from his old Leveller allies, too, at this point. Indeed, given that he was happy to repudiate a longstanding friendship with Lilburne to keep on good terms with providence, it is no surprise that Elizabeth Poole, apparently a traitorous member of his congregation, found herself excommunicated. No wonder, either, that Poole's views found publication and probably readers. Although the controversy does not disclose how close Poole now was to the Levellers, she was far from Kiffin. And fragments of circumstantial evidence connect her to people (the Calverts, publishers of *The Agreement of the People*) and possibly to some events connected with Lilburne. We can, though, position Poole in general terms on the Leveller side of the post-regicide split between saints and Levellers and other opposers of the regicide. And we can see something of the political importance, at times power, of the congregations.

---

[57] Patricia Higgins, 'The Reactions of Women, with Special Reference to Women Petitioners', in *Politics, Religion and the English Civil War,* ed. Brian Manning (London: Edward Arnold, 1973), pp. 178–222, esp. 200–4. See *Humble Petition of divers wel-affected Women* [E.551 (14)].

[58] *an Agreement of the Free People of England* (1649) [E.571 (10)].

A second strand of Poole's political and religious associations can be traced from clues in the pamphlets and elsewhere. These clues take us into the printing fraternity in London and to the religious groupings of Abingdon and thereabouts. As has been argued, nonconformist connections and communications seem to have played an important part in fostering and changing sectarian politics.[59] Let us turn to Abingdon. Poole's pamphlet included a substantial letter from T.P., 'A Friend to truth'.[60] The letter's author has been identified as Thomasine Pendarves, the wife of John Pendarves, the Baptist preacher of Abingdon. In 1648 John Pendarves had been given a substantial stipend to preach away from Abingdon. The published letter, dated 6 March 1649, suggests that his wife had intercepted a letter sent by Kiffin to her absent husband. She offers her own contact address: 'if you please to send me a word of an answer, leave it with M. *Calvert*, at the Black spred Eagle at the West End of *Pauls*'.[61] As the introduction to the letter tells us, since her appearance at the Council others had been before it to testify against Poole:

that it should be given into the Councel by your two witnesses, that the said Mrs. *Poole* should say, that you cast her out for differences in judgement; and when Coll. *Reeth* [Rich?] and Coll *Harrison* asked to whom she spake it, they said to some of *Abington*: now indeed my husband said to you, that he thought such a thing, but when he came home and see so little ground for his thoughts, I think he had but little comfort in telling you so.[62]

The writer of the letter sees Poole being murdered piecemeal by the campaign of false witnesses (identified elsewhere in the pamphlet as W.K.—Kiffin—Mr. P, probably Pendarves, and Mr John Fountain), but also defends her truth from those who, seeking to asperse the 'message', attack the messenger.[63] T.P. recommends that Poole's opponents, principally William Kiffin, be merciful—'mercy is required of us towards our Sister', not the cruelty of the Pharisees. T.P. reminds her 'brethren' that God can manifest himself in unexpected and undesired places, and tells

[59] Michael Frearson, Nesta Evans, and Peter Spufford 'The Mobility and Descent of Dissenters in the Chiltern Hundreds', in *The World of Rural Dissenters 1520–1725*, ed. Margaret Spufford (Cambridge: Cambridge University Press, 1995), pp. 273–331, esp. 276–87.

[60] Poole, *Alarum* [E.555 (23)], pp. 7–8.   [61] Ibid., p. 14.
[62] Ibid., p. 10.   [63] Ibid., p. 7.

them, 'I cannot but wonder at it, that is, how you durst so peremptorily to judge the woman that shee brought a delusion for a vision of God.'[64] Like Walwyn, T.P. condemns persecutory ministers. Poole's own introduction to the pamphlet also has a millenarian inflection, calling upon the vision of the woman clothed in the sun in Revelation and referring to the sin of these '*latter dayes, viz. selfe-love*'.[65] To halt self-love would, she asserts, be a great '*stop and let to the Independent designe, viz. the taking away the life of the King*'.[66] Thus, T.P. and Poole address the effects of witnesses against Poole appearing at the General Council in a worldly context, but also in terms of God's selection of vessels for grace in these moments. In this context Poole singles out the Independents as her political enemies.

Manfred Brod has followed these hints of the subdivisions of the saints into the context of Abingdon, and he presents a fairly convincing case that Poole had associations likely to dismay her former Baptist teacher, Kiffin. Brod traces the initials T.P., linked with 'the Saints at *Abingdon*' in Abiezer Coppe's *Some Sweet Sips, of some Spirituall Wine* 'freely dropping'.[67] Printed by Giles Calvert, *Some Sweet Sips* pre-dates Coppe's two *Fiery Flying Rolls*. It is a composite text, drawing on Boehmist imagery to address the times and exhort its addressees to '*arise out of Flesh into Spirit, out of Form into Power, out of Type into Truth*'. The call to abandon formalism, and embrace grace, is dramatically expressed: '*Every* Forme, *a persecutor, but the spirit free from persecuting any.*' The '*knowing of men after the flesh*' is to be replaced by '*Christ in Spirit*'—brought in, ironically and punningly, by the violence of the '*Lord Generall*'.[68] Epistles follow, one of which is an extract from a letter from T.P. recounting one of her 'visions of the night' by which 'of late' the 'Father teacheth me'. The recounted vision is Edenic, prelapsarian:

I was in a place where I saw all kinds of Beasts of the field; wilde and tame together, and all kinde of creeping wormes, and all kinde of Fishes—in a pleasant river, where the water was exceeding cleere—not very deep—but

---

[64] Ibid., p. 13.   [65] Ibid., p. 7.   [66] Ibid.
[67] Abiezer Coppe, *Some Sweet Sips of some Spiritual Wine* (London: Giles Calvert, 1649), title page, in *A Collection of Ranter Writings*, ed. Nigel Smith (London: Junction Books, 1983), pp. 42–72; Brod, 'Dissent', pp. 164–81.
[68] Coppe, *Sweet Sips*, pp. 44–5; *A Fiery Flying Roll* (London, 1649).

very pure—and no mud, or setting at the bottome, as ordinarily in ponds or rivers. And all these beasts, wormes, and Fishes, living and recreateing themselves together, and my selfe with them; yea, we had so free a correspondence together, as I oft-times would take the wildest, as a Tiger, or such-like, and brought it in my bosome away...

T.P.'s vision-self 'at last' takes 'one of the wildest, as a Tiger, or such like, and brought it in my bosome away from all the rest, and put a Collar about him for mine owne, and when I had thus done it, it grew wilde againe, and strove to get from me, And I had great trouble about it.'[69] She concludes:

I am not altogether without teachings in it. For when I awoke, the vision still remained with me. And I looked up to the Father to know what it should be. And it was shewen me, that my having so free commerce with all sorts of appearances, was my spirituall libertie...

T.P requests an explanation, which, she believes, 'might be of great use to the whole body', but she also offers her own. The vision itself is permitted and Godly, 'a very glorious libertie, and yet a perfect Law too'. The tamed beast signifies her contrasting 'weaknesse'.[70] While 'the whole body' which might benefit is certainly her Christian fellowship, she may also imply the nation. Her interpretation is politicized as it acts to mediate God's revelation to the world.[71] Coppe writes, 'I know that Male and Female are all one in *Christ*, and they are all one to me. I had as live heare a daughter as a sonne prophesie.'[72] Coppe's publication of T.P.'s dream indicates the way the crisis of 1648–9 at times reshaped the world as vision. Relatedly, it discloses a network in which women enunciate political and spiritual crisis. The question of form and formalism in religion so forcefully taken up by Coppe is pursued in part through the seriousness with which he takes the visionary power of dreams and visions.[73] And, significantly, the question of gender is directly addressed.

---

[69] Coppe, *Sweet Sips*, p. 63.   [70] Ibid., p. 65.   [71] Brod, 'Dissent', p. 177.
[72] Coppe, *Sweet Sips*, pp. 66, 72.
[73] Reid Barbour, 'Liturgy and Dreams in Seventeenth Century England', *Modern Philology*, 88, No. 3 (1991), pp. 227–42, and *Literature and Religious Culture in Seventeenth-Century England* (Cambridge: Cambridge University Press, 2002), p. 92; Nigel Smith, *Perfection Proclaimed: Language and Literature in English Radical Religion 1640–166* (Oxford: Clarendon Press, 1988), pp. 83–4.

Coppe and T.P. lead us, as Brod notes, to other associates of Poole. In 1654, when the minister and Boehmist John Pordage was ejected from his living, a deponent against Pordage asserts:

We professe we do not know, neither can we learn of any that he [Pordage] hath entertained, but Abiezer Copp, notorious for blasphemy and *rantisme*, in whose behalf this Dr appeared before the Committee at *Reding*; and being opposed by one of us, replied, (*but with much meeknesse*) *that we should follow shortly after our dear brother* Love. Or *Coppin*, to whose book that crawls with blasphemy, the Dr gave his approbation. Or *John Tawney*, or *Everard*, who let their mouths wide open against God and man: or *Elizabeth Pool*, or Goodwife *Geffreys*, who even stink above ground: we that live round about him, do not know any godly person but shuns him as a very *monster*...[74]

If it is true, this list places Poole as a close associate of the powerful radicals disenfranchised at the end of the republic. Abiezer Coppe, by this later date, was notorious for his publication of the *Fiery Flying Roll* (1649). The other figures mentioned were equally troubling to property-owning church worshippers: William Everard was with the diggers at Cobham, and published *A Declaration and Standard of the Levellers of England* (1649); Richard Coppin was associated with Coppe. In April 1649 Winstanley had led the Diggers to St George's Hill. Calvert published over half of Winstanley's writings.[75] However, fifth monarchist elements were also very active in the area, as we know from the riots and surveillance attendant on the funeral of John Pendarves in Abingdon in 1656. So, at least by 1654 and in the late 1640s when her associate Thomasine Pendarves knew him, Poole was in the same circles as Coppe.

Poole and Pendarves were not the only women in this circle publishing in the late 1640s. In 1649 a member of John Pordage's circle, self-described as 'M.P. a Member of the Body', published *The Mystery of the Deity in the Humanity; or the Mystery of God in Man*. Attributed to both Mary Pococke and John Pordage's wife Mary, *The Mystery* was devoted to showing the threefold state of man.[76] He is traced first '*as he proceeds*

---

[74] Christopher Fowler, *Deamonium Meridianum. Satan at Noon* (London, 1655), pp. 60–1; Brod, 'Dissent', p. 177.

[75] Altha Terry, 'Giles Calvert's Publishing Career', *Journal of the Friends Historical Society*, 35 (1938), pp. 45–50.

[76] Ariel Hessayon, 'Pordage, John (bap. 1607, d. 1681)', *DNB* (Oxford: Oxford University Press, 2004). There are other possible candidates for authorship. <www.oxforddnb.com/view/article/22546>, accessed 3 June 2005.

out of the hands of God in his Paradisical Form and Being, through the Fall to '*restauration*'. This was printed by Giles Calvert, and the copy I have seen is in an early modern, probably seventeenth-century, binding with Abiezer Coppe's *Some Sweet Sips, John the Divines Divinity*, and John Warr's *Administrations Civil and Spiritual*.[77] It seems likely that whoever decided on such a grouping considered the texts as having political as well as spiritual implications. The way in which Poole and M.P. link the spiritual and the political is strikingly similar. As we have seen, like Poole, M.P. describes herself as a 'Member of the body'. Also like Poole, in so far as M.P.'s mystical programme is turned outwards, it concerns 'restauration' (we recall Poole's demand that the army take carefully the step to 'restauration'). Significantly, M.P. says that she has two gifts—she has visions and can interpret them:

This vision being declared to man in man, we Mary-like cast in our mindes, what maner of salutation this should be. Hence ariseth wide mistakes, For the Visions from God to man is one thing, the gift of Interpretation of them is another thing; both the Visions, and Interpretations of Visions must be from God, not from our selves, that we may not be found amongst the dreamer[s] of dreams. It seems good to me, being moved thereunto, though but a silly damosel, yet not as a slothful servant, to hide my talent in a napkin; but thought it necessary to shew, to declare the Interpretation of the Mystery of this Vision, concerning this King, Man, in his paradisical Kingdom, as he came out of the hands of God; which God hath both discovered, and interpreted unto my soul many years since; which now in these days calls for it, to be by me proclaimed on the house top, that the glory of my Lord and Master may by me, the least of all his saints, be advanced.[78]

M.P. presents herself as duty bound to interpret her vision. Determinedly employing political language to describe the rule of the son in terms of the King in Parliament and the King as a husband of 'this Parliamental *Eve*', her words, like Poole's, seek on their own terms to show the workings of the Lord for the world.[79] In the *Alarum* Poole interprets her own visions and sees them as likely to steer the political process. If Poole and M.P. claim to interpret visions then, we remember, so did Thomasine Pendarves in her correspondence with Coppe. Each

[77] M.P. (Mary Pococke), *The Mystery of the Deity in the Humanity; or the Mystery of God in Man* (London: Giles Calvert, 1649). In the Bodleian this is misclassified under Mary Pennington: class mark Vet A3, fo. 306. See Fowler, *Daemonium*, pp. 7, 15, 39.

[78] Pococke, *Deity*, A4[r-v].

[79] Ibid., pp. 31–2.

addresses the status of women as visionaries and interpreters of the 'mystery' in the commonwealth. For each, true interpretation is crucial if the world is to be restored to God's ways. While the languages of the three differ, and T.P.'s and Pococke's words have a much heavier mystical inflection than Poole's, they share a form of mystical politics which requires that the interpreter read both the vision and the world appropriately.

That the female dreamer and visionary was something under consideration in the late 1640s, and that the interpretation of women's dreams might indeed affect the commonwealth, is clear. The debate was long-lived and circled the promise in Joel that sons and daughters should prophesy; Luther and Milton are among many commentators on this issue.[80] That at the time and soon after women's involvement in proposals for government linked to the attack on form in religion *was* noticed is indicated by the Blasphemy Act of 1650, condemning 'divers men and women who have lately discovered themselves to be most monstrous in their Opinions' and 'rejecting the use of any Gospel Ordinances, do deny the necessity of Civil and Moral Righteousness'.[81] In *Paradise Lost* (1667) Milton gives Eve a morally depraved dream of 'flight' and 'high exhaltation' (V, 89–90) and no power of interpretation. Adam blames fancy; when Reason retires 'mimic fancy wakes | To imitate her; but misjoining shapes, | Wild work produces oft' (*PL* V, 110–12). Eve's second dream, divinely inspired, foretells her role in bearing Christ. If by Book XII Eve is allowed a vision, she is still frightening because susceptible and, importantly, unfit to interpret. The newly distant Adam hears Eve's dream of restoration, but it is not to be developed: 'So spake our mother Eve, and Adam heard | Well pleased, but answered not; for now too nigh | The Archangel stood' (*PL* XII, 624–6).[82]

---

[80] e.g. Susan C. Karant-Nunn and Merry E. Weisner-Hanks, *Luther on Women* (Cambridge: Cambridge University Press, 2003), pp. 61–3 and *passim*; David R. Como, 'Women, Prophecy, and Authority in Early Stuart Puritanism', *HLQ* 61, No. 2 (2000), pp. 203–22.

[81] *An Act against several Atheistical, Blasphemous and Execrable Opinions* (9 Aug. 1650), in *Acts and Ordinances of the Interregnum, 1642–1660*, ed. C. H. Firth and R. S. Rait (London: HMSO, 1911), II, 409–12.

[82] Quotations are from Alastair Fowler's edition of *Paradise Lost* (London: Longman, 1968; repr. 1971), pp. 286–8.

For Milton, then, female visions have no ready route into political action. However, in the crisis of sacred rule which *Paradise Lost* is in part recalling, Poole, Pococke, and Pendarves (assuming it is they) elaborate a position opposite to Milton's. Each makes an important connection between vision and interpretation; interpretation, for Poole, is the way in which God's truth can influence the actual events in the world—her vision, rightly understood, offers a better political path than the one being taken. It is a means towards true 'restauration'. M.P. might, perhaps, be an unlikely Leveller, but Elizabeth Poole *is* sharply aware of the relationship between the mystery and circumstances. In this—as we have seen—she is not entirely isolated but involved with the Abingdon visionaries. But she is also politically aware: if she is a mystic, she is no quietist. Dream, interpretation, and politics are linked, and they link Pendarves, Pococke, and Poole.

Pendarves and M.P. as well as Poole are each connected to a further, potentially crucial but shadowy, scene. The two groups of Poole's associates—those around Abingdon and her more indefinite, possible, connections with Levellers—are each associated with the London print trade and very specifically with the printers and booksellers Giles and Elizabeth Calvert. These two were well-known radical publishers—we have already encountered Giles Calvert as the publisher of the 1 May 1649 *Agreement of the People* and as T.P.'s forwarding address. Amongst Calvert's many publications in 1648–9 was a voice from the dead with sentiments remarkably close to Poole's: Saltmarsh's widow Mary edited her husband's posthumous yet 'seasonable advice', exhorting Cromwell, 'let not the wisdom of the flesh intice you under the disguise of Christian prudence'.[83] The posthumous Saltmarsh pamphlet is suggestive about a politico-religious grouping in London in 1648–9. But the Calverts were prolific—they published the theologian Jacob Boehme, Familist material, Quakers, Gerrard Winstanley, Joseph Salmon, Laurence Clarkson, William Walwyn. In 1653 Giles Calvert was appointed with Henry Hills and Thomas Brewster as printer to Council of State. In 1656 Giles Calvert's sister Martha Simmonds (much vilified in Quaker history) was implicated in egging on James Nayler in his entry into Bristol. At the Restoration the Calverts continued to print

[83] *Englands Friend Raised from the Grave* (London: 1649), sigs. A2^r, A3^v.

anti-monarchical writing. Elizabeth Calvert died in 1675, and her wish was to be buried among the Baptists.[84]

What little can be gleaned of Poole's later career supports this placing of her as both mystically engaged and politically active. In the proceedings against John Pordage in the 1650s Mary Pococke, like Poole, was mentioned as close to the magus. Just as *Pragmaticus* and the Clarke papers juxtapositionally imply an association between Poole and the Levellers, specifically Lilburne, later reports reinforce this. What we know or can guess of Poole's later movements supports our understanding of Poole as radical in religion, politically active, and moving in the circles of the radical London book trade. In July 1653, when the Barebones government was coming into being and John Lilburne was on trial for his life, we read of a woman named Poole, possibly but not certainly this one, who invaded the pulpit at Somerset House, possibly more than once. In some reports this is immediately followed by discussion of the women's petition on Lilburne's behalf.[85] Finally, on 28 April 1668, an Elizabeth Poole was arrested and committed to the gatehouse for printing unlicensed books and having a printing press. Elizabeth Calvert, radical publisher and widow of radical publisher Giles Calvert, also of the Mint Southwark, was committed to the same place, for the same offence, on 29 April. In May, Poole petitioned the King for release, claiming she 'was imprisoned because having let an outer room of her house to a printer, books and papers were found there tending to the prejudice of public concernments'. We can believe her if we choose to. On 8 May, Elizabeth Calvert petitioned Arlington that her family be allowed to visit her.[86] It seems quite possible that Poole supported Lilburne. And it does seem more than likely that in 1668 Poole was more closely connected with Calvert than she admitted.

---

[84] Terry, 'Giles Calvert', pp. 45–50, and 'Giles Calvert: Mid-17C English Bookseller and Publisher', MA thesis, Columbia University, 1937. As Terry notes, 600 publications bear this imprint. Henry R. Plomer, *A Dictionary of Booksellers and Printers* (London: Bibliographical Society, 1907).

[85] Brod, 'Politics', pp. 400–1. *Severall Proceedings*, No. 199, 14–21 July 1653, p. 3149 (mispag.) (E.217 (2)); *The Faithful Post*, No. 122, 19–26 July 1653, p. 1096 (E.217 (7)); *The Dutch Diurnal*, No. 20, 19–26 July 1653, p. 11 (E.707 (6)); *Weekly Intelligencer*, 19–26 July 1653, p. 930 (E.707 (7)). The *Weekly Intelligencer* names 'Mistris Anne Pool'.

[86] *CSPD* (1667–8), pp. 363, 369, 373. Brod, 'Politics', 395–412; Maureen Bell, '"Her Usual Practices": The Later Career of Elizabeth Calvert, 1664–75' *Publishing History*, 35 (1994), pp. 5–64: 27.

In directing our attention to the writings emerging from the congregations, Poole's story tells us about the importance, sometimes power, of both the congregations collectively and their individual members. Poole's writings clearly find a context in the splits between saints and Levellers in 1648–9. Seeing Poole in this context, and asserting the interpretation of visions—including women's visions interpreted by themselves—as a key to the 'restauration' of God's plan (a familiar pattern for mid-century thinkers), allows us to see her as one amongst several women, some known to each other, asserting the importance of visionary interpretation for the commonwealth. Poole's story and its personnel, then, tell us not simply that Poole was a puppet at the General Council, but that there are reasons to understand her pamphlets as making a considered intervention in a particular debate, being likely to find readers and pointing us towards a set of women and men who were considering the import of visions for the commonwealth. Poole's story reminds us, then, that part of what has happened in the interpretation of women's relationships to politics is that, in allowing the contexts and relationships to drop away, perhaps in isolating women from the men who were around them, we have cut away the clues that connect the prophetic and the political.

WOMEN, POLITICS, AND THE SECTS: TELEOLOGY AND ITS DISCONTENTS

In order to draw out the implications of the social and political exchanges traced we need to consider, first, the specifics of the relationships to politics suggested in the material discussed and, second, the traditions of interpretation which frame our investigation of the politics of sectarian women's writing. In canvassing the relationship between religion and politics, and women's place in the printed polemic of the 1640s, these two chapters have focused on the writings and events associated with Sarah Wight and Elizabeth Poole rather than the more often studied writings of figures who stand out more clearly as individuals, such as Anna Trapnel. The chapters have, therefore, explored not solely texts by women emerging from the gathered churches but teased out some of the contextual factors influencing those writings and how they might have been received by contemporaries—the questions of congregations and ministers, print and permission; above all the different ways in which political and religious languages influence one another.

In each case, I have argued, gender is a factor in shaping the way they address the world and the way in which their writings are read. When Manfred Brod tells us that Poole was 'ideally placed' to take a message to the General Council of the army and that 'there was nothing surprising in her being selected to do so' his remarks implicitly address the problematic way in which Poole's sex has been used to render her simultaneously extraordinary (what is a *woman* doing at the Council and who brought her there?) and negligible (one critic writes amusingly of Poole's 'rambling lucubrations').[87] When one is seeking to address the strange situation in which Poole spoke, at the Council, it is disconcerting to find most discussion of events circling around who sponsored her initial appearance there. In such circumstances it might be tempting to argue that Poole's sex was not significant. However, the evidence suggests otherwise. Not only do all the comments we have on her emphasize her sex, but her own writing puts the issue of gender at the heart of her description of power relations, and so uses it to build her relationship to the political and spiritual crisis she sees enveloping the army and nation. While opinion varies on what might be considered the 'source' of Poole's visionary political vocabulary, she clearly uses highly resonant, perhaps quasi-mystical, gendered language (even though she saw no angel, as she freely admits) to articulate political and spiritual crisis.[88] In doing so, Poole both indicates her separateness from the secular programme of the Levellers—her intervention is grounded in some kind of inspiration—and, exactly as the Levellers were doing, puts forward political arguments against regicide. Poole's use of the idea of female disobedience to characterize the army's wifely relationship to the king is not, it seems, best understood in terms of whether it challenges or articulates patriarchal rule. Rather, we can see it as plaiting together significant factors in the controversy over regicide: Poole's own status as a woman, the relationship between contractual and mystically guaranteed

---

[87] Brod, 'Dissent', p. 169; Stevie Davies, *Unbridled Spirits: Women of the English Revolution* (London: The Women's Press, 1998), p. 138.

[88] On links to Joseph Salmon's *A Rout, A Rout* (1649) see Brod, 'Dissent', pp. 177–9.

authority, and the situation of the actual players—army and King. Moreover, once we look at the world into which Poole's message was sent, its dual status as part of an event at the General Council of the army (where it was initially favourably received) and its status as a pamphlet printed in three versions in the post-regicide controversy between the sects and the Levellers, we have a sharper apprehension of how it might have been received and how it shaped Poole's relationship, as a woman, to changing events.

As I have suggested, Poole's use of the language of embodiment, her careful shaping of the image of wife and husband, enabled these political metaphors to do a lot of work for her. Rather, then, than finding Poole imprisoned by or challenging binaries, we can see her words as part of a complex web of sacralized and politicized languages. Her metaphors, figures, and visions act like a net, drawing together women, politics, and mystical spirituality; her words, ideas, and images have a doubly spiritual and political force. At the same time, precisely because Poole seems to support something close to the Leveller position from within the sects, her pamphlets enable us to see more clearly the way in which in 1649 the Leveller project was decisively cut away from the gathered churches—while leaving supporters, like her, in a problematic relationship to congregation on the one hand and political aims on the other.

Where Wight seeks to demarcate realms of politics and spirituality, as we have seen, Poole uses the genre of the vision to articulate political ideas. If Poole uses overlapping sacred and secular vocabularies of rule, Wight tries to keep her discussion of obedience to God clear of politics. The relationships between language and politics are different in each case. Taken together, though, the groups of texts associated with Wight and Poole do have some wider implications for sectarian women's relationship to politics. They suggest that interwoven in the contextual, social and cultural, influences on the production of the texts are both local (internal, sectarian, congregational) politics and wider (national) issues. As Phyllis Mack argues, women needed male approval yet the power relations of women's public interventions were complex rather than unilateral.[89] Different as they are from each other, the political interventions of sectarian women in the 1640s are marked by the complex dynamic of relations between ministers and congregations,

[89] Mack, *Visionary Women*, p. 97.

by the nature of spiritual claims but also by their political impact, by the shifting relationships between gathered churches and other institutions. These conditions of political relationships, not just views on political situations articulated in print, shape women's writing. The stories of Wight and Poole's place in congregations and in political contexts are incomplete, even fragmentary, but their relationships with men and women within and outside the sects are what helps us to follow some of the passages between a woman's experience of grace or her vision and the wider issues of national good, the place of the sects in government, the regicide.

In discussing Wight's and Poole's printed contributions to religious and political debate I have been concerned to offer a nuanced account of the complex relationships of the spiritual and political, to understand the role of printing and dissemination in enabling spiritual as well as political words and events to do work in the world, and to offer a careful account of the ways in which specific contingencies shape women's relationship to politics. This analysis has attempted to historicize the ways in which gender impacted on religious and political languages in specific contexts. Accordingly, my discussion has tried to avoid, first, judging the effects of that language in the long term or, second, offering a speculative evaluation of whether or not involvement in such writing constituted the emergence of a feminist discourse. However, this last has been and remains a key issue in the historiography of sectarian women's writing. How can we productively articulate the political implications of this writing? Or, to put the issue in very polarized terms: is placing this writing in a teleology of feminism simply succumbing to myth, or is historicizing an arid, even depoliticizing, academic exercise?

The parameters of the debate on women and the Civil War sects were to an extent set by Keith Thomas's approval of R. A. Knox's opinion that 'the history of enthusiasm is largely a history of female emancipation'.[90] For Knox, enthusiasm was 'a recurrent situation in Church history', a pattern, 'always repeating itself', where 'an excess of charity threatens unity'. Studying the philosophy and psychology of schism, Knox is also primarily concerned with the times in which he is writing—'the modern

---

[90] R. A. Knox, *Enthusiasm: A Chapter in the History of Religion* (Oxford, 1950; repr. London: Collins, 1987), p. 20, quoted in Keith Thomas, 'Women and the Civil War Sects', *PP* 13 (Apr. 1958), pp. 42–62: 50.

religious situation in England'.[91] He signs up women (with others) to his explanation of the present. In the case of writing on women and the sects, while Hilary Hinds, James Holstun, Ann Hughes, and Phyllis Mack, offer rich contextualizing studies, this material has as often been used in teleological narratives, either acknowledged or implicit. Thus, Dorothy P. Ludlow offers a synoptic statement of the political valency of women's preaching and visions within the sects: 'Men could live with the presence of women visionaries, provided that their dreams and trances were politically innocuous or exclusively spiritual. Intrusion into the male preserve of politics, however, was considered dangerous or suspicious.'[92] As Ludlow's own work implies, we also need to ask, when is speech or writing 'intrusion'? What is 'innocuous', and to which bodies of men and women? What is 'exclusively spiritual' (or indeed 'political') and in what context?

Many visionary, exegetical, or even just passionate texts, indeed, seem to reveal, or at least promise to reveal, shifts in the significance of female political agency at moments of national crisis. Characterizations of mid-century women as passionate about politics—both, to polarize, radical and royalist—are surely right. It seems as though we must decide whether, or to what extent, we interpret such shifts as presaging the present. A scholar's decisions about this both depend on and determine the kind of argument the evidence serves. The issue of the extent to which it is helpful to think of these texts and events *developmentally*—in terms of an evolving, or emerging, feminism—is complex. The terms on which such discussions bring the reader to the question of gender and the Civil War can tend to pre-empt the ways in which gender is considered at the time (in so far as that is recoverable) by making it part of a teleology. When women's participation in written and spoken polemic in the Civil War texts is placed as part of the longer narrative of the development of the discourse of feminism, it tends to follow that relations between the sexes are seen in terms of women's struggle in a way that is a reflection of a struggle for rights even though the terms are not deployed. Thus one critic ends a recent article, 'My unanswered question is, Can we see a coherent statement, detect a prevailing logic of the sex system, in the

---

[91] Knox, *Enthusiasm*, pp. 1, 589.

[92] Dorothy P. Ludlow, 'Shaking Patriarchy's Foundations: Sectarian Women in England 1641–1700', in *Triumph Over Silence: Women in Protestant History*, ed. Richard L. Greaves (Westport, Conn.: Greenwood Press, 1985), pp. 93–124: 103.

range of responses to women in public? Was the English Revolution an "advance" for women?'[93] While there is no reason not to ask such questions, it may be that by asking others which do not pre-emptively situate the women prophets as signifying solely as part of a history of feminism, we may be able to produce questions which that material does not force us to leave wholly 'unanswered'.

The frequency with which critics want to answer questions about the development of late modern feminism on the terrain of women's writing in the Civil War—given the foundational importance of the early modern period in the historically saturated narratives (and myths) of contract theory, feminism, government—is not surprising. If we want to make those answers, I think, we need to consider at least two further issues. First, the question of women's changed place in the public—and explicitly political—sphere during the franchise debates of the nineteenth century, which form part of the basis for women's participation in modernity. These debates both extended and transformed forms of political consciousness and the political imaginary. Our political world is not that of seventeenth-century London or Abingdon. Accordingly, evidence available which permits us to trace a path from prophets to the House of Commons is fascinating—but richly dialectical and marked by the effects of epochal shifts on the interpretability of language, particularly metaphor. Second, it is significant that R. A. Knox, whose remark is at the start of this debate, is writing a narrative history of the long term. To what extent do we want to continue to bring to Civil War history the teleological, even allegorical, debates in which analysis of the period has so long been steeped, of which writers on the wars accuse one another and which we find hard to diagnose or acknowledge in our own writing? If we follow Knox in seeing the significant effects of this history as issuing in modernity, do we risk leaving unexplored the contingencies and motivations of past actions and texts—potentially leaving unexplored the specific terrain of the gendering of politics in the seventeenth century?

The present study's response to the issue of how to relate historicist and wider feminist or developmental concerns in enquiring into the relationship of women and politics is shaped by its attempt to understand the

---

[93] Sharon Achinstein, 'Women on Top in the Pamphlet Literature of the English Revolution', *Women's Studies*, 24 (1994); repr. in *Feminism and Renaissance Studies*, ed. Lorna Hutson (Oxford: Oxford University Press, 1999), pp. 339–72: 365.

seventeenth-century political realm more fully. As I have been arguing, to ask of these texts *only* questions about improvement in the lot of women would produce readings bound to a teleology substantially outside the interpretative frameworks of the text and founded on an understanding of the public sphere as secular and modern. Certainly, the language examined here has, at times, implications for the improving or declining status of women, but the terms which might be related to this—like the metaphors of marriage and the body—tend to carry other, broader and more immediately received, meanings as well. What prophecy tells us about the future fortunes of women is not the only or even, always, the best place to begin if we want to reveal something of the constellation of women's writings in relation to the political arena at the time of writing.

In attempting to tease out the issues of contemporary reception it has become clear that, while men like Kiffin actively attempted to silence women like Poole, we also need to remind ourselves that the rediscovery of sectarian women as part of 'a history of female emancipation' itself forms particular conditions of reception. That these women have no place in the canon of political theory or the literary canon does not mean that their texts had no impact at the moment of publication or subsequently. Wight's text has a history of being read by dissenters as a spiritual document; a little research into the way Poole was writing and the people she was writing about suggests good reasons why there might have been—as seems to be the case—several versions of her pamphlet in circulation. The contextualizing methodology offered here has suggested, then, how these writings were both shaped by and shaped their circumstances. We have found them imbricated in political and spiritual networks, positioned by their sex indeed; but also negotiating a contribution to political events to which history and historiography, not their variously sympathetic, hostile, or baffled contemporaries, have been deaf. Women's sectarian writing has, arguably, been dramatized as marginal by late modern writers as much as by its contemporary readers, though for distinct reasons.

As Stephen Greenblatt reminds us, in trying to listen to the past we cannot help but hear ourselves.[94] And we can speculate that a part of the reception of these writings as marginal comes from the questions we ask

[94] Stephen Greenblatt, *Shakesperean Negotiations: The Circulation of Social Energy in Renaissance England* (Oxford: Clarendon Press, 1988), pp. 1, 20.

it about our 'route' to the present—questions to which seventeenth-century material is sometimes only partially responsive. That said, these women are going to go on having an active, if marginal, life in historically saturated myths of the emergence of feminism, and they certainly belong there. As western feminists, we have chosen them as bit-players in a narrative with Joan of Arc, Simone de Beauvoir, Angela Davis as the heroines. (From this perspective, given their prose, history—or myth—has done them proud.) However, this narrative does not have that much to tell us about the specifics of how politics was understood and imagined in seventeenth-century England, nor about women's place in that. Perhaps, though, we do not have to choose between myth and historicism, but rather acknowledge their discursive power and, as far as possible, try to consider the aims of specific readings and interpretations. When W. S. Graham asks 'What is the language using us for?' he can remind us that, when we seek to answer questions about political languages, whether deriving a path to the present from sectarian writing or seeking to imagine more fully a contemporary context for those texts, part of our task is to consider what our own languages and expectations bring to the evidence. Later in this study I will return to the question of the way in which the political charge of spiritual writing has fared in transmission. In the next chapter I continue the discussion of the limits of political writing and women's use of poetic vocabularies in political struggle.

III

THE POLITICS OF GENRE

5

Poetry and Politics: Anne Bradstreet and Lucy Hutchinson

> I renounce not even ragged glances, small teeth, nothing
>
> (John Berryman, *Homage to Mistress Bradstreet*, 56)

This and the following chapter examine women's place in the mid-seventeenth-century understanding of politics, what might be called the political imaginary, from distinct, even opposite, vantage points. This chapter pursues the question of the way women's poetry imagines politics; the next chapter examines the way in which one particular woman's place in the political world was imagined. Discussing the poetry of Anne Bradstreet and Lucy Hutchinson, this chapter investigates the political and poetic projects of these far from royalist poets during the upheavals of the 1650s and 1660s. What do we find when we attend to their poetry, and the contexts in which it was produced and read? How might we reconsider critical and political categories in the light of such poets? Certainly, literary history has a bearing on how we come to them. For many years the history of Civil War poetry was synonymous with the history of the 'cavalier' lyric.[1] As the category of royalism itself has come under increasing analytical scrutiny, critics have teased out the specific local and intellectual contexts of royalist writings. Attention has been drawn to the ways in which writers' positions, strategies, and vocabularies responded to changing events—particularly the crises marking regicide, Protectorate, and Restoration.[2] As Hero

---

[1] Earl Miner, *The Cavalier Mode from Jonson to Cotton* (Princeton: Princeton University Press, 1971), pp. x, 5, vii. For the naturalization of Cavalier ideology see e.g. Alfred Harbage, *Cavalier Drama* (New York: MLA, 1936); *Cavalier Poets*, ed. Thomas Clayton (Oxford: Oxford University Press, 1979).

[2] James Loxley, *Royalism and Poetry in the English Civil Wars* (Basingstoke: Macmillan, 1997); Lois Potter, *Secret Rites and Secret Writing: Royalist Literature, 1641–1660*

Chalmers argues, during the mid-century period royalist women poets used royalism in a range of ways to legitimate public writing, and the strategies they shared with male poets produced for them enduring models of legitimately politicized authorship.[3] However, while royalist poetry is no longer understood as either isolated or wholly dominant, poetry written by women within the complex and distinct, yet related, alliances which might be broadly characterized as Puritan, parliamentarian, or republican, remains less examined than material by poets whose alignments, though complicated, are broadly royalist—such as Katherine Philips and Margaret Cavendish.[4] More generally, the association of royalism with aesthetics, and Puritanism with barbarism, has also endured.[5] While some poets did see the court and royalty as the sole keys to political life and related to one another through those terms, the assumption that this is how politics operates has also sometimes simplified connections and oppositions. A blunt or cover-all understanding of royalism both effaces complexities within that term and adversely affects our ability to recognize poets not covered by an equivalent branding but who, obviously, also had complicated and driving political commitments.[6] Bradstreet and Hutchinson have been such poets. Bradstreet's

(Cambridge: Cambridge University Press, 1989), p. xiii and *passim*; Timothy Raylor, *Cavaliers, Clubs and Literary Culture* (Newark: University of Delaware Press, 1994); Kevin Sharpe, 'Cavalier Critic? The Ethics and Politics of Thomas Carew's Poetry', in *Politics of Discourse*, ed. Kevin Sharpe and Steven N. Zwicker (Berkeley: University of California Press, 1987), pp. 117–46; Robert Wilcher, *The Writing of Royalism, 1628–1660* (Cambridge: Cambridge University Press, 2001).

[3] Hero Chalmers, *Royalist Women Writers 1650–1689* (Oxford: Oxford University Press, 2004), pp. 1–2, 5–15, 86–104.

[4] Margaret Cavendish is critical of the Stuarts. See e.g. *The Lives of William Cavendishe, Duke of Newcastle, and of his wife Margaret Duchess of Newcastle*, ed. Mark Anthony Lower (London: John Russell Smith, 1872), pp. xxxiii, 122–37; Hilda Smith, ' "A General War Amongst the Men ... but None Amongst the Women": Political Differences between Margaret and William Cavendish', in *Politics and the Political Imagination in Later Stuart Britain*, ed. Howard Nenner (Rochester: University of Rochester Press, 1997), pp. 143–60. On Katherine Philips's royalism see *The Collected Works*, ed. Patrick Thomas (Essex: Stump Cross Books, 1990), vol. I and *passim*. See her 'Upon the double murther of K. Charles, in answer to a libellous rime made by V.P.', and Vavasour Powell's manuscript libel, probably 'Of ye late K. Charles of Blessed Memory by Vavsour Powell', National Library of Wales, Aberystwyth. See also Chalmers, *Royalist Women Writers*, pp. 82–104.

[5] See David Norbrook, *Poetry and Politics in the English Renaissance* (Oxford: Oxford University Press, 2002), pp. 1–15.

[6] Carol Barash, *English Women's Poetry, 1649–1714* (Oxford: Oxford University Press, 1996).

writings have also been further isolated by the disciplinary split between scholars of American and English writing; her poetry has at times been excluded from evaluations of English women's writing. For example, in studies of Civil War women's poetry we usually find contemporary writing coded as English, such as Margaret Cavendish's, replacing rather than being compared with Bradstreet's—even though the latter's poetry was brought to London and published there.

It is in part because of the literary history of such 'non-royalist' poetry that we do not yet have a fuller sense of both royalist and other women's relationships to politics and poetry in the Civil War. It is, though, possible to tease out some of the complex investments of poets who were, say, republican (but also Calvinist), or parliamentarian (but also critical of disputes within the English church and state). What has been obscured is in part simply material, and Hutchinson, particularly, is now the object of historical and critical attention. The process of 'recovery' is itself important, but with whom, exactly, can or should Bradstreet and Hutchinson, very different from each other, be grouped? In what contexts can their poetry be seen? What methods show the interrelationships between politics, gender, and poetry in their writings? My assumption is that under the Republic and during the Protectorate poets did dispute social, political, and personal visions and the power of particular forms to project these. While there is no doubt that poets saw themselves writing in relation to traditions, these were generic and contingently politicized. Although 'context', of course, is attributed rather than natural, each poet requires fairly detailed textual and contextual discussion. As I hope to show, seen in this way Bradstreet's and Hutchinson's poetry reveals the building and reception of strikingly complete, though different, political visions.

POETRY AND MILLENNIUM: ANNE BRADSTREET AND ELIZABETH AVERY

The Tenth Muse Lately sprung up in America, published in London in 1650 but written in New England, turns poetry towards the cause of Protestant reformation; Bradstreet makes claims to write historical poetry and to associates herself, broadly, with a Sidneyan Protestant poetics.[7] *The Tenth Muse* was a notable event in the publication and circulation of Puritan poetry in the year after the regicide. Significantly, the full title of her volume—*Wherein especially is contained a compleat discourse and description of The Four Elements, Constitutions, Ages of Man, Seasons of the Year. Together with an Exact Epitomie of the Four Monarchies, viz. The Assyrian, Persian, Grecian, Roman. Also a Dialogue between Old England and New, concerning the late troubles*—foregrounds just those poems marginalized by current critical opinion (see Figure 7).[8] Much work on Bradstreet takes its cue from assessments by Perry Miller and, more directly, Adrienne Rich. Apart from *The Tenth Muse*'s 'technical amateurishness', impersonality, and failure to treat 'theology', Rich accuses Bradstreet of ignoring the 'indelible impressions' of New England, and of writing, Rich asserts, 'by way of escaping from the conditions of her experience, rather than as an expression of what she felt and knew'. For Rich, 'New England' appears in *The Tenth Muse* only 'as a rather featureless speaker in a "Dialogue Between Old and New England"; the landscape, the emotional weather of the New World, are totally absent'. Rich concludes, 'These long, rather listless pieces seem to have been composed in a last compulsive effort to stay in contact with the history, traditions, and values of her former world; nostalgia for English culture, surely, kept her scribbling at those academic pages, long after her conviction had run out.' Worst of all, Rich finds 'Personal history—marriage, childbearing, death—is similarly excluded from the book.' Rich is, of course, a poet seeking forebears. And one can have some sympathy with the poet John Berryman's similar assessment: 'all this bald | abstract didactic rime I read appalled'.[9]

---

[7] The order of the poems in the 1650 volume may be Bradstreet's. See Margaret Ezell, *Social Authorship and the Advent of Print* (Baltimore: Johns Hopkins University Press, 1999), pp. 46–51.

[8] *The Tenth Muse Lately sprung up in America. Or Severall Poems, compiled with great variety of Wit and Learning, full of delight. Wherein especially is contained a compleat discourse and description of The Four Elements, Constitutions, Ages of Man, Seasons of the Year. Together with an Exact Epitomie of 'the Four Monarchies', viz. The Assyrian, Persian, Grecian, Roman. Also a Dialogue between Old England and New, concerning the late troubles.* With divers other pleasant and serious Poems (London, Pope's Head Alley: Stephen Bowtell: Popes Head Alley, 1650). On the alley see Maureen Bell, 'Hannah Allen and the Development of a Puritan Publishing Business, 1646–51', *Publishing History*, 26 (1989), pp. 5–66: 7. Bradstreet is in need of a scholarly edition. This chapter relies on the first edition in the Thomason tracts. See also *The Tenth Muse (1650)*, ed. Josephine K. Piercy (Gainesville, Fla.: Scholars' Facsimiles and Reprints, 1965).

[9] Sonnet 12 in *Homage to Mistress Bradstreet* (New York: Farrar, Straus & Cudhay, 1956), unpaginated.

THE
TENTH MUSE

Lately fprung up in AMERICA.
OR

Severall Poems, compiled
with great variety of VVit

and Learning, full of delight.
Wherein efpecially is contained a compleat difcourfe and defcription of

The Four ⎰ *Elements,*
　　　　 ⎱ *Conftitutions,*
　　　　 ⎰ *Ages of Man,*
　　　　 ⎱ *Seafons of the Year.*

Together with an Exact Epitomie of
the Four Monarchies, *viz.*

The ⎰ *Affyrian,*
　　 ⎱ *Perfian,*
　　 ⎰ *Grecian,*
　　 ⎱ *Roman.*

Alfo a Dialogue between Old *England* and
New, concerning the late troubles.
With divers other pleafant and ferious Poems.

By a Gentlewoman in thofe parts.

Printed at London for *Stephen Bowtell* at the figne of the
Bible in Popes Head-Alley. 1650.

7. *The Tenth Muse* (1650), title page

Nevertheless, much is lost in Rich's failure of historical imagination. Understood thus, all the poetry published in Bradstreet's lifetime and therefore perhaps ambiguously, with her consent, as opposed to the additional verses added to the posthumous edition of *The Tenth Muse*, fails in a poetic duty to be personal, and, above all, to express her world as an American and as a woman poet.[10] Rich's assessment of Bradstreet as moving from stultified Anglophile imitation (*The Tenth Muse*) to later intimate, American, feminist poetry ('the later poems which have kept her alive to us') has been influential in shaping a critical debate in which Bradstreet's personal voice is set against and prized over public, tropes of modesty are interpreted solely in terms of feminine submission or rebellion, and her status as 'American' is repeatedly canvassed.[11] However, it is also possible to situate Bradstreet's poetry more carefully in complex cultural and historical contexts, and when we begin to do this there are reasons to read *The Tenth Muse*.[12]

Relationships within New England, and between New and old England, were complex, as recent scholarship suggests.[13] In Atlantic New England

[10] Adrienne Rich, Foreword, in *The Works of Anne Bradstreet*, ed. Jeannine Hensley (Cambridge, Mass.: Belknap Press, 1967), pp. ix–xxxv, esp. pp. xiv–xv.

[11] 'The second Edition Corrected by the Author, and enlarged by the Addition of several other Poems found among her Papers after her death.' *The Tenth Muse* (Boston, 1678), title page. See Perry Miller, *Errand into the Wilderness* (Boston: William & Mary Quarterly for the Associates of the John Carter Brown Library, 1952), pp. 12–13; *Errand into the Wilderness* (Cambridge, Mass.: Harvard University Press, 1956), pp. 9–10. Following, see e.g. Wendy Martin, *An American Triptych: Anne Bradstreet, Emily Dickinson, Adrienne Rich* (Chapel Hill: North Carolina University Press, 1984), pp. 15, 16, 17; Alicia Oistriker, *Stealing the Language: The Emergence of Women's Poetry in America* (London: Women's Press, 1987), pp. 15–22; Theresa Freda Nicolay, *Gender Roles, Literary Authority and Three American Women Writers* (New York: Peter Lang, 1995), pp. 1–2; Agnieszka Salska, 'Puritan Poetry: Its Public and Private Strain', *ELA* 19, No. 1 (1984), pp. 107–21: 115, 116. Compare Jane Donahue Eberwein, 'The "Unrefined Ore" of Anne Bradstreet's Quaternions', *ELA* 9 (1974), repr. in *Critical Essays on Ann Bradstreet*, ed. Pattie Cowell and Ann Stanford (Boston, Mass.: G. K. Hall, 1983), pp. 166–73. See also Rosamond Rosenmeir, *Anne Bradstreet Revisited* (Boston: G. K. Hall, 1991), pp. 1–5.

[12] See Jeffrey A. Hammond, *Sinful Self, Saintly Self: The Puritan Experience of Poetry* (Athens: University of Georgia Press, 1993), pp. 83–5, 99–100, and *passim*; Sara Eaton, 'Anne Bradstreet's "Personal" Protestant Poetics', *Women's Writing*, 4, No. 1 (1997), pp. 57–71; Patricia Pender, 'Disciplining the Imperial Mother: Anne Bradstreet's "A Dialogue Between Old England and New"', in *Women Writing 1550–1750*, ed. Jo Wallwork and Paul Salzman, *Meridian*, 18, No. 1 (2001), pp. 115–31; Nancy E. Wright, 'Epitaphic Conventions and the Reception of Anne Bradstreet's Public Voice', *EAL* 31, No. 3 (1996), pp. 243–63.

[13] Philip Gura, *A Glimpse of Sion's Glory: Puritan Radicalism in New England, 1620–1660* (Middletown, Conn.: Wesleyan University Press, 1984); Andrew Delbanco, *The*

twenty years after the establishment of the colony, things were indeed new; given 'American' identity's status as at most an embryonic category, Rich's call for Bradstreet to express it seems quixotic. However, New and old England were entities in the consciousness of thinkers and writers—as William Spengeman notes, English texts and Milton in particular were influential in seventeenth-century New England—and these linked the two sides of the Atlantic. *The Tenth Muse* actively participated in the literary and poetic cultures of Civil War England and New England. Indeed, that the 'Dialogue between Old England and New' was specifically advertised on the title page of her book might encourage us to see her text as comparing old and new. Yet at the same time that the very title claims Bradstreet as an additional muse, representing a 'new' part of the world, 'America'.[14]

The relationship between New England settlers and the English Church was complicated and uncertain; the 'errand into the wilderness' was troubled from the first.[15] New England offered a refuge from hated church practices without leaving the settlers open to the accusation of separatism, yet to undertake such a journey spoke loudly of rejection of English clerical practice; as voyagers to a distant land where many of their number died, how would the early settlers feel certain that they were fulfilling God's providence?[16] Attempting to understand and assess the colony, Bradstreet's father, Thomas Dudley, had written back to the Countess of Lincoln in March 1631, describing their relations to England in dialogic terms. Planters, he writes, need to be 'endued

---

Puritan Ordeal (Cambridge, Mass.: Harvard University Press, 1989); Janice Knight, *Orthodoxies in Massachusetts: Rereading American Puritanism* (Cambridge, Mass.: Harvard University Press, 1994), p. 2. On studying early American literature see William C. Spengeman, *A New World of Words: Redefining Early American Literature* (New Haven: Yale University Press, 1994), pp. 1–50.

[14] Stephanie Jed, 'The Tenth Muse: Gender, Rationality, and the Marketing of Knowledge', in *Women, 'Race', and Writing in the Early Modern Period*, ed. Margo Hendricks and Patricia Parker (London: Routledge, 1994), pp. 195–208: 196–7.

[15] See e.g. Samuel Danforth, *A Brief Recognition of New England's Errand into the Wilderness* (Cambridge, Mass., 1671).

[16] Susan Hardman Moore, 'Popery, Purity and Providence: Deciphering the New England Experiment', in *Religion, Culture and Society in Early Modern Britain*, ed. Anthony Fletcher and Peter Roberts (Cambridge: Cambridge University Press, 1994), pp. 257–89. Compare Perry Miller, *The New England Mind: The Seventeenth Century* (Cambridge, Mass.: Harvard University Press, 1939), pp. 365, 474–88; Sacvan Bercovitch, *The Puritan Origins of the American Self* (New Haven: Yale University Press, 1975).

with grace', but also 'furnished with means to feed themselves and theirs for eighteen months, and to build and plant'.[17] New England is indeed defined in relationship to geography and landscape. But that landscape is also inhabited by figures which suggest the complexity of Protestant history in England and New England—'Indians', those who transgressed the laws of the colony (such as Thomas Morton, the author of *New English Canaan* (1634)), as well as the worldly and the Puritan members of the old world. We find those who had left England calling for a Puritan reform of the Church, not a separation from it. While Dudley does discourage those who might come to New England for worldly ends, he nevertheless ambivalently acknowledges that New England is related to the old as a commercial, as well as spiritual, venture.

In the twenty years between Dudley's letter and the publication of his daughter's poems relations between old and New England had become more complex.[18] In New England fears of antinomianism were powerful after the trial of Anne Hutchinson, and the exile of John Cotton and the treatment of the Quakers, banished and beaten, vividly shows how those fears might find expression. While Morton's criticisms of the colony in *New English Canaan* could be dismissed as maverick, by the time Bradstreet was writing the views of Roger Williams on religious toleration and on the Indians, including his dictionary *A Key Into the Language of America* (1643), had initiated a whole other set of views on toleration, cultural difference, and the new world—views against which Dudley had set his face. A self-penned epitaph, said to have been found by Cotton Mather in Dudley's pocket at his death in 1653, reads:

> Let Men of God in Courts and Churches watch
> O're such as do a *Toleration* hatch,
> Lest that Ill Egg bring forth a Cockatrice,
> To poison all with Heresie and Vice.

---

[17] 'Dudley's Letter to the Countess of Lincoln', in *Chronicles of the First Planters of the Colony of Massachusetts Bay, from 1623 to 1636* (Boston: Charles C. Little and James Brown, 1846), pp. 323–4. See *The Puritans in America: A Narrative Anthology*, ed. Alan Heimert and Andrew Delbanco (Cambridge, Mass.: Harvard University Press, 1985), p. 98, and also Michael Leroy Oberg, *Dominion and Civility: English Imperialism and Native America, 1585–1685* (Ithaca: Cornell University Press, 1999), pp. 82–4.

[18] See Gura, *A Glimpse of Sion's Glory*, pp. 126–52.

If Men be left, and otherwise Combine,
My *Epitaph's* I, DY'D NO LIBERTINE.[19]

Clearly the governors of the New England colony, of which Dudley was one, saw it as overrun by uncontrollable, protean, religious, political and social movements and debates whose purchase spanned the old world and the new. Libertinism was felt to threaten church practice and order. Millenarian fervour needed to be kept separate from toleration, and so tensions between ranting and discipline (though these were not always tied to doctrinal disagreements) were crucial in shaping the colony's identity. Thus, in 1650 the political identity of New England was bound, though not exclusively, to the histories of the old world just as it was tied to, and partly disavowed, the geography of the new. This is the context in which Bradstreet's Atlantic identity as a poet can be understood.

Bradstreet begins her volume with a poem to her father, to whom her poems were 'humbly presented':

> TD on the
> Deare Sir, of late delighted with the sight,   four parts
> Of your* four sisters, deckt in black & white   of the
> Of fairer Dames, the sun near saw the face,   world
> (though made a pedestall for *Adams* Race)
> Their worth so shines, in those rich lines, you show.
> Their parallels to find, I scarcely know...[20]

Often interpreted as solely a gesture of modesty by Bradstreet, the opening does foreground her father's precedence. But in acknowledging him through his poem, on 'the four parts of the world', she also recognizes the importance of spatial positioning, including implicitly her own as 'Tenth Muse', and begins to signal her own contrasting turn to history; the relationship between history and place is one of tension rather than a mutually exclusive choice.

---

[19] Revd Cotton Mather, *Magnalia Christi Americana; or the Ecclesiastical History of New-England* (London, 1702), bk. II, p. 17. Quoted in Elizabeth Wade White, *Bradstreet: The Tenth Muse* (New York: Oxford University Press, 1971), pp. 296–7.

[20] Bradstreet, 'To Her Most Honoured Father *Thomas Dudley* Esq; *these humbly presented*', in *Tenth Muse*, p. 1. Except where otherwise indicated, the edition used is the 1650 edition of *The Tenth Muse* in the Thomason Collection at the British Library: E.1365 (4).

Bradstreet's avowals of modesty and disavowals of politics pose problems of interpretation. The question of whether they should be taken at face value is raised, if not answered, in the very next poem, 'The Prologue'. Her claim, here, that she is unworthy 'To sing of Wars, of Captaines, and of Kings, | Of Cities founded, Common-wealths begun'—'Let Poets, and Historians set these forth, | My obscure verse shall not dim their worth'—must be considered against the fact that these topics are precisely the main poetic focus of the first section of her volume. The partial irony of her disclaimer seems to be emphasized by her address to the critics: 'And oh, ye high flown quils . . . If ever you daigne these lowly lines, your eyes | Give wholesome Parsley wreath, I aske no Bayes'.[21] Taking its lead from her father's poem on the four parts of the world, the first part of the volume analyses in fours: elements, humours, ages of man, seasons. Most significantly, the longest poem, over a hundred pages in the original edition, 'the Four Monarchies of the World' analyses sacred meaning and the power of rule.[22]

How are we to read this long poem published by a woman in England the year after the regicide and clearly addressing the place of monarchy, Protestantism, and republic? Describing it as 'a barren exercise in rhetorical ingenuity, unreadable by present-day standards', Elizabeth Wade White also noted the 'abrupt' ending.[23] However, a poem using the four monarchies—Assyrian, Persian, Greek, and Roman—to interpret history was far from barren to a seventeenth-century reader. As Bernard Capp reminds us, fifth monarchist thinking was widespread in England in the 1640s; it had both academic and ecstatic roots in different interpreters of the Bible's prophetic books, especially Revelation and Daniel, and it was brought to the fore by the execution of Charles I.[24] Fifth monarchism was a framework which mixed interest in the classical world with the biblical by applying the prophecies of Daniel to world history. The narrative of the four, succeeding, empires degenerating to the end of the Roman empire, after which would come the millennium, both offered a pattern to history and, by the 1640s, a terrain of political and religious debate: when would the end be, what was to be

---

[21] *Tenth Muse*, pp. 3, 4.   [22] Ibid., pp. 65–179.
[23] Wade White, *Bradstreet*, pp. 236, 229.
[24] Bernard Capp, *The Fifth Monarchy Men* (London: Faber & Faber, 1972), pp. 14, 17–49. On English publication see Carla G. Pestana, *The English Atlantic in an Age of Revolution 1640–1660* (Cambridge, Mass.: Harvard University Press, 2004).

interpreted as the fourth monarchy in mid-seventeenth-century England?[25] Such questions invited comparison between the prophecies of Daniel and the present state of England during the crises of war, and, to many, the chaos of war suggested that the end might come in the near rather than distant future.[26] Puritans of Bradstreet's father's generation, leaving England, called on apocalyptic imagery and contemporary crises in government, such as the Thirty Years War, to express their sense that, as Thomas Hooker put it 'As sure as God is God, God is going from England.'[27] Bradstreet puts this motivating pattern to work within the shape of a history poem which also draws on Sir Walter Raleigh's *History of the World* and, to an extent, considers itself in relation to Joshua Sylvester's translation of du Bartas's *Divine Works and Weeks*. That Bradstreet's poem sets out to elucidate the divine understanding of the meaning of human time—history—may go some way to illuminate her use of an intermittently dull metre.[28] In such a poem aesthetic concerns are clearly subordinate to an understanding of history past and present.[29]

In appealing to history's divine but veiled pattern, the poem presents examples of crises generated by monarchy.[30] The examples make up much of the body of the poem, but the reader is clearly invited to trace the logic of degeneracy whereby each monarchy fades. Thus, repeatedly, the poem recognizes the fall of princes, sometimes placing it alongside

[25] See Jane Donohue Eberwein, 'Civil War and Bradstreet's "Monarchies" ', *EAL* 26, No. 2 (1991), pp. 119–43.

[26] Capp, *The Fifth Monarchy Men*, pp. 20–1.

[27] Thomas Hooker, 'The Danger of Desertion', *circa* April 1631, in *Writings in England and Holland, 1626–1633,* ed. George H. Williams, Norman Pettit, Winfred Herget, and Sargent Bus Jr. (Cambridge, Mass.: Harvard University Press, 1975), pp. 221–70, esp. 225, 244. On John Cotton's sermons and the book of Daniel, see Ann Stanford, *Anne Bradstreet: The Worldly Puritan* (New York: Burt Franklin, 1974), p. 60. On Hooker, Mrs Drake, and his failure to find a living in England see Knight, *Orthodoxies,* p. 63.

[28] See Achsah Guibbory, *The Map of Time, Seventeenth-Century English Literature and Ideas of Pattern in History* (Urbana: University of Illinois Press, 1986); Gerald M. MacLean, *Time's Witness, Historical Representation in English Poetry 1603–1660* (Madison: University of Wisconsin Press, 1990).

[29] Lucy Hutchinson makes this point quite explicitly in her investigation of divine time. See *Order and Disorder,* ed. David Norbrook (Oxford: Blackwell, 2001); Norbrook, 'A Devine Originall: Lucy Hutchinson and the "Woman's Version" ', *TLS,* 19 Mar. 1999, pp. 13–15.

[30] MacLean, *Time's Witness,* pp. 157–8.

other Protestant literature on the same topic: 'as . . . doth (well read) Raleigh write', Darius the last Persian king 'from the top of the worlds felicity; | He fell to depth of greatest misery, | Whose honours, treasures, pleasures, had short stay; | One deluge came and swept them all away.'[31] A central example, Alexander the Great, first ruler of the third, Grecian, monarchy and simultaneously a high and low point of the power of monarchy, occupies a pivotal and central section of the narrative. Perhaps because Alexander is thematically and structurally important, it is at this point that Bradstreet reminds the reader that the examples traced are seen in relation to a millenarian Protestant structure and particularly the prophecies of Daniel. She notes that Alexander was actually shown these at Jerusalem, an occasion the text marks as a lost opportunity for true interpretation.[32] The overall shaping role of Daniel's prophecy is further foregrounded at the end of the Greek empire—'The affinities and warres *Daniel* set forth'—at which point she is forced to consider the implications of dealing with the fourth, and last, monarchy.[33]

Bradstreet's use of examples invites a dialectical reading. The reader is encouraged to set each example against a trajectory of repeated monarchical degeneracy and to draw conclusions about the past and the crisis of monarchy and Protestantism. The text's opening passages make this dynamic clear:

> When Time was young, and World in infancy,
> Man did not strive for Soveraignty,
> But each one thought his petty rule was high,
> If of his house he held the Monarchy:
> This was the Golden Age, but after came
> The boysterous Son of *Cush*, Grand-child to *Ham*,
> That mighty Hunter, who in his strong toyls,
> Both Beasts and man subjected to his spoyls.
> The strong foundation of proud Babel laid,
> *Erech*, *Accad*, and *Calneh* also made;

By opening her poem with Nimrod, Bradstreet's account of the birth of political time fuses biblical and classical accounts of a period before rule, a regime destroyed by 'boysterous' Nimrod, the 'mighty Hunter' of Genesis.

---

[31] *Tenth Muse*, p. 118.   [32] Ibid., p. 127.   [33] Ibid., p. 171.

This dark descendant of Ham was a builder of cities, first king and designer of Babel, ender of the Golden Age. For Bradstreet, as for others, Nimrod's rule figured the start of tyranny, not merely kingship.[34] As David Norbrook indicates, Nimrod's presence, strongly associated with the Tower of Babel, echoes through the anti-monarchical writings of the Commonwealth and Restoration, appearing in Andrew Marvell's 'Upon Appleton House' and his 'The Character of Holland', and in Milton's *Areopagitica* (1644).[35] Bradstreet's poem can be seen in a tradition of Protestant poetry including *Paradise Lost*, where the shift from post-Edenic calm (men living 'With some regard to what is just and right', XII, 16) to the rule of Nimrod is dramatized in Michael's prophecy:

> Long time in peace, by families and tribes,
> Under paternal rule; till one shall rise
> Of proud ambitious heart, who not content
> With fair equality, fraternal state,
> Will arrogate dominion undeserved
> Over his brethren, and quite dispossess
> Concord and law of nature from the earth...
>
> (ll. 23–9)

Milton's politicization of Nimrod's epithet, 'mighty hunter' (l. 33), implying 'empire tyrannous' (l. 32), is more direct than Bradstreet's, yet the poets clearly share a Protestant interpretation of human time where human labour 'reaping plenteous crop | Corn wine, and oil' is violently disrupted by the arrival of the rule of kings. Structurally positioned at the very opening of Bradstreet's poem, her account of Nimrod's career suggests simultaneously the awesome sway of great empire and the kernel of destruction lodged within that very power. Balancing Nimrod's tyranny at the opening of the poem is the Babylonian queen Semiramis, an example

[34] Capp notes the popularity of Daniel's vision of the rise and fall of four successive monarchies (Babylon, Assyria, Greece, Rome), and notes also 'The concept too blended with the widespread theory of a Roman Golden Age from which all later history represented a continuous decline lasting till the world's end' (*The Fifth Monarchy Men*, pp. 20–1). As an influence on Bradstreet see Walter Raleigh, *The History of the World* (London, 1614), pp. 37–8.

[35] David Norbrook, *Writing the English Republic: Poetry, Rhetoric and Politics 1627–1660* (Cambridge: Cambridge University Press, 1998), pp. 290, 296, 411, 463–7.

of degenerate monarchy. Semiramis is represented by Bradstreet as a monster made of power who 'usurp'd the throne', and 'like a brave Virago, play'd the rex, | And was both shame, and glory of her sex'.[36]

Semiramis and Nimrod exemplify modes of tyranny, but in counterpoint with the use of example we find politicized commentary. When Bradstreet discusses 'The inter-Regnum between Cambyses and Darius Hyslapes' which leads the Persian Darius's kingship by election, she writes:

> A Consultation by the States was held.
> What forme of Government now to erect,
> The old, or new, which best, in what respect,
> The greater part, declin'd a Monarchy.
> So late crusht by their Princes Tyranny;
> And thought the people, would more happy be,
> If governed by an Aristocracy.
> But others thought (none of the dullest braine,)
> But better one, then many Tyrants reigne.
> What arguments they us'd, I know not well,
> Too politicke (tis like) for me to tell . . . [37]

Political opinion here is again both asserted and retracted. Criticizing tyranny and aristocratic government, the poem implies monarchy as a solution (chosen by those of sharper brain) but notes also its degenerate form. Having made the discrimination and drawn out implications, the poem goes on to insist on the author's incapacity to make political judgements of any kind: the 'arguments they us'd' are 'Too politicke' for her to tell.

The pattern of political assertion and withdrawal marks many of the poems in *The Tenth Muse* and takes on growing significance in the latter part of 'The Four Monarchies'. It offers, I suggest, a way to reinterpret what has usually too readily been understood as Bradstreet's 'exhaustion' and self-confessed inability to provide a full-length version of the fourth monarchy. Having seen all the other quaternions to completion, as well as three of the four monarchies, why would Bradstreet suddenly become exhausted when faced with the well-known story of Rome? One answer concerns the part the Roman monarchy has to play in Bradstreet's

---

[36] John Milton, *Paradise Lost*, ed. Alastair Fowler (London: Longman, 1968; repr. 1971), pp. 610–11; *Tenth Muse*, pp. 67, 68.
[37] *Tenth Muse*, p. 93.

structure. Indeed, the final moments of the third monarchy clearly recognize that the fourth monarchy demands that she bring political problems within the frame of contemporary history. She writes that 'these Three Monarchies now have I done, | But how the fourth, their Kingdoms from them won; | And how from small beginnings it did grow, | To fill the world with terrour and with woe'. However, the fourth monarchy obviously presents specific problems which, she writes, her 'tired braine' will 'leave to a better pen'. And she explicitly acknowledges that it leads her into the realm of politics—'This taske befits not women, like to men'. Ultimately, it is the sublimity of the political implications which she claims defeats her: 'The Subject was too high, beyond my strain'.[38] Clearly, what is so daunting about the fourth monarchy is its implications for the present.

However, as in the rest of *The Tenth Muse* Bradstreet's insistence that she will not, cannot, make political comment is not the whole story. Between the third and fourth monarchies a passage offers an account of her decision to continue:

> *After some dayes of rest, my restlesse heart,*
> *To finish what begun, new thoughts impart*
> *And maugre all resolves, my fancy Wrought*
> *This fourth to th'other three, now might be brought.*
> *Shortnesse of time and inability,*
> *Will force me to a confus'd brevity;*
> *Yet in this Chaos one shall easily spy,*
> *The vast limbs of a mighty Monarchy.*
> *What e're is found amisse, take in best part,*
> *As faults proceeding from my head, not heart . . .* [39]

The desire to tackle the politically difficult Roman monarchy is in tension with the sheer difficulty of dealing with the subject, and further complicated by the required shift to a potentially immodest register of overt political engagement. The last line implies a resolution of this problem by the attribution of error to weak and unable reason, not to a 'heart' which is politically true, though exactly what a true heart might be is left open. Within the eschatology of the four monarchies it

[38] Ibid., p. 174.   [39] Ibid.

stands at the end, and its end signals the end of the world. That the Roman monarchy is the last, yet time continues, provokes the political and religious question of the relationship between the Roman monarchy and the present, troubling the relationship between Bradstreet's moment of composition and time's end. If the Roman monarchy began 'Anno Mundi 3212', when, and how, is it to end?

Opening with 'Stout *Romulus*, *Romes* Founder, and first King' Bradstreet tracks his transformation of pastoral into city:

> Where Shepheards once had Coats, and Sheep their Folds,
> Where Swaines, and rustick Peasants made their Holds.
> A Citty faire did *Romulus* erect:
> The Mistris of the World, in each respect.
> His brother *Remus* there, by him was slaine,
> For leaping o're the Walls with some disdaine;
> The Stones at first was cimented with bloud,
> And bloudy hath it prov'd, since first it stood:[40]

Rome's associations with the 'Citty faire' which replaces Babylon, and on the other hand with fratricide, civil strife, and the Roman church 'cimented with bloud' indicates clearly that discussion of the fourth monarchy is bound to touch on contemporary religious and political issues. Thus, the material introducing Rome and its treatment invite the reader to look for links between past and present. Indeed, Bradstreet closes the whole poem with Tarquinius Superbus and Sextus, his son, who did:

> *Lucretia* force, mirrour of chastety;
> She loathed so the fact, she loath'd her life,
> And shed her guiltlesse blood, with guilty knife,
> Her Husband, sore incens'd to quit this wrong,
> With *Junius Brutus* rose, and being strong,
> The *Tarquins* they from *Rome* with speed expell,
> In banishment perpetuall, to dwell;
> The Government they change, a new one bring,
> and people sweare, ne're to accept of King.[41]

The poem started with Nimrod and Semiramis, the earliest tyrants, and it ends with Tarquinius Sextus's tyranny defeated by Lucretia's chastity and the foundation of the Roman republic. The treatment of

---

[40] *Tenth Muse*, p. 175.   [41] Ibid., p. 179.

the fourth monarchy, then, though truncated, is fully considered and highly self-conscious. The conclusion of the poem is preceded by a sequence of disclaimers of knowledge, further supplemented in the 1678 edition by a subsequent '*Apology*', claiming 'Essays I many made, but still gave out, | The more I mus'd the more I was in doubt'. In this edition Bradstreet also gestures towards the loss of her papers in a fire in1666.[42] Arguably, leaving the story at the establishment of the Roman republic allows Bradstreet to avoid controversy. However, the patterning of the poem overall, using Nimrod's emergence as a tyrant at the opening of the poem and setting this against closure on the inauguration of the Roman republic, was hardly without political implications. When Bradstreet's poems travelled to England in 1647, the issue of the nature of tyranny was of urgent significance, and by the time they were published England was a republic, with a reading public highly alert to the contemporary significance of arresting the four monarchies at a moment when the temporary defeat of monarchy might seem to prefigure the present English crisis.

Exemplarity, discussed in the first chapter of this study, is so evident throughout 'The Four Monarchies' that it must also give us pause here. Lucretia, as example, no doubt serves the rhetorical function of putting women in relation to politics; that to a modern reader her self-murder appears masochistic must not blind us to its power as political martyrdom in the early modern period. Bradstreet's claim to tiredness is not artless. The breaking off of the poem is itself a kind of ending and one which, however ambiguously, ensures that the quaternions halt at a moment of female exemplarity and political martyrdom. A breaking off it may be, but it is also, inevitably, a culmination. It is not so much that in the hands of a woman writer Lucretia's use is transformed; rather, it is clear that Lucretia could put women in relation to politics for both men and women writers and that as an example, as here, her presence is explicitly political and a final point of force. Lucretia's exemplary power crosses over from a diegetic role to call attention to writing, the world, gender, and politics.[43]

[42] *Several Poems* 'by a Gentlewoman in *New-England*': 'The second Edition, Corrected by the Author and enlarged by an Addition of several other Poems found amongst her Papers after her Death.' (Boston, 1678), p. 191.
[43] For a discussion of the supplement see Jacques Derrida, *Of Grammatology*, trans. Gayatri Chakravorty Spivack (Baltimore: Johns Hopkins University Press, 1977), p. 144.

Thus, 'The Four Monarchies' positively invites interpretation in terms of the writing of Protestant poetic history. The poem seems to refuse to address the pressing question of the present. Its ending (in narrative terms) with the rape of Lucretia and the death of the last Roman King Tarquin and (thematically) with a foregrounding of poetic agency, serves to emphasize the status of its subject matter as highly politicized. However, it leaves the reader in no doubt that the poem addresses the crisis of Civil War. In terms of the quaternions, Bradstreet builds up from the elements, humours, and ages to the most sophisticated and troubling of her interpretative frameworks, and the one in which it is both most important and hardest to see the hand of God—history.

The question of the divine pattern in history, including the role of providence, was an urgent one for other writers. One poem (circulated from 1621, printed in 1642) appeals to the figure of Elizabeth I, begging her to 'save this *Sodom Britain* from the fire' for '*Egypts* ten plagues we have indur'd twice told' since her death.[44] Similarly, the poem immediately following 'the Four Monarchies', 'A Dialogue between Old *England* and New, concerning their present troubles', explicitly addresses the problems of civil government in the present, but also in the developing pattern of Protestant history. Addressing '*Sodom* Britain' from the perspective of New England, the 'Dialogue' represents the force of the past in the present in the form of the conversation between mother and daughter. Taking up the popular Civil War form of the dialogue, the poem uses analysis of the crisis of the Civil War to throw into relief different ways in which the relationship between Old and New England could be understood in the 1640s. Old England treats New as still incorporate, an extension ('and thou a childe, a Limbe, and dost not feele') and the poem suggests that this view is a product of Old England's decadence. Throughout the poem, the pair's distinct relationship to the true church is used to indicate their separateness. In a mixture of bodily, medicinal, and religious vocabulary, Old England claims New England's loyalty: 'by my wasting state dost think to thrive?' New England turns to historical discourses rather than medicinal to diagnose Old England's trouble:

---

[44] *The Humble Petition of the Wretched and most contemptible, the poore Commons of England* To the blessed ELIZABETH of famous memory (London, 1642), pp. 5, 3. Bodl. MS Malone 23. I am grateful to Michelle O'Callaghan for information on the manuscript.

'What, hath some *Hengist*, like that *Saxon* stout, | By fraud, and force, usurp'd thy flowring crown?'[45]

Old England admits that her troubles stem from her mistaken role in frustrating Protestant history, 'Ile shew the cause | Which are my Sins, the breach of sacred Lawes':

> Church Offices are sold, and bought, for gaine,
> That Pope, had hope, to finde *Rome* here againe;
> For Oathes, and Blasphemies did ever eare
> From *Beelzebub* himself, such language heare?
> What scorning of the Saints of the most high,
> What injuries did daily on them lye;
> What false reports, which nick-names they did take,
> Not for their owne, but for their Masters sake;
> And thou, poore soule, wast jeer'd among the rest,
> Thy flying for the Truth I made a jeast;
> For Sabbath-breaking, and for Drunkennesse,
> Did ever Land prophannesse more expresse?[46]

Old England finds that for past sins—'crying bloods'—she, too is to be punished: 'Now sip I of that cup, and just 't may be, | The bottome dregs reserved are for me.' New England's reply, is 'Your fearful sinnes, great cause there's to lament, | My guilty hands (in part) hold up with you, | A sharer in your punishment's my due'. No longer incorporate, and only in part taking responsibility for Old England's sin, New England's voice emerges as independent and authoritative:

> Blest be the Nobles of thy Noble Land,
> With (ventur'd lives) for truths defence that stand,
> Blest be thy Commons, who for Common good,
> And thy infringed Lawes have boldly stood.[47]

New England has the last word, closing the dialogue with a valediction and clear political advice: 'Farewell dear mother, Parliament prevail, | And in a while you'l tell another tale'.[48]

The rest of the volume enlists the political and religious heroes of the Tudor Reformation. Elegies on Protestant heroes including Elizabeth

---

[45] *Tenth Muse*, p. 181.   [46] Ibid., pp. 183–4.
[47] Ibid., p. 188.   [48] Ibid., p. 190.

I and Philip Sidney, as well as Joshua Sylvester, resonate with the implications for the 1640s. For Bradstreet Sidney is 'Philip and Alexander both in one'—biblical and classical, national and Protestant, past and present are bound together.[49] As Henry Vane put it, the prophetic discovery of the 'inward and spiritual meaning' of events is designed 'not to exclude thereby their literal and historical sense, but to shew how well both may stand together'.[50] The inescapable connection between history and the present is emphasized in the penultimate poem, 'David's Lamentation for *Saul* and *Jonathan*, 2 Sam.I.19', sometimes interpreted as a lamentation for Charles I. Certainly the poem returns to the relationship between old and New England in the current crisis. The biblical verse, 'The beauty of Israel is slain upon thy high places: how are the mighty fallen', appears to refer once again to the old and new worlds, here figured fraternally: the chapter ends, 'I am distressed for thee my brother'. Bradstreet's volume ends with a self-undoing gesture—a poem 'On the vanity of all worldly creatures'. Yet vanity itself is used to turn the volume towards true Protestantism; 'This satiates the soul, this stayes the mind, | The rest's but vanity and vain we find.'[51]

The Tenth Muse gives a disciplined typological poetic history, starting with elements and humours, and building up to an analysis of national histories that uses fifth monarchist ideas. 'The Four Monarchies' meditates deeply about how to express the 'true' relationship between the prophecies and Bradstreet's own time. Rather than offer conclusions on this, *The Tenth Muse* traces implicit, potential but powerful, connections between biblical promises and their present realizations. An important aspect of this narrative involves putting New England into a spatial, historical, and familial relationship with English politics and the English Church. However, as suggested by the first edition's advertisement of 'The Four Monarchies' and John Woodbridge's insistence on Bradstreet's being 'honoured, and esteemed where she lives, for her gracious demeanour, her eminent parts, her pious conversation', circumstances suggest more than the poems alone about the volume's

---

[49] 'An Elegie upon that honourable Knight, Sir Philip Sidney', 'His Epitaph', *Tenth Muse*, p. 195.

[50] Henry Vane, *Retired Mans Meditations* (London, 1655), a4ᵛ; see also Nigel Smith, *Literature and Revolution in England, 1640–1660* (New Haven: Yale University Press, 1994), p. 124.

[51] *Tenth Muse*, p. 207.

intervention in the Atlantic politics of 1650. This context I will now explore, particularly the personnel involved in sending Bradstreet's volume into the world. Fifth monarchism is one factor here. Another is that the same group of people who supported Bradstreet can be found censuring another female author—Bradstreet's aunt by marriage. These previously unnoticed circumstances tells us more about the views of a particular group on women's political and religious affiliations. To see this clearly we need to examine some of the details of Atlantic and local English political and religious relations.

Fifth monarchist ideas were long-lived, widespread, and part of controversies over church discipline and the future of the republic. One writer on these ideas, Thomas Parker, arrived in New England in May 1635, and became assistant to Nathaniel Ward at Aggawam. Thomas was the son of Robert Parker who, fleeing England in 1607 after having published a controversial tract, went to the Netherlands, where he met Henry Jacob, known to us already as the founder of the Jacob church. Robert Parker spent the rest of what remained of his life controverting the role of the minister, congregation, and synod in church organization. Ultimately, though not without discussion or unconditionally, he threw in his lot with the Presbyterians, who emphasized the judgemental role of the synod. Parker died in 1614 leaving three children. Thomas, his only son, took on some of his ideas. After coming to New England, he moved to incorporate the township of Newberry with his nephew—John Woodbridge. John and his younger brother Benjamin Woodbridge, of Stanton-Fitzwarren in Wiltshire, were the sons of Thomas Parker's sister, Sara or Sarah, by her first marriage. While Sarah's second husband, Thomas Baylie, a minister in Wiltshire, was ejected at the Restoration and accused by Anthony à Wood of fifth monarchism, there is no sense that John and Benjamin Woodbridge were fifth monarchists; rather, John was both a minister and civil magistrate and returned to New England, while Benjamin was ejected from his living in 1662 and licensed as a Presbyterian preacher in 1672.[52] John Woodbridge—the man who probably

[52] See *DNB*. I am very grateful to Tim Wales for discussion of this point. See Dorothy Parker's will, 10 Oct. 1649, and H. F. Waters, *Genealogical Gleanings in England* (Boston: New England Historic Genealogical Society, 1901), I, 7–8. The will indicates that Sarah Bayly, as the name appears, is also the mother of John and Benjamin Woodbridge. It also names Elizabeth Avery's husband as Timothy Avery.

brought Bradstreet's poems to England—had, of course, married Anne Bradstreet's sister, Mercy. The third Parker sibling was Elizabeth, whose married surname was Avery.[53] So the poet Anne Bradstreet was related by marriage to the prophet Elizabeth Avery. And in 1650 Thomas Parker and the Woodbridge brothers were, records indicate, instrumental in the contrasting reception of Bradstreet's and Avery's writings.

In 1646 Thomas Parker's *The Visions and Prophecies of Daniel Expounded* was published in England. The next year his sister, Elizabeth Avery of Newbury in Berkshire, through our old friend Giles Calvert, published *Scripture-Prophecies Opened, Which are to be accomplished in these last times, which do attend the second coming of Christ; In several Letters Written to Christian Friends*. If Bradstreet wrote in relation to the unfolding pattern of Protestant history, what did prophetic scripture promise to her relative, Elizabeth Avery? Perhaps the same events prompted Avery to publish as had precipitated Jessey and Wight's circulation of *The exceeding Riches*. She links the 'arbitrary' 'Monarchical power' with the disappointing Parliament, recalling 'the violence done to the Saints' in the spring of 1647.[54] Avery refers explicitly to these in her first letter—addressed 'to some particular Christians'—on the subject of Babylon. 'Babylon and Antichrist', she tells us, 'is over all States which govern by an Arbitrary power, and over all Churches, whether National or others, and all worships, whether the worship of Heathens, or Antichristian Worship.' Indeed, 'Babylon is in the purest Worship that is most agreeable to the letter of the Word, because the Saints have no rule for what they practise in taking up the Ordinance.'[55] While her brother, Thomas Parker, regarded himself as *explicating* Daniel's prophecies, Elizabeth Avery saw herself a visionary prophet: she concludes her last letter, on the topic of the resurrection of the dead, 'the main thing God will speak by me at present'.[56] Avery's writings are most vividly informed by both millenarian and mystical interpretation

---

[53] See John Rogers, *Ohel or Beth-shemesh. A Tabernacle for the Sun: Irenicum Evangelicum. An Idea of Church Discipline* (London, 1653), pp. 402–3. In a marginal note Rogers tells us: 'Mr *Parker* was her father, that able Duvine that writ *De Eccles. Polit.* So largely; but she married Master *Avery* a Commissary in *Ireland.*' On the church and presbytery at Newberry see *A History of New-England* (London, 1653), ch. 31, pp. 68–70.

[54] Avery, *Scripture-Prophecies Opened* (London: Giles Calvert, 1647), p. 15.

[55] Ibid., p. 2.

[56] Ibid., p. 36.

of the kind associated perhaps with Jacob Boehme, more obviously with familism, and Ranterism.[57] She writes of 'that vail of Darknesse which covers all flesh, *Isa*.25.7' and, although God promises to remove it, at present 'the spirit of Errour doth reside in the flesh more than ever, even in the Saints themselves as well as others'. Avery expresses the relationship between flesh and divinity in mystical locutions, such as 'Flesh must die, when God appeareth in it.' The nature of her expression may, possibly, suggest links to the circle which included the radical Abiezer Coppe: in 1647 Coppe (discussed in Chapter 4) was somewhere on his trajectory from Baptism towards radical, visionary Ranterism. He was collecting followers close to the area in which Elizabeth Avery lived.[58] On Monday, 18 September 1654 John Pordage, associate of Abiezer Coppe and Elizabeth Poole amongst many others—and whose mystical political circle was discussed in the last chapter—was required to appear at the Bear in Speenhamland near Newbury to give evidence to the commissioners for scandalous ministers. Pordage, who had been convening a circle of Boehmist mystics in Bradfield and who certainly was also associated with Diggers and other politicized protests, elicited both support and hatred from his local community. The first article against Pordage, exhibited in a paper, included the accusation that he had asserted '*the fiery deity of Christ mingleth, and mixeth itself with our flesh*'. Later in the proceedings the commissioners exasperatedly demand of Pordage, 'is *England* Babylon?'[59] While such linguistic resemblances are far from conclusive connections, the language attributed to Pordage is very like that of Avery in the 1647 prophecies. It is worth observing, too, that none other than Benjamin Woodbridge was an assistant to the commissioners against scandalous ministers—those who pursued Pordage.

---

[57] On the place of grace in antinomianism see Dewey D. Wallace, *Puritans and Predestination* (Chapel Hill: University of North Carolina, 1982), pp. 112–57; on Boehme see Nigel Smith, *Perfection Proclaimed: Language and Literature in English Radical Religion 1640–166* (Oxford: Clarendon Press, 1988), pp. 185–6; see also pp. 144–84; see also Manfred Brod, 'Dissent and Dissenters in Early Modern Berkshire', Diss., Oxford, 2002.

[58] Avery, *Scripture-Prophecies Opened*, pp. 1, 2–3, 5; *A Collection of Ranter Writings*, ed. Nigel Smith (London: Junction Books, 1983), p. 11.

[59] Christopher Fowler, *Daemonium Meridianum. Satan at Noon* (London, 1655), A2ʳ, pp. 166–7.

Benjamin Woodbridge, brother of Bradstreet's brother-in-law, was not an especially significant divine. He is, though, important in understanding the way in which political writing was gendered by the associates who sponsored *The Tenth Muse*—associates who were politically and spiritually linked, and, geographically, both close, even local, yet also Atlantic. Woodbridge's career suggests how this group might make the distinction between *The Tenth Muse* (Bradstreet's acceptable poems) and Avery's unacceptable, mystical prophecies which drew upon themselves the accusation of antinomianism. In 1649 Benjamin Woodbridge, rector of Newbury (Berkshire) wrote an introduction to his uncle's vituperative response to his sister's prophecies: *The Copy of a Letter Written by Mr Thomas Parker of Newbury New England to Elizabeth Avery* of 'Newbury in the County of Berks'. The letter is dated November 1648. In his introduction to his uncle's letter Woodbridge noted that John Cotton, John Wilson, and James Noyes (of Newberry, New England, Parker's cousin) had sent similar letters—supplying us with three other Atlantic connections.[60] In the body of the text Parker bellows at Avery: 'Why do you not then dictate Oracles immediately from Heaven?' '[Y]our printing of a Book', he tells her, 'beyond the custom of your Sex, doth rankly smell; but the exaltation of your self in the way of your Opinions, is above all.' Supplying a further suggestion that she is connected to Coppe or others, he begs her to 'cast off the Masters and Fomentors of your Heresies' even though '*It will be grievous to you to renounce that Society which hath furthered you in your new and horrid Opinions.*'[61] Parker writes that Avery 'will not come to Ordinances, nor willingly joyn in Private prayer with your own Husband, but onely condescend to his infirmities; for you say you are above Ordinances, above the word and Sacraments, yea above the Blood of Christ himself, living as a glorified Saint'. He sees her dividing herself from 'the glorious church of *New-Jerusalem*', taunting her with a comparison to the Apostles: 'Why do you not infallibly Prophesie of the Times? Why do you not work Miracles as they did?' He criticizes her poor reasoning and asserts, 'Let me tell you plainly, I doubt there was some grievous sin at bottom, as the Pride of Women, or Spiritual Pride . . . that

---

[60] Thomas Parker, *The Copy of a Letter Written by Mr Thomas Parker* (London, 1649), A2^r.

[61] Ibid., pp. 6, 13, 16.

God hath suffered you so horribly to fall away.' Ultimately, Parker wants to know where 'Is the Doctrine of your Reverend Father, and of Dr *Twisse*, and the Doctrine of the holy Martyrs?'[62] Dr William Twisse was the former rector of Newbury and could be described as a Presbyterian fifth monarchist and an associate of John Cotton. Philip Gura reminds us of Thomas Parker's 'open presbyterianism'.[63] Parker's invocation of Twisse returns us to the Woodbridge family in the years preceding the publication of *The Tenth Muse*: Benjamin Woodbridge's ministry in Newbury, Berkshire, in Dr Twisse's old parish, began on 18 May 1648. It combined encouragement to godly sobriety and controversy. As one of those who thought that the 'antinomians' pushed grace and predestination too far (as Dewey D. Wallace reminds us), Benjamin Woodbridge both wrote against the Antinomians and defended Richard Baxter against the charge of 'Arminian moralism'.[64] In 1652 he published *Justification by Faith: or, Confutation of that Antinomian Error, That Justification is before Faith*.

If Avery's detractors might be characterized as a group that emphasized church discipline—ordinances—but also grace, then Avery's own path was both disturbed and visionary. For example, in 1653 John Rogers published Elizabeth Avery's confession of her spiritual trajectory and conversion, given to his church in Dublin, including material on the loss of her children.[65] In her conversion narrative, Avery's account of her prophetic period discusses how 'I was in a *trance* for a while, but after I awakened *full of joy*; and yet for all this, I was somewhat under *bondage* (me thoughts) but the *Word* and *Means* of *Grace* did *confirm me* and *comfort me*.' She was 'brought out of *Egypt* into the *Wilderness*', 'for I had his *Spirit*, his *voice* speaking *within me*, and *God* alone was with me, and no *strange god*'. It was 'when the *wars* began to cease' that Avery experienced her greatest trouble 'for I had forgot how *God* had *taught* me within before'. In a carnal distortion of the bridal language of grace used in Song of Songs, she writes, 'Yet I *followed* and *hunted* after my *lovers*, having *mens persons in admiration*.' On Colonel Lambert's advice

---

[62] Thomas Parker, *The Copy of a Letter Written by Mr Thomas Parker* (London, 1649), pp. 15, 6–7, 10, 12.

[63] Gura, *A Glimpse of Sion's Glory*, pp. 131–2.

[64] Wallace, *Puritans and Predestination*, pp. 135–6, 146–7.

[65] Rogers, *Ohel*, pp. 402–3.

she went to Oxford, possibly while he was briefly governor there in
1646. She 'heard *their disputes* between Master *Kiffin* and others, very
hot, but saw nothing of God there'. It is this, in the end, which prefaces
a conversion:[66]

Then I *writ down* what *God* had *done* for me, and *writ* about it to *my friends*; but
yet I was *struck* in the *flesh* again, *which I wonder at*; and then I heard *the voice*
again say, *It was sin that was suffering in me, and the flesh as the punishment of sin*;
and so I *found* it was, for the *destruction* of the *flesh*; and ever after that *I found
Christ in me*, ruling and reigning, and taking *all power to himself*, and he hath
caught the *man-childe* up to God, which I brought forth. *i.e. The flesh* (by his
incarnation) and *I have found* in me (and do yet) his *judgement-seat fit*, to *judge*
and *sentence sin*, and *lust* and *corruption*, and his *throne* is there for *himself* to *sit*,
and to *rule* by his own *Laws*:[67]

This language, markedly like that of the prophecies, invokes mystical
incarnation, infusion of spirit into flesh to express union with God. It may
well be coincidence that in 1654 the fifth article against Newbury's local
mystic, John Pordage, concerned his interpretation of Genesis: '*That by
male, and female* Genesis the 1. *we are to understand by male, the Deity, and
by female, the humanity, and therefore that these two become one flesh.*'[68]
Nevertheless, the claim of Avery's language is mystical. Yet if the Atlantic
Presbyterianism of Noyes and Parker seems to have been articulated
differently from that found in England in the 1650s, Bradstreet's relative
Benjamin Woodbridge joined with Parker, John Cotton, John Wilson,
and James Noyes in condemning Elizabeth Avery, and the wider implications of their censure involves concern for church government.

What does all this evidence suggest about *The Tenth Muse* and the way
in which women were bound into political controversy? When we put
together writers about Bradstreet and Avery we find that probably two—
Benjamin Woodbridge and possibly John Wilson—wrote both in favour
of Bradstreet and against Avery. Benjamin Woodbridge (assuming he is
'B.W.'), his brother, John Woodbridge, and Nathaniel Ward provided
commendatory poems to *The Tenth Muse*. Elizabeth Wade White thinks
that John Wilson—cited in Benjamin Woodbridge's introduction as also
having written a letter against Elizabeth Avery—may well have composed

---

[66] Rogers, *Ohel*, pp. 403–4.   [67] Ibid., p. 405.
[68] Fowler, *Daemonium*, p. 33.

the commendatory anagram to *The Tenth Muse*.[69] H.S., she thinks, might be Henry Stubbs, whose patron, Henry Vane, sent him to Oxford.[70] It is tempting to speculate on some of the other initials to commendatory verses: could N.H. be the Nathaniel Holmes or Homes on whose work Henry Jessey drew in interpreting Sarah Wight's words? An even longer shot, could R.Q., who seems to write as a labouring man, and who writes on time, be Richard Quelch, a clockmaker from the same area?[71] Certainly, N.H. picks up the question of the fifth monarchy, describing the 'divine and lucid light' which 'Revives all things so obvious now to th' eye', that the reader 'Shall see what's done in all the world before'.[72] However, as the classical inflection of most of the commendatory verses makes clear *The Tenth Muse* was sent into the world as an aesthetic, not a prophetic, achievement. Further research is needed.

A comparison between Parker's and Woodbridge's reactions to Bradstreet and to Avery makes clear the literary and religious culture of a group of influential Puritans whose very Atlantic formation indicates that Bradstreet was not isolated. There existed in New England in the 1630s and 1640s a group of those who emphasized free grace and were 'avid millennialists', hard at work for the second coming. The historiography of New England, Janice Knight argues, has marginalized this group; she reminds us of the literary and linguistic implications of these views and the importance of a millennial literary culture in New England. Like other writers in or connected to this culture, Bradstreet's *Tenth Muse* and its New England commendors blend classical and religious ideas.[73] The fifth monarchist inflection of Bradstreet's poetry and the political impetus of its millenarianism was welcome, indeed apparently familiar and acceptable, within their circles. Any serious consideration of Bradstreet's poems themselves makes it obvious why

[69] Wade White seems to think that John Wilson might have composed the anagram *Anna Bradstreate* (*Bradstreet*, p. 266). Harold Stein Jantz thinks John Wilson may have composed the anagrams to *Tenth Muse*. *The First Century of New England Verse*, American Antiquarian Society Proceedings 53, pt. 2 (Worcester: American Antiquarian Society, 1882), pp. 14–15, 30–3, 496.

[70] Wade White, *Bradstreet*, pp. 264–5.

[71] Capp, *The Fifth Monarchy Men*, pp. 51, 94, 104, 260.

[72] 'In Praise of the author, Mistress Anne Bradstreet, Virtues True and lively Pattern, Wife of the Worshipful Simon Bradstreet Esq., At Present Residing in the Occidental Parts of the World in America, Alias Nov-Anglia', *Tenth Muse*, A7ʳ.

[73] Knight, *Orthodoxies*, pp. 3–4.

John Woodbridge, seeing in them religious and political as well as aesthetic value, would understand them as finding their moment for publication in 1650. Social decorum, discipline, and millenarian ideas were linked in such a grouping.

The 'public' arena of print, as interpreted by the New England and English Woodbridges, can, evidently, tolerate secular publication by women. But our understanding of what that publication meant is brought to life when we find the same group that commended Bradstreet attacking her aunt by marriage. The countervailing example of Elizabeth Avery and her treatment shows us, very precisely, the religious and political limits of this religio-political grouping, borders which are made explicit in Avery's transgression of them. Setting mystical language against reason, revelation against exegesis, and emphasizing grace over discipline, Avery's language, even as it envisioned the radical transformation of England, did not—for Parker or Woodbridge—speak truth to Christians. Their reaction to the prophecies suggests, by reverse, what they liked about Bradstreet. The comparison gives an insight into the politics of the publication of *The Tenth Muse* in 1650, at a high point of millenarianism. It would be speculation to suggest that the printing of *The Tenth Muse* in the same year as Parker's attack on his sister offers a positive model of feminine publication—rational, religious, politically informed, and learned—which deliberately counters Avery's perceived antinomianism. Intentional or not, though, the interconnection of these texts published between 1647 and 1650 reveals the ways in which women might, and might not, build their relationship to politics and the millennium. Bradstreet's poems claim political and aesthetic space. Set against the prophecies of Elizabeth Avery some of the boundaries to that space come into view, and they are religious and political limits as well as limits of gender. For this group, it seems, prophecy and poetry are distinct, and prophetic interpretation (as undertaken by Avery's brother and condemner) is different again from experiential prophecy.

The contrasting receptions of Bradstreet and Avery suggest that Avery transgressed a decorum concerning the linking of religious and political time: Avery puts herself at the centre of a drama of revelation whereas Bradstreet gives a carefully historicized narrative of the succeeding monarchies. Aesthetic achievement was, it seems, infinitely more welcome than the refusal of forms and ordinances. We can see a religious and literary public sphere at play in the reception of the two texts by the readers we can trace, and these readers tell us, explicitly, why one is good, one bad. The context of either strong or more diffuse fifth monarchist thought meant that both *Scripture-Prophecies* and *The Tenth Muse* made, and were understood by readers as making, political interventions. Bradstreet takes care to eschew prophecy, emphasizing the difficulty of the interpretation of the fourth and fifth monarchies. The contrast between these two texts allows us to see more clearly—*pace* Rich—the way that Bradstreet's published volume engages with ideas at the very heart of the political issues of the Civil War. We can see in Bradstreet's engagement with poetic genres, and her building up from elements and humours to a typologically Protestant present, the potential of poetry as situated between the aesthetic, religious, and political in a way that permits Bradstreet, at least, to engage with political issues absolutely throughout the volume.

It seems, then, that Bradstreet's disciplined use of reason, engagement with old and New England, and emphasis on proper church discipline, form, and general decorum was approved by the family, whereas the New and old England Woodbridges and Parkers found Elizabeth Avery's insistence on grace, self-reliance, and revelation dangerously antinomian. Her writings called for and received printed denunciation. While the pattern that emerges here is not exactly surprising, given the ever-reviving fear of antinomianism in New England, it is significant in offering contexts for the reception of *The Tenth Muse*. It makes clear that *The Tenth Muse*, amongst other things, was considered politicized poetry. And if we already knew that Bradstreet's relatively secular volume was acceptable to, indeed sponsored by, this section of the New England elite, our increased recognition of the depth of its political import tells us more about the significance of that acceptance: the controversial publication context of *The Tenth Muse* gives new body to our understanding of it as politically charged. We can see the volume is endorsed by some English millenarians as well as the New England elite. And the simultaneous condemnation of Avery shows the nature of a certain literary, religious, and political formation: women in the Woodbridge family can be political writers but not visionaries. This, in turn, suggests that a literary-political sphere existed between the old and New Englands and that women were sometimes participants. In this case, too, the old chestnut that it is 'safer' for women to write in religious than

secular-political modes is far from true: it is Bradstreet's views, the
political cast of her writing, and the claims of poetry that stimulate
admiration.

It could be argued that Bradstreet may have had little or no control
over *The Tenth Muse*. However, the 1650 arrangement is wholly logical,
using genre and topic to shape a reader's consciousness of the historical
patterns, and the present importance of reforming Protestant
poetics, and to articulate the different responses of old and new worlds
to the Civil War. Bradstreet's poems themselves, written in the New
England context, might not appeal to post-Romantic sensibilities, as
Rich and other commentators rather relentlessly tell us, but they are not
nostalgic revisions. On the contrary, they evidently engage with ways of
thinking and genres current in the metropolis in which they were
published and current in old and new worlds. They relate old England's
cataclysm to New England by contrasting the two and by implying that
New England is the inheritor of a true Protestant tradition. Moreover,
the *Tenth Muse* does consistently attempt to mediate the relationship
between European history (a category indissoluble from literary and
religious traditions) and her place in a new world.[74] In aligning the
Parliament, Protestant rule, and poetics with the rejuvenated Protestantism of New England *The Tenth Muse* advertises that literary form is
always a political as well as an aesthetic choice. In *The Tenth Muse*
history offers a chance to reinterpret and annex the past, and to understand the present for, in Raleigh's words, history 'hath triumphed over
time, which besides it nothing but eternity hath triumphed over'.[75]

While critical commentators tend to see Bradstreet as concerned for
the cause of true Protestantism, yet, drawing back from regicide and
deep criticism of the Stuarts, there is much evidence in *The Tenth Muse*
that Bradstreet embraces a critical attitude to monarchs encouraging
'Romish clergy'; 'The Four Monarchies' is, clearly, critical not only of
Rome but of the degenerative potential of monarchy. A sharper contrast,
in the New England context, is perhaps with antinomianism as recalled
from the 1630s and as found, by Bradstreet's circle, in Elizabeth
Avery. That Bradstreet was understood by contemporaries as attacking

---

[74] See Myra Jehlen, *American Incarnation: The Individual, the Nation, and the Continent* (Cambridge, Mass.: Harvard University Press, 1986), p. 5.
[75] Raleigh, *History of the World*, preface, A2ᵛ.

monarchs who fail to support Protestantism is suggested by some of the alterations to the reprinted text of *The Tenth Muse*.[76] Bradstreet's poetry offers an image of Protestantism in crisis, but her consideration of this crisis from her position in a new world, which offers some answers to some of the problems of the old, puts her in a different position from English poets. Lucy Hutchinson, to whom I shall now turn, was pressed by circumstances to look to the future of English Protestantism and, although at immense personal cost, she consistently saw it as bound up with the potential of republicanism in England.

LUCY HUTCHINSON: POETRY, POLITICS, AND MOURNING

Lucy Hutchinson is relatively unusual because of her deep and rigorous engagement with the materials of elite masculine culture. Hutchinson, the wife of the parliamentarian, soldier, and republican John Hutchinson, whose political opinions she shared, contrasts with Bradstreet in that most of her extensive writings—including the well-known life of her husband, her translation of Lucretius, her own life, advice to her daughter, poetry, and notebooks—remained in manuscript throughout her life.[77] In these writings, amongst many other things, we can trace Hutchinson's analysis of the relationships between politics, gender, and poetry. Her voiced distaste for feminine transgression and her apparently self-effacing self-presentation as narrator of the life of her husband have led to her being seen as an obedient wife. However, as Neil Keeble has rightly noted, Hutchinson's submissive persona coexists with highly opinionated narration in the *Memoirs* of her husband.[78] Similar paradoxes mark some of her poetry; Hutchinson did not allow her identity as a modest wife to

[76] Wade White, *Bradstreet*, p. 246.

[77] See Margaret W. Ferguson, 'Renaissance Concepts of the "Woman Writer"', in *Women and Literature in Britain*, ed. Helen Wilcox (Cambridge: Cambridge University Press, 1996), pp. 143–68. See Lucy Hutchinson, *On the Principles of the Christian Religion, Addressed to her Daughter* (London: Longman, Hurst, Rees, Orme & Brown, 1817); *Lucy Hutchinson's Translation of Lucretius' De rerum natura*, ed. Hugh de Quehen (London: Duckworth, 1996). On print and manuscript see Arthur Marotti, *Manuscript, Print, and the English Renaissance Lyric* (Ithaca: Cornell University Press, 1995).

[78] Lucy Hutchinson, *Memoirs of the Life of Colonel Hutchinson*, ed. N. H. Keeble (London: Everyman, 1995), pp. xxiv–xxvi. See also *Memoirs of the Life of Colonel Hutchinson*, ed. James Sutherland (London: Oxford University Press, 1973), p. xviii.

inhibit her use of highly politicized cultural forms, from her translation of
Lucretius to history, memoir, elegy, and satire. Hutchinson's understanding of proper femininity clearly affected her religious and political writings in complex ways. For example, she first claimed and then repudiated
Epicurean ideas. At some point in the Interregnum she translated *De
rerum natura*, with its claim that 'by no designe | The world was made,
but moving atoms hitt | On that conjunction which produced it'.[79]
While earlier some had argued, indeed, that the idea of creation from
atoms was more readily Christianized than the idea of humours, an
interest in Epicurus or Lucretius was also a strong cultural marker; at
the Restoration such positions were associated with the likes of John
Wilmot, Earl of Rochester, or the translator of Lucretius, Thomas
Creech: Lucretius was, Hutchinson tells her patron, no proper topic for
female skill.[80] However, that Hutchinson did first make and then repudiate her translation—while preserving it—indicates the depth of her
involvement with processes of political transformation and the changing
Calvinist cultures of the 1650s and nonconformist 1660s and 1670s. Just
as in *The Tenth Muse* Bradstreet imagines a world built up from the
elements and humours to the most sophisticated, if catastrophic, political
systems, so Lucy Hutchinson's engagement with creation from atoms is
articulated with her political ideals in complex ways. Hutchinson required that she be taken seriously; she hated the idea that as a Calvinist she
might be satirized as a 'Puritan'. Where atheism implies libertinism,
Puritanism spoke of hypocrisy.[81] As we might expect, Hutchinson's
complex attitudes mark her poetry.

Much work has now been done on the way this paradoxical figure
strove to integrate her Epicurean reading with providential Calvinism.[82]
Here the focus is on her own poems possibly written in the 1650s and her
Restoration elegies. For between her translation of Lucretius and her long

[79] *Lucy Hutchinson's Translation of Lucretius*, ed. de Quehen, bk. I, p. 29; Reid
Barbour, 'Between Atoms and Spirits: Lucy Hutchinson's Translation of Lucretius',
Renaissance Papers (1994), pp. 1–16: 1.

[80] Reid Barbour, 'Lucy Hutchinson, Atomism and the Atheist Dog', in *Women,
Science and Medicine 1500–1700*, ed. Lynette Hunter and Sarah Hutton (Stroud: Sutton,
1997), pp. 122–37: 129.

[81] Reid Barbour, *English Epicures and Stoics* (Amherst: University of Massachusetts
Press, 1998), pp. 240–68.

[82] See N. H. Keeble, '"The Colonel's Shadow": Lucy Hutchinson, Women's Writing
and the Civil War', in *Literature and the English Civil War*, ed. Thomas Healy and
Jonathan Sawday (Cambridge: Cambridge University Press, 1990), pp. 227–47.

poem on the Christian creation myth, *Order and Disorder*, Hutchinson wrote poems that vividly chart women's relationship to politics. The poems she wrote in the 1650s and after the death of her husband show her analysing the personal and political implications of her changing relationship to public good and her ability to lead a good life, as she inhabits shifting forms of religious retirement. In their sophisticated, and unresolved, canvassing of political identity Hutchinson's poems show her using, refusing, and rebuilding the available political languages.

Huchinson's writings come to us mainly in manuscript. However, she certainly took part in the internecine poetic controversies of the 1650s. Indeed, bound to the various circumstances of social life, the manu-script circulation of poetry cannot be understood as simply private.[83] Hutchinson wrote a satirical riposte to Edmund Waller's 'A Panegyrick to my Lord Protector', a poem which she copied into her commonplace book, the survival of which enables us to trace her procedures as a writer.[84] When Cromwell seized power in 1653 it was a blow to both royalists and those who had fought for, or who believed in, a radical change of government. Waller, however, chose to greet the Protector as a military leader, close to Caesar and to Augustus, protecting the war-torn English from their own internecine quarrels: 'with a strong, and yet a gentle hand | You bridle faction, and our hearts command'.[85] Such a characterization of Cromwell as rescuer, builder of national unity, and military hero was guaranteed to infuriate opponents of the Protectorate. A royalist reply, *The Anti-Panegyrike Answering the Panegyrike*, parodied Waller's poem stanza by stanza. Another response, probably by Hutch-inson, uses the same technique:[86]

> Whilst with a smooth yet a servile Tongue
> You Court all Factions, and have sweetly sung
> The Triumphs of yo[r] Countreys Overthrow
> Raysing the Glory of her treacherous Foe.[87]

[83] Marotti, *Manuscript, Print, and the English Renaissance Lyric*, pp. 1–2.

[84] David Norbrook, 'Lucy Hutchinson versus Edmund Waller: An Unpublished Reply to Waller's "A Panegyrick to my Lord Protector"', *The Seventeenth Century*, 11, No. 1 (1996), pp. 61–86. See also *Lucy Hutchinson's Translation of Lucretius*, ed. de Quehen, pp. 6–7; *Order and Disorder*, ed. Norbrook, pp. xii–lii.

[85] Norbrook, *Writing the English Republic*, p. 306.

[86] *The Anti-Panegyrike Answering the Panegyrike* (n.p., 1655).

[87] 'To Mr Waller upon his Panegirique to the Lord Protector', printed in Norbrook, 'Lucy Hutchinson versus Edmund Waller', pp. 73–85.

The royalist attack begins with its focus on Cromwell, but Hutchinson has Waller in her sights, particularly the treacherous servility with which he has deployed his 'sweet' and 'smooth' poetic style. Hutchinson's response to Waller shows her poetic character—she is acid, adroit, and attacks her opponents on the terrain of their politicized vocabulary. Her poem also indicates the importance of circulated manuscript satire, as well as the ways in which print and manuscript overlapped. In many politicized manuscript texts the idea of, or desire for, 'privacy' is in tension with the drive for publication. Manuscript satire, Harold Love reminds us, functioned as 'privileged information'; bound into patronage relations and connections amongst near social equals, circulated manuscripts can be considered a kind of delimited publication—both making known and attempting to control who knows.[88] In the 1640s and 1650s Hutchinson used classical texts as active agents in her literary and political production and, as here, a favoured technique was to expose as false the languages of those she opposes.[89]

For poets of the Commonwealth and Protectorate the implications of pastoral retreat, often implying an enforced retirement from political affairs as much as a retreat to the good life, were mediated by Horace—himself an admirer of Epicurus.[90] Hutchinson analyses retirement in a poem which clearly engages with many of the tropes of pastoral poetry of the 1630s, particularly Ben Jonson's 'To Penshurst', where the virtuous man is represented as lord of his manor.[91] The poem becomes a study in the psychology of ambition and kingly power, and in the possibilities of finding within available poetic languages an analysis of power relations. It opens:

> All sorts of men through various labours press
> To the same end, contented quietness;

[88] Harold Love, *The Culture and Commerce of Texts: Scribal Publication in Seventeenth-Century England* (1993; repr. Amherst: University of Massachusetts Press, 1998), pp. 177–242 and *passim*. See also Marotti, *Manuscript, Print, and the English Renaissance Lyric*, pp. 82–94.

[89] See Norbrook, 'Lucy Hutchinson versus Edmund Waller', p. 63; commonplace book, Nottinghamshire Archives DDHU1, fos. 251–8. Significantly, the book also includes long passages from royalist appropriations of Virgil: John Denham's *The Destruction of Troy* (1656) and Sidney Godolphin's *The Passion of Dido for Aeneas* (1658).

[90] See e.g. Norman Wentworth DeWitt, *Epicurus and his Philosophy* (Minneapolis: University of Minnesota Press, 1954), pp. 298, 300.

[91] Printed in *Memoirs*, ed. Keeble, pp. 389–40. See Loxley, *Royalism*, pp. 202–3.

> Great princes vex their labouring thoughts to be
> Possessed of an unbounded sovereignty;
> The hardy soldier doth all toils sustain
> That he may conquer first, and after reign;

Enumerating the desires of the king, soldier, and merchant who 'ploughs the angry seas', Hutchinson replaces pastoral's emphasis on the willingness of the natural world to give up its fruits with an idea of labour. The opening, while invoking Georgic poetry with its emphasis on country labour in terms such as 'ploughs', directs the reader's attention to work and worldly endeavour as predominantly concerned with power, particularly over others ('sovereignty', 'reign'), expansion of the self at cost to others, producing unequal relations, and empire, in the broad sense. The 'restless passions' of the 'court hung round with flaring lights' foster desires, nightmares, and a system of psychic and economic bondage:

> Ambition doth incessantly aspire,
> And each advance leads on to new desire;
> Nor yet can riches av'rice satisfy,
> For want and wealth together multiply:
> Nor can voluptuous men more fulness find,
> For enjoyed pleasures leave their stings behind.
> He's only rich who knows no want; he reigns
> Whose will no severe tyranny constrains;

Firmly located in the experience of the courtier, the poem delineates the psychology of courtship as a treadmill of desire, while also deftly gesturing outwards, beyond the court. '[W]ant and wealth together multiply' in the desires of the ambitious subject, but also, literally, in the accumulation of wealth by individuals. In accord with the poem's questioning pursuit of power relations, its earlier claim that 'only private lives are free from care' is given an explicit contextualization:

> He's only rich who knows no want; he reigns
> Whose will no severe tyranny constrains;
> And he alone possesseth true delight
> Whose spotless soul no guilty fears affright.
> This freedom in the country life is found,
> Where innocence and safe delights abound.
> Here man's a prince; his subjects ne'er repine

> When on his back their wealthy fleeces shine:
> If for his appetite the fattest die,
> Those who survive will raise no mutiny:
> His table is with home-got dainties crowned,
> With friends, not flatterers, encompassed round;
> No spies nor traitors on his trencher wait,
> Nor is his mirth confined to rules of state;

The language of rule, 'reigns', is redescribed in terms of freedom from tyrannous constraint, and rule over others is replaced by temperate self-rule within a medical and political economy of equal, perhaps fraternal, relations—'friends, not flatterers'. Although it is clear that republicanism, for Hutchinson, implies patrician estate management as an aspect of noble virtue—her representation of country rule is hardly a levelling vision—yet within the wider political framework actual rule is problematic: the 'spotless soul', for Hutchinson, can legitimately rule over—sheep. The boundary between men and animals, and God's decree that animals exist for men, for Hutchinson set the absolute bounds of human dominion; but to be subject to another is to be constrained by 'tyranny', to be willingly so subject is to be not only a servant but, like Waller, 'servile'.

Profoundly disillusioned by the Protector's seizure of power, John Hutchinson had spent the Protectorate in retirement at Owthorpe. Critical opinion dates the poem from this period or, perhaps a less likely moment, from the time of his retirement at the Restoration. The poem's probable context, therefore, alerts us to the likelihood that Hutchinson's apparently simple poem engages with the different interpreters of Horace. Sir Richard Fanshawe, probably the best-known English translator of Horace, was pro-Stuart and used Horace in a poem supporting Charles I, in 1630.[92] Fanshawe published translations of Horace in 1647 and in the 1648 volume of *Il Pastor Fido*. Following the translation of two of Horace's odes on Rome's civil wars, Fanshawe's 'Summary Discourse of the Civill Wars of *Rome*' (dedicated 'To the Prince His Highnesse') describes Horace: 'this same despairing *Horace* did live to see, and particularly to enjoy, other very different *times*, when the Common-wealth, after the defeat of *Mark Anthony* at the Battell of *Actium*, *being now quite tired out with civill Warres*,

---

[92] Norbrook, *Writing the English Republic*, pp. 65–6, 252.

submitted her selfe to the just and peacefull Scepter of the most Noble Augustus.[93] In 1652 Fanshawe published a selection from Horace, and his translation of the second epode was reprinted at the Restoration. However, using the 'Horatian Ode' to analyse Cromwell's position, Marvell explores a more enigmatic potential of Horace: his poem was so contentious that it was not published until 1776.[94]

Hutchinson's poem is apparently something of a pastiche and—partly for this reason—both puzzling and potentially illuminating of her poetic procedure. Her loose reworking of the idea of *beatus ille*, or 'happy man', seems to draw on a tradition of interpreting Horace as a moralist, one expressed in Casimere Sarbiewski's interpretations and translations. Maren-Sofie Rostvig has discussed the combination of classical Latin and the intensely religious, even Platonic, approach which characterized Casimire's poetry.[95] Humphry Moseley, the publisher of much royalist poetry, brought out a translated selection of his *Odes* (1646), but Hutchinson seems to have been reading him in the Latin—the epigram she translated in her commonplace book was not available in English.[96] The 1646 translation contains Casimire's palinode, or response to Horace's second epode: 'A Palinode *To the second Ode of the book of Epodes of* Q.H. Flaccus. *The praise of a Religious Recreation. Ode 3. Lib.Epod*'.[97] The poem, like Hutchinson's, contrasts court and country (Denham, contrastingly, compares city and country). In the 'dispers'd flock' Casimire Christianizes the various animals caught

---

[93] Sir Richard Fanshawe, *Il Pastor Fido, the faithfull Shepherd* (London, 1648), title page after p. 223 and p. 310. See also *The Poems and Translations of Sir Richard Fanshawe*, ed. Peter Davidson, 2 vols. (Oxford: Clarendon Press, 1997,1998), I, 139–40, II, 371.

[94] Sir Richard Fanshawe, *Selected Parts of Horace* (London, 1652), pp. 62–4; *The Poems of Horace Translated into English by several Persons* (London, 1666), pp. 155–9; includes Fanshawe's translation and 'A Paraphrase on the same'. See J.S., *The Lyrick Poet: Odes and Satyres Translated out of Horace into English Verse* (London, 1649). See also Luis de Camões, *The Lusiads*, trans. Richard Fanshawe (London, 1649), ed. Geoffrey Bullough (London: Centaur Press, 1963), pp. 37–53.

[95] Maren-Sofie Rostvig, *The Happy Man: Studies in the Metamorphoses of a Classical Ideal* (Oslo: Norwegian Universities Press, 1962), p. 79.

[96] Casimire Sarbiewski, *The Odes of Casimire*, trans. G. Hils (London, 1646). Lucy Hutchinson, commonplace book, fo. 206, translates 'XXXIV *Fortis est ut mors dilectio. Cant 8*', which can be found in *Mathie Casimiri Sarbievii. Lyricorum libri IV. Epodon Lib. unus alterq epigrammatum* (Antwerp, 1634), p. 182.

[97] Sarbiewski, *Odes*, p. 125.

in Horace's epode, lodging them in the conscience of a retired hermit. But it is in the use of light to figure distinct spiritual worlds that there seems to be a more direct analogy with Hutchinson's analysis of the happy man. The stars stand as a metaphor for the end of spiritual darkness, showing him how to redeem his soul:

> At evening when the harbinger of night
>   The torches of the sky doth light,
> How he admires th' immortall rayes breake forth,
>   And their bright Orbes, more large than earth;
> How through his trickling teares, he helps his sight,
>   Unto the open courts of light
> Which with thy selfe, o Christ, thy self in pray'r
>   He adores, t'Eternall life an heire!
> The Starres with golden wheels, are hurried by,
>   And let their prostrate exile lye...

Hutchinson's emphasis on light, contrasting the court 'hung round with flaring lights' and the 'bright constellations' which 'hang above' the head of the retired soul, may suggest her reading, or use, of Casimire's poem and more particularly her sympathy with his moral interpretation of Horace. In sum, Hutchinson's model of religious retirement in this poem adapts the Horatian ideal of a good life to that of Christian virtue. It continues her 1650s project of making classical languages of political behaviour Christian, and, in a significant sense, 'national'. Her Horatian and georgic language serves an evident purpose in putting a substantial and important mode of classical thought about virtue and retirement at the disposal of an overriding understanding of the world as lit by God's grace, ordered by his divine schema.

Hutchinson's Virgilian meditations and Horatian verses, though hardly her sole or main engagement with classical learning, are significant as part of the poetry she composed as opposed to that she translated. The engagement with Waller, the use of the ballad forms we find in her commonplace book, her engagement with pastoral all show her working to counter political positions and vocabularies. We see how closely intertwined are reading and writing for Hutchinson, and the ways in which she understands language as a resource of political identity. Hutchinson's close grappling with political and linguistic issues has implications for her character as a writer: her combative engagement with the rhetoric of others means that both her ability as poet (because parody and appropriation require an emulation which outdoes that which it is addressed against) and her political identity are at stake when she writes. The poems we have looked at show Hutchinson meditating, possibly in the 1650s, on key issues which, in Restoration material, she explores more fully and differently: the good life, religious retirement, public good. Central to her Restoration poetry and writing was the fate of the English Republic and that of her husband. But what happens to Hutchinson's contestatory poetic voice at the Restoration?

The Restoration transformed the political landscape. But it seems that from 1660 to 1662 changes seemed to contemporaries likely to be reconciliatory, or at least less cataclysmic than they later proved. A regicide and republican, Colonel Hutchinson nevertheless initially tried to make peace with the restored monarchy. When the Convention Parliament, of which Hutchinson was a member, met on 1 May 1660 and decided to recall the King, debates ensued on the trial of Charles I. A proclamation was issued requiring all regicides to surrender themselves. Soon after Charles II entered London on 29 May, Lucy Hutchinson sent a letter to the Speaker of the House of Commons and later the Colonel himself petitioned, setting in motion a train of events which resulted in his pardon and inclusion in the Act of Oblivion. However, despite his retirement to Owthorpe, in 1663 Hutchinson was arrested and conveyed to the Tower on suspicion of conspiracy. He died in September 1664 in the wrecked and unhealthy Sandown Castle, on the coast of Kent. Lucy Hutchinson's surviving writing from the period of his death attempts to interpret the defeat of the republic, to understand how the decadent Stuart monarchy might have been allowed to triumph, to shape her husband's image as a republican patriot, and to submit herself to God's incomprehensible providence. The famous *Life* was central in this endeavour, and in writing the Colonel's life Hutchinson works to maintain coincidence between republican and religious virtue so that, as is often remarked, the Colonel is represented as a paragon of all human perfection. The elegies, contrastingly, explore a different kind of political memory: they focus substantially on the elegist or writing subject, and explicitly address the dual crises of Restoration and death. By the time Hutchinson came to write these poems she had every reason to despair: 'Sorrow age death rewin' had, she wrote, left her 'a dimme expiring snuffe'.[98] If Bradstreet's elegies in *The Tenth Muse* (1650) publicly memorialize and revive a Protestant past which still has promise, Hutchinson's lament the lost Republic.

Hutchinson's attempts to reconcile the fact of the Restoration, providential history, personal humiliation, and despair expose some explosive tensions: God had permitted the defeat of the Republic, and of her husband, and he looked down on her own misery. The form of the elegy is used to confront, simultaneously, the implications of mourning for the elegist, the ideal life, political memory, and providence.[99] In these elegies, written up in another's hand in a manuscript book, we can trace Lucy Hutchinson's attempt to build a poetic monument to her husband and to rebuild an operative political poetic vocabulary. How was the image of her husband as virtuous republican patriot, fashioned for the next season of political struggle, to be reconciled to her own situation?

'Leave of yee pittying friends; leave of in vaine | Doe you perswade ye dead to live againe' (ll. 1–2).[100] So opens the first elegy. Their comforts are pointless because 'not he; twas only I That died' (l. 4). The opening discussion distinguishes worldly love and divine union by literalizing the earthly as deathly. It presents the earthly and the spiritual worlds as inverted images, reversing the positions of living and dead:

> In That Cold Grave which his deare reliques keepes
> My light is quite extinct where he but sleepes
> My substance into ye dark vault was laide
> And now I am my owne pale Empty Shade
> If this y:^{r} mirth or admiration moove
> Know tis but the least meracle of Love
> The effect of humane Passion such as mine
> Which ends in woe & death:
>
> (ll. 5–12)

---

[98] David Norbrook, 'Lucy Hutchinson's "Elegies" and the Situation of the Republican Woman Writer (with Text)', *ELR* 27, No. 3 (1997), pp. 468–521: Elegy 11, 'On my Visitt to W.S. w:ch I dreamt of That Night' (p. 508, ll. 40, 28). I have emended *i* to *u* and *j* to *v*. References to Elegies below give poem number and page number in this edition.

[99] 'Elegies', p. 471.

[100] 'Elegies' 1 (pp. 487–8).

The elegist's passion 'ends in woe and death' but the colonel's 'Love devine'(l. 12) has 'Maide Carnall reason freely to lay downe' the symbols of her rule—'her Scepture & her Crowne' (ll. 21–2). The Colonel disciplines 'rebell sence' (l. 20) so that, though in prison he is free: 'Despising his oppressors rage while They | By lusts enslavd in Sadder [Thralldome] lay' (ll. 54–6). The imagined rejection of earthly delights enables the colonel to give 'Calamity a lovely face | And put on honours Crowne upon disgrace' (ll. 61–2), but it leaves the elegist an unredeemed ghost. Giving a forceful articulation of John Hutchinson's project as fulfilled despite his enemies, but also evoking the psychic— and political—displacement of widowhood, this elegy initiates one of the sequence's main dynamics.

If the reader of the 'Elegies' recognizes Lucy Hutchinson's strong republican politics this is in tension with a sense of personal despair: political martyrdom is accompanied by a distinct crisis of poetic voice. For instance, 'To the Sun Shineing into her Cham:'' uses both the 'Bright [day] starre' (l. 1) (suggesting hope) and, unusually, the sun to illuminate the elegist's political and personal darkness. Addressing the sun, Hutchinson writes about light in a way directly related to the ruin of political fortunes:

> Thou Sawest my Desolation made
> And Comest Thou now my rewin to upbrade
> Let me and my Just greifes alone
> Goe guild ye tyrants bloody Throne
> Cast lustre on The Strumpets face
> Reveale Their glories in full grace
> And lett The Greate ones by Thy Light
> Act crymes w:^{ch} Used to black the Night... [101]

The sun is ambiguous here. It does suggest the light of divine truth, able to illuminate like plain day the sexual and political crimes of the 'tyrant' and his mistresses. Yet, paradoxically it is a warming sun which Hutchinson begs will 'keepe away' from her 'Secret' tears, 'silent Streames'. The colonel's death and the Restoration are public and political calamities whose significances eclipse the mourner's desire for secret tears, private consolation—she is 'Wayling a *Publick* funerall'.

---

[101] 'Elegies' 2 (p. 489).

The sun, suggesting the public nature of calamity, frustrates the desire for private mourning. At the same time, the very open daylight in which acts that she sees as criminal—the dispatching of 'Noble Patriots' to 'Prison and Exile'—leaves her struggling to assert an opposed justice which is forced by circumstances to seem like darkness and conspiracy. Perhaps the poem also echoes John Donne's more familiar bid for darkness in 'The Sunne Rising'.[102] In Donne's poem political vocabulary is established in order to be collapsed into the erotic intimacy and dominion of the bed—'Aske for those Kings whom thou saw'st yesterday, | And thou shalt heare, All here in one bed lay' (ll. 19–20). Hutchinson's poem reverses this strategy, banishing the sun from the bedroom to the public and political world. Sharing some of the sexual urgency of the Donne, as well as evoking a political world, this poem suggests a 'desolation' which is sexual as well as private and political. Exposed by the open way in which the 'unthankfull Land' has transformed patriots into criminals, Hutchinson is also struggling with the way the public nature of that change is in itself part of the Restoration regime's claim to justice. The end of the patriots, not just Hutchinson, is a 'public funeral' because of the very public way in which they are removed, yet that very publicness, the wrong kind of ritual, inhibits both personal and political mourning. As in the Horatian 'Verses', in the elegies the use of light and dark suggests complex connections between political and spiritual concerns. Light at times signals spiritual comfort, even at times her husband, but at times the royalist image of the sun suggests the problematic Restoration regime.[103] Yet the very mobility of the implications of light within the sequence of elegies indicates (and is used to signal) the depth of the crisis in the moralization of images which mark the elegies.

The triad 'Upon two pictures one a Gallant man dressed up in Armour The other y:ᵉ Same Honorable P'son looking Through a Prison Greate & leaning on a Bible' takes two images of John Hutchinson as a way to canvass the nature of the well-lived life in relation to public and

---

[102] Donne, *Poetical Works*, ed. Herbert J. C. Grierson (1971: repr. Oxford: Oxford University Press, 1977), p. 10.

[103] 'Another Night': 'Elegies' 9 (p. 503); 'On the Spring 1668': 'Elegies' 14, l. 25 (p. 513). For an incisive discussion of Hutchinson's use of light and dark in terms of mystical and earthly union see Erica Longfellow, *Women and Religious Writing in Early Modern England* (Cambridge: Cambridge University Press, 2004), pp. 192–4.

spiritual good and the subject's own relation to these.[104] The first poem traces John Hutchinson from his military career (when he wore 'killing weapons', 'Not to destroy but to Restore' (ll. 9–10)) to his greater triumph over 'Prison and death' (l. 3). Using techniques we saw in Hutchinson's response to Waller, these poems clearly endeavour to re-evaluate the ideologically freighted vocabulary of Restoration. We see John Hutchinson's portrait in armour:

> The table you here See presents
> A true-borne Princes Lyneaments
> No Vulgar hands sett on his Crowne
> Nor could they cast his Empire downe
> Whose Soule [Stoopt] not to servile Things
> But triumpht over foyld Kings . . .
>
> (ll. 2–6)

John Hutchinson's self-government can be seen as true empire, not that of kings: 'Temperance was leiftenant of ye tower | Who Captive kept ye Passions rebel Power' (ll. 29–30). Self-government as key to active virtue is given its political meaning when 'tirannique powr' with 'violence' 'Ore flowed his Native land' to precipitate his courageous 'Victorie' and then his kindness to foes, 'Releiving vanquisht foes who prostrate lay' (ll. 45–6, 55–6). Moreover, his attempt to 'Restore' the subject's liberties works by opposites to imply the destructive qualities of the 'Restoration' of the Stuarts. In the other picture, imagining political defeat, the Bible with which he is pictured contains a world of virtue. It:

> Brings to his viue old Prophetts martyred Saints
> Shewes him his one returne from gredy death
> His foes Consumed by Gods fiery streaming breath . . .
>
> (ll. 27–9)

In 'Opening' God's 'grace' to Hutchinson the Bible 'Swallowes up ye horrors of The place' (ll. 31–2) and, unusually in the 'Elegies', Lucy Hutchinson is willing to invoke the greater schema of God's providence—even the promise of the prophetic books so important in the 1640s and under the Protectorate. The poem very deliberately engulfs human time (and suffering) in divine time which, though in

---

[104] See 'Elegies' 4, 5, and 6 (pp. 494–8).

the present offering but little comfort to benighted humans, does come with a promise which it is the task of humans to truly apprehend and which can be felt in 'grace' (l. 31) and 'love' (l. 33). Asserting John Hutchinson's 'patient meekness' (l. 41) as divinely sanctioned—something close to martyrdom, but more vengefully expressed—the poem finds him 'Spite of his foes Crownd in his funeral' (l. 55). The three poems indicate the way in which Hutchinson's need to deal with the morality or otherwise of her husband's taking up arms in civil war is changed by the Restoration and moulded by the genre of elegy. Defence of participation in civil war is encapsulated in justification of the individual and the poems, while implying John Hutchinson's virtuous heroism, resolve the moral problem of participation in war with recourse to her husband's Christian virtues. The good life and public good are put in a different relationship by the Civil War struggles being in the past.

One elegy, 'To the Gardin' at Owethorpe, takes the reader into the terrain of Epicurus—his school was said to have been established in a garden—in order to mourn its master.[105] This poem again characterizes John Hutchinson as her teacher of virtue and learning; here he 'planted in me all y:ᵗ yelded prayse' (ll. 3, 14). Evidently blending Christian and Epicurean associations, the poem's characterization of the garden as itself available for reuse by 'Annother Gardiner' in 'another Spring' (l. 35) contrasts with the elegist's self-description as a tree 'dead at roote' (l. 40). It seems that Epicurean as much as Christian consolation fails the poetic subject. In a later epitaph, Hutchinson condenses philo-sophical and political points more coherently. The 'Consecreated Attomes treasured' are of one who:

> ... his whole life one fixt designe pursued
> T'advance Gods glory and the Publique good
> His Acts & Sufferings both w:ᵗʰ Victory crownd
> From heaven equall testimony found...
>
> (ll. 7–10)[106]

Moreover, she asserts 'Nor yet can his descendants wholly fall | Exalted still in Their Originall' (ll. 23–4). The epitaphs memorialize a 'great Patriot' (l. 1).[107] Here, Hutchinson's tendentious revaluation of

---

[105] 'Elegies' 7, 'To the Gardin att O' (pp. 499–500).
[106] 'an Epitaph', 'Elegies' 15 (p. 515).
[107] 'Elegies' 16 (p. 516).

Restoration political language coexists with what seems to be an attempt to integrate her earlier philosophical and political interests into the writing of mourning.[108] However, the vision of mourning as a successful integration and a turn to the future ('descendants') is short-lived—not only is the marble certainty of epitaph undermined by several other elegies, but in the arrangement we have it gives way to final poems of extreme doubt. So, if the elegies do build a monument for their object, John Hutchinson, how do they work to shape a political language and identity for their subject?

As Reid Barbour suggests, the Restoration changed Lucy Hutchinson's relationship with the classical authors with whom she had earlier engaged, particularly Lucretius. She seems to have experienced 1660 and perhaps also the death of her husband as establishing new lexical conditions within which poetry operates as a linguistic and political refusal. In 'Upon two pictures', likening her husband ultimately to 'Sampson', we see both the assertion of the strong form of a Calvinist narrative of providence and predestination and an intransigent refusal of the Restoration at the level of the very words which express what it might mean.[109] Thus, in an appropriation of the language of rule, she makes virtue princely but the 'true-borne Prince' (l. 2) is not vulgarly crowned as tyrants are, nor is he 'servile' (l. 5). Even more significantly, she appropriates the key term of Charles II's regime when she asserts that Colonel Hutchinson fought 'not to destroy but to restore' (l. 10). The elegies, like the longer poem published as *Order and Disorder*, partake of an astringent precision of expression which is theological and political as much as poetic. Besides building a poetics of desolation, Hutchinson's contestation of vocabulary challenges and re-evaluates the foundational language ordering her world. In a broad way Hutchinson's re-evaluative poetic vocabulary is analogous to Katherine Philips's building of a language of friendship during the Civil War, but it operates very differently: rather than a world elsewhere, or within, Hutchinson's poems both recognize their status as now outside the sphere of influence, and contest the dominant tropes describing the Restoration world.

---

[108] See 'To the Gardin att O': 'Elegies' 7 (p. 499).

[109] 'Upon two pictures one a Gallant man drest up in Armour The other y:e Same Honourable Prson looking Through a Prison Greate & leaneing on a Bible': 'Elegies' 4 (p. 494).

In Hutchinson's elegies we see a highly systematic poetry casting human tyranny within the larger frame of godly justice; we also see on a smaller scale the elegiac persona's differentiation between subject and object. The two 'pictures', depicting versions of the active and the contemplative life, are shown by the poetic voice inviting 'you' to examine them. 'See him in prison' we are told in the first and third poem, but the implied speaker, the 'I' which directs the 'you', remains unvoiced with most of the poems using the third person. The elegies on the sun and elsewhere focus on an 'I'. However, the triad of poems on pictures builds a relationship between its object and religious and political virtue; they strongly refuse—and counter—other vocabularies of military heroism and virtue. Yet the triad, too, is marked by the problem of the elegiac subject. The displaced mourner of the first elegy also inhabits the triad of poems on the picture. While the challenge to vocabulary and the canvassing of the different modes of life are precisely and clearly shaped in the poem, the subject's relation to the world—the implied but unspoken 'I' paired with the 'you' to whom the images are shown—is comparatively enigmatic and shadowy. Both uncertain and understated, the nature of the poetic 'I' invites a form of attention distinct from that of the political project in the poem. This merely hinted subjective presence troubles the otherwise sparely reasoned memorial. It returns us to both the question of Lucy Hutchinson's writing self so much canvassed by critics, and to one of the central issues of this study—the ways in which writings build, or fail to build, a political identity for their speakers.

Like *The Tenth Muse*, Hutchinson's book of elegies ends with poems on the vanity of human endeavour, a theme which undermines poetic artifice even as it sustains it by providing its pretext. Hutchinson's and Bradstreet's poems are tellingly different. Bradstreet's final poem, though it might provoke the reader to consider the potentially problematic relationship between aesthetic endeavour and Christian worship, suggests that the volume as a whole has a place in a spiritual purpose. Hutchinson's two final songs, by contrast, make only minimal concessions to the ability of the spiritual life to endow worldly actions with significance, and in consequence these poems offer a conclusion to the volume which bleakly maintains the paradox of endeavour and pointlessness. 'A Song', opening 'What boots it This Pale Corpse to Crowne | Since Death has Cast Its Empire downe', returns the reader to despair: the poetic 'crown' is for the corpse alone as all his power and sway are removed. 'As Livelesse Ecchoes fainter growe | The ofter Theyre repeated', so in the end 'Heroes no more mention have | Than ye obscure Vulgar in ye Grave' (ll. 25–6). Despite its position (whether effected by Hutchinson's hand or not) at the end of the sequence the poem maintains the relationship between the world and spiritual consolation as one of tension rather than resolution, as the complex final stanza suggests: 'Glorie itt Selfe is a vaine Thing' which is not remembered. It 'flowes not from ye eternall spring' (ll. 33–4),

> But [that] wch God to Mortalls gives
> Att once in him both dies & lives
> Soe Marriadge floods ye lesser streames
> Looseing Their owne gett nobler names
> Thus men There Consum[m]ations have
> Thus are redemed from ye darke grave...

Redemption by being melded into the mixing streams of humanity, just as a woman's name is lost in marriage, is a memorialization hardly distinguishable from complete oblivion. The finally positioned 'Another Song', bidding farewell to joy and to mourning, reinforces the inability of the subject to act on past, future, or present.[110] Memory of joy, 'Hasty flashes | Sunk in Ashes' (ll. 3–4) leave behind 'Successive Sorrow' (l. 6):

> Tempt me no more ye poysond bate
> Doth yet my Sick heart ulcerate
> Sad woe farewell
> Life's torturing hell
> Farewell my teares
> Vane Care vane feares
> Which for ye past arrive to late
> And future ills Anticipate
> And make ye present torture more
> While woes Care not w^t They deplore...
>
>   (ll. 7–16)

---

[110] 'A Song', 'Elegies' 22 (pp. 520–1): 'Another Song', 'Elegies' 23 (p. 521). This may not be the volume's planned conclusion: see 'Elegies', p. 485.

Far from being released from mourning, the subject in this poem relinquishes tears and cares not because of any resolution, but because misery has an internal, and pointless, psychological momentum in which grieving itself, startlingly, involves a lack of care for their object: 'woes Care not w^t They deplore'.

The elegies, while building a monument to John Hutchinson and rebuilding a political vocabulary in response to the Restoration, open and close by hinting emphatically at the impossibility of that monument and returning to the irresolvable grief of the subject. At points, the narrative of the Colonel's religious commitment seems to be triumphant, yet the elegist is unable to use that narrative to transcend private grief or to describe the completion of what Peter Sacks, following Freud, calls the elegy's work of mourning.[111] Memory, for this elegist, is represented as both seductive and annihilating, first taking her out of, and then returning her to, the world of the present, in which 'woes sault floods' (l. 13) are accompanied by 'Fretting remorce & guilty dread' (l. 15).[112] Throughout the sequence Lucy Hutchinson's failure to resolve her own crisis by memorializing her husband casts a reflected doubt on the power of the elegy to act as a monument.[113] Taken as a whole, the elegies show her building a political language in circumstances which deprive her of a sphere in which that language can work. Her poetic use of John Hutchinson shows both the fluency of her political thought and the limits of female purchase on a political sphere—for the loss of her husband, as well as the changed world, block any movement from thought to action.

Ernesto Laclau, writing of political subjectivity, argues that the taking up of a political position can be understood as 'the point of crystallisation of a tension, of an undecidable alternative *between* subject and object'.[114] For Laclau, forms of political commitment involve an act of identification founded on the subject's lack, while that very act brings with it a destabilization of the object identified with.[115] Laclau's

[111] See Peter Sacks, *The English Elegy* (Baltimore: Johns Hopkins University Press, 1985), pp. 1–37.

[112] 'The Night 8th', 'Elegies' 8 (p. 501).

[113] Compare 'Elegies' 9 (p. 504).

[114] Ernesto Laclau and Lilian Zac, 'Minding the Gap: The Subject of Politics', in *The Making of Political Identities*, ed. Ernesto Laclau (London: Verso, 1994), pp. 11–39: 12.

[115] Ibid., p. 14.

suggestion that the taking up of a political position does not solve but 'crystallises' the tension between the subject's desires and demands, and the political system or organization to which they subscribe, is illuminating in considering the connected personal and political discourses in Lucy Hutchinson's elegies. Laclau's insight, explicitly about the subject's relationship to political systems, helps us to see the double loss in the elegies. The Colonel of the elegies is not simply an embodiment of a political position—republican virtue; his loss is part of a sweeping away of that order which he was part of and, crucially, in which he gave Hutchinson a place. The fabric of that world has been torn down, but we see Hutchinson building an oppositional poetic vocabulary from the lexicon of the Restoration, subtly and overtly challenging the way the words are made to fit the case in the apparent plain day of the Restoration. This linguistic re-making, far from being consolatory, expresses the contrast and tension between past and present. In its forced relation to the dominant terms of the Restoration, Hutchinson's lexical critique demonstrates, at least for the present, its impotence. Paradoxically, Hutchinson's elegiac language notes the loss of John Hutchinson as the removal of a world, even as she manages to make a political language in which to remember him. Her identification with republicanism is with an ideology recently defeated: she can build the Colonel's memorial, yet his political culture and the interpretative community that would give it meaning have gone. The Colonel's removal takes away her relationship to a world which, in any case, is no more. Hutchinson's assertion of her status as shade in her own life has political, as well as personal, significance. Perhaps articulated most fully in the elegies is her sense of removal from the political sphere. The languages of memorialization, the transvaluation of Restoration tropes, and the crisis of the elegiac subject dissolved by grief work together to build a relationship to the Restoration political sphere—even as that relationship is understood as impossible.

The amount of work these elegies have to do to find a language with which to build a monument, and the way in which political and passionate work are bound together in doing so, do not alone account for the subject's insistence on inconsolable loss. But it does seem that the elegies imply that, although they can find a language for the Colonel, they cannot find one for his wife. This hinted failure of language is, of course, a political intervention, albeit one partly highlighted for the

reader by the use of elegy. Hutchinson's use of elegy in the making of a
political relationship with the world, while simultaneously asserting that
such a relationship cannot be made, is sophisticated, complex, vexed.
Like her partial repudiation of Lucretius, it is revealing in the way it
enacts the paradoxes of women's relationship to politics—both there
and, of course, forbidden, seen, and invisible. Lucy Hutchinson's 'shade'
is perhaps one fitting metaphor for women's haunting political, as
well as emotional, place: a shade may not be there, but it makes its
presence felt.

The elegies, though they here sit at the centre of a discussion of
the expression of Hutchinson's poetic and political vocabulary and subjectivity, are not Hutchinson's last poems nor her longest. *Order and Dis-*
order, part of which was anonymously published (as *Order and Disorder*,
licensed in March 1678/9), turns to Genesis to give poetic 'meditations
upon the Creation and the Fall'. In many ways this long poem returns to,
and redeems, what she had come to regard as mistakes. Concentration on
the Christian creation myth replies to her own youthful translation of
Lucretius; the poem has been compared to *Paradise Lost* in its achievement and its address to key theological issues.[116] It could be argued that
Order and Disorder tells us about Hutchinson's changing views on libertinism and the creation while the elegies show us the struggle for political
subjectivity. Yet we find some of *Order and Disorder* copied into the book
of elegies. In words reminiscent of Lady Mary Wroth's evocation of the
labyrinth of love, Eve speaks:

> Wherever I, my eyes or thoughts convert,
> Each object adds new torture to my heart.
> If I look up, I dread heavens threatning frown
> Thorns prick my eyes when shame hath cast them down,
> Dangers I see, looking on either hand,
> Before me all in frightening posture stand.
> If I cast back my sorrow drownéd eyes,
> I see our ne'er to be recovered Paradise,
> The flaming sword which doth us thence exclude,
> By sad remorse & ugly guilt persu'ed . . .

[116] Norbrook, ' "Devine Originall" ', pp. 13–15.

Eve wishes that she had 'but sind' & dyed alone'. Gazing on herself, she is horrified to see her 'spots', but looking at her beloved, 'Confusion doth my shameful eyes deject, | Seeing the man I love by me betrayed'.[117] Just as it is hard to read *Paradise Lost* without remembering the debates of the Civil War, so it is hard to read the voices of Adam, Eve, and the narrator without recalling the personal and political disaster that struck Hutchinson at the Restoration and which is so vividly explored in the elegies. It should come, perhaps, as no surprise to find that Hutchinson has little sympathy with the betrayer, Eve.[118] Yet in Eve's unproductive desire to return to an earlier moment, in her 'remorce', 'sorrow', and 'guilt', we can hear echoes of the political and personal complaint, perhaps despair, of the elegies.

WOMEN, POLITICS, POETRY

The writings of Bradstreet and Hutchinson tell us both about the issue this chapter began with—the place and affiliations of anti-Stuart women's poetry in the 1640s and after—and also suggest some more general questions. Bradstreet, considering the origins and formation of the world, puts to work humoral theory, Protestant history, the Bible, and millenarian interpretations of time: she blends politics with religious resources to address herself to the world. And she clearly anticipates that she will be read. The nature of Bradstreet's achievements may suggest constraints produced by her remoteness from books and libraries. Yet her poems, and the testimonials accompanying them, also show her active connection with religious, political, and aesthetic networks. In education and affiliations, Bradstreet is grounded in Atlantic culture and illuminates the local and Atlantic connections of religious writings. Like

---

[117] Quotation here from Hutchinson, *Order and Disorder*, ed Norbrook, canto 5, ll. 421–34; see also 'These verses transcribed out of my other Book JH': 'Elegies' 2A (pp. 490–1). According to F. E. Hutchinson's transcription of the elegies, this poem is in the hand of Julius Hutchinson, grandfather of the first editor of the memoirs. Norbrook, 'Elegies', p. 490.

[118] A contrast is offered by a similarly disputatious poet, Katherine Philips. When her Cromwellian husband faced the embarrassment of her royalist poems being circulated, she defended herself (*Collected Works*, ed. Thomas, I, 346–7). See Philips, 'to Antenor, on a paper of mine wch J. Jones threatens to publish' (ll. 5–6, 11–12), *Collected Works*, I, 116–17; Smith, *Literature and Revolution*, pp. 267–75.

many other writers of the 1640s and 1650s, she attends to the potentially millennial shape of time and the meaning of biblical and literal history. There is no doubt that Bradstreet and Elizabeth Avery sought to influence those around them, but in the roles of those who published and responded to their work we can see a significant difference between these women and poet-politicians. In sum, from their closest readers their words elicit (and in Bradstreet's case anticipate) responses which judge, morally and politically, the nature of their approach to politics.

If much of Hutchinson's poetry is clearly oriented towards influencing public affairs, it also responds to the shaping circumstances of the Protectorate and Restoration by attempting to memorialize the past and its republican values. The death of her husband did attenuate her relationship to the legitimate political sphere, and we see in her elegies the resources she used to attempt to build a political identity in the wreckage of political and personal hopes. Hutchinson, like Bradstreet fascinated by creation myths and the relationship of the present to a larger pattern of meaning, draws on the resources of the high Renaissance—Lucretius (albeit disavowed), Virgil, Horace, classical history. In *Order and Disorder*, like Milton in *Paradise Lost*, she essays an interpretation of Christian creation. In terms of education, cultural entitlement, and achievement Hutchinson is 'reassuringly expensive'.[119] She has classical languages, is well read in Roman history and contemporary poetry, is at the forefront of intellectual debate. At last, we might think, we find ourselves dealing with an immensely talented female intellectual, not a princess—indeed, a republican—who has successfully laid claim to an education usually exclusively the preserve of men, successfully internalized its rules (something which Margaret Cavendish does not seem to have quite wanted to do), and, above all, excelled in ways valued highly by cultural arbiters. Yet Hutchinson's successful acquisition and mobilization of cultural capital—and how we might respond to the way it facilitates comparison with some of the greatest poets in the language—invites questions as much as offering answers about the nature of processes of canon formation as well as women's political engagement and poetic and intellectual abilities.

---

[119] Advertising for Stella Artois lager, 1990s/2000s.

Hutchinson, engaging so ably with convention and form, undoubtedly offers an example with which to challenge any assumption that all women were solely or simply deprived of intellectual resources, confined to the sphere of religion, wholly sexualized, or silent. Her example allows us to return to writers such as her most obvious parallel, Margaret Cavendish, and look for their philosophical and political engagements with renewed confidence. A longer study would compare Cavendish, Philips, Bradstreet, and Hutchinson in greater detail. But by the same token it would be unproductive—indeed, a poor use of this poet—to allow her achieved status as an intellectual and her able political commentary to separate her from other interests she shares with her less well resourced contemporaries, men and women. In being religious, even theological, these links are important intellectually. Hutchinson was a classical scholar, but also an Independent in religion; she was fascinated by parliamentary business and gossip as well as by high culture; she shared republican politics with her husband and Independent religion with a range of the authors discussed in this study. Hutchinson sounds a rich and distinctive chord in mid-century political poetry, but if we decide to understand her solely as Milton's contemporary then we will, once again, obscure some of the active religious and political connections which motivate her. If Hutchinson shares the topic of Eve with Milton she also shares it with the royalist Katherine Philips and many others. That Hutchinson's erudition and ability certainly overshadow many of her contemporaries need not blind us to what she shares with them.[120] Elite education and access to elite genres are here crucial in allowing these poets' contemporaries as well as later critics to recognize fully women's interventions in politics. Writers like Bradstreet and Hutchinson, who share some of the aesthetic as well as political attributes of Fulke Greville, or John Milton, or Andrew Marvell, are visible—part of a sub-canon of politicized poets. However, religious faith is important in facilitating their political claims: in some ways their writing does have connections, even if hostile ones, to the polemical religious writings examined in the last two chapters. Women poets do, indeed, attempt to influence 'public affairs', but like their male contemporaries (as the exception of Hutchinson reminds us), some of them (like

---

[120] See David Loewenstein's discussion of Milton's associations in *Representing Revolution in Milton and his Contemporaries: Religion, Politics and Polemics in Radical Puritanism* (Cambridge: Cambridge University Press, 2001), pp. 242–4.

Anna Trapnel) use resources distinct from those recognized by the educational and cultural elite. When they were writing though, in the 1640s, 1650s, even in the 1660s, an array of political and religious languages existed, including prophecy, Calvinism, and republicanism. Priority was troubled and disputed rather than hierarchized. Not only is the *naturalized* triumph of royalism as the language of political poetry a later event, but so is the separation of the concerns of, say, millenarians and parliamentarians, Calvinists and republicans. For writers of the 1640s and 1650s these issues were strongly disputed and so connected. Bradstreet's and Hutchinson's politico-religious analyses locate them in specific milieux, but also in quite a wide field of political and religious struggle.

What do these investigations suggest about women, poetry, and politics? Restoring politics to poetry David Norbrook reminded his readers that 'Some of the greatest English Renaissance poets were politicians, and all of them tried to influence public affairs through their writings.' Norbrook also argues forcefully that critical commentary on sixteenth- and seventeenth-century poetry has always had political implications; indeed, 'much modern criticism has given a distorted picture of the political complexion of Renaissance poetry'.[121] It is suggestive to measure Hutchinson and Bradstreet, as women writing poetry in the 1650s and 1660s, against the political engagements of their predecessors and contemporaries, and to do so illuminates some of the ways in which each poet articulated political concerns. The relationships to politics suggested by Hutchinson's and Bradstreet's poetry is very different from that envisaged by Aristotle or, in the English Renaissance, Sir Philip Sidney. Neither lawgivers nor heroes themselves, writing about lawgivers and heroes is also different for them from their male precursors and contemporaries. If the poems of Bradstreet and Hutchinson share the contemporary apprehension of political poetry as attempting to influence a (broadly conceived) public good, the writings of each poet also remind us of the crucial legitimizing roles of men in women's political poetics—both literally as gatekeepers and as political exemplars (as in Bradstreet's use of Philip Sidney as an example, or Hutchinson's use of her husband). In this chapter we have seen women articulating political aims yet not, of course, with the autonomy

---

[121] Norbrook, *Poetry and Politics*, p. 1.

of the statesman-poet who—though himself subject to the bounds of patronage, friendship, and honour—is in dialogue with masculine equals and superiors. Each poet registers the fraught conditions under which she makes claims to political and poetic status, and the fragile, because in some senses dependent, hold each has on an audience.

Finally, does politics itself need to be redefined before we can assess the poetry of women like these? Yes and no. As we have seen, several factors influence this answer, particularly the specificity of the mid-seventeenth century, and the nature of literary influence and resources. To return, briefly, to David Norbrook's formulation: attempting to influence worldly affairs through their poetry, the writing and publication history of each of these poets, in distinct ways, raises the question of women's relationship to *both* poetry and politics. Each addresses political issues, 'public affairs'. Yet the nature of each poet's address is marked by awareness (in Bradstreet's case) of the geographical and gendered restrictions on thought, and (in Hutchinson's case) of the way in which women's words have the power of memorialization rather than desired political influence. To generalize from these poets about the relationship between anti-Stuart women, poetry, and politics in the 1650s would be a problematic undertaking. What these two poets, writing almost at the same time, do seem to share is their sharp self-awareness in attempting to negotiate, poetically, the public nature of the political world. The next chapter examines the relationship of women and politics from a different angle. It canvasses the question of women's relationship to the political sphere through an examination of what was written about a particular woman, asking what that tells us about ideas, and fantasies, about women, men, and politics.

6

Rule and Representation: The 'Libertine' Case of Queen Christina

'I understand you have seen the Queen of Sweden, and beg you to send me word if you find what people say about her person and disposition is true. I should be very glad to know it.'

(Henrietta Maria to Charles Stuart, 29 October 1655)

Readers who may be scandalized at Christina must remember that she lived in an age when everybody, and especially men, were unrestrained both morally and physically. With the pre-natal influence and the upbringing of a man and the sexual capabilities of a highly emotional woman, in an era of licence and excess, it is impossible to judge her by our standards and our conventions.[1]

So wrote Barbara Cartland in her 1956 biography of Christina, Queen of Sweden. That Cartland, launched on a highly successful career writing romance, wrote of Christina at all is testimony to the Swedish queen's enduring status as an object of curiosity and judgement, interpreted repeatedly according to prevailing fashions. For most modern writers Christina has signalled principally a *sexual* conundrum and scandal.[2] However, although her contemporaries also felt that Christina's behaviour demanded comment, her significance for them was religious, at times philosophical, and political, as well as sexual.

This chapter explores the relationship between women and politics from the vantage point of representation. It examines writings which draw on one figure who, for those who saw or heard of her, put women, politics, and philosophy together in unpredictable ways. In doing so it

---

[1] Barbara Cartland, *The Outrageous Queen: A Biography of Christina of Sweden* (London: Frederick Muller, 1956), foreword (unpaginated).
[2] Sarah Waters, '"A Girton Girl on a Throne": Queen Christina and Versions of Lesbianism, 1906–1933', *Feminist Review*, 46 (1994), pp. 41–60, esp. 58, 43.

draws on Joan Wallach Scott's insight that gender is one of the main ways in which power is signified, and therefore known and discussed.[3] Specifically, as work on the competition for representation over Elizabeth Tudor indicates, much of political and cultural significance can be gleaned from study of the representation of women and rule.[4] For her contemporaries, Queen Christina demanded comment. Throughout the latter part of the 1650s and into the Restoration the ideas of liberty which emerged so forcefully in the 1640s put women and politics into the same frame for consideration, and writing on Christina is an index of the explosive potential of this perceived proximity. That, to many of her contemporaries, Christina seemed 'a Queen so unlike a woman' made her an ideal focus for men and women to test their own political ideals.[5] While in the 1650s Elizabeth I had become a figure who called up happier times and whose place in Protestant history was contested, Queen Christina was a more immediately present conundrum.[6] Henrietta Maria and 'Queen' Cromwell were the targets of praise and blame, but Christina's 'foreign' status meant that she occupied a more distant, and so—perhaps—intriguing, position for English writers. As, in England, Republic gave way to Protectorate and then Restoration, Christina embarked on her own course of political cataclysm. Discussions about Christina are informed by concerns about the British Civil War, but not always in obvious ways.

Christina also allows some exploration of the potential paradoxes in women's political power. Do distance and proximity seem to affect the ways in which women are seen in relation to politics? What does the case of Christina suggest about theory and pragmatism in imagining but also dealing with women in politics? Contemporary reactions to Christina do recycle prejudice and stereotype, but she also prompted writers to consider and discuss the relationship between women and political

[3] Joan Wallach Scott, 'Gender: A Useful Category of Historical Analysis', repr. in *Feminism and History*, ed. Wallach Scott (Oxford: Oxford University Press, 1996).

[4] Helen Hackett, *Virgin-Mother, Maiden-Queen* (Basingstoke: Macmillan, 1995); Susan Frye, *Elizabeth I: The Competition for Representation* (Oxford: Oxford University Press, 1993).

[5] *Memoirs of Mademoiselle de Montpensier*, trans. anon., 3 vols. (London: Henry Coulburn, 1848), II, 53.

[6] See Frye, *Elizabeth I*; *Ideology and Politics on the Eve of Restoration: Newcastle's Advice to Charles II*, ed. Thomas P. Slaughter (Philadelphia: American Philosophical Society, 1984), pp. 50, 57–8.

power. Indeed, one characteristic which arguably links the very different kinds of writing that draw on the idea of the Swedish queen—from panegyric to sexual scandal—is that they often seem to be at the very limits of what their understanding of the place of women allows them to interpret.[7] Whether as an apparently Lutheran queen in her early life in Sweden or in her later European travels, whether as a virgin queen or a wanton murderer, observers found Christina a particularly rich, but also disturbing, subject for meditation. 'She'—or the writing which imagines her—lend themselves to a study in representation. In this chapter, the questions that arise when women and liberty are put in the same frame are explored in the languages of diplomacy, satire, and utopia. We here find English writers engaging with a wider world. The focus is on Bulstrode Whitelocke's *Journal*, John Bargrave's *College of Cardinals*, and Margaret Cavendish's *Blazing World* and *Female Academy*. It is with Whitelocke's *Journal*, a text which was drafted in close proximity to Christina, that I begin.

DIPLOMACY: QUEEN AND REPUBLIC

On 23 August 1653, in the fourth year of the English republic, Whitelocke received a letter from his agent in London telling him that he was 'named by the councell of state to goe ambassador to Sweden', to the court of Queen Christina, and he arrived in Uppsala before Christmas.[8] This was a second summons. Though he had opposed the trial of Charles I, immediately afterwards Whitelocke had been deeply involved in making the new republic legally viable. So when he had been informed that he was to be ambassador to Holland he had been disappointed that someone (Cromwell?) wanted to send him on a dangerous mission. Although Whitelocke managed to talk his way out of the appointment (the man who was sent, Dr Isaac Dorislaus, was indeed murdered by royalists) it would hardly have been politic to refuse the Swedish

---

[7] See Waters, ' "A Girton Girl" '; Susanna Akerman, *Queen Christina and her Circle* (Leiden: Brill, 1991). Recent biographies include Veronica Buckley, *Christina Queen of Sweden* (London: Fourth Estate, 2004) and Bernard Quillet, *Christine de Suède* (Paris: Fayard, 2003).

[8] Bulstrode Whitelocke, *A Journal of the Swedish Ambassy*, 2 vols. (London: T. Becket & P. A. de Hondt, 1772), I, 2. Subsequently cited as *Journal*.

post as well.[9] In Sweden his task was, in theory, clear—he was to persuade the Queen to sign a treaty against the Dutch and the Danes to open the shipping of the Sundt. However, the circumstances of the embassy held both known and unforeseen complexities. From his home in England Whitelocke could see that several things required negotiation besides the treaty itself: the significance of Christina's place as a female ruler, the significance of England's troubles, the political foundations and nature of the established republic.

A prolific 'recorder' of his times and what it meant to pragmatically oppose Charles I, Whitelocke is now best known for his *Memorials*, but he covered many pages in notes, meditations, briefs, annals, diaries.[10] Whitelocke's ambiguous consideration of women's political natures is revealed in papers he wrote before his departure. His preparations canvass the role and intentions of an ambassador and, amongst a range of texts, he discusses Genesis 24, in which the aged Abraham sends his servant to find a wife for Isaac, and the servant returns with Rebecca. Whitelocke contrasts Rebecca's frank willingness to be married with modern women:

> how different was this from the demeanor & scornfullness of young women in after times, who will be sick if the servant doe butt putt on his hatt before them, & must not be spoken to, but att a distance, they must not presume to propound their suit, butt in great veneration of their Mistris.[11]

For Whitelocke, anticipating his place at Christina's court, the Old Testament servant's actions offer a model.[12] The literature of diplomacy customarily drew on biblical and Homeric sources, but Whitelocke's use of examples is specific both to his own religious formation and, from that perspective, to the way he imagines negotiation with a young woman.[13] He makes a story of family and marriage also the story of nations, as the conduct of Abraham and his relatives fluidly represents the nation or the family. And 'father... children... servants' need to be like Abraham's family—not 'debauched' but praying.[14]

[9] Ruth Spalding, *The Improbable Puritan: A Life of Bulstrode Whitelocke* (London: Faber & Faber, 1975), pp. 114–17.

[10] Ibid., pp. 262–5.

[11] BL MS Add. 37346, fo. 8.

[12] BL MS Add. 37346, fo. 1b.

[13] Garrett Mattingly, *Renaissance Diplomacy* (London: Jonathan Cape, 1955), p. 219.

[14] BL MS Add. 37346, fo. 12.

At almost the same time as he was characterizing the modern young woman as foolish, Whitelocke wrote a dialogue between himself and his 'Wife' on the subject of his selection for this diplomatic task. In 1649 Whitelocke's beloved second wife, Frances, had died, but by August 1650 he had married Mary, the widow of a parliamentarian (his first wife was called Rebecca).[15] This is the 'Wife' who asks, 'why should you adventure your selfe for those that doe not wish you well? butt rather that you may never returne, as I thinke the Gen[era]l & his party doe'. Whitelocke 'records' his counter-argument that 'a refusall at this time, added to their former distasts of me, would increase the interest of my ennemies', whereas to accept will 'greatly advantage my selfe & relations'. Yet, while his dialogue makes 'Wife' voice the obligations of hearth and family, she also thinks about politics:

Wife. So you had his letter that they would impose nothing on you, and yett you see how earnestly they presse this uppon you, hee means no good to you, butt would be rid of you.

Wh. why should he desire to be rid of me, when I may be servicable to him heer?

Wife. though you are servicable in some things, yett you are not through paced in all things, which they would have you to do, you refused to act in the great busines, you opposed the breaking of the Parlam[en]t & other unjust things.[16]

Responding to 'Wife's' conspiracist suspicion of Cromwell, Whitelocke asks, 'what further designes can he have? hee exercises more power than any king of England ever had or claymed.'[17] The two manuscripts make clear the importance of gender relations in Whitelocke's thinking about the world and imply, it seems, that while he is at ease discussing politics in private with his wife, he is very anxious about encountering a woman, particularly a young one, who exercised regal power. Cromwell's 'designs' were to become clear while Whitelocke was in Sweden.

Arriving at the Swedish court, Whitelocke was forced to accommodate theory to practice. He successfully pressed to have his audience with Christina before Christmas ('much observed in this country'). Making notes which translate from the court's French,

[15] Spalding, *The Improbable Puritan*, p. 127. His wives were Rebecca Benet, Frances Willoughby, and Mary Wilson (née Carleton).

[16] BL MS Add. 4994, fo. 6ᵛ.

[17] BL MS Add. 4902, fo. 6.

Whitelocke describes his first meeting on 23 December. The Queen, 'very attentive',

coming up close to him, by her looks and gestures (as was supposed) would have daunted him; but those who have been conversant in the great affairs in England are not so soon as others apalled with the presence of a young lady and her servants . . . [18]

While Whitelocke uses the incident to illustrate his worldly experience and ground it in Civil War military virtue, it is evident that he is responding to Christina's own tactics.[19] He sees the Queen's desire for political dominance. In his initial address to Christina Whitelocke makes a telling analogy:

the present happy government under your majesty, which remembers unto us those blessed dayes of our virgin queen Elizabeth, under whom, above forty years, the people injoyed all protection and justice from their prince, and she, all obedience and affection from her people.

He continues, 'Nor had it been lost in those who followed queen Elizabeth, butt through their own ill government.'[20] That the language of monarchy came readily to supporters of the Commonwealth has been taken to indicate that in republican England patterns of political thought were saturated with the idea of monarchy.[21] Yet the precise nature of this compliment to Christina tells a slightly different story. Elizabeth's status as a Tudor enabled Whitelocke to imply the absolutist ambitions and personal failings of the Stuarts, and so the comparison enables him to discriminate good from bad monarchs. That 'ill government' can forfeit a throne is a position Whitelocke poses subtly here, and which he often reiterated. He tells the Swedish archbishop:

Wh. . . . Selfe preservation goes farre with mortall men . . . it is not the right of a king to governe a people, but the consent of a people that such a king shall governe them; which, if he do not according to justice and their law, they hold,

---

[18] *Journal*, I, 233.

[19] *The Diary of Bulstrode Whitelocke 1605–1675*, ed. Ruth Spalding (Oxford: Oxford University Press for the British Academy, 1990), p. 317.

[20] *Journal*, I, 237.

[21] Kevin Sharpe, ' "An Image Doting Rabble": The Failure of Republican Culture in Seventeenth-Century England', in id., *Remapping Early Modern England* (Cambridge: Cambridge University Press, 2000), pp. 223–65.

that the people for whom, and for whose good, and for preservation of whose rights, he is instructed as the supream officer, may, if they please remove him from that office: and uppon this ground the people's deputies in our supreme councell, the parlement, thought fitt to take away the government by kings and to make it a republique.[22]

The example of Elizabeth allows Whitelocke to suggest all this to Christina in a tactful compliment. He repeats to the Chancellor his justification of the people as the base of political authority, arguing, 'Every government, which the people chooseth, is certainly lawfull.'[23] Endorsing English and Swedish forms of government simultaneously, Whitelocke's use of Elizabeth indicates that Queen's exemplary importance during the Commonwealth, not only as an object of nostalgia but as a chosen tool of the Republic's self-representation.[24] Standing before Christina, the example of Elizabeth, Protestant virgin queen, must have seemed to Whitelocke a perfect comparison. With hindsight it seems less convincing. What Whitelocke did not know—it seems certain— was that though a virgin queen, Christina was far from the specifically Protestant heroine which he imagined her to be. Within a month the situation in England and in Sweden was to have changed dramatically and, for all Whitelocke's boasting of the excellence of the English intelligence, he was in a position where he had to explain Cromwell and the English to the Queen, to his diplomatic 'family', and perhaps to himself as well.

At a private audience, on 5 January, Christina told Whitelocke, 'I believe that your generall will be king of England in conclusion.' Whitelocke's protest—'that cannot be, bicause England is resolved into a common-wealth'—was to seem foolish. On 12 January the ambassador received 'the great news of the dissolving of the parlement in England, and that the generall was made supreame governour'.[25] Christina was an admirer of Cromwell, describing him as 'one of the gallantest men in the world; never were such things done as by the English in your late war'. She continues, 'the prince of Condé is next to him, but shortt of him. I have as great a respect and honour for your generall as

---

[22] *Journal*, I, 391.   [23] Ibid., p. 321.   [24] Discussed in Ch. 5.
[25] *Journal*, I, 296, 323.

for any man alive; and I pray, lett him know as much from me.'[26] It seems that his elevation to Protector pleased the Queen:

Qu. Par Dieu, I beare the same respect, and more to your generall and to you then I did before; and I had rather have to doe with one then with many.

Wh. I may very well believe it; and returne thanks to your majesty for the continuance of your respects to England, and to my generall, and to his servant: your majesty understands he hath a new title, butt his power was not meane before.[27]

The court, Whitelocke observed, was 'very much pleased with it'.[28] Christina found 'your affayres in England are much amended, and better established, by this change then before'.[29]

The change also allowed the Queen to press, even provoke, the hitherto staunch republican on the nature of a 'protectorate'. When Christina asks, 'Is your new government by a *protector* different from what it was before as to monarchy?' Whitelocke replies, not wholly accurately, that 'government is the same as formerly, by successive representatives of the people in parlement', only now 'the protector is the head, or chiefe magistrate'. Returning to the issue, Christina asks:

Qu. Why is the title, Protector, when the power is kingly?

Wh. I cannot satisfy your majesty of the reasons of this title, being att so great a distance from the inventors of it.

Qu. New titles, with soveraign power, proved prejudiciall to the state of Rome.[30]

The Queen's prediction of Cromwell's accumulation of power echoes those in the discussion with Whitelocke's wife. Asked if Cromwell's 'power is the same with that of king, and why should not his title have bin the same?' Whitelocke fudges a reply—'It is the power which makes the title, and not the title the power; our protector thinks he has enough of both.'[31] Evidently groping for a new political rhetoric, the ambassador is at a disadvantage. But the crisis in England was, for Whitelocke, a dual problem. He needed 'to see how this newes be relished att court', but simultaneously he had to justify his whole position as ambassador to his diplomatic 'family'.[32] Christina might make capital from political

---

[26] *Journal*, I, p. 251. [27] Ibid., p. 324. [28] Ibid., p. 325.
[29] Ibid., p. 326. [30] Ibid., pp. 326–8. [31] Ibid., p. 329.
[32] Ibid., p. 333.

change, but his household had serious objections. Ambassadorial manuals were much exercised about the question of loyalty to the prince and the intertwined relationship between moral action, the good of Christendom, and the good of a prince. As Tasso put it, to be a perfect ambassador one must first have the perfect prince.[33] Cromwell's actions and his treatment of his ambassador brought home these issues to the whole English entourage who had 'divers objections' to continuing the embassy.[34] Some felt vehemently that it was invalid to work for the new Protectorate.[35] Whitelocke's rationale for continuing was fidelity to his nation, not to government.

The transformation of English governance was hardly resolved when, on 21 January, Whitelocke was caught up in a Swedish crisis which provided an uncanny comparator for the English one:

> *Qu.* Sir... I have it in my thoughts and resolution to quitt the crowne of Sweden, and to retire myselfe unto a private life, as much more suitable to my contentment, then the great cares and troubles attending uppon the government of my kingdome; and what thinke you of this resolution?[36]

So the Queen broke to Whitelocke, 'under secrecy', news of her abdication.[37] Whitelocke responded that he hoped 'your majesty is pleased only to drolle with your humble servant', and continues:

> *Wh.* I beseech your majesty deferre that resolution still, or rather wholly exclude it from your thoughts, as unfitt to receive any intertainment in your royall breast; and give me your pardon, if I speake my poore opinion with all duety and plainness to you, since you are pleased to require it: can any reason enter into a mind, so full of reason as yours is, to cause such a resolution from your majesty?
> *Qu.* I take your plainness in very good part, and desire you to use freedome with me in this matter. The reasons which conduct me to such a resolution are: bicause I am a woman, and therefore the more unfitt to governe, and subject to the greater inconveniencies; that the heavy cares of governement do outweigh the glories and pleasures of it, and are not to be imbraced in comparison of that contentment, which a private retirement brings with it.[38]

---

[33] Mattingly, *Renaissance Diplomacy*, p. 222, citing *Il Messagiero* in *Opere*, VII, 111.

[34] Mattingly, *Renaissance Diplomacy*, p. 219.

[35] Objections included that Cromwell's power had no legal base, so to serve him was 'unlawfull'. See *Journal*, I, 333.

[36] *Journal*, I, 361, and see pp. 360–2.

[37] Ibid., p. 360.

[38] Ibid., pp. 361–2.

Whitelocke's replies, and the areas of Christina's reasoning over which he passes in silence, tell us something about his position as an ambassador (part courtier, part civil servant) but also about the tools he used to think about his world. He does not record directly addressing her reiterated point that she was a woman, 'I desire that more service to God, and more good to the world may be done, then I, being a woman, am capable to performe', arguing rather that 'the higher your station is, the more opportunity you have of doing service to God, and good to the worlde'.[39] He says: 'Butt, madame, you that injoy the kingdome by right of descent, you that have the full affections and obedience of all sorts of your subjects, why should you be discouraged to continue the reines in your own hands? how can you forsake those, who testify so much love to you, and likeing of your government?' She suggests that it is her 'love to the people' which prompts her to find 'a better governor for them then a poore woman can be' besides 'somewhat of love to myselfe, to please my own fancy, by my private retirement'.[40] And, significantly, Whitelocke is not a courtier speaking but the ambassador of a republic, and a man who counselled Cromwell against taking the throne.[41] If the relationship between Christina and Whitelocke reflects Cromwell's usurpation of power in England, it does so in an unpredictable way. However, it seems certain that it was circumstances rather than theory which generated Whitelocke's response to Cromwell's seizing power and Christina's plan to relinquish it. At the same time, the *Journal* is concerned to produce an image of Whitelocke himself as dealing well with what he encounters.

The *Journal* is marked by anecdotes indicating closeness to the Queen. Perhaps aware of the political and national complexities of the exchange, Whitelocke records using the example of masculine familial authority to mirror the Queen's situation to her. Visiting terrain familiar from *King Lear* and Montaigne's essay on the relationship between fathers and sons, Whitelocke tells a story of inheritance. An 'old English gentleman' relinquishes management of his estate to his son, 'reserving only a pension'.[42] At the moment when the agreement of transfer was being drawn up, the father 'taking tobacco in the better

---

[39] *Journal*, I, p. 362.   [40] Ibid., pp. 362–3.   [41] Ibid., p. 349.
[42] Ibid., p. 364; see Michel de Montaigne 'Of the Affection of Fathers to their Children', in *Essays*, trans. John Florio, 3 vols. (London: Dent, 1910), II, 65–89.

roome' was desired by the son 'to take the tobacco in the kitchen, and to spitt there, which he obeyed'. Understanding the implications of the incident, the father at once took back his agreement and resumed the reins of power. Whitelocke uses this example to remind the Queen of her own 'eminent place and power', similarly decreed by God and equally dangerous to relinquish. Using a homely example of inheritance to teach the Queen, Whitelocke associates himself with both the gentry his anecdote describes and with the idea of paternal counsel. Once again, political exchange between Queen and ambassador is gendered in a deep, yet implicit, way.[43]

Even taking into account Whitelocke's desire to gloss his own performance for potential readers, it seems that Whitelocke and the Swedish queen were able to work together, and in ways Whitelocke had not imagined. More generally, Whitelocke's diplomatic writings at this moment suggest the major part played by court structures and proximity. Far from having recourse to political theory, Whitelocke mentions entertainments and music as offering opportunities for the ambassador to assert the value of his own culture while also offering the Queen his abilities in music, theatricals, and festivities.[44] 'Matters of ceremony are here in great observance', he writes, 'and the neglect of them highly resented and offensive. This caused a great wariness in Whitelocke not to offend in that omission, the performance whereof was cheap and easy.' Seeing how much the Queen enjoyed festivities, and perhaps recognizing the political potential of shared intimacy, he writes that, having stayed away on Sunday, 'being now again solemnly invited from the Queen herself to a ball this night at Court, he thought, if he should again refuse to come to it, the Queen might be distasted, and think her favour slighted. He therefore resolved to go.'[45] Whitelocke records that when Christina asked his opinion he criticized her own practice of Sunday dancing since it would be 'most becoming to a Queen' to 'restrain and punish the sin of prophanation of the Lord's day', 'as likewise swearing and debauchery'.[46]

---

[43] See Sarah McKenzie, 'Death, Inheritance and the Family: A Study of Literary Responses to Inheritance in Seventeenth-Century England', Diss., University of Warwick, 2003.

[44] Whitelocke records his own love for music: *Journal*, I, 239, 279.

[45] Ibid., p. 292.

[46] Ibid., p. 298.

Although Whitelocke's opinions in his *Journal* are sometimes marked by a bullying assertion of English ways which seems calculated to appeal to an English reader, his notes also suggest a willingness to become immersed in the ways of the young Queen's court. In his own eyes, Whitelocke's diplomatic effectiveness is definitely enhanced by his integration into Swedish court life and his abilities in courtship.[47] Accordingly, the *Journal* expands into a full discussion a brief diary note that he 'found visits to Ladyes not unnecessary'.[48] '[E]specially in the court of a queen,' he writes 'their influence in the highest affayres is not to be despised.' In his view, he fed the Queen's women such matters as he was willing should 'come to the queen's eare'.[49] Whitelocke's self-satisfied assessment of his manipulation of ladies in dallying, roundabout, negotiation contrasts strikingly with the method that he prescribed for himself before he set off for Sweden. The story of inheritance seems to have been much more practical help than that of Rebecca.

Writing about the philosophical tradition of friendship, something closely linked to diplomacy, Jacques Derrida repeatedly reminds his readers that friendship is a category of power and politics. In this literature, 'friendship' is invoked at the point where hostility might become formalized; it is a fraternal quality associated with the republic and, like the political sphere itself, a realm and language regarded as unavailable to women.[50] At a tangent to its own purposes, the politically inflected tradition of theorized friendship (and enmity) reminds us of women's exclusion from the languages and theories of political process. However, texts like Whitelocke's *Journal* confirm that the exclusion of women from political languages was qualified or countermanded by contingency.[51] As a tool with which to analyse the political significance and position of women, political theory offers us only one language amongst many which enunciate women's relationship to the political sphere—and one likely to give an idealized, systematized, stabilized fantasy of women's political role.

---

[47] Whitelocke, *Diary*, 22 Mar. 1653/4, p. 343.
[48] Ibid., 3 Jan. 1653, p. 321.
[49] *Journal*, I, 293 (3 Jan. 1653).
[50] Jacques Derrida, *The Politics of Friendship*, trans. George Collins (London: Routledge, 1997), pp. 72, 173, and *passim*.
[51] On women's involvement in diplomacy see J. C. Russell, *Diplomats at Work* (Stroud: Alan Sutton, 1992), e.g. pp. 9, 94.

Most obviously, Whitelocke's writings indicate to us that in considering the presentation of women's relationship to politics the distance between the writing persona and its object is very important. As we might expect, writing generated for or in the proximity of women acting politically—whether within the family or the court, or even in a siege—is marked by an assumed acceptance of such roles. One implication is that operational political languages seem to have been distinct, and perhaps acknowledged as such, from the theoretical material with which they coexist and on which they draw. Whitelocke shows us the factors that went into consideration of women's political roles in practice. Against his detailed theoretical assessment of the situation using the Bible as his guide we can set the way in which he interpreted discussions with his wife and with the Swedish queen: in his case, the discussion and practice of politics required different materials and ideas from those elaborated in theoretical or idealized understandings of the gendering of the political sphere.

Whitelocke's *Journal* conveys a relative intimacy, careful negotiation, and willingness to imagine her point of view that are, as we shall see, quite distinctive in writing on Christina. After her abdication and her flight in men's clothes, the figures used to describe her, and the purposes of such descriptions, change dramatically. She was, it seems, more discussed in abdication than in rule. As will become clear, the ambassador of the English Republic gives one of the most intimate and sympathetic accounts of the Queen in English. It is also an account which in several ways shows us the mediation of theory and practice in women's political involvement.

SCANDAL: 'STRANGE STORIES' AND POLITICAL IDENTITY

We hear strange stories of the Swedish queen with her amazonian behaviour, it being believed, that nature was mistaken in her, and that she was intended for a man, for in her discourse, they say, she talks loud and sweareth notably.

So wrote Cromwell's spymaster, John Thurloe, in August 1654.[52] Thurloe's disgusted representation of Christina's Amazonian behaviour

[52] 28/18 Aug. 1654: John Thurloe, *State Papers*, 7 vols. (London, 1742), V, 451.

was probably intensified by political disappointment: an abdicated, Catholic ex-queen was politically useless. It seems that as early as 1652 Milton had commented that Christina 'may abdicate the Sovereignty, but she will never lay aside the Queen'.[53] Regal behaviour without a throne was an invitation to gossip and satire, and Christina was now reported as extraordinary, without proportion. So she was said to have asserted that 'The English have cut off the Head of their King, whom they did not Value, and they have done well.'[54] In fact, Christina's abdication and her reception into the Catholic Church generated a whole new wave of writing on this former 'virgin queen' and the stories about her became increasingly exotic and scandalous. Thus, when she was entertained with a comedy after she 'publickly abjur'd the Lutheran Religion' she was retrospectively reported as telling the guests, 'It is very fit that you should give me a Comedy, after I have given you a Farce.'[55] It is not uncharacteristic of later reporting of the abdicated Queen that she is made to speak her own shame in a cynical libertine register. Though far from the nuanced diplomatic interchanges of Whitelocke's diary, the satire on the abdicated queen is nevertheless evidently deeply engaged with issues of sex and politics. What does this suggest about the role of gender in shaping political identities and identifications of English Protestant men?

The ceremony which made Christina a member of the Roman Catholic Church was, it seems, witnessed by at least one Protestant Englishman: John Bargrave.[56] Testifying to the extent and nature of the English appetite for news of Queen Christina, Bargrave's report also invites us to ask what political purposes the libertine characterizations of her served and, concomitantly, reveal some of the tensions in his own religio-political identity. Bargrave, 'Cannon of Christ Church Canterbury', was among the royalists who toured Europe during the Civil War and its aftermath. During intermittent self-imposed exiles in

[53] G. Masson, *Life of Milton* (London, 1877), IV, 599; quoted in Akerman, *Queen Christina*, p. 291.

[54] *The Miscellaneous Remains of Cardinal Perron, President Thuanus, Monsr St. Evremont* (London, 1707), p. 243.

[55] Ibid., p. 244.

[56] Stephen Bann, *Under the Sign: John Bargrave as Collector, Traveller, and Witness* (Ann Arbor: University of Michigan Press, 1994), pp. 115–16, 146 n. 26. My account follows Bann.

the 1650s, he repeatedly visited Rome. His travels were somewhere between tour and perverse pilgrimage. Bargrave's attitude to Rome was marked by fascination and abhorrence in the intense form precipitated by Civil War conflict, but also, as Stephen Bann notes, by a deep desire to understand the historical circumstances of his own life and the tempests that had shaken the English Church's worship.[57] As Bann describes it, Bargrave's enterprise during and after his exile was 'living symbolically'; he collected manuscripts and artefacts (surviving in cabinets in Canterbury cathedral archives) which he used to make sense of his experiences.[58] This is why Christina makes her appearance in his strange manuscript, 'College of Cardinals'. The 'College', describing the Roman cardinals, brings together information and hearsay on their histories. It is not clear for whom, exactly, Bargrave wrote up this text. However, he was employed by the Restoration Church and his experience of travel was put to use in a mission to redeem 300 British captives in Algiers—so it seems likely that this written aspect of his travels was shared with others.[59]

Bargrave supported neither the cleansing of images from church nor the Laudian reordering of the liturgical space, but his support for his idea of the English Church was strenuous nonetheless. His religio-political position was built around his veneration for Charles the martyr, combined with a view that Civil War and regicide were a conspiracy.[60] In the 1650s (as at earlier points in English history) situational logic made radical Protestants and Catholics—particularly Jesuits—look similar. Thinking this way, Bargrave writes, 'in all probability [the Jesuits] were the men that ruined the king and kingdom under the new name and cheat of INDEPENDENT'.[61] Accordingly, the Civil War could be seen as 'a war of religion, to bring in Popery'. Animated by swirling anxieties

---

[57] Ibid., pp. 117–19. On Bargrave's Anglicanism as far from Laudian, see pp. 57–8.

[58] Ibid., p. viii.

[59] On 2 Aug. 1660 Bargrave recovered his fellowship at Cambridge. In May 1662 he petitioned the Crown to be prebend at Canterbury; Sheldon (then bishop of London) helped him to it. Sent off to redeem 300 British captives in Algiers. See James Craigie Robertson, *Pope Alexander the Seventh and the College of Cardinals* (London: Camden Society, 1868), pp. xii–xvi.

[60] John Bargrave's 'College of Cardinals' exists in manuscript, Canterbury Cathedral Archive, Lit MS E.39.a, and in James Craigie Robertson's edition. See 'College', ed. Robertson, in Robertson, *Pope Alexander*, p. 20; Bann, *Under the Sign*, p. 120.

[61] 'College', ed. Robertson, p. 20. See also Bann, *Under the Sign*, pp. 120–1.

about the English Church and fantasies uniting Rome with Independency, Bargrave finds a ready focus in the conversion and career of the Swedish queen. For Bargrave, Christina's behaviour must, surely, give evidence of the Jesuit conspiracy. However, even as he condemns her abandonment of Protestantism Bargrave, piquantly, *shares* Christina's fascination with Rome. If, as seems to be the case, Bargrave sought to observe and know Rome as the antithesis and enemy to the true English Church, testing his own truths against an all-too-familiar other, Christiana, made things more complicated.

Bargrave's 'The Pope, and Colledge, or Conclave of Cardinalles living when I was my fourth and laste time at Rome, wheare I bought them in sheets Ano 1660' devotes a side to each cardinal (and one to Christina), maximizing scandalous detail.[62] Christina's point of entry into the Roman hierarchy is her association with Cardinal Azzolino, who some thought was Christina's lover. Azzolino's 'Amours to all kinde of Ladies Eclipse all his parts.' A 'certayne Fryer his Pandor' used to supply him 'certayne Doxies', but these Christina eagerly replaces. Cardinal Azzolino's putative relationship with Christina gives Bargrave an instance confirming what he 'knows' already; if Rome is a whore the converted Christina out-Romes Rome. And so the abdicated Queen appears among the Catholic hierarchy, a lone convert in a 'conclave'. Bargrave's insertion of Christina into his 'college', as well as being a bizarre detail, offers a clue to the way in which he formed his own identity as an Anglican, an Englishman, for it connects the text specifically to his own witness testimony. It also tells us something about the difficulties contemporaries encountered and the strategies they required to address Christina's paradoxical status and behaviour.

Bargrave's description has its roots in personal experience. Either by luck or planning he had witnessed Christina's reception into the Church on her route to Rome; it was an event perfectly designed to sharpen his fascination and prejudice.[63] As he puts it, the Queen, 'brought up a Protestant in the Lutheran way, Quitted her Crowne and her Religion too, Turning Papist and was Received at Inspruck'. Her conversion from Lutheranism to Roman Catholicism illuminates the terms of his own struggle against the enemies called Independency and

---

[62] Canterbury Cathedral Archive, Lit MS E.39.a, fo. 34^{r-v}.
[63] Bann, *Under the Sign*, p. 116 n. 26, p. 146.

Catholicism—abominations which, while appearing to be polar opposites, are in fact distinct faces of the same Hydra of heresies. The border of Italy and Germany was the place chosen for her to 'renounce her former Religion of a Lutheran Protestant, and to be Received into the bousome of the Church of Rome'. At that time Bargrave made his own drawing of her.[64] He notes his capacity as witness, 'I was Present, staying there a month for that purpose', and asserts, 'All most all the Emperors Court and other Nobility were there.' Indeed, Pope Alexander VII sent another Lutheran convert, 'Monsigr Lucas Holstenius', also Bargrave's 'Courteous Acquaintance', to 'Admit her into the Roman Fayth'.[65]

Christina was closely observed. How was this ceremony of renunciation and reception to be understood? Bargrave, like everyone else, notes her restless carriage in church—'very scandalous':

laughing and giggling and curling and trimming her locks, and motion of her hands and body was so odd, that I heard some Italians that were neere me say E Matta per Dio: by God Shee is mad, and truly I thought so too, There being in her no signe of Devotion, but all was to her, as if shee had binn at a play, whilst shee Received the Sacrament in Roman moade, and all the time of the short Sermon, But shee had short Sermons all the weeke after: Every day in a severall language, all which shee understood well, as I was told there by Monsig Holstenius the Popes internuntio, with whom I was often: That night she was entertained wth a most excellent Opera, all in Musick, and in Italian, The Actors of that Play being all of that Nation, and as some of them selves told me, they were 7 Castrati or Eunuchs, the rest were whoores, moncks, Fryers, and Priests. I am sure it lasted 6 or 7 hours, with most strangely excellent scenes and Ravishing Musick...

Bargrave has even been able to obtain a copy of this diabolic entertainment, 'a book in Italian, which I have now in my study, with all the Scenes'.[66] The analogy between the mass and playing draws on Christina's reputation for loving theatricals but also expresses Bargrave's deep

---

[64] Lit MS E.39.a, fo. 34ᵛ.

[65] Lucas Holstenius, 'Keeper of the Vatican Library', gave Bargrave three sheets of ceremony, from which the Queen read 'very readily in a lowe manly voice undauntedly'.

[66] The piece was apparently Marco Antonio Cesti, *L'Argia*. See *The Travel Diary of Robert Bargrave, Levant Merchant 1647–1656* (London: Hakluyt Society, 1999), p. 244 n. 1; *New Grove Dictionary of Music*, XX, 581–2.

fear of the possible relationship to faith and ceremony that Christina's behaviour indicates. Bargrave, like others, was troubled by the way the Queen's extreme actions—conversion and abdication—were accompanied by flippant behaviour—'no signe of Devotion'—during the very ceremony which was understood as key to her actions (the 'Sacrament in Roman moade'). Indeed, other accounts claim Christina did not take the sacrament until she could receive it at Rome.[67] Why she would treat with apparent contempt that for which she had relinquished a throne seems to have been beyond the comprehension of several contemporaries.

At mass Christina behaved 'as if shee had binn at a play'. Her light conduct is reprehensible, truly, but more importantly the Catholic ritual is, Bargrave hints, play. The actual entertainment which follows the ceremony emphasizes, for Bargrave, that—whether it is the mass or an opera—Catholic ritual is dangerous theatre. While the very 'actors' are in themselves deceivers—'whoores, moncks, Fryers, and Priests', the music is 'ravishing'. For Bargrave, deceitful, Catholic ceremonial has power. Christina, here, is hybrid or fractured; a strange being made up of apparently incompatible opposites. Her ability to combine behaviours—faith and play, serious purpose and extreme flippancy, masculinity and femininity—is clearly profoundly troubling. And in watching the ceremony Bargrave witnesses the efficacy of Romish power, not its diminution. When Christina stays on for a 'variety of Entertaynement', including shooting chamois in 'whole Droves' with 'smale Canons', Bargrave stays too, to gawp and criticize. A chamois horn in his collection testifies to his presence.

Bargrave's response to Christina is reminiscent of that of observers at the court of Henrietta Maria who, as Erica Veevers has discussed, made constant play on the idea of a masque and the deceits of Catholicism.[68] Henrietta Maria brought to court both masques and masses. Moreover, her prominent involvement in court masque can be seen as a complex continuation of and response to Anna of Denmark's—Protestant—use of masque in English court politics. Puritan satire on Henrietta Maria pinpointed with the accuracy of finely tuned politicized enmity the link

---

[67] 'College', ed. Robertson, p. 69.
[68] Erica Veevers, *Images of Love and Religion* (Cambridge: Cambridge University Press, 1989), pp. 205–6.

between the Queen's religious and theatrical activities, and Veevers cites a printed image of her religious life 'described under the figure of a dance or masque'.[69] What, then, does Bargrave's engraving of Christina actually commemorate? As in the rest of his writing and collecting, one key point for him is that *he was there*. Coexisting with the importance of his claim to witness history was a more analytical interest in the way in which the activities and manners of Christina exposed to him the secret truth of the Roman Catholic Church. Her behaviour—as an ex-Protestant queen—was evidence of the far reach of Rome. In building his own identity as a loyal churchman and displaced traveller, Bargrave found Christina's behaviour meaningful enough to be collected for future reference—he sketches her even as her actions are repudiated. At the Restoration, interested in building an image of Anglicanism past and present as true Protestantism, Bargrave perhaps uses Christina in the 'College' to illuminate the path of one who did not return to a true way. Yet, her significance seems to exceed this: his writing is scarcely able to keep control of the fascinating details. Bargrave seems to struggle to stabilize what this encounter really meant.

Like Bargrave, others saw Christina through the lens of the English political crisis. A substantial quantity of material about her was circulated, and some translated into English in the 1650s. One of these pamphlets was published in 1656 as *A Relation of the Life of Christina Queen of Sweden*, possibly translated by James Howell, later to be historiographer to Charles II. The *Relation*, like the Dutch publication of the French texts, presents together two rather different accounts of Christina. The shorter and more scandalous of the two, the 'Brief Life' interests itself in the meaning of Christina's abdication and, specifically, canvasses the question of her reputation. In this account, supposedly written by 'one of her Domesticks' (promising 'ample account' of Christina 'in her glory' and 'after her eclipse') her career is organized around the transformation of reputation whereby having 'worthily obtained the repute of being not so great and glorious, as wise and vertuous', upon embracing Spanish counsel she 'became quite changed;

[69] Veevers, *Images of Love*, p. 205. See Clare McManus, *Women on the Renaissance Stage: Anna of Denmark and Female Masquing at the Stuart Court 1590–1619* (Manchester: Manchester University Press, 2002).

and her Court, which was formerly a School of Vertue, was now a Nursery of Vice'.[70] We read:

> Never was the World so gull'd in their opinions of any one person, as of this Princess, who whilst she was esteemed the Phoenix of the Age, became insensibly a prodigous monster; and from a Lady of great renown, she is become a Lady Errant, seeking Adventures in strange lands.

Not surprisingly, the pamphlet concentrates on the same moment that fascinated Bargrave—her entry into the Roman Church.[71]

Eccentric as Bargrave was, his explanation of the Civil War as a Jesuit conspiracy was not that unusual. If his 'College' reveals the specificity of his attempts to symbolize political and religious trauma, his acts of pilgrimage and witnessing also partake of, and perhaps feed into, more widely held, and elsewhere more fully realized, uses of Christina as a symptom of political crisis. Bargrave's witnessing and testimony suggest some of the political work done by gender in the 1650s. For Bargrave, Christina suggests both the causes and the effects of civil crisis. Standing for and being evidence of the usually secret connections between Rome and sectarianism, 'Christina' is a very specific example, but one which takes on much of the symbolism associated with the Civil War figuring of rebellion as female. Obviously printed satire and accounts like Bargrave's—forensic yet partly allegorized, true yet always overdetermined—are not an index of any freedoms gained by women in the English Civil War. Yet, at the same time as Bargrave's meditations on Christina strive to make her public, political, religious actions symbolize conspiracy, secrecy, and sin they perforce acknowledge women's political participation.

The complex diplomatic discussions which Whitelocke used to engage with a powerful woman involved in political process stand in a stark contrast to the operations of fame after she abdicated. In the *Aeneid* we find that fame is 'monstrous, deformed, titanic'; with 'as many tongues and buzzing | Mouths as eyes, many pricked up ears'.[72] Christina, as the object of fascination reported by Bargrave and scores of printed pamphlets, in the 1650s became a feminized figure of fame.

---

[70] *A Relation of the Life of Christina Queen of Sweden* (London, 1656), A2^r, A2^v.

[71] Ibid., p. 24.

[72] Virgil, *Aeneid*, trans. Robert Fitzgerald (London: Random House, 1981), bk. IV, ll. 249, 251–2.

Everyone wanted to know about her. Those who met her—like the two French aristocrats Madame de Montpensier and Madame de Motteville who wrote of their encounters with Christina during her invited, and uninvited, stays in France—offer complex pictures of her. But generally, from the point of her flight in masculine clothing, the tension about the ethical import of Christina's behaviour as a queen, now abdicated, exacerbated by the distance of any actual events, is transformed in print into characterizations of her as libertine.

The investments revealed by such satirical representations, obviously, also disclose the contours of female political activity: a political threat is sometimes also a sexual threat, and vice versa.[73] Certainly, there was a figural reciprocity and intimacy between the symbolic values of female and general rebellion for early modern readers and writers. However, Bargrave's account of Christina stops short of allegory or full symbolization. It shows us in process the struggle to obtain, or make, political knowledge, and in this Christina holds a partly symbolic, partly forensic place. Bargrave's use of Christina shows femininity in the process of satirical political image-making yet, perhaps because of his very strategy of witnessing, that image seems restrained from fully stereotypical attack. The partial symbolization in Bargrave's account valuably discloses some of the literal ways in which thinking put together women and politics, drawn on the one hand towards closure on the symbolic and on the other to complex and continuing events. In Bargrave's and the pamphlets' struggles to know Christina we can trace a tense, and overdetermined, acknowledgement of the symbolisms and actualities of female rule as overlapping, but not contiguous or seamlessly joined. It remains to explore a key factor in the representation of Christina: her philosophical, religious, and sexual libertinism. This was as important as her Protestantism, Catholicism, and homicide for some contemporaries measuring themselves against the Swedish queen. In 1656 Queen Christina described her religion as 'best represented in Lucretius' *De Rerum Natura*' and we will now turn to the political implications of female libertinism.[74]

[73] Neil Hertz, 'Medusa's Head: Male Hysteria under Political Pressure', *Representations*, 1, No. 4 (Fall 1983), pp. 27–55: 27.
[74] Akerman, *Queen Christina*, p. 73.

UTOPIA: CAVENDISH, THE EMPRESS, NEW WORLDS

A consideration of Queen Christina and Margaret Cavendish together illuminates the way Cavendish's political, utopian, secular, and sexual ideas are intertwined. Taking the representation of the Swedish queen more figurally, this section takes a tour through Cavendish's thinking on similar topic before returning to the Queen herself. Bargrave and Whitelocke found the Swedish queen rich material with which to consider their own worlds and the connections between women and rule. Margaret Cavendish, it seems, found Queen Christina good to think with in a very different way: she uses utopia. Sharing with Christina a tendency to tendentious praise and blame of women, Cavendish explores in much more detail than can be found in Christina's own fleeting comments the ideal and degraded political potential of women. Moreover, part of Cavendish's project as a writer is, clearly, her self-construction as 'singular', Margaret the First. So while her writing gives every impression of drawing upon contemporary women as they were in relation to politics—most obviously Henrietta Maria and Queen Christina—she eschews direct homage or criticism. How do Cavendish, Christina, politics, religion, and libertinism touch one another?

A distinctive feature of Cavendish's writing is that, although she sees sexual implications in libertinism, she considers it to have philosophical and perhaps political implications. Her *Description of a New World Called the Blazing World*, initially published as a 'companion piece' to her *Observations Upon Experimental Philosophy* (1666), takes seriously the claims of the same thinkers that influenced Christina.[75] Published at a time when the King held court in the Countess of Castlemaine's apartments and satirical pornography was an important and politicized genre, Cavendish's freedom in her utopia is very different from the licence of the court represented in scandalous novels or porno-political satires. However, philosophically and politically inflected as it was, Cavendish's utopia did also imply a version of sexual liberty. As Stephen

---

[75] Margaret Cavendish, *The Blazing World and Other Writings*, ed. Kate Lilley (London: Penguin, 1994), p. xii.

Clucas writes, 'In her witty defenses of the "honest liberty" of philosophical discourse' Cavendish can be seen as England's 'first woman libertine philosopher'.[76] Certainly, for Cavendish, moving in philosophically if not sexually libertine circles, the Swedish Queen's libertine concerns would have seemed familiar. The issues that preoccupied that Queen—including pleasure, female rule, learning, the physical and philosophical apprehension of the world, and to a lesser degree, the relationship between Protestantism and Catholicism—also either touched Cavendish's life or were amongst her significant preoccupations. To see how Queen Christina, liberty, thought, and politics are related in Cavendish's imagined world we can first explore the contexts of her writings and some of the writings themselves.

Though he was to die before her story truly began to unfold, Descartes serves as the first specific connection in the libertine matrix which held both Margaret Cavendish and Christina. Descartes corresponded with Christina herself and wrote about her to Hector-Pierre Chanut, French resident in Sweden (in 1645–9) and later ambassador to Holland (1653–5). Although, as he confided to Chanut, Descartes was wary of Christina, he was not perhaps wary enough, allowing himself to be transported to her court, where he died.[77] In her approaches Christina had asked Descartes to expound his 'view of the supreme good understood in the sense of the ancient philosophers'. Descartes responded that, as knowledge of what is good is often beyond us, what humans can control is will. So, one should 'by a firm and constant resolution' perform what one judges to be best: this 'constitutes all the virtues' and produces 'contentment'. In this way, he continues:

I think I can reconcile the two most opposed and most famous opinions of the ancient philosophers—that of Zeno, who thought virtue or honour the supreme good, and that of Epicurus, who thought the supreme good was contentment, to which he gave the name of pleasure.[78]

[76] Stephen Clucas, 'Variation, Irregularity and Probabilism: Margaret Cavendish and Natural Philosophy as Rhetoric', in *A Princely Brave Woman: Essays on Margaret Cavendish Duchess of Newcastle*, ed. Stephen Clucas (London: Ashgate, 2003), pp. 199–209, p. 207.

[77] René Descartes to Chanut, 26 Feb. 1649, in *The Philosophical Writings of Descartes* ed. John Cottingham, Robert Stoothoff, Dugald Murdoch, and Anthony Kenny, 3 vols. (Cambridge: Cambridge University Press, 1991), III, 368.

[78] René Descartes to Queen Christina, 20 Nov. 1647: ibid., III, 324–6: 325.

Descartes goes on to prove that the good use of free will produces contentment—a judgement which successfully unites many of Christina's own concerns. Descartes knew the Cavendishes too. In 1647 or 1648 the Marquess of Newcastle gave a dinner in Paris at which Descartes was reconciled with his critics, Thomas Hobbes and Pierre Gassendi.[79]

In 1647 Margaret and William had been married for two years. They had been married by the Anglican chaplain to Henrietta Maria's court, John Cosin, in the private chapel of the ambassador, Sir Richard Browne.[80] Judging from Cavendish's extremely halting letters to William and her own account of her early years, much of her education began when she met him.[81] Between meeting Newcastle at Henrietta Maria's court in Paris and her first publications almost a decade later, Margaret Cavendish seems to have absorbed an education from the thinkers around her.[82] It would have been hard to find an educational milieu more threatening to the restricted ideas of female education sometimes expressed in conduct literature and educational theory than the Newcastle circle in the late 1640s. The education Cavendish acquired was not only late but potentially improper. Certainly its effects in her later writing could be considered so. That Cavendish consistently presented her writing as what Kate Lilley calls 'a conjugal effect', part of an elaborate and competitive romance of status, marriage, and education, may say more than her direct comments on the influence of Newcastle and his circle.[83] When Cavendish entered their circle, in the 1640s and 1650s, several of Newcastle's intimates had published

---

[79] René Descartes to Queen Christina, p. 389; Kathleen Jones, *A Glorious Fame: The Life of Margaret Cavendish, Duchess of Newcastle, 1623–1673* (London: Bloomsbury, 1988), p. 60; see also Anna Battigelli, *Margaret Cavendish and the Exiles of the Mind* (Lexington: University Press of Kentucky, 1998).

[80] Jones, *A Glorious Fame*, pp. 51–2.

[81] *Letters of Margaret Lucas to her Future Husband, William Cavendish*, ed. R. W. Goulding (London: Roxburghe Club, 1909). On education see Sarah Heller Mendelson, *The Mental World of Stuart Women: Three Studies* (Brighton: Harvester, 1987), pp. 12–31; Katie Whitaker, *Mad Madge: The Extraordinary Life of Margaret Cavendish, Duchess of Newcastle, the First Woman to Live by her Pen* (New York: Basic Books, 2002), pp. 14–28.

[82] On London see Hero Chalmers, *Royalist Women Writers 1650–1689* (Oxford: Oxford University Press, 2004), pp. 16–21.

[83] Kate Lilley, 'Contracting Readers: "Margaret Newcastle" and the Rhetoric of Conjugality', in *A Princely Brave Woman*, ed. Clucas, pp. 19–50.

or were considering atomism.[84] As Clucas reminds us, the philosophical differences amongst those in the Newcastle network—Thomas Hobbes, Walter Charleton, Kenelm Digby, as well as Sir Charles Cavendish, René Descartes, Pierre Gassendi, and, of course, Margaret Cavendish— were more important than the similarities.[85] Thus, drawing on the Epicurean and Lucretian thinking so important at the English Stuart court, Cavendish developed her interests in atoms, politics, government. Significantly, she understood motion in a way that paid little attention to the prime mover or the divine: her insistence that 'atoms, *of themselves*, could make a world' was heterodox, indeed, close to heresy.[86]

Religion, apparently so important, and possibly so unimportant, to the Swedish Queen, also played an enigmatic role in Cavendish's writing and, although Cavendish's comments on religion initially take us away from Christina, they also bring us back to the Queen. By 1656, when Christina described her religion as 'best represented in Lucretius' *De Rerum Natura*', Margaret Cavendish was living in Antwerp with her husband. There they lived amongst other exiles, including Edward Hyde, in whose chapel she and the Duke worshipped, and who had an influentially low opinion of Newcastle's political abilities.[87] Cavendish was establishing her reputation as a writer, and in her early literary attempt, *The Worlds Olio* (1655), she debates religion and

---

[84] Pierre Gassendi revitalized Epicurean atomism in Christian form. More significant, though, for the Newcastle circle was Walter Charleton's *Physiologia Epicuro-Gassendo-Charltoniana* (1654). See Stephen Clucas, 'The Atomism of the Cavendish Circle: A Reappraisal', *The Seventeenth Century*, 9 (1994), pp. 247–73: 254–6.

[85] Clucas, 'Atomism', pp. 265–7. Charleton wrote extensively on Epicurus. See e.g. his libertine discussion in *The Ephesian Matron* (London, 1668; 1st published 1653), introd. Asach Guibbory, Augustan Reprint 172 (Los Angeles: William Andrews Clark Memorial Library, 1975), A3ʳ; *Epicurus's Morals* (London, 1656). Reconciling Epicurus with a Christian life see *Physiologia Epicuro-Gassendo-Charltonia: or a Fabrick of Science Natural, Upon the Hypothesis of Atoms*, ed. Robert Kargon (New York and London: Johnson Reprint Corporation, 1966).

[86] See Robert Kargon, *Atomism in England from Hariot to Newton* (Oxford: Clarendon Press, 1966), pp. 63–75: 75; Clucas 'Atomism'. See also Lisa Sarashon, 'A Science Turned Upside Down: Feminism and the Natural Philosophy of Margaret Cavendish', *HLQ* 47, No. 4 (1984), pp. 289–307; Susan James, 'The Philosophical Innovations of Margaret Cavendish', *British Journal for the History of Philosophy*, 7, No. 2 (1999), pp. 219–44.

[87] Richard Ollard, *Clarendon and his Friends* (Oxford: Oxford University Press, 1987), pp. 143–5; Mendelson, *The Mental World of Stuart Women*, pp. 39–40.

politics.[88] First she contrasts the likely inabilities of a prince 'born to a just title' with the observant wisdom of an usurper. An hereditary prince, 'thinking his rights to his Crown, is a sufficient warrant' is likely to be careless: 'he may put the asse where the fox should be, and the sheep where the Lion should be, the serpent where the dove should be, and thus misplacing of men in several offices, and commands, is many times the ruine of a kingdom'.[89] Hardly calculated as an endorsement of the Stuarts, this passage is preceded by a discussion of the subject with equally critical implications. Cavendish asserts, 'a solitary life is the happiest' but 'I do not mean so solitary as to live an Anchoret'. Rather, she suggests an Epicurean tranquillity: to be content 'persons must be as free from all bonds, as their mindes must be from all wandering desires'.[90] A substantial analysis of 'Monastic life' follows this endorsement of secular solitariness; she finds it 'very profitable to the Common-wealth, whatsoever it bee for the soul, for it keepes peace and makes plenty, and begets a habit of sobriety which gives a good example'. Although, she concedes, religion requires other forms of evaluation, 'rationally one would think that God should not take delight in shaven heads; or bare and dirty feet, or cold backs, or hungry stomachs'.[91] Cavendish's own history lends significance to her sarcasm about religion generally, but also about Catholicism specifically. As Battigelli comments, Cavendish's expressions of scepticism about religion had both personal and, importantly, political sources.[92] As a member of Henrietta Maria's court Cavendish was familiar with Catholic ritual and the Queen's commitment to female monasticism. We know that from 1651 Henrietta Maria spent as much time as possible in the convent of Chaillot.[93] We also know that, at the time of her marriage to Newcastle, Cavendish was on poor terms with the Queen.

[88] On Cavendish, religion, and politics see Hilda Smith, *Reason's Disciples* (Urbana: University of Illinois Press, 1982), pp. 61–3 and *passim*; Anna Battigelli, 'Political Thought/Political Action: Margaret Cavendish's Hobbesian Dilemma', in *Women Writers and the Early Modern British Political Tradition*, ed. Hilda Smith (Cambridge: Cambridge University Press, 1998), pp. 40–55 and Smith's introduction, esp. p. 4; Battigelli, *Margaret Cavendish*, pp. 50–61.

[89] Margaret Cavendish, *The Worlds Olio* (London, 1655), pp. 47–51: 48.

[90] Ibid., p. 27.

[91] Ibid., pp. 29, 30.

[92] Battigelli, *Margaret Cavendish*, p. 55.

[93] Alison Shell, *Catholicism, Controversy and the English Literary Imagination, 1558–1660* (Cambridge: Cambridge University Press, 1999), pp. 148–56.

Cavendish criticized monasticism from close to the Queen's circle, and her anti-Catholic sentiments were noted by at least one attentive reader who was possibly herself a part of that circle. One Du Verger, probably Susan du Verger, in 1657 published *Du Vergers Humble Reflections Upon Some Passages of the Right Honourable the Lady Marchioness of Newcastles Olio*.[94] Starting with Cavendish's attack on the monastic life and those in it as 'drones', the response mounts a trenchant defence of Catholicism and monasticism. This author seems to be an Englishwoman. On reading Cavendish's *Olio*, she writes, 'my sharpe appetite greedily tooke down those unaccustomed cates, and that with much satisfaction and delight (eyeing in it the honour of our nation, and sexe, wherein we have had but few arguments of such abilitie)', but then she finds the attack on monasticism—and has to reply.[95] Du Verger responded vehemently and at length. And Cavendish's later writings seem equally, if anything more, explicitly hostile to Catholicism. The whole incident prompts us to think about the politics of Cavendish's relationship to that religion as it can be partly tracked in her repeated literary working over of the (for her) twin questions of female rule and female communities.

The nature of Susan du Verger's writings leads us to the contested relationship between Christian religion and Epicureanism. Du Verger was a translator; her first translation had been published in 1639 and was dedicated to Queen Henrietta Maria.[96] Du Verger's other signed translations were of the moralized yet also complex and often sexualized romance tales and other writings of the Bishop of Bellay, Jean-Pierre Camus. In the dedication of her first translation, to Henrietta Maria, du Verger quotes the Jesuit Nicholas Caussin's *Holy Court* where she finds Caussin enthusiastically approving the Bishop. Caussin was an authority calculated to appeal to Henrietta Maria, but also one implicated in the

---

[94] (?)Douai, 1657.

[95] 'Epistle', ibid. (unpaginated). See *Susan du Verger*, ed. Jane Collins (Aldershot: Scolar Press, 1996).

[96] *Admirable Events: Selected Out of Foure Bookes,* Written in French by the Right Reverend John Peter Camus, Bishop of Bellay Together with morall Relations, written by the same Author And translated into English by S. Du Verger (London, 1639), dedication to Henrietta Maria, A3ʳ; 'Trans. Susan du Verger', A5ᵛ. This probably indicates that the same person translated *Diotrephe or, an Historie of Valentines* (London, 1641).

debates about Epicurean pleasure and tranquillity which the Newcastle circle was addressing. His *Holy Court*, itself dedicated to Henrietta Maria by the author who held the place of Louis XIII's confessor, engaged with Epicurus. As Reid Barbour writes, Caussin was ready to denounce the Epicures, but also gave Epicurean thinking a prolonged reappraisal in his consideration of the place of pleasure at the court. Caussin's particular disapproval is for the tendency of Epicurean thinking to produce 'utopian fantasies'.[97] For Caussin, even though God gave men, women, and animals intense forms of pleasure (such as 'delectation'), a good life could not be reconciled with Epicurean pleasure.[98]

The textual relationship between Margaret Cavendish and Susan du Verger, then, illuminates three issues. First, for all that Cavendish wrote little and unenthusiastically about religion in general, she did make negative comparisons between Catholic monasticism and other ways of life. Second, we can speculate that du Verger, herself apparently associated with Henrietta Maria's circle, may have been in a good position to recognize an implicit hostility to the Stuarts in Cavendish's comments. Third, taking into account du Verger's reading of Cavendish and both Cavendish's and du Verger's other writings, we can glimpse a role played by Epicurean thought, or more precisely the idea of Epicurean thought, in finessing the potentially cataclysmic distinctions between Catholic and Protestant at the courts of Henrietta Maria in London and Paris. *The Holy Court* itself shows clearly the limits of the engagement between Epicureanism and Catholic ideas of the good life. It is also notable that Cavendish's treatment of religion in terms of its social influence has something in common with Christina's apparent use of it as a theory of origins and moral code. Queen and Duchess seem to share an understanding of religion as social and political—important as a set of functions, codes, ceremonies, and possibilities. For all that

---

[97] Reid Barbour, 'The Early Stuart Epicure', *ELR* 23, No. 1 (1993), pp. 170–200, esp. 188–90; id., *English Epicures and Stoics*, pp. 101–5.

[98] Nicholas Caussin, *The Holy Court*, trans. Thomas Howard, vol. IV (London, 1638), p. 127. One of the British Library copies seems to have been owned by Thomasine Aston. Brilliana Harley records being sent it 'from Worster'; Letter XXII (1 Feb. 1639), in *Letters of the Lady Brilliana Harley* (London: Camden Society, 1854), p. 27.

Christina was a convert, neither she nor Cavendish seems to have approached religion as strictly a question of belief.[99]

Cavendish's espousal of philosophical liberty for herself—the liberty to think and rule her own thoughts—is far from the Holy Court's circumscribed understanding of pleasure. Yet her analysis of female pleasure and quasi-conventual life does traverse some of the same terrain. Cavendish's ideas on female liberty and rule are increasingly fully realized in the writings of the later 1650s and 1660s. In writings such as *The Female Academy* (1662), *The Convent of Pleasure* (1668), and *The Blazing World* (1666), she visits and revisits the scene of female education, political organization, and rule.[100] For Cavendish the scene of sequestered female education is clearly compelling. Certainly, scenes from *The Female Academy* show that female education, because it is out of reach of the world, brings a strong charge of freedom. Yet Cavendish marks for the reader the contrasts and resemblances between her academy and brothel, conventicle, or convent. Women academicals, sent to the convent-like academy by their mothers to be 'virtuously and wisely educated', learn rhetoric and to debate on themes.[101] Men, increasingly furious because unable to attract the women's attention, 'rail extremely that so many fair young ladies are so strictly inclosed' (II. iii) and, after setting up their own academy, plan to use trumpets to distract the women speakers. Cavendish's imagined cloister is sexually and politically double-edged.[102] From the start the play acknowledges the tendency of a school to seem like the brothel found in the parallel

[99] See Susan James, *Margaret Cavendish: Political Writings* (Cambridge: Cambridge University Press, 2003), p. xxviii.

[100] On politics, retreat, and education in Margaret Cavendish's drama see Sophie Tomlinson, '"My Brain the Stage"', in *Women, Texts, and Histories*, ed. Clare Brandt and Diane Purkiss (London: Routledge, 1992), pp. 134–63; Irene Dash, 'Single-Sex Retreats in Two Early Modern Dramas: *Love's Labour's Lost* and *The Convent of Pleasure*', *Shakespeare Quarterly*, 47 (1996), pp. 387–95; Annette Kramer, '"Thus by the Musick of a Ladyes Tongue": Margaret Cavendish's Dramatic Innovations in Women's Education', *Women's History Review*, 2, No. 1 (1993), pp. 57–80; Julie Sanders, '"A Woman Write a Play!": Jonsonian Strategies in the Drama of Margaret Cavendish', in *Readings in Renaissance Drama by Women*, ed. S. P. Cerasano and Marion Wynne-Davies (London: Routledge, 1998), pp. 293–305.

[101] Margaret Cavendish, *Playes* (London, 1662), p. 653.

[102] See Julie Sanders, '"The Closet Opened": A Reconstruction of "Private" Space in the Writings of Margaret Cavendish', in *A Princely Brave Woman*, ed. Clucas, pp. 127–40: 133.

literature of sexual or erotic 'education'. The opening scene offers us this exchange:

2 Lady. The Female Academy, what is that?

1 Lady. Why a House, wherein a company of young Ladies are instructed by old Matrons; as to speak wittily and rationally, and to behave themselves handsomly, and to live virtuously. (I. i)[103]

As virtue rubs up against handsome behaviour, Cavendish, rather than resisting the resemblances between sexual desire and the liberating experience of educational speech, reminds the reader of them. As the women speak freely they are watched through a grate by the men, who soon begin to make smutty jokes about how the 'Grave Matrons' would be put to work as 'midwives' if men were to be let in, and admit that they can think of nothing but women. While the women speak, passionately engaged and at first oblivious, they are surrounded by hearers and viewers who comment on the sexual economy—a subject addressed by the women only in a late speech on the subject of courtship. Obviously by splitting men and women, speaking and hearing, virtue and violence, Cavendish shapes the plot towards the tentative reuniting of suspended opposites—men and women—at the end of the play. Yet, of course, the very plotting and narrative tension which tug the reader or hearer towards the rebalancing conclusion of men and women reintegrated in comic courtship mean that, throughout, the audience must be aware of both the desirability produced by sequestration and the erotic charge of pedagogy. Readers of *The Female Academy* are taught that sequestration of women offers intellectual freedom *and* increases women's sexual desirability. The polarization of men and women in an educational and sexual drama coexists with an understanding of femininity as unstable.

If sequestration in Cavendish's female academy implies intellectual liberty from men it also hints at the alliance between conventual life and the seraglio. But Cavendish's female educational community needs to be distinguished from other analogues besides the brothel—specifically, Cavendish distinguishes her world from the female discussion and preaching in the gathered churches of Civil War London.[104] Cavendish

---

[103] Cavendish, *Playes*, pp. 656, 653.
[104] On Cavendish in London, see Whitaker, *Mad Madge*, pp. 136–7.

is self-consciously and polemically engaged in the political struggles of the Civil War; her writings obliquely and explicitly replay her own family's trials and those of her husband. She was personally involved in those struggles over ethos, money, and power when she visited Republican London in an attempt to settle her husband's estate. In *The Female Academy* this appears in the brief, punitive, drama of the Citizens' Wives. In insistently condemning them, Cavendish's *Female Academy* acknowledges the significance of a politically engaged lower stratum of women of the kind involved in petitioning and other activities. Initially presented as desiring education, the Citizens' Wives want to hear the women discourse. However, the Citizens' educational project is immediately and forcibly redirected. One comes on to the stage saying:

3. *Wife*. . . . the Door-keeper beat me back, and said there was no room for Citizens Wives, for the room was only kept for Ladies, and Gentlewomen of Quality.
2. *Wife*. Well, we may come to be Ladies one day, though not Gentlewomen, and then we shall not so often be beaten back.
1. *Wife*. Let us go to the Gentlemens side, they will receive us, and use us kindly. (II. xi)[105]

The implications of the scene turn on the word 'ladies'. The porno-political satires of the 1640s and 1650s used this term, among many, for whores. Thus *News from the New Exchange* (1650) gives notice to readers of 'certain *Ladies*, called *Coursers*, whose Recreation lies very much upon the *New Exchange* about 6 a.clock'. At the same time, we are told to beware of 'my Lady *Sandys*; for she sweeps the *Exchange*, like a Chain'd Bullet, with Mr. *Howard* in one hand and *fitz James* in the other'.[106] Here the term 'Ladies' is used to designate a sexual progress through the ranks, and it is similarly used by Cavendish to discriminate between virtuous and sexual education. The play here briefly draws on the scenarios and language of porno-political pamphlets.[107]

---

[105] Cavendish, *Playes*, p. 662.
[106] Henry Neville, *News from the New Exchange* (London, 1650), collected by Thomason 30 Jan. 1649 [E.590 (10)], p. 20.
[107] See Susan Wiseman, '"Adam, the Father of all Flesh": Porno-Political Rhetoric and Political Theory in and after the English Civil War', in *Pamphlet Wars: Prose in the English Revolution*, ed. James Holstun (London: Frank Cass, 1992), pp. 134–57; James Grantham Turner, *Libertines and Radicals in Early Modern London: Sexuality, Politics and Literary Culture* (Cambridge: Cambridge University Press, 2002), p. 110.

It seems to be doing so, however, to keep at bay satiric and pornographic interpretations of the academical ladies, as the Citizens' Wives absorb the pornographic potential of the educational situation. Thus, Cavendish responds to the sexual and satiric potential of her own comic plot by writing *in* satire on sex and status which, being directed against the Citizens' Wives, ensures the contrasting 'innocence' of the academy.

Cavendish's use of the Citizens' Wives to stabilize several difficult aspects of her drama points towards other resemblances that she recognized as troubling, most obviously one canvassed in the text: the unclear border between a female academy and a cloister. The Matron addresses the Gentlemen and the audience:

> *Matron.* Gentlemen, pray give me leave to inform you, for I perceive you are in great Error of mistake, for these ladies have not vowed Virginity, or are they incloystred: for an Academy is not a Cloyster, but a School, wherein are taught how to be good wives when they are married. (V. xxix)[108]

The academy—because of the grate—must be considered as on the very border of private and public; the nature of the women's confinement needs to be distinguished from Catholic ideals. Constantly aware of the potential of a female community to seem like a convent, for a school for wives to seem to be a school for whores (something Cavendish plays on from the opposite side in 'Assaulted and Pursued Chastity' where the bawd reads the young Lady 'lectures of nature'), Cavendish nevertheless repeatedly visits these scenes. What does her interest suggest about the relationship between women and politics?[109]

If *The Female Academy* demonstrates Cavendish's linking of female power and thought, this is explored more fully in *The Convent of Pleasure*, published in her second volume of plays (1688). In part a rewriting of *The Female Academy* which heightens the sexual and political tensions of the earlier play and locates them in central, indeed ruling, figures—Lady Happy and the Princess that she admits into her retreat. The Princess (Prince) and Lady Happy elaborate Cavendish's interest in the self-validating aristocratic pair—but with an additional frisson supplied by the doubleness of the Princess as a she *and* a he. *The Convent of*

108 Cavendish, *Playes*, p. 679.
109 Margaret Cavendish, 'Assaulted and Pursued Chastity', in *The Blazing World*, ed. Lilley, pp. 47–118: 49.

Pleasure provides an exploration of the mental states of men and women experiencing female retreat. The term 'convent' signals that the play is again considering the status of religious retreat and its apparent antithesis—'pleasure'. Pleasure's associations with Epicurean philosophy invite us to see the play as framed, paradoxically, by both Epicureanism and Catholicism. Within this problematic, Lady Happy's utopian project is used to explore the question of the good life and, particularly, how that category can be interpreted for women:

> *L. Happy.* . . . I will take so many Noble Persons of my own Sex, as my Estate will plentifully maintain, such whose Births are greater than their Fortunes, and are resolv'd to live a single life, and vow Virginity: with these I mean to live incloister'd with all the delights and pleasures that are allowable and lawful; My Cloister shall not be a Cloister of restraint, but a place for freedom, not to vex the Senses but to please them. (I. i)[110]

The play's project is to complicate but not wholly undermine this utopian analysis of female community and powerful rule, retirement, and pleasure. The play opens with Lady Happy's plans for a 'retiredness' which bars nothing else from life but—men. Lady Happy's interlocutor objects:

> *Med.* O yes, for those that incloister themselves, bar themselves from all other worldly Pleasures.
> *L. Happy.* The more fools they.
> *Med.* Will you call those Fools that do it for the gods sake?
> *L. Happy.* No Madam, it is not for the gods sake, but for opinion's sake . . .
> (I. i.)[111]

At this point, using the more generalized 'gods', Lady Happy repeats the critique of monastic life Cavendish had offered in *The Worlds Olio*, asking why 'the gods' should be pleased by men lying 'uneasily' on the hard ground.

There has been much discussion of the central scenes of *The Convent of Pleasure* where, after the Ladies watch a dystopic play of marriage, the Prince, disguised as a Princess, successfully makes love to Lady Happy.

---

[110] Margaret Cavendish, *Plays Never Before Printed* (London, 1668), p. 7. See also Anne Shaver, *The Convent of Pleasure and Other Plays* (Baltimore: Johns Hopkins University Press, 1999).
[111] *Plays Never Before Printed*, p. 4.

Deep in love melancholy, Lady Happy wanders in pastoral garb asking herself, 'why may not I love a Woman with the same affection I could a Man?' (IV. i). She forbids herself such a love on the grounds that 'No, no, Nature is Nature, and still will be | The same she was from all Eternity.' However, in the scene which follows, liberty and knowledge rather than nature are at issue. The Princess (i.e. the disguised Prince) enters, '*in Masculine Shepherd's Clothes*', and Lady Happy confesses that she fears 'our Goddess Nature' will 'punish me, for loving you more than I ought'. Sexual pedagogy ensues:

Prin. Can Lovers love too much?
L. Happy. Yes, if they love not well.
Prin. Can any Love be more vertuous, innocent and harmless then ours?
L. Happy. I hope not.
Prin. Then let us please our selves, as harmless Lovers use to do.
L. Happy. How can harmless Lovers please themselves?
Prin. Why very well, as, to discourse, imbrace and kiss, so mingle souls together.
L. Happy. But innocent Lovers do not use to kiss.
Prin. Not any act more frequent amongst us Women-kind; nay, it were a sin in
    friendship, should not we kiss: then let us not prove our selves Reprobates.
They imbrace and kiss, and hold each other in their Arms.
Prin. These my Imbraces though of Femal kind,
    May be as fervent as a Masculine mind. (IV. i)[112]

Although the scene does of course draw on conventions of disguise from romance and stage, it also shows, in part, the seduction of one woman by another. The audience or reader, though they do not know the Princess to be a Prince, is pressed into a position of knowledge which is potentially both generic (the pornographic seduction) and involves a more worldly understanding of the implications of same-sex desire than is explicitly voiced in the seductive dialogue. Lady Happy's desire for the Princess indicates her own inadequate sense of the implications of the cloister, for she learns that desire does not invade from the outside but is stimulated by proximity and acquaintance. Learning about desire she also learns about friendship and implicitly about Platonism, so she (innocently?) recognizes that the body is implicated in the desire to 'mingle souls'. While *The Convent of Pleasure* is resolved in marriage, Lady Happy plans to preserve the convent for virgins and widows: the

---

[112] *Plays Never Before Printed*, pp. 32–3.

utopian project is not abandoned but to be re-established in the light of a greater understanding of desire. In reworking *The Female Academy*, *The Convent of Pleasure* concentrates much more fully on the questions of female rule within the community, the good life, desire, and the philosophy of pleasure. What the inhabitants of the convent learn is their vulnerability to desire which—of course—rather than being suppressed (as in religious communities), needs to be philosophically schooled if it is to make the right kind of woman.

With the question of female rule and female desire we can return explicitly to women's relationship to politics and Cavendish's use of Queen Christina as we examine the politics of the paired rulers—the Empress and the Duchess—in *The Blazing World*. The rule of Lady Happy shows her exploring and becoming more knowledgeable about the good life. It also shows her making a world and setting it to work. In *The Blazing World* the scene of world-making and rule replaces the issue of education and sequestration as the main focus, and the two female rulers are evidently in possession of an education which enables them to build a world: utopia takes off from the end point of the drama's more agonistically dialectical account of the education of the female ruler. It would be possible to argue that the Empress is, literally, modelled on Queen Christina; such a figure, for a contemporary reader, resembles Christina. And in exile, of course, Christina and Cavendish did indeed have an empire nowhere. The text, however, shows us not Christina but, in an impulse not often realized in Cavendish's fiction, empire shared; the authorial Duchess and indeed the diegetic Duchess are happy to share power with a figure who has libertine commitments and interests, travels, and imagines rule. Significantly, then, the rulers in *The Blazing World* offer a literary representation of the interests shared by Christina and Margaret Cavendish—and the ideas, indeed, are a model for rule. If, as Clucas suggests, Margaret Cavendish is a libertine thinker, then her Empress represents a realization of a libertine figure in utopia. Moved from the architecturally imagined enclosures of academies and convents to the intercommunicating and self-transforming worlds of the utopia, the ruling female is given greater sway and more philosophical as well as political liberty. In *The Blazing World* what Mary Campbell calls Cavendish's interest in the 'immanent interior of the person' is explored in part in the form the external powers. A utopia bound to the languages of natural philosophy by its position in her *Observations on Experimental*

Philosophy and its representational premises, *The Blazing World* is none-theless not solely an atomist treatise; rather, it stretches that vocabulary to fit the building and ruling of fictional worlds by an Empress and her scribe.[113] It is in *The Blazing World*'s utopian mind-empires that Cavendish puts before us figures that both address and, by magic indeed, offer a fantasy of the positive resolution of female political power.

Not precisely a sexual couple, like Lady Happy and the Princess, the Empress and her scribe are more fully rulers than the convent princesses in the plays.[114] In Cavendish's utopia the representation of women as rivals is resolved in the persons of two platonic soulmates, willingly sharing their time in the Duke's soul. Empress and Duchess are trapped in worlds which they both need to, and in various ways *can*, make and remake. Without the danger attendant on solely female communities, the two rulers are also at a facilitating distance from their subjects. Within a fictional frame they are, like Christina and Cavendish, philosophers, natural scientists; they are influenced by libertine not Christian thinking. Having initially asked for the soul of a dead philosopher as scribe—'Aristotle, Pythagoras, Plato, Epicurus' or a modern 'Galileo, Gassendus, Hobbes'—these being unsuitable the Empress settles for Margaret Cavendish. When the Empress chooses the Duchess as her scribe we are reminded of the potential of female intimacy; far from offering no cause for jealousy 'platonic lovers' are 'very dangerous, as being not only very intimate and close, but subtle and insinuating'.[115]

In *The Blazing World* Cavendish liberates the potential of the philosophical heroine to rule over the land. Coming to *The Blazing World* from considerations of Christina, it is clear that the Empress is a

---

[113] Mary Baine Campbell, *Wonder and Science: Imagining Worlds in Early Modern Europe* (Ithaca: Cornell University Press, 1999), p. 182 and *passim*.

[114] On rule and utopia in *The Blazing World* see Catherine Gallagher, 'Embracing the Absolute: The Politics of the Female Subject in Seventeenth Century England', *Genders*, 1 (1988), pp. 24–9; Rachel Trubowitz, 'The Re-enchantment of Utopia and the Female Monarchical Self: Margaret Cavendish's *Blazing World*', *Tulsa Studies in Women's Literature*, 11, No. 2 (1992), pp. 229–46; Ellayne Fowler, 'Margaret Cavendish and the Idea of Commonwealth', *Utopian Studies*, 7, No. 1 (1996), 38–48; Rosemary Kegl, ' "The World I have Made": Margaret Cavendish, Feminism, and the Blazing World', in *Feminist Readings of Early Modern Culture: Emerging Subjects*, ed Valerie Traub et al. (Cambridge: Cambridge University Press, 1996), pp. 119–41; Marina Leslie, 'Gender, Genre, and the Utopian Body in Margaret Cavendish's *Blazing World*', *Utopian Studies*, 7, No. 1 (1996), pp. 6–24.

[115] *Blazing World*, ed. Lilley, p. 181.

representation of a female ruler-philosopher of the kind which, at points, Christina aspired to be. The political and gendered obstacles to female rule are substantially effaced by the generic power of utopia to reconsider morsels of culture as an idealized whole. At the same time, I think, we can see a use of the figure like Christina which makes productive and, unusually, positive use of the political and philosophical potential of the female libertine. It would be possible to work through a literal mapping of Christina and Cavendish—both cross-dressed, both were projective fantasists and valued the power of fantasy, commentators found each presenting unstable versions of femininity. Such detailed or biographical parallelism would yield different insights; my concern here has been to suggest some of the ways in which Cavendish, Christina, politics, religion, and libertinism do intersect. Consideration of the freedom—as well as the problems—implied in Christina's career undoubtedly illuminates our sense of rule and freedom in Cavendish's writings.

[A]lthough the Ladyes have their faces masked, nevertheless one may sometimes spie parts that doe not lesse add to their luster, I wished you a sight of it truly, as well as of the Queene of Sweden who surely deserves it if any woman does, I doe not meane for the beautie of her face, but for that Majestie that appeares in it, as likewise in all her actions & comportments wch savour far more of a man than of a woman, wch sex she resembles in nothing more than in her inconstancie, for in truth I conceive her to be as weary of her new religion as of her old one as is plainly seene by her postures, gestures, & actions at the Masse, before wch I think at any time she would preferre a good Comedie, and a handsome wittie Courtier before the Devoutest Father.

So wrote a correspondent who may be William Russell, the future Rye House conspirator, in the mid-1650s.[116] Russell was among many who wondered whether Christina was man or woman, heroine or criminal, devout or degenerate. We have not pursued her career into France where Madame de Motteville, biographer of Anne of Austria, and Madame de Montpensier, also a writer of utopias, had much to say about her.[117] Nor

---

[116] MSS Duke of Devonshire at Chatsworth: William Russell's Early Letters, from Augsburg, 27 Dec. 1656.

[117] Françoise Langlois de Motteville, *Memoirs of Madame de Motteville on Anne of Austria and her Court*, trans. Katharine P. Wormeley, 3 vols. (London: William Heinemann, 1902), vol. II *passim*; Anne Marie Louisa, Duchesse de Montpensier, *Lettres de Madamoiselle de Montpensier, de Mesdames de Motteville et de Montmorenci*, ed. Leopold Collin (Paris, 1806).

have we delved into the scandalous pamphlets which, plagiarizing and expanding upon one another, inflated her doings—grand or sordid—to huge proportions and blew them around Europe. Rather, in examining three English writers, we have seen three very different uses of one particular figure in thinking about politics, and particularly women's relationship to politics. Following the ways in which three writers used the Swedish queen has given us information about the place of distance and fantasy versus intimacy and experience in the conceptualization of women's relationship to rule. As well as telling us about the specific concerns of the three writers, Whitelocke's, Bargrave's, and Cavendish's engagements with Christina indicate the ways in which individual views are always in communication with the cultural assumptions around them. Cavendish has idiosyncratic concerns but also sees potential in a kind of (fairly) chaste libertinism. Bargrave participates in an apprehension of papal conspiracy as well as being an eccentric. Whitelocke modifies theory by practical involvement. This mixture of specific obsessions with wider cultural concerns at particular moments is what makes productive the study of a particular figure.

Yet, before I conclude, I must mention one figure whose views have so far been ignored: Christina. Inevitably, the Queen left her own views on the world in, amongst other forms, memoirs, maxims, and an assessment of Alexander the Great.[118] Apparently identifying with Alexander the Great she described him as 'an object worthy heroick emulation' for:

Alexander was a man, and therefore we ought to pardon his faults upon the account of his great virtues.... The faults of great men are ... richly worth the virtues of the vulgar. It is also past doubt that envy and calumny spare none. They fasten inseparably upon the most illustrious lives. It is not therefore to be wonder'd, that they have not spared Alexander.[119]

She comments on Alexander's relationships with ambassadors that it is 'obvious that princes are liable to be flatter'd' and 'embassadors know how to make their court, and do not always speak as they think'.[120] It is tempting to see in the Queen's reflections on Alexander an assessment of her own career. Her own is one voice amongst the many interpretations

---

[118] *The Works of Queen Christina*, trans. from the French (London: D. Wilson & T. Durham, 1753).
[119] Ibid., pp. 1, 36, 137.
[120] Ibid., p. 141.

of what her political and sexual career might 'mean'. We might expect a radically different perspective. Yet Christina, too, seems to be responding to the circulation of material on the topic of her sexual and political significance. The Swedish queen was acknowledged as a figure against which views and stereotypes of gender and politics were tested. Indeed, as a queen, a celebrity, and because of her very overt transgressions of decorum (not least in abandoning her Lutheran kingdom for Rome) Christina is distinguished from almost all the other figures studied in this book. It is only tangentially that her own political identity is under consideration; the focus of discussion is how she was represented and interpreted. What do the uses of Christina suggest about women's relationship to politics in seventeenth-century England?

As we have seen, representation of Christina indicates the way in which circumstances remodel theory, iconography, and stereotype. Writing on her shows us some of the tensions experienced by writers in the gendering of politics. Thus, Bulstrode Whitelocke's records suggest that his preconceptions, theories, and plans about diplomacy at the court of the Swedish queen were transformed when he actually encountered her. His writings, generated as Cromwell was taking power and Christina relinquishing her throne, suggest the importance of (and by extension we must assume the pressure on) the theoretical, experiential, and rhetorical role of the paternal household as a stable ground and example. While discussions of regicide often invoke the crisis of the father-king as initiating a crisis in the paternal family, Whitelocke's writings generated by Christina offer a more complex and nuanced picture, in which the collapse of higher-level conceptual frameworks see him bringing into play the idea of the household. As well as showing the contradictions political theory and modelling encounter in actual situations, Whitelocke's writings on Christina tell us more about the connotations of the father and the ruler in the 1650s, and the pressures on these. Whitelocke's writings suggest a distinct political formation was in play because of the actualities and paradoxes of distance and closeness at play in the Swedish court.

Like Whitelocke's, Bargarve's writings on Queen Christina demonstrates the tension between theory or ideal and experience. They also, like Whitelocke's, suggest some of the ways in which witnessing can complicate an individual's relationship to cultural givens—in this case about women and particularly women and politics. Bargrave's strenuous attempts to use Christina to symbolize Rome, femininity, and the conspiracy against the English Church encounter the way in which he finds her not only troubling but also impressive and fascinating. While his writing draws on the printed scandal describing her life, we can see, I think, in his writing a failure to fully realize his image of Christina as stereotype. Indeed, Queen Christina seems to have forced those who thought about her to consider the nature of rule itself, in part through her extraordinary activities. What may be Cavendish's use of Christina in the overtly fictionalizing genre of utopia is of course very different from the others—Christina is not discussed. Nevertheless, the Empress and her servant exist in relation to the same array of stereotypes of good and bad womanhood and, once again, these are challenged; the utopian genre enables the author to render that challenge in positive fictional and idealized terms as the two female rulers are allowed the political and imaginative liberty not only to invent their own positions in control of all forms of representation in their kingdoms but also, as those kingdoms are imaginary, to resolve their own position in relation to politics and virtue.

This analysis of the representation of rule has revealed the connections between women and libertinism, religion, and national politics to be more complex than perhaps we might have anticipated. Political theory is one among many discourses describing the political situations examined here. Christina, an exception in herself, illuminates thinking on both widely held ideals and the fraught yet present potential for women's involvement in political philosophy. We have seen in action three writers with very different agendas working with the stable ideologies of femininity, stereotypes of good and bad female rule, and literary genres to say something about women's relationships to politics. This chapter has begun to explore the claims to political truth implied by a diary, testimony, witnessing. It remains for the two chapters that follow to explore more fully the ways in which gender and claims to legitimacy interact in writing from the later part of the seventeenth century.

IV

LEGITIMACY AND SCANDAL

7
Martyrdom in a Merchant World: Elizabeth Jekyll and Mary Love

MEMORY AND NARRATIVE

'Something is branded in, so that it stays in the memory', a philosopher observes, 'only that which *hurts* incessantly is remembered.'[1] Politics, and political language, are concerned with legitimacy and with undermining the claims of others, and in this and the next chapter the place of gender in the dynamics of scandal and legitimacy is explored. This chapter looks at the remembering and forgetting of the particular circumstances of politics, and at the part the writing and transmission of women's biographical texts played in the making of memory. In Restoration nonconformist political and religious memory martyrdom is the dominant figure for the ceaseless pain of the past, and its meanings in the present. Yet, for a memory to operate as a prompt to political action in the present it must be freed of some of its ties to the past— a branding *in* of memory involves, inevitably, a burning *out* of some details of the originary event. Here I explore the genealogy of a particular event from 1651, the trial for treason of the Presbyterian Christopher Love, as it was recorded in the narratives of two women, Elizabeth Jekyll and Mary Love. In doing so I argue that these texts, which circulated after the Restoration, indicate that we need to re-evaluate the place of

---

[1] Friedrich Nietzsche, *On the Genealogy of Morals*, trans. Douglas Smith (Oxford: Oxford University Press, 1996), pp. 42–3. See also Wendy Brown, 'Wounded Attachments: Late Modern Oppositional Political Formations', in *Feminism, the Public and the Private*, ed. Joan B. Landes (1993; repr. Oxford: Oxford University Press, 1998), pp. 448–74.

narrative produced by women in building Restoration nonconformist culture. The process of political memorialization and amnesia which Elizabeth Jekyll's and Mary Love's manuscripts facilitated was complicated and is here discussed in three stages: the 'event' (Christopher Love's trial and his Lilburnian claims to citizenship); the women's narratives; their Restoration editing and significance. At each stage the 'meanings' of the event are changed.

This case study of these two narratives has implications with regard to wider critical concern about the impact of the Restoration on what became nonconformist writing and on women's texts within radical and nonconformist circles. Accounts of women and radicalism in the 1640s and 1650s have tended to follow an established historiography within which the Restoration is seen as a retreat for radicals.[2] Accordingly, critics have drawn attention to women's productivity in those decades and contrasted this with an apparent withdrawal from public activity after the Restoration.[3] Although the genres used by nonconformists can certainly be seen to change at 1660 and during the Restoration, the still dominant story of this as a shift to quietism needs to take into account also the developments of the 1670s and 1680s which saw what contemporaries felt was a return of the political questions of the 1640s. Moreover, the narrative of radical retreat at the Restoration has dovetailed all too neatly with a tendency within women's history to see women's lot as either improving or declining. Recent challenges to this framework note its narrative overdetermination in repeatedly finding women 'not only oppressed, but more oppressed than they were in the past', or vice versa.[4]

[2] Christopher Hill, writes: 'many radicals lapsed into silence'. See *The Experience of Defeat: Milton and Some Contemporaries* (London: Faber & Faber, 1984), p. 19; see also pp. 15, 21. See also Richard L. Greaves, 'The Puritan-Nonconformist Tradition in England, 1560–1700', *Albion*, 17, No. 4 (1985), pp. 449–86: 468–9. As Greaves notes, although 'historians have been partial to a "vertical" approach to the Puritan-nonconformist tradition, they have often been hesitant to extend their studies across the great watersheds of the period, 1640 (or 1642) and 1660', and this periodicity, too, tends to be duplicated in some studies of women's place in Puritan/nonconformist history.

[3] Especially helpful on sectarian writers is Elaine Hobby, *Virtue of Necessity* (London: Virago, 1988), pp. 26, 49, 85, 88.

[4] Amanda Vickery, *The Gentleman's Daughter* (New Haven: Yale University Press, 1988); Margaret W. Ferguson, 'Moderation and its Discontents: Recent Work on Renaissance Women', *Feminist Studies*, 20, No. 2 (1994), pp. 349–66: 351.

This chapter aims to nuance the relationship between religious radicalism before the Restoration, and citizenship, Presbyterianism, and nonconformity afterwards. The Presbyterians analysed here offer an opportunity to reconsider the way in which texts by women were used in the 1650s and the 1680s. As I will argue, these texts invite a rethinking and extension of the way in which women can be understood as participating in Civil War and Restoration culture not because they articulate explicit demands for citizenship, but because they use their very position of exclusion from politics to tell a political story.

TESTIMONY AND CITIZENSHIP: LILBURNE, LOVE, AND JOHN JEKYLL'S TESTIMONY

The event which the narratives I am examining take as their starting point involved complicated, perhaps confused, political and religious allegiances. Christopher Love, the main actor in the treason trial which also embroiled Elizabeth Jekyll's husband, was a Presbyterian minister. His trial followed hard on that of John Lilburne in 1649. Love, accused of organizing to 'stir up a new and bloody war, and to raise insurrections, seditions, and rebellions within this Nation', was arraigned for high treason under the Act of 26 March 1650, which made it illegal to send letters to those organized against Parliament.[5] Procedure had changed since Lilburne's trial before a jury, and Love faced judges.[6] Nevertheless, following Lilburne's example, Love sought to shape his trial as an issue of rights rather than treason. As the two trials were significant in shaping the idea of the citizen under the republic, it is worth looking in some detail at what Love took—or tried to take—from Lilburne.

At his trial Lilburne insisted on 'ancient rights' and asserted natural law inflected as the inalienable right of the individual to defend himself.[7] In texts connected with the case Lilburne mobilized legal and

---

[5] T. J. Howell, *Complete Collection of State Trials* (London, 1816), V, 51 (subsequent references are to *ST*); obviously *State Trials* is far from objective reporting. See also Cynthia Herrup, *A House in Gross Disorder* (Oxford: Oxford University Press, 1999), pp. 138–42.

[6] Thanks to Professor Fritz Levy for this point.

[7] Richard Tuck, *Natural Rights Theories* (Cambridge: Cambridge University Press, 1979), pp. 147–9.

biblical vocabulary; Lilburne himself is often associated with Christ, persecuted by the law which should defend him. Lilburne made his trial a legal spectacle which invoked the law in its absolute and quotidian manifestations, and an understanding of law as double—ideal and interested, absolute and quotidian—irradiates Lilburne's writing and trials and allows him to produce an image of himself as the citizen martyred.[8] In reading 'Lilburne', as Nigel Smith reminds us, the reader inhabits the world of the apprentice and of mercantile London, a world bathed in the glow of martyrological typologies.[9] A powerful pattern for the idea that the law was itself tested in its treatment of the citizen was found in the martyrological narrative of Foxe's *Acts and Monuments*, and reinforced in the 1640s and 1650s by the Leveller claims to citizenship in *The Agreement of the People*.

On trial for his life at the Guildhall, the records of the trial preserve the way Lilburne adapts the language of martyrdom to assert his claims to citizenship. He promises emotively that, if deprived of 'The benefit of the Law and Liberties ... by my birth-right And inheritance is due unto me', he will nevertheless 'leave this Testimony behind me, That I died for the Laws and Liberties of this nation, and upon this score I stand, and if I perish I perish'.[10] In Lilburne's defences at the trials themselves, in his relationship with those who attended them, and in the published narratives surrounding the trials, the doubleness in the law, shifting between the quasi-religious and the quotidian, came to shape a particular concept of the citizen. Lilburne's accounts offer the citizen-as-martyr, not necessarily actually murdered by law but made visible as a citizen, paradoxically, by the very refusal of the law to recognize him as at the centre of its world—a refusal coupled with its rejection of its higher, transcendent, role as truth or justice. Thus, linking himself to St Paul when he argues, 'I crave but so much liberty from you as was given to Paul when he pleaded for his life before the heathen Roman judges, which was free Liberty of Speech to speak for himself', Lilburne infused the law with the glow of biblical precedent, overlaying his position

---

[8] *An Act For the Establishing an High Court of Justice*, with 'An Act declaring what Offences shall be adjudged Treason' (London, Nov. 1653), p. 197.

[9] Nigel Smith, *Literature and Revolution in England, 1640–1660* (New Haven: Yale University Press, 1994), p. 132.

[10] John Lilburne's trial for high treason on Thursday, 24 Oct. 1649: *ST* V, 1270–1.

as a claimant of true law disenfranchised by interest with the affecting properties of the narratives of Christian martyrs.[11]

The law, as Lilburne recognized, was on trial as much as he. Lilburne's trial, some nine months after the death of Charles, was the first fruit of a new legal system. In it we can see in operation the new system of justice, notionally uniting the nation under the Great Seal, but also being tested by a totemic figure and, as was reported at the time, before a huge audience who loved Lilburne. The question of the place of the 'free-born Englishman'—that mobile but evocative concept—before the law of 'his' Commonwealth was implicitly at stake. Lilburne's call upon the rights of the free-born Englishman is a reminder of the true law betrayed by the court and an assertion of the natural right of self-defence.[12] For the substantial audience supporting Lilburne and those who read about the trial, Lilburne's defence was unforgettable as an occasion on which natural law was asserted and quotidian law was forced to compromise. Lilburne was not executed. He was acquitted by the jury and, as if to prove the overlap of law and community, bonfires were lit, a medal was struck, a day of thanksgiving was appointed.[13]

Christopher Love seems to have taken up Lilburne's claim to disenfranchised citizenship. The publication of Love's trial, by 'John Farthing, Citizen of London, who took the Trial in the said Court for Mr Love, and at his own Request', suggests that Love had learned the connection between liberty and publicity.[14] The court thought he had learned it from Lilburne, the Attorney General accused him of attending Lilburne's trial because 'he thought his time might come', and the court was 'informed, that since he hath been in the Tower, Lilburne hath

[11] *ST* V, 1271. See also Joan Webber, *The Eloquent 'I'* (Madison: University of Wisconsin Press, 1968), p. 68; John Knott, *Discourses of Martyrdom in English Literature 1563–1694* (Cambridge: Cambridge University Press, 1993), p. 144.

[12] This sense of 'law' as Magna Carta, the Bible (Old and New Testaments), and Coke's *Institutes* consistently underwrites Lilburne's more quotidian uses of 'law'. The much-circulated and resonant, if repetitive, language of Lilburne's defence, the published image of him reading Coke's *Institutes* back to the court that tries him, and his use of the law in his own defence is what is remembered about the trial. The specific occasion of it as a test for the nature of the law of the English republic has been lost, effaced with the removal of those laws from the statute book. Yet understood together the two crystallize a moment in the invention of the citizen, or at the least the story and image—as in the image of Lilburne in the court—of the citizen.

[13] Pauline Gregg, *Free-Born John: A Biography of John Lilburne* (1961; repr. London: Dent, 1986), pp. 300–1.

[14] *ST* V, 43.

been his counsel'.[15] Both Love and the court agreed that his trial was connected to Lilburne's, but was the connection to be understood as one of criminal influence or the free defence of the rights and liberties of the free-born Englishman?

In court, Christopher Love modelled his claim to citizen-martyr status on Lilburne's. The opening sallies of his defence show clearly his highly self-conscious attempt to appropriate the position which Lilburne had been able to shape for enunciation of the grievances of the citizen disenfranchised by the law:

> Mr *Love*: I hope you will not be more severe to a Minister than you were to Lieut. Col *John Lilburne*. When you were at the court at *Guild-hall* at the trial of *Lilburne*, you gave him the liberty of two hours to plead before he pleaded guilty or not guilty.
>
> L. *Pres.* To a Minister, you say well; but I tell you, we do more to a christian then to a minister; and we are all christians, and your ministry is but an Office; and therefore what *Mr. Lilburne* had, it was the favour of the court then; but time is spent, and pray do not you follow that now.[16]

Love argued that Lilburne had given 'the Narration of his doings and sufferings that he might not be misrepresented to the Court', asserting, 'I insist on that liberty that Mr Lilburne had'.[17] A Lilburnian telling of a 'narrative' of circumstances, a desire to read a 'paper', was a central plank in Love's attempt to shape the trial as a Lilburnian defence of rights:

> Lord *President*. How many leaves is it?
>
> M. *Love.* But two or three; and if this court be more strict and severe to me, than that was to Mr. *Lilburne* I cannot help it.
>
> Att. Gen. Sir, not before you plead.
>
> M. *Love.* Yet I have the liberty, that when matters of law ariseth in the Indictment, to make a motion, and to move for counsel, and to shew the illegality of it; and though I confesse I am extreamly ignorant of the Law, yet I understand, that after I have pleaded, I am not capable of counsell.
>
> L. *Pres.* You are mistaken Mr *Love*.
>
> M. *Love.* I suppose I am not mistaken: For in the third part of Judge *Cooks* Institutes, I find it thus: *The prisoner, when he pleads not guilty, whereby he*

---

[15] *ST* V, 54.   [16] *The Whole Triall of Mr Love* (London, 1652), p. 3.
[17] Ibid., pp. 3, 4.

denies the fact, after the plea of not guilty, can have no counsell; but if he have any matter of Law to plead before it he may urge it.
L. Pres. He pleads he is ignorant of the Law, and yet can make use of it.
M. Love. I am to plead for my life, and I am to use Scripture, Law, and any other lawfull means to save my life. *Paul* did plead in the *Roman Law.*[18]

Perhaps Lilburne did school him in the Tower: Love, like Lilburne, reads a paper, reads from Coke's *Institutes*, claims to be like St Paul. As significantly, he uses the law in the same way as Lilburne to put in play patterns of martyrdom simultaneously with the claim to 'rights' enunciated from the position of the disenfranchised. As John Knott has argued, the discourses of martyrdom in the 1630s enabled those in prison to assimilate their experience to that of the martyrs in Foxe's book, a strategy with psychic dimensions in that it staved off despair as well as offering a 'pattern' for resistance.[19] Love's use of Lilburne's trial as a pattern offers an extension of such modelling which would have been understood by contemporary readers of accounts published 'for Publick satisfaction'—a patterning made more vivid precisely because of the newly made status of the law.

Love was no insignificant figure. Later remembered within nonconformist circles as one having both strong admirers and strong detractors, a sense of his own power within the City seems to have been behind his demand that his trial, held in Westminster, should be by a jury from his 'neighbourhood', 'of London'.[20] The world Love inhabited outside the courtroom is sometimes palpably present to the reader of the trial, visible in the tasks, desires, and oppressions which some witnesses testifying about Love's engagement with royalists bring into the room with them. Love's house was the centre of a group of men, including some esquires, an alderman, and Love's main co-accused, William Drake, an eminent Puritan divine, who was also described as a mercer.[21] Royalist agents moved in and out of this environment. Trial testimony derived from those around Love included those who felt keenly their

---

[18] Ibid., p. 4.   [19] Knott, *Discourses*, p. 144.
[20] John Quick, 'Icones Sacrae Anglicanae' (Dr Williams Library, MS 38, fos. 34, 35), collated much material from the 1650s on Love and writes of him as 'a man exceedingly beloved by som, & hated by others, who was highly honoured by his friend, & as much despised by his Enemys' (fo. 279). See *ST* V, 54.
[21] *Whole Triall*, p. 1; *ST* V, 43.

subservient relationship to the minister in the narrow streets of the City, some miles away. One such was Elizabeth Jekyll's husband, John, of St Stephen Walbrook, a general dealer of good family whose work took him to Bristol and Hull where, in the years of Civil War, his wife's diary records his adventures. John Jekyll met Titus, the royalist agent, through William Drake who introduced them 'in a cheese-monger's house in Newgate-Market'.[22]

Jekyll's courtroom testimony and behaviour indicate fear of the law, but also terror of neighbourhood slander and damage to his reputation.[23] Jekyll's evidence against Love is marked by extreme anxiety about both the oath and the nature of bearing witness. On the second day of the trial Jekyll was called into the court:[24]

Master Jaquel was called into the Court, and the Clark tendered him his oath; and Mr Jaquel spoke to the Court to this purpose: That there were many oaths abroad, and he could not tell what to say to them; and he desired to be excused. The Lord President told him that he could not be excused. Mr Jaquel said he was a Prisoner, accused of the same offences that Mr Love was accused of; and that he conceived he was not a competent witness against him. The Court again pressed him to take his oath. Mr Jaquel said that he durst not in conscience swear against Mr Love; and therefore desired it might not be pressed upon him. The Court still persisted in it, that he must take his oath and witness what he knew. He answered, he would speak the truth of what he knew as well as if he were under an oath. The Court told him he could not be; for if he did not swear, what he should say could not be received as anything in matter of Evidence. Mr Jaquel still persisted in his refusal. When the Court saw he could not otherwise be prevailed with, they fined him 500l for refusing to swear. And Mr Jaquel after he was withdrawn out of the Court, was called in again, and pressed to take his oath; and was told that the Court had fined him 500l for refusing to swear; and again asked him whether he would swear. Mr Jaquel then, when the oath was read to him, did not swear in that manner as the other witnesses did, but only put his hand to his buttons. And when Mr Love asked him if he was under an oath, he answered that he was as good as

22 *ST* V, 113.

23 See Laura Gowing, *Domestic Dangers: Women, Words and Sex in Early Modern London* (Oxford: Clarendon Press, 1996).

24 *CSPD* (1651), p. 6; 4 Nov. 1651: Council of State day's proceedings. On 3 Aug. 1652 the Council of State heard a report from the Committee of Examinations and debated the reward of Adams, now in danger from his enemies, for his part in bringing Love to the attention of the authorities. *CSPD* (1652).

under an oath. But the Court not being satisfied with this answer, pressed him further; and then he did say he was sworn, and as under oath.[25]

As a witness Jekyll lacked entirely the discursive resources and boldness demonstrated by Lilburne and attempted by Love. His comi-tragic play with the buttons was to haunt him throughout the trial, for Love continued to taunt Jekyll saying, 'this witness, I cannot call him so, but this informer'.[26] Days later, when it came to the summing up of his defence, Love referred back to the question of Jekyll's oath, asserting that 'Mr Jaquel himself, since he was sent away from the court, hath said he was not under an oath.'[27]

John Jekyll's 'oath' and his play with his buttons had clearly been under discussion in and out of the court and his vacillation leads us into the neighbourhood and citizen world beyond the court, one in which Love had power as a minister. Jekyll, himself accused of treason, as his wife recorded in her diary—in great 'danger being accused by the State for Treason against them'—may have bought his way out of trial by testifying against Love.[28] His behaviour suggests the urgent anxieties of those caught up in the trial. Jekyll was desperate, and could not, at least in the theatre of the courtroom, make the claims of citizenship or martyrdom. Love could make the claims, as we have seen, but not successfully. Love's deliberate Lilburnianism wearied the court and, for all that he had access to Matthew Hale, when he asked to speak the Lord President told him, 'you have not spoken at any time yet, but you have hurt yourself more than anybody else hath; and yet your language is so liberal, that no man shall escape the lash of your tongue'.[29] On 5 July 1651, having in his testimony of 25 June told the court of hearing treason without revealing it to the magistrate—misprision of treason— Love was sentenced to die. After the unexpected failure of petitions, he

[25] Jekyll was called immediately after Love had silenced Mr Cobbet, an army major, on the grounds of his connection with Captain Adams, the man who had told the Council of State about the conspiracy. *ST* V, 113.

[26] *ST* V, 154, also pp. 113–18; day 3, pp. 138, 154. Love accuses Jekyll of 'not any taking of an oath; but fearing his fine' (pp. 244–6).

[27] *ST* V, 154.

[28] The diary of Elizabeth Jekyll, Beinecke Library, Osborn Collection, Box 58 [H]20, fo. 18.

[29] *ST* V, 246.

was executed on 22 August.[30] Love's last words were published, and his works were published by his executors.[31]

Love was much less successful than Lilburne in his attempt to put the issues of rights and citizenship at the core of his trial. Where Lilburne's own writing dominates understanding of his trial, the political 'meaning' of Love's martyrdom was brought into being not so much by his own attempts as by the efforts of others to memorialize his death—those of the ministers who were Love's executors, that of his wife Mary, in the testimony and published letter of John Jekyll, and in the diary of Elizabeth Jekyll. It is in two of these four imbricated testimonies, rather than in legal testimony, that I will trace the interrelationships of citizenhood, disenfranchisement, and the powerfully moving narrative of the subordinate.

The significance of Love's treason and trial grew and changed in the world beyond the court. With Love's death another story begins, but this story, like the interwoven quality of the trials of Lilburne and Love, reinforces the point that politics, like law, can be understood in part as 'a language and imagery of transmission'.[32] Love became a Presbyterian martyr. The words of memorializers, written by those less able and equipped than Lilburne, drew attention to Love's, and the writer's, complex suffering and disenfranchisement before the law. The diary of Elizabeth Jekyll and the narrative of his own wife Mary Love make the event and its aftermath a case study in the circulation of narratives of citizenship.

---

[30] Petitions Love and his supporters presented and a long debate in the Commons generated a reprieve, so he did not die on the appointed date, 15 July. *ST* V, 43. By 12 August relations with Scotland were so tense that an additional, temporary Act Prohibiting Correspondence with Charles Stuart or his Party had made such contact treasonable: *Acts and Ordinances of the Interregnum*, ed. C. H. Firth and R. S. Rait (London: HMSO, 1911), II, 550–1.

[31] Presbyterian associates circulated his sermons. His executors issued *Grace, the Truth and Growth and Different degrees thereof* (fifteen sermons) (1652). At least six other publications generating a corpus of material associated with him as a martyr. His executors were Edmund Calamy, Simeon Ashe, Jeremiah Whitaker, William Taylor, and Allan Geare. Other publications included seventeen sermons in *Heaven's Glory, Hell's Terror* (1653); *The Soul's Cordial* (1653); *A Treatise of Effectual Calling* (London, 1653); *Scripture Rules to be observed in Buying and Selling* (1653); *A Christian's Duty* (1653); *The Hearer's Duty* (1653).

[32] Peter Goodrich, *Languages of Law: From Logics of Memory to Nomadic Masks* (London: Weidenfeld & Nicolson, 1990), p. vi.

Reshaped, with the emphasis shifted from law to the pain of the private citizen, Love's trial becomes a story of radical (yet obedient) suffering told in the female voice. The question of citizenship and rights, so consistently foregrounded by Lilburne, remained central to the story because of women's complex relationship to citizenship. Spiritually equal but politically indefinable, women held a poignantly imprecise relationship to natural law. Subordination, tempered with a claim to a wider reaching political as well as spiritual authority, made 'her' narratives (always themselves in an ambiguous relation to the public sphere) imaginative vehicles which for the voicing of 'the gaps and absences in the citizen's story . . . the body of feelings and affects that people bring' to the making of political change.[33]

MARY LOVE AND ELIZABETH JEKYLL: WOMEN TELL TALES OF LOVE

For the Rump, Love's defeat and death was a more solid victory than that over Lilburne. It was a political triumph, ending clerical resistance to the rule of the Republic.[34] But news of his execution, like Lilburne's acquittal and continued campaign, entered the 'neighbourhood' world outside the courtroom. The critically neglected accounts by the wives of Love and Jekyll—notionally on opposite sides of the trial—show how the past of the Republic came to be figured in nonconformist memory, and the place of feminine narration in that. Each text deserves fuller discussion than it has yet received, both in terms of the stories told and because of the way in which each manuscript received highly politicized editorial shaping by other hands.

Mary Love's narrative of her husband's life seems to have been fashioned later in the 1650s or in the 1660s, probably after she had remarried and moved away. 'The Life of Mr Christopher Love' responds to the claims, trial, and execution of her husband but, except in digressions, avoids direct discussion of the causes of the trial itself, thereby avoiding

---

[33] Carolyn Steedman, 'A Weekend with Elektra', *Literature and History*, 3rd ser., 6, No. 1 (1990), pp. 17–40: 21.

[34] See Richard L. Greaves, *Saints and Rebels* (Macon: Mercer University Press, 1985), p. 33; Blair Worden, *The Rump Parliament* (Cambridge: Cambridge University Press, 1974), pp. 243–8.

discussion of royalist conspiracy amongst the Presbyterian ministers. This suggests that it was written, if not circulated, before the Restoration. In Mary Love's story the trial barely features, though knowledge of it and its injustice is the justification for the telling of Love's life, beginning with his upbringing in Cardiff and never, quite, reaching the end.

Using the model of an exemplary life, the narrative also invites us to read Love's behaviour in terms of the failure of secular, and the success of spiritual, authority figures. Hearing no sermon before the age of 15, when 'one Mr Erbury' came to preach, Love, 'among others was taken with the novelty of it'; and 'although (as he would say him self) he went only to see a man in a Pulpit which hee never saw before, yet there God was pleased to meet with him'.[35] Coming home 'with an Hell in his Conscience', his struggle to pursue his faith began. He refused 'his old companions' and 'his usuall Games of Carding and Diceing (in which he would with grief say he was soe expert his father would have put him forth to have played with the greatest Gamesters in the Countrey) but now the very thoughts of them as Daggers in his Hart'.[36] Instead, escaping paternal vigilance, he puts a cord out of the window, 'Sliding downe by it, and soe went unto the Congregation'; 'and now this young Convert lyes under the unsupportable thoughts of an offended father in Heaven and a displeased father upon Earth'.[37] Although Erbury's radical opinions would, at least later, make him an unlikely spiritual guide for the Presbyterian Love, he remained Love's chosen mentor. What could be seen as Love's search for a chosen, rather than a given, paternal authority eventually leads him to Oxford, then to London, where he meets the narrator.

As the time of his trial and death approaches, his martyrdom becomes a palpable textual presence. Love is likened to both Joseph and Jeremiah, and his Presbyterian ordination becomes the occasion for play on his

---

[35] BL MS Sloane 3945, 'The Life of Mr Christopher Love', fo. 80[r]. Erbury eventually 'fell ... into very loose, dangerous & damnable opinions' (as John Quick put it), but Love continued to regard him as his 'spirituall father'. John Quick, 'Icones Sacrae', fos. 271, 279. See Richard L. Greaves and Robert Zaller, *Biographical Dictionary of British Radicals* (Brighton: Harvester Press, 1982), I, 253–4. In discussing Mary Love's 'Life' the holograph Sloane manuscript is used to discuss her text while that of T.H. is taken from the clearer copy in Dr Williams Library, 'Life of Christopher Love' PP. 12.50*.4(21) in an unknown 17th-century hand, checked against MS Sloane 3945.

[36] BL MS Sloane 3945, fo. 80[v].   [37] BL MS Sloane 3945, fo. 81[r].

martyrdom and that of others, when the narrator tells us of his humility and anticipatorily martyr-like qualities:

being asked whether he thought he could suffer for those truthes of Christ which he had then made profession of his answer was that he trembled to think what he should do in such a case especially when he considered how many had boasted what they could suffer for Christ and yet when it came to it they did rather deny Christ and his truths then suffer for them, making mention of Peter and amongst many others he produced that instance of Mr Pendleton who said he at a conference in the Countrey seeing that famous martyr Mr Saunders that was in danger with him assaulted with many fears lest he should not be able to hould out the ffirie Tryall he said Brother bare up for I am not at all afraid to think that this fat selfe of mine shall frye in the ffire and yett when they both came to the tryall he that came trembling suffered couragiously for Christ but he that came confident in his own strength recanted and could not burn for Christ, and then said he if such tall cedars as these shrinke what may such a shrub as I do Therefore I dare not boast what I shall do but if this gift be given me of God, then I shall not only be willing to be bound but to dye for the truths name and sake of the Lord Jesus.[38]

The reader is left in no doubt of Love's own graces: as the narrator tells us, 'here ye see him like unto the blessed disciples of Christ that did not know their own graces' and she finds him, 'with Joseph under all his Tryalls and temptations and suffrings'.[39] Offered reference points including the disciples, Joseph, and the English Protestant martyrs, the reader's interpretation of Love's status could hardly be more clearly directed. Love's life is dramatically contrasted with the attempts of his enemies, whose 'blacke mouths' and 'tongues were set on fire by hell' and who circulated 'horrid slanders' so that 'his death [would] not [be] so much lamented'.[40]

The shaping of the narrative as martyrdom intensifies towards the end of the text, as the narrator explains Love's qualities. She justifies him as one accused of being 'a man of contention yet his Relations to his family and acquaintance did know his to be a Moses for meekness and a Job for Patience'; 'of a humble self condemning spirit, that low Grace of Humility it was very tall in him'.[41] The humble, passive, aspects of martyrdom, what might be thought of as the lower Christian virtues, are combined with the martyr's certainty in his final days:

[38] BL MS Sloane 3945, fo. 102ʳ⁻ᵛ.   [39] BL MS Sloane 3945, fo. 102ʳ–103ᵛ.
[40] BL MS Sloane 3945, fos. 101ᵛ, 108ᵛ, 113ʳ.   [41] BL MS Sloane 3945, fo. 106.

as he said himself that he did never know what it was to have a full assurance till he had received that sentence of death at the Barr, & at that very minute (he said to his wife[)] that God came in with such ravishing manifestatcons of Love upon his Soule That said he I feare it was to much discovered in countenance, and may be misinterpreted as if I smiled in a contemptuous way upon my Judges but said he it was no such thing for I pitied them in my very Soule to think what wrong they had don themselves in being instrumentall of so much good unto me, and, I wish that they may have that Comfort when they come to dye which I had when I received sentence of death from them, which strong consolation remained with him to the last.[42]

Carefully described as initially doubting his own powers, strong yet gentle, right yet humble, forgiving yet by example condemning his captors, this narrative inflects Christopher Love as a martyr-citizen. Mary Love's account carefully makes political as well as affective points: the judges who condemn Love also condemn themselves in their misuse of the law. Thus, drawing on the type of the martyr, the story sees Love in legal and political terms. The affecting story fuses religious and political implications.

However, the martyred Love shares the focus of his text with the narrator. Mary Love's comments, for example that she has not 'the least revenge upon my spirit', serve to establish the narrator as the reader's focus and remind the reader that Love's death has continued significance for those who survive him. The text's recursive movement between memory and a present-of-writing *after* the trial calls the reader's attention to the trial's effects—on Mary Love's husband, but also on her. The narrator's role in producing the martyrdom for the reader, inserting the significance of a past event into the reader's present, invites identification and empathy. That the text so carefully places the narrator as subordinate to the martyrdom, yet as inhabiting a present shared with the reader was, I would suggest, significant in making it suitable for circulation after the Restoration. Mary Love's story uses the figure of the narrator to bind together past and present, and quietly, yet insistently, emphasizes the importance of these specific events for the reader.

If Mary Love's tale claims her husband as a martyr by a narrative retelling of his exemplary life (with gaps and digressions), then Elizabeth Jekyll's text gives a more spiritually inflected, abstract, and, in the early

---

[42] BL MS Sloane 3945, fo. 107^r.

passages, intensely providential account of the Civil War and Republic. However, like Love's, though by different means, Elizabeth Jekyll's writings from the 1640s and 1650s are shaped to use the female voice in which they are told to play upon the sentiments of a Restoration reader. This text has been discussed by David Underdown in the context of politicized reading during the Civil War, and the manuscript has received fuller notice from Elizabeth Clarke, who rightly describes it as 'spiritual and dogmatic'.[43] The emotional dynamic this text employs to give a spiritual account of political change from 1643 to 1653, its political implications, and its complex provenance and compilation invite detailed discussion. The manuscript opens:

I desire in the beginning of this booke to blesse god for unsought mercies that have done me good against my will, which are his Afflictions which I would nere have suffered to do me good if I could possible have helpt it.[44]

Since 1643 at least Elizabeth Jekyll had been keeping an analytical record of God's providences, apparently something between a commonplace book and a diary in which the spiritual and the political were interwoven.[45] The text as it stands begins to list God's providences in 1643. The opening page, although it is 'signed' 'Elizabeth Jekyll, 1643' at the end, seems to anticipate what is to be told later and may have been added later. It has the effect of framing any reading of the manuscript by Jekyll's 'desire', repeated in four blocks of text, to thank God for his mercies. However, the text has also been edited by a later hand, as is made clear by the inclusion of Alice Lisle's trial of 1685.[46] Although it is clear that Elizabeth Jekyll's words make up the text, omissions and editorial emendations cannot be checked. It seems more than likely—as I shall show—that the editor was making a self-consciously significant compilation of narratives of feminine suffering, culling the manuscript for politically poignant detail.

---

[43] David Underdown, *A Freeborn People* (Oxford: Clarendon Press, 1996), p. 110; Elizabeth Clarke, 'Elizabeth Jekyll's Spiritual Diary: Private Manuscript or Political Document?', in *English Manuscript Studies 1100–1700*, No. 9, ed. Peter Beal and Margaret J. M. Ezell (London: British Library, 2000), pp. 218–37.
[44] Osborn Collection, Box 58 ᴴ20, fo. 2.
[45] Underdown, *A Freeborn People*, pp. 110, 130–1.
[46] See also Clarke, 'Elizabeth Jekyll's Spiritual Diary', p. 229.

The opening framing (editorial, authorial, or both) invites the reader to interpret the text as a shaped set of fragments leading to a conclusion, rather than an unshaped notebook. The textual shaping is continued in a 'definition of believing' and of 'conscience', where Jekyll defines conscience as 'my hart and mind and Brain indued wth knowledge and grounded upon the word of God'.[47] As Patricia Crawford reminds us, questions of conscience moved between realms construed as private and public. Meditating on the state of the soul might subject highly public issues to a process of thought simultaneously highly analytical, structured, and open to the prompting of God; and so it proves in Jekyll's text.[48]

The rest of the manuscript mixes notes, meditations, and narrative. Registering roughly three political-spiritual phases, it opens by focusing on God's providences during the Civil War as found in national and familial 'mercies and deliverances'. The first recorded is a 'deliverance' and is of her husband in Bristol, July 1643. The King 'being there at that time' her husband:

was taken hold of by one of the Kings Souldiers, which not long before was our very next neighbour, a Sugar Baker his name was—Worme, who pulld him by the Coate and asked him what he did there, Whereupon my husband answer'd him, that he came about business, and this fellow tould him he would see that, and he imeadiatly called his companions about him and tould them that my husband was the greatest Roundhead in all the parish and that he kept open his shop on Holy dayes, and the like frivlous things, and then he takes my husband as his Prisoner to his Lodgings, where the hand of God in Mercy was much seen.[49]

John Jekyll is refused permission to write a note to a Bristol friend, but nevertheless 'the Mercy of God is seen' for God limited the power of the interrogators, so that:

they had power to ask him but 2 questions, i whether he did not take up armes against the king att Brentford, to which he truly Answered hee did not, for as it pleased the Wise Disposer of Heaven and Earth to order it, hee was att that time

---

[47] Osborne Collection, Box 58 ^{H}20, fo. 2.

[48] Patricia Crawford, 'Public Duty, Conscience, and Women in Early Modern England', in *Public Duty and Private Conscience in Seventeenth-Century England*, ed. John Morrill, Paul Slack, and Daniel Woolf (Oxford: Clarendon Press, 1993), pp. 57–76, esp. 57.

[49] Osborne Collection, Box 58 ^{H}20, fo. 3.

in Lincolnshire about his business; ii they askt him whether he did not dig a pass att the works to which the Lord gave him an answer, for he was then in Hull therefore he could truly answer them he did neither of those things . . . had they but askt whether he had taken the Covenant [illegible] then they had secured him, for he just took it ye Sabbath day before he went.[50]

Much of Jekyll's meditation on political events and her canvassing of her conscience is, as here, mediated by her thoughts on her husband's activities in the world. Her narration emphasizes her self-consciously secondary position, yet, as the opening passages concerning her knowledge of God's mercies make clear, the diary is not, exactly or solely, 'about' her husband but about her reaction to the political cataclysm that they are both involved in. To a greater degree than in Love's narrative the authorial consciousness is the focus of the reader's interpretation, for the meanings of the events described are related to Jekyll's salvation. While 'Elizabeth' is a narrating presence rather than an actor in most of the events described (many of which are her husband's doings), these events register in relation to her own spiritual state; the narrator is both self-effacing and, in claims to sympathy and to articulate her relationship to God, the emotional focus of the text.

Jekyll's providential narrative technique, melding national events with her life, invites comparison with the writings of Nehemiah Wallington and other Puritan interpreters of the early 1640s.[51] Jekyll's mode is to weld together her husband's affairs, those of the nation, and her own—subordinate, but for the reader all-important—interpretative role in locating the workings of God's providence. This technique produces a narrator ambiguously subaltern and marginal to events, yet also the focus of them. As the text (and events) unfold the initial assumption that the Christian can rely on God's providences is undermined. An hiatus emerges between events and their interpretability by the godly, and the narrator's state of mind and soul moves to the centre of the text.

In August 1650, after the execution of Charles, Elizabeth Jekyll analyses something which happened to her husband: 'my husband was combing the horse [which] threw him and he pitcht upon his shoulders wth little hurt, which was a verie great Mercie that the bone was not out which would have been very sad'. She interprets the event, 'thus doth

50 Osborn Collection, Box 58 ^{H}20, fo. 4.
51 Nehemiah Wallington, *Historical Notices*, 2 vols. (London, 1869).

god but shake the rod over us being unwilling to strike without there be no other way' to provoke 'repentance' in 'his people'.[52] The passage suggests that the incident may indeed be an ill omen. The earlier faith in providence guiding self, Parliament, and nation seems to have dissolved and regicide, implicitly at least, invites God's punishment. The failure to repent, or the wrong form of repentance, will bring worse consequences.

In the shaping of the manuscript this incident of 'pitching' stands as a textual precursor to the main drama of Love's trial. While her husband, 'accused by the State for Treason', was testifying against Love apparently in order to save his life, Elizabeth examined her conscience:

I have heard the slanders of many fear was on Every side while they took councell together Against mee they desired to take away my life, but I trusted in the Lord, I sayd thou art my god, my synnes are in thy hands, deliver thou me from the hands of my Enemies, and from them that persecute me, Make thy face to shine upon thy Servant, Oh save me for thy mercies sake. Let me not be Ashamed O Lord for I have called upon thee be Ashamed, and let them be silent. Let the proud lips be silent that have spoken against thee, O, how great is thy goodness, which thou hast laid up for them that fear thee, for them that trust in thee, before the Sons of men ... [53]

Surviving the trial and the 'slander' associated with it, and presumably the shame of her husband's conduct, Jekyll left a relatively abstract retrospective analysis. Rather than recording happenings, the text uses the language of the Bible, prayer, and meditation to discuss the problem of interpretation presented by events. Significantly, acknowledgement of the difficulty of tracing the connection between God's will and political or worldly action replaces previously confident providentialism. Situated in the middle of the manuscript, the account of the trial is a turning point. The stylistic shift in the diary's method of building links between spiritual and quotidian worlds both intensifies the sense of the interpenetration of the spiritual and material and indicates the complexity and difficulty of spiritual self-examination.

---

[52] Falls from horses seem to have signified in popular and elite culture, in so far as such distinctions can be made, having classical antecedents and currency in popular literary and theatrical texts such as Fletcher's *Valentinian*, in which Aetius is thrown from his horse as he is about to fall from favour. See Osborn Collection, Box 58 [H]20, fo. 17.
[53] Osborn Collection, Box 58 [H]20, fo. 22.

How, though, was the writer to interpret the events of the trial? Although, she reasons, 'the Lord doth not willingly Afflict nor greave his people', nevertheless 'Judgement is his' and his creatures were subject to the 'tryall of Grace'. 'Afflictions', Jekyll writes, 'have a voice which we must harken to.'[54] But how is that voice to be interpreted? What particular sin is this 'physick of Afflictions' sent to punish?[55] While God often makes punishment suit the sin, yet 'that is not an infallible rule For I knowe that sometimes that God afflicts to show his soverainety over the creature and for the tryall of Grace and the Excercise of faith, yet most commonly we shall find some sin in us to which our Affliction is suited'.[56] God's apparent sadism allows Jekyll to prove, once again, that she is amongst his chosen: for 'he bringeth into troubles that he may show his power in delivering out of troubles, he brings his people into straits that he may show them he alone can bring them to comfort'.[57]

Yet the logic of God's demonstration of his power, and the subject's deliverance from peril, only ultimately gives coherence to the experience as, retrospectively, she is able to find a cause. She writes, 'upon due Exammination I found my heart to[o] Much sett upon my Deare Husband who is most dear to me', a sin about which she decides to 'Avoyd particulars Lest my pen should do as my hart has done run beyond bounds'. Her excessive devotion to her husband, in the way of the creature, she argues may have caused God to chastise her by punishing him:

I only say he is worthy of all Affections yt are lawfull to be given to a Creature, but hee was and is too much my failing I did I fear look upon him in a higher nature than creature should be and for that cause I persuade my self that God hath Afflicted me but God is wise and I Adore him for all his works of Wisdom . . . [58]

Thus, the trial holds a lesson on 'the vanity of the Creature', and 'that there is no more in the Creature than he can bring down'. 'I trust', she writes, that the experience has 'in some measure blunted the Edge of my desire to worldly comforts' so that she can 'comfortably resigne my Soul

[54] Osborn Collection, Box 58 ^{H}20, fo. 19.
[55] Osborn Collection, Box 58 ^{H}20, Jekyll, fo. 18.
[56] Osborn Collection, Box 58 ^{H}20, fo. 19.
[57] Osborn Collection, Box 58 ^{H}20, fo. 18.
[58] Osborn Collection, Box 58 ^{H}20, fo. 20.

into his hands with understanding'. Only once a cause is located can self-condemnation give way to rejoicing, as she uses the language of the thirtieth psalm, 'I will Exalt thee O Lord for thou hast lifted me up and hast not made my foes to rejoyce over me. O Lord my God I cryed unto the and thou hast healed me', concluding, 'Weeping may Endure for a night but Joy cometh in the morning.'[59] The textual shift from recording providence to attempting to articulate crisis brings the narrator to the fore as a victim of political circumstance and the empathetic centre of a reader's experience.

The third, or final, phase of the text is relatively fragmentary, but seems to offer some form of assessment of what has happened. Jekyll resolves her understanding of the trial:

Still I must speak of Gods multiplyd goodness for me and mine In his delivering my husband from great danger being accused by the State for Treason against them. God beyond my thought nay beyond my weak faith was pleased to give him a deliverance from all his and my fears, therefore while I live my lips shall preach the praises of my god which alone is Worthy to be feared and alone to be praised, he bringeth into troubles that he may show his power in delivering out of troubles, he brings his people into straits that he may show them he alone can bring them to comfort... [60]

This conclusion, however, also seems to involve a shift in her attitude to God's providence.[61] Although this passage may be notes on a sermon or an analysis of another text, it is the last piece of prose in the manuscript and may offer a shaping and conclusion. Repentance, we read 'Encreases and marks godly sorrow for sins past, brings to our remembrance the history of our life':

The horrid indignities offered to y[e] Majesty & justice of god,
The odious contempt of his holy will and soverraine Authority...
The high provocation of his jealousy & displeasure...
These things should make us look wth self abhorrence on our selves... [62]

---

[59] Osborn Collection, Box 58 [H]20, fo. 21. She quotes 1–2 and then adapts some of the rest to suit her situation.
[60] Osborn Collection, Box 58 [H]20, fo. 18.
[61] Osborn Collection, Box 58 [H]20, fos. 29, 31, 37. This section offers a partly biographical passage on 'What is Originall Sin' in which she discusses her miscarriages, memoranda of her 'wofull misery', poems, 'Upon Death', and 'Upon Prayer'; the rather fragmentary section concludes with a passage entitled 'Upon Repentance'.
[62] Osborn Collection, Box 58 [H]20, fo. 37.

'Sanctification', she concludes, is 'no less than for a man to be brought to an entire resignation of his will to the will of God'.[63] Working its way from faith in providence to resignation via political trial, Jekyll's understanding of the interrelationship of personal, national, and godly history has changed substantially by the end of the text. Personal and political 'history' offer evidence not of God's providences to a chosen people, but of God's mercy despite 'horrid indignities', 'odious contempt', 'high provocation', and the firm situation of the language of majesty in the description of God suggests that, at the end of the text, she is thinking of the regicide: 'O poor England', she writes or copies, 'how low art thou brought by the pride of ignorant zealotes.'

These final pages, even if they are copied from another source, look back in spiritual terms, obliquely, over the political upheavals of her life. They offer a retrospective analysis of the spiritual significance of her suffering, addressed to her children. 'Above all be sure you get down this pride of your heart forgett not all the sermons I preached to you against this sin.'[64] The text ends with a list of the children born during the years in which she kept her book.[65] In taking up the book, apparently as Elizabeth had intended, the copyist turns her text to the ills of the next generation. Whether copied verbatim or extracted, Jekyll's meditations trace a rethinking of the relationship between religion and politics. By 1653 she finds that submission and repentance rather than the interpretation of God's providences are the central duty of the Christian, and implicitly her earlier providentialism is understood as the efflorescence of pride.

In the pages of Jekyll's diary an understanding of God's providence as guiding the political world, and herself and others as agents prompted by God to action in his divine drama, coexists with a growing sense of the dangers of spiritual pride and need for obedience to God. It is the coexistence of the two positions, as well as the sadness of her story and unwarranted suffering, which offer the reader a drama of a subordinate suffering unfairly. These qualities made her text, like that of Mary Love, available for copying and circulation (whether merely within the family

63 Osborn Collection, Box 58 ᴴ20, fo. 39.
64 Osborn Collection, Box 58 ᴴ20, fo. 41.
65 Thomas Jekyll (1646), later a divine, Elizabeth (1647), John (1648), Sarah (1649), and Jacob, born 13 Sept. 1651, just after Love's death.

or beyond) as a martyrological prompt to political action. For the next generation the stories of Mary Love and Elizabeth Jekyll could be used as proof that dissent in religion (Love's Presbyterianism) could combine with loyalty to the Crown (Love's 'conspiracy'). Significantly enough in terms of memory and forgetfulness, it seems that this could happen even though John Jekyll and Christopher Love had been on opposite sides in the trial. Elizabeth Jekyll's diary and Mary Love's narrative could hardly fail to call to mind the struggles and defeats of royalist religious radicals, for in the 1660s the history of Love was, in some circles, as vivid a memory as Lilburne's.

Each woman takes up a position subordinate to a husband who is, himself, arraigned by the law which arguably should have been protecting him. In taking up the position of the wife of a disenfranchised yet loyal citizen, the narrators articulate the pain of political conflict in a voice which is all the more affecting for being politically disenfranchised. The narrative of disenfranchised citizenship taken up by Love from Lilburne is given a particular poignancy by narration in the marginal feminine voice, enabling the reader to locate the pain of political process in the private, affective sphere.

Jekyll's and Love's text were probably circulated at the Restoration as part of the binding together of a post-Restoration political culture of disenfranchised nonconformity. Such lives—of men and women—were significant in shaping Restoration nonconformist martyrologies. Thus Samuel Clarke's compilation of martyrs included various pious women including, for instance, Elizabeth Wilkinson, who 'kept a *Diary* of Gods dealings with her'.[66] While such texts were hardly lacking in political implications, the emotional drama of Elizabeth Jekyll's diary—at least as we have it—offers a spirituality easily read in politicized terms. Indeed, that Jekyll's and Love's affecting stories had, or at least were thought likely to find, a politicized readership is indicated by the way both were editorially shaped and augmented after the Restoration. Both the surviving copies of Mary Love's speech include an introduction written after 1660 which gives a very full sense of how such narratives played a part in shaping political culture after the Restoration. Moreover, returning us to the context of the violent outcomes of political trials,

---

[66] Samuel Clarke's martyrology went through many editions. See for instance *A Collection of Ten Eminent Divines* (London, 1662), p. 513.

in the same hand as Jekyll's text, in the same manuscript, can be found the scaffold speech of Alice Lisle, executed in Winchester market place on 2 September 1685 for harbouring refugees after the defeat of the Duke of Monmouth at Sedgmoor.[67]

A POLITICS OF TEARS: FEMININE NARRATIVE AND CITIZENSHIP AFTER THE RESTORATION

What is Alice Lisle's 'dying speech' from the Bloody Assizes of 1685 doing at the end of Elizabeth Jekyll's text? What connections might a copyist have implied between the two stories? The Restoration crisis in nonconformity, and dissenters' complex responses to being disenfranchised, offer some answers to these questions. For the godly, who had prospered in the 1650s, 1660 seemed like a 'good time to die'. It brought career disaster as they were thrown out of livings and the gradual horrified realization that 'they would never again be a prominent part of a national church', a realization in part acknowledged in 1672 when many took up the opportunity to become licensed congregations.[68] The question of citizenship denied was central for the nonconformists, and loyalty to Protestantism was in increasing tension with loyalty to the Crown as the crisis about the succession deepened.

Alice Lisle's trial opened the notorious Bloody Assizes after the rebellion at Sedgmoor, where many were convicted on shaky evidence. Lisle, the wife of the regicide John Lisle, called 'Lady' because her husband had been in Cromwell's House of Lords, returned to England after her husband was shot in Lausanne in August 1664. On 20 July 1685, two weeks after the battle of Sedgmoor, she was at her home, Moyles Court in Hampshire, when she received a request from the dissenting preacher John Hicks that he might shelter at her house. By

[67] Alicia Lisle, *Madam Lisle's Last Speech* (London, 1685), *The Dying Speeches of Several Persons* (London, 1689), *The Second and Last Collection of the dying Speeches of those Eminent Protestants Who Suffered in the West of England* (London, 1689). For discussion of the possibility that women's scaffold speeches had special propaganda value, see Lois G. Schwoerer, 'Women and the Glorious Revolution', *Albion*, 18, No. 2 (1986), pp. 195–218: 214.

[68] Thomas Hall, quoted in Ann Hughes, 'The Frustrations of the Godly', in *Revolution and Restoration*, ed. John Morrill (London: Collins & Brown, 1992), pp. 70–90: 88–9.

2 September, Hicks's visit was to have caused her death. He was found at Lisle's house by Colonel Penruddock, whose father had been sentenced to death by her husband. She was tried by special commission, and Judge Jeffries sentenced her to death for harbouring a traitor. In 1689 her daughters, one of whom was married to Lord James Russell, the fifth son of William Russell first Duke of Bedford, had the attainder reversed by Act of Parliament.

The publication of Lisle's 'Dying Speech' (printed in 1685 and 1689) offers a story of Restoration revenge on Civil War enemies.[69] If John Lisle had not killed Colonel Penruddock's father, it seems, Penruddock might not have waited, deliberately, for the refugees from Sedgmoor to enter her house. Lisle's story is also, like Elizabeth Jekyll's, one of feminine suffering and political injustice, likely to prompt the reader's sympathy. Alice Lisle was old and infirm and, as Robin Clifton indicates, the six hours needed to coach reluctant witnesses, Lisle's age, 'limited offence . . . and social status' made her a ready figure for martyrdom.[70]

By the time Lisle suffered and died, though, Elizabeth Jekyll was long dead, dying soon after her manuscript closes. There is no living connection between Elizabeth Jekyll and Lisle, but it is possible that Jekyll's husband, John, would have seen reasons to put them together. John Jekyll's career from the Restoration to his death in 1690 offers a possible context for his wife's narrative, for he was active in political and nonconformist circles throughout the period. Indeed, he was not only alive during Lisle's trial, but still politically active. At the age of 74, he was considered dangerous enough to be arrested himself, briefly, in connection with the Monmouth rebellion.[71]

In 1663, as the persecution of nonconformists (like Jekyll) was intensifying, *Love's Name Lives*, a sequence of letters and petitions first published by Mary Love in 1651, was republished. This text sits at the

---

[69] *Dying Speeches*; For extensive discussion of the role of local revenge in shaping Restoration politics see Ronald Hutton, *The Restoration* (Oxford: Oxford University Press, 1985).

[70] Robin Clifton, *The Last Popular Rebellion* (London and New York: Maurice Temple Smith/St Martin's Press, 1984), pp. 231–4, 245–6; Andrea Button, 'Royalist Women Petitioners in South-West England, 1655–62', *The Seventeenth Century*, 15, No. 1 (2000), pp. 53–66: 58.

[71] DRW MS R. Morrice Entring-Book I, fo. 476. On John Jekyll see also Clarke, 'Elizabeth Jekyll's Spiritual Diary', p. 233.

inception of the nonconformist Restoration strategy of asserting loyalty to the Crown (indeed invoking a past martyrdom for Charles II), while simultaneously urging the truth and needs of nonconformists in the present. The royalism of the Presbyterian protagonists in the Love drama, coupled with their religious conviction, offered a perfect combination; the publicizing of Love as a martyr for the royal cause implied that religious dissent should be understood within a framework of Protestant loyalty.[72] The epigraph, from Psalm 112, makes the aim clear: '*The Righteous shall be had in everlasting remembrance*'. Besides the letters and petitions of Mary Love this text contains a startling letter from John Jekyll, described on the title page as 'one of the witnesses against him', begging forgiveness of Christopher Love.[73] Jekyll writes of his heart 'so full, that I know not how to empty it':

but in tears before the Lord for you night and day. And oh, that the remembrance of the seventh and the one and twentieth of *June* might often come into my thoughts, to keep my heart humble for my folly, in taking my own, and carnall friends counsell, and not the counsell of those that are right godly;

Jekyll argues that his testimony against Love was given because he was 'informed, it would do you good and not hurt, being but Misprision at the most'.[74] Of Elizabeth, Jekyll writes, 'my dear wife, whose heart (I know) bleeds for you, and her eyes run down with tears to God for you'.[75]

Here John Jekyll is (if problematically) associated with Love, and the reprinted pamphlet uses evidence from the 1650s to reinforce Love's status as a Presbyterian martyr. Through Charles II's return Love, as a Presbyterian royalist conspirator, could assume the status of a true patriot. His example showed why the government was wrong to exclude Presbyterians from the new church settlement, but it also implicitly justified nonconformist resistance. The tension between obedience and treason in the nonconformist position was to intensify and culminate in the rebellion of 1685. The reprinting—suggesting that Love's trial was of interest beyond the circle of his close associates—is also evidence in

---

[72] '*Love's Name Lives* or, a Publication of divers PETITIONS presented by Mistris LOVE to the Parliament, in behalf of her HUSBAND' (London: 1651; repr. 1663). For Mary Love's petitions, see also *CSPD* (1651), p. 9.
[73] 'Mr *Jaquel* his Letter to Mr *Love*', in *Love's Name Lives*, p. 3.
[74] Ibid.   [75] Ibid., p. 4.

support of Greaves's suggestion that the extent and nature of opposition to Charles II's government during later 1660s and mid-1670s has an imprecise relationship to religious groupings: Presbyterians and Baptists, for example, had complex relationships and at points worked together.[76] While he may have mistaken his way in '51, Jekyll stood firm throughout the Restoration, appearing in the state papers during periods of intense persecution of nonconformists or nonconformist activity. Jekyll was a member of Common Council in 1661–2, 1668–70, and 1681.[77] In 1670 he and Alderman Hayes were both imprisoned, apparently as 'jurymen that were fined for finding not guilty the Quakers'.[78] In this connection the King ordered Jekyll to be brought before him at the Council.[79] Renewed nonconformist protests and defiance followed Charles's proclamation against conventicles of 3 February 1675. In 1676 Guy Carleton, Bishop of Bristol, gave his view of Jekyll to Sheldon. For him, Jekyll was 'solicitor general for the fanatick party', the King had no 'woorse subject' and 'The father of Lyars never begott a sonn more like'; 'This is the man to whom all our aldermen that are disaffected to ye present government civil & ecclesiastical repaire for advise, and assistance.'[80] In 1683, after the arrests of

---

[76] R. L. Greaves, *Enemies Under his Feet* (Stanford: Stanford University Press, 1990), pp. 245, 247.

[77] See SP/29/417 (pt. 3), 'Votes in Councill', which associates him with strong players in petitioning the Crown to disappoint Roman Catholic 'hopes of a popish successor' such as Papillon, Dubois, Player. See also Mark Knights, *Politics and Opinion 1678–81* (Cambridge: Cambridge University Press, 1994), pp. 280, 330–1; J. R. Woodhead, *The Rulers of London 1660–1689* (London: London and Middlesex Archaeological Society, 1965), pp. 98, 100. John Jekyll was the son of Thomas Jekyll, described an an 'antiquary'. For his collection of manuscripts, some of which were passed on to his grandson Nicholas Jekyll, see Cyril Ernest Wright, *Fontes Harleiani* (London: Trustees of the British Museum, 1972), p. 204. I am grateful to Michelle O'Callaghan for this information. See BL MS Harley 5191 for Elizabeth.

[78] *CSPD* (1670), 4, 9, and 27 June (pp. 300–1, 312), 22 Nov. (p. 545), 7 Dec. (p. 566); *CSPD* (1671), 18 July (p. 386). Jekyll is also mentioned *CSPD* (1671), p. 497, as part of a plot against the king, revealed by Blood. The text this is drawn from is described by the calendar as 'Notes by Williamson', 'in parts illegible', and the same sentence is read by Greaves as referring to Captain Roger Jones. Greaves, *Enemies*, p. 211.

[79] *CSPD* (1670), p. 312.

[80] Bodl. MS Tanner 40, fo. 37, 'Character of John Jekel' (1676). Letter from Dr Guy Carleton, Bishop of Bristol, to Archbishop Sheldon. In 1677 he is mentioned in connection with the mayoral election of Robert Cann; in 1681 he was involved in the furore around the choosing of a London mayor.

the Rye House plotters, Jekyll was informed against.[81] Jekyll, it seems, participated in the crossover between City and aristocracy facilitated by the Earl of Shaftesbury.[82] He came to the attention of the King and certainly had connections amongst the high-ranking Whigs. By 1675 John Jekyll, still a force to be reckoned with, had been joined in public life by his son Thomas (his other son, not with Elizabeth, Joseph Jekyll went on to become Master of the Rolls; it was to him, ironically enough, that the papers of John Thurloe discovered in a false ceiling, were sent).[83] By 1685, then, Jekyll had been active in politics for at least forty years. He was aware not only of contemporary claims that Whigs were 'true' Protestants, 'true' patriots, 'truly' loyal, and, therefore, right in contravening strictures against them, but also of the history of the sufferings of Presbyterians and others because of their claim to be true, though disenfranchised, citizens of England.

By 1685 the position of the true Protestant was to coincide with that of the rebel, made to do so by the various acts restricting their partici-pation as citizens—including the Corporation Act, Conventicle Act, Five Mile Act, and the Act of Uniformity. The response to these Acts and to the reactivation of these policies in the later 1670s shaped the nature of various nonconformist groupings. The Presbyterian claim to recognition by monarch and church and the repeated unfairness of their treatment formed their consciousness of present and past. In circum-stances of disenfranchisement, as N. H. Keeble has argued, the written word, collective reading, and circulation preserved nonconformist net-works.[84] Love's and Jekyll's texts would have offered a particularly appealing version of the narrative of personal suffering to Presbyterians, and it seems likely that both were circulated within Presbyterian circles.

---

[81] Greaves, *Enemies*, p. 231; *CSPD* (1683), p. 356. This was in a list of those seen at the house of Sir Thomas Player—a list including Francis Jenks the linen draper (who in June 1676 had been urging the Lord Mayor to call Common Council in order to petition Charles II to call a Parliament) and the Duke of Monmouth.

[82] Clifton, *The Last Popular Rebellion*, p. 138.

[83] *Collection of the State Papers of John Thurloe*, ed. Thomas Birch, 7 vols. (London, 1742), 'a series of papers discovered in the reign of king William, in a false ceiling in the garrets belonging to secretary Thurloe's chambers'. Although Thomas was ordained in the Church of England, he was mobbed in January 1675 in Bristol over a speech he was to have given, and in 1682 he was to have preached an inflammatory sermon before the Duke of Monmouth entitled *True Religion Makes the Best Loyalty.*

[84] N. H. Keeble, *The Literary Culture of Nonconformity* (Leicester: Leicester University Press, 1987), pp. 78–82.

Thus, the addition of Alice Lisle's scaffold speech to Elizabeth Jekyll's text seems to have prepared it for circulation by aligning it with the martyrdoms of 1685, and connecting it to subsequent martyrology. This martyrology was constructed in part immediately after Sedgmoor, but also later in the context of the Glorious Revolution of 1688.[85] Martyrologies were published in 1689, 1693, and 1705.[86] The politico-religious path traced within Jekyll's text (from the political and religious providentialism of 1643–5 through the crisis of the regicide, to the terrible crisis of the treason trial in 1651) would have served what appears to have been John Jekyll's agenda. In 1653 Elizabeth Jekyll's text suggests obedience as well as providentialism, but also makes it clear that the government was cruel—a political ambivalence perfect for the atmosphere of 1685. Radicalism, innocence, and martyrdom are, by the combination of the two texts, turned into an affecting history of misunderstood religious radicalism and make claims simultaneously to religious truth and political obedience at the moment of 1685. The manuscript seems to have been prepared to support the political positions of 1685, but would also have found an audience after the Glorious Revolution. Although we cannot be certain that Jekyll's story was circulated beyond the family, wider circulation seems very likely. For her story, especially once carefully joined to Lisle's, offers to a nonconformist reader a pointed examination of citizenship denied, martyrdom, religious self-examination and a story which, because told by an innocent and powerless protagonist, victim rather than agent of political change, allows the reader the pleasures and pains of meditating on the continuing significance of religious oppression in the present.

Mary Love's narrative, which exists in two copies, offers more precise information about circulation. It seems to have been prepared for publication and was certainly known, and used, in the shaping of nonconformist history and martyrology. John Quick, recognized as a builder of intellectual coherence in the nonconformist project, used Mary Love's memoir in making up his 'Iconaes Sacrae', part of which

---

[85] Melinda Zook, '"The Bloody Assizes": Whig Martyrdom and Memory after the Glorious Revolution', *Albion*, 27 (Fall 1995), pp. 373–96, writes of 'the interplay between memory, radical propaganda, and reader expectations' in Whig polemic after the revolution (p. 374).

[86] Ibid., p. 377

was a life of Christopher Love.[87] The text John Quick used might have been the one lodged at the Dr Williams Library, or another. Thus, at least three known uses of the manuscript exist between Mary Love writing the text and 1700—the two copies of the introductory material and Quick's quarrying of it.[88]

Each of the two known manuscripts of Mary Love's story is accompanied by prefatory material which gives a relatively detailed political context for the intended circulation. This material includes an address on behalf of Mary Love, though nowhere in her hand, inviting the 'Christian Reader' to kindly 'receive this unexpected Birth from a Woman, the Conception was long since (I may say) form'd tho I cannot say perfected'.[89] The discourse of maternity, whether deployed by Love herself, or, as seems more likely by T.H., who is planning to circulate the text, establishes the text's feminine voice as its authenticating ground.[90] The reader is invited to respond by identifying with the experiences of the author:

I know not how far it may work upon thy on Bowells or affections (If thou pleases to look upon it while it weeps) Surely all mine were moved in the working of it; Yet the debt I owed unto the truth, the testimonie I owed unto Grace of God, and the memorie of his servant suffered me not to decline, either

---

[87] Held at the Dr Williams Library, where there is also a full copy of the Sloane manuscript, bound in with a set of nonconformist funeral sermons including one by Quick (*Sermon Preached at Meeting House in Bartholomew Close Jan 16 1697*) and others, 'Iconaes Sacrae Anglicanae' was to have been published with the aid of another survivor of the Civil War, William Russell, fifth Earl (later first Duke of Bedford) and the father of the William Russell executed in connection with the Rye House plot. However, in 1700, just as publication was about to take place, the Duke died. A week later Quick himself was disabled, so he could not collect subscriptions, and the project languished in manuscript.

[88] Quick incorporates also the poem of the nonconformist Northamptonshire wit, Robert Wild (ejected from Aynhoe, Northamptonshire, in 1662). 'The Tragedy of Christopher Love', incorporated by Quick, seems to have been written in 1660. Wild is another figure combining royalism with Puritanism at the problematic moment of the Restoration.

[89] Dr Williams Library, PP. 12.50*.4(21), fo. 3.

[90] T.H. is at present unidentified. Faith Lanum identifies Mary Love as dying in 1663; Elizabeth Clarke, 'Beyond Microhistory: The Use of Women's Manuscripts in a Widening Political Arena', in *Women and Politics in Early Modern England, 1450–1700*, ed. James Daybell (Aldershot: Ashgate, 2004), pp. 211–27: 214, 225 n. 14. See Melinda S. Zook, *Radical Whigs and Conspiritorial Politics in Late Stuart England* (University Park: Pennsylvania State University Press, 1999), pp. 39–56.

the sorrowes which by such a rehearsall were renewed in me or the Censure which for it and its imperfections may possibly light upon mee.[91]

The affective properties of the text are central to the reader's response, which is invited as empathetic with the sufferings of Christopher (in martyrdom) and with Mary in rehearsing events to make the reader weep. But the reader is to weep for specific reasons. The narrative:

might goe, and crye (when it comes abroad & is once understood) that none know better how to love their King even to the death than they who best know how to love their God and a good conscience, and this much I hope it will speak, & in time to be believed:[92]

The address frames the text, emphasizing the true 'good conscience' of the nonconformists who (like Love) know loyalty, 'even to the death'. Notably, the story of the past is oriented towards the future: 'this much I hope it will speak, & in time to be believed'. Linking the affective properties of the text to present and future politics, the introduction inflects the Presbyterians as loyal precisely because of their religious choices, and claims the purpose is 'to provoke thee to love, Loyaltye and good works'.

However, that 'good works' might include various forms of resistance is made clear by the following address by T.H. T.H. links past and present, describing the story as, '(at least in the Tragicall part thereof)' likely 'to make a most deepe and bitter wound bleede afresh'.[93] Knitting together past and present, familial and spiritual, T.H. tells us that Mary Love:

breaks not the bande of silence, but upon the impulse of a most just affection to preserve the Life of his memory who was both a Husband and a spirituall father, and lost his life in an enterprise adjudged then a capital crime; but now universally owned as a Duty.[94]

The political capital of Love's story for nonconformist claims to truth and loyalty is clear:

His [Love's] only transgression wherewith he was burdened, even to death, was Loyalty, discerning and practising that Duty so long agoe and so freely whereunto necessity hath now at the long runne made so many Prosslytes.

91 PP. 12.50*.4 (21), fo. 3ʳ.   92 PP. 12.50*.4 (21), fo. 3ᵛ.
93 PP. 12.50*.4 (21), fo. 4ʳ.   94 Ibid.

As T.H. can see, the Restoration, when Charles II seemed favourably disposed to acknowledge the loyalty of those who became dissenters, might have been a good moment to make public Love's story of exemplary loyalty and dissent. He writes: 'I know not how the intention was frustrated of sending forth this narrative, about the time of his Maties Restauration, When all harts and eyes' were absorbed by 'contemplation of the adorable Providence' who disposes human affairs. The Restoration itself, 'the greatest Revolucion', was brought about 'in such a manner that even they acknowledged causes of high Thankfullness in it, who as to the matter were most averse or fearfull of it'. There were 'no Garments rolled in blood about it, but only a wonderfull conquest wrought upon a wonderfull consent in the spirits of men to accomplish this great change'. He (if it is he) ends, however, by noting that men must look to 'our God; that we provoke him not to use sharper expedients, to make severer experiments upon us'.⁹⁵

Thus, discussion of when 'this little History' might have been published leads to an ironic commentary on its relationship to the wider history of nonconformity, loyalty, and radicalism—precisely the formation which is generating his renewed attempt at circulation. T.H.'s prefatory material signals the explicitly political purpose of Mary Love's narrative in the present. As T.H. exhorts the readers, 'Let us learne to improve our present opportunities', and 'Let us learne alwaies to be Zealously affected in a good thing...sufferers triumph, Triumphers suffer.'⁹⁶ Mary Love's text as prepared for circulation illuminates the ways in which the narrative of the citizen as disenfranchised was considered a prompt to political action, to the improvement of present opportunities. In sum, what the addition of Alice Lisle's speech does for Elizabeth Jekyll's text T.H.'s introduction does for Mary Love's. Under the politicized hand of their editors these 'tragicall' memoirs are made to weave together politics and passion. Editorial shaping enables these women's memoirs to lodge sadness at the heart of political culture and to connect discourses on political rights, law, and justice to empathetic reading.

⁹⁵ P.P. 12.50*.4 (21), fo. 4ᵛ.   ⁹⁶ Ibid.

MARTYRS AND MEMORY IN THE
RESTORATION PERIOD

The existence, adaptation, circulation, and use of Love's and Jekyll's texts have implications for critical thinking on wider questions, most particularly the nature of political memory at the Restoration, concepts of citizenship and women's relation to them, and connectedly, the place of texts by women in Restoration political culture.

The kind of political memory these carefully shaped manuscripts are calculated to provoke is complex. Memory, not solely 'a function of the thinking parts', involves both recollection and amnesia, and as Giorgio Agamben has argued, political transformations alter not only the world but the experience of time.[97] Memory is 'a reminder', though not necessarily of the event as it seemed at the moment.[98] The claims Jekyll and Love made on their Restoration readers played on the interpenetration of remembering and forgetting to allow a narrative of disenfranchised nonconformity to be made from Love's trial—a trial which, from another point of view, looks very like royalist conspiracy under the republic. Love's story was consistently shaped as that of a martyr through the printing of his sermons, circulation of his letters, and narratives of the trial. The trial is the pretext of the women's texts, but in their production they set up a new set of concerns with martyrdom, politics, and the position of the sufferer while the question of citizenship, so important to Lilburne as taken up by Love, becomes sublimated in the affective politics of the text.

At the Restoration the edited texts, mixing memorialization and forgetting with a prompt to action, exemplify a very specific use of political memory to provoke present action. Central to their ability to do this, I have argued, is their sublimation of the question of citizenship within female narration. Importantly, these stories are told in female voices—in the voices of subjects participant in certain ways in political

---

[97] Aristotle, 'On Memory', in *The Complete Works of Aristotle*, rev. trans. ed. Jonathan Barnes (Princeton: Princeton University Press, 1984), pp. 714–21: 715–16; Giorgio Agamben, *Infancy and History: The Destruction of Experience*, trans. Liz Heron (1978; London: Verso, 1993), p. 91.

[98] Aristotle, 'On Memory', pp. 714–16.

culture and yet specifically excluded from actual citizenship. As Melinda Zook notes, affective martyrologies shaped Protestant memories of the Bloody Assizes and, in the 1690s, the vividly misremembered accounts of Protestant martyrdoms were lodged at the heart of Whig political culture. The texts I have analysed participated in building a mode of reading which associated past and present sufferings, used feminine subjectivity to articulate the powerless position of the disenfranchised citizen, and used that position to invite the reader's empathy with the sufferings of the martyr and the subordinate survivor, suffering—like Mary Love, Elizabeth Jekyll, and Alice Lisle—for politics without ever being fully included in a political arena. The story I have traced suggests that women's ambiguous relationship to citizenship gave their voices a particular—ambiguously recognized, politicized—poignancy at the Restoration.

Natalie Zemon Davies has pointed out that in early modern Europe citizenship was not a clear category for men or women.[99] It was though, uncertainly, under discussion. Particularly significant for male citizenship in this period are the arguments about natural law, what Richard Tuck calls 'inalienable right', in terms of the defence of a larger social body against its ruler and, as significantly, in terms of the claims of the individual's inalienable rights ('every man by naturall instinct aiming at his owne safety and weale' as Richard Overton put it). Demands from the Levellers and others at the Putney debates for government by constitution were embodied in the different versions of *The Agreement of the People*. Such demands indicate that the category of the citizen, though the term itself might not be used, was coming into sharp focus in the period where debates about the rule of Charles I gave way to those over the establishment of the republic. As C. B. Macpherson notes, the Leveller demand that the franchise be extended to include all men who were not servants or beggars (doubling the number of voters) would have been enough to concentrate the minds of lawyers, MPs, and soldiers on the question of the nature of 'citizenship'.

[99] Natalie Zemon Davies, in *A History of Women in the West*, ed. N. Z. Davies and Arlette Farge (Cambridge, Mass.: Belknap Press, 1994), p. 169. Compare Merry Weisner's assessment of 15th-century female citizenship in the cities of the Holy Roman Empire, 'The Holy Roman Empire: Women and Politics', in *Women Writers and the Early Modern British Political Tradition*, ed. Hilda Smith (Cambridge: Cambridge University Press, 1998), pp. 305–23: 316.

In this analysis of the place of subaltern narratives, particularly women's narratives, in political cultures, the imprecision which Natalie Zemon Davies locates in the concept of citizenship in early modern Europe is both confirmed and qualified. For women, as Davies notes, the question of the franchise remained vague. Yet, in the 1640s and 1650s, as the nature of political authority was debated with increasing intensity, women were repeatedly used as examples of the political *subject*—the one who must be subject to legitimate political authority. Even as the conceptual supports of Charles's authority crumbled, the woman, as subject to the authority of the household, became the most obvious example of legitimate authority with which political theorists and polemicists might illustrate their examples.[100] As Constance Jordan puts it, in being subject to obedience 'Hers is the position of the quintessential political subject, forever bound to honour divine law and also to assiduously obey her human superior.'[101]

The presence of the law, and specifically the trial and martyrdom, is significant in relation to this question of subjecthood and citizenship in all the different stages through which Jekyll's and Love's stories pass, and the addition of Lisle's dying speech—yet another drama in which the law is not only unrelenting but violent—indicates that the Jekyll compiler was alert to the power of invoking the law when shaping a drama of citizenship—or subjecthood—denied. For the reader, the ambiguities between both protagonists' spiritual authority and political marginality link political and affective worlds. Subordinate to the story they tell, yet claiming the reader's sympathy, the female narrators invite the reader's empathy, prompting them to remember the past and its relationship to the present.[102] The purpose of the circulation of these feminine tales of male martyrs is, in part, to allow an empathetic response, for the story is both a political history of nonconformity told in terms of reactions to political change and also therefore, in a sense, the reader's own history.

---

100 Tuck, *Natural Rights Theories*, pp. 147, 148–9; Richard Overton, *An Appeale from the degenerate representative body* (London, 1647), in *Leveller Manifestoes of the Puritan Revolution*, ed. Don M. Wolfe (1944; repr. New York: Humanities Press, 1967), p. 162; C. B. Macpherson, *The Political Theory of Possessive Individualism* (1962; repr. Oxford: Oxford University Press, 1990), p. 117.

101 Constance Jordan, *Renaissance Feminism: Literary Texts and Political Models* (Ithaca: Cornell University Press, 1990), p. 308.

102 Steedman, 'A Weekend with Elektra', p. 23.

For the reader is in each case addressed as the heir to a troubled present, illuminated by a past of heroic struggle. The affecting first-person narratives of women's relationship to political cataclysm combine the force of masculine martyrdom in a drama of claimed and refused citizenship with their own innocence and status as victims. They offer a history of the struggles of nonconformity and Protestantism but, simultaneously, embody a carefully calculated balance between religious challenge and political subordination and obedience. For the reader, the stories of martyrdom offer an opportunity to weep over the history of the movement, and invite an empathetic relationship to political change. Moreover, they offer an identificatory narrative standing in, in some ways, for that of the suffering self.

How is the circulation of texts of martyrdom in the feminine voice to be set against other accounts of the place of women in nonconformist religion in the Restoration? Such texts, while they do indicate the participation of women in political culture, do not articulate demands for change in that position. Rather, they use the position of exclusion from politics to tell a political story. While the very circulation of such texts prompts us to question the apparent quietism of those excluded by the violent Restoration settlements of church and government, it does so by inviting us to complicate and extend both what we consider to be literary participation in political culture and the kind of texts that can be understood as shaping such culture. These texts invite us, particularly, to emphasize connections between Civil War and Restoration recognized by contemporaries. The reprinting of Foxe's *Acts and Monuments* indicates clearly enough the vivid felt applicability of this kind of narrative, and further examples of Restoration use of such feminine narratives exist.[103] Clearly, a model of Restoration retreat needs to be replaced by one which recognizes the political power of affective narrative and the centrality of femininity—of course precisely because outside the precise parameters of citizenship—in articulating the changes, rememberings, and misrememberings, which shaped nonconformist narratives of the

---

[103] e.g. *A Brief Historical Relation of the Most Material Passages and Persecutions of the Church of Christ* out of Foxe coll. by Jacob Bauthumley (1676) dedicated to the 'Mayor and Aldermen' of Leicester who have made a 'publick Library' of which Bauthumley was keeper (A4ᵛ). An example of a similar narrative genre preserved in a Restoration nonconformist collection is 'Of an Auncient Protestant called Mr. Jo. Petite', Dr Williams Library, Roger Morrice MSS, L.Xi.9, fos. 12–13.

1640s and 1650s as transformed by Restoration politics. Lilburne's influence on Love, in terms of the assertion of rights and emphasis on the citizen disenfranchised by the law echoes, if indirectly, through the feminine retellings.

8

Legitimizing Conspiracy: Anne Halkett, Rachel Russell, Aphra Behn

when we contend about things and matters, all things else except demonstrations are needless. And yet they greatly prevail upon deprav'd Auditories.

(Aristotle)

VIRTUE: See, my dear Astrea, as we approach the capitol, how busy Intelligence appears, like a courtier new in office! She bustles up and down, and has a world of business upon her hands; she is first lady of the bedchamber to the Princess Fame, her garments are all hieroglyphics.

(Delarivier Manley)[1]

SHADOW-POLITICS: MEN, WOMEN, CONSPIRACY, AND WRITING

'[J]ust such I fancy'd fam'd *Lucretia* was, when *Tarquin* first beheld her'; so Philander describes a newly desired beauty in Aphra Behn's *Love-Letters Between a Nobleman and his Sister* (1684–7).[2] That Behn makes Philander identify with Tarquin is an example of the lively connection

[1] *Aristotle's Rhetoric*, III. i, trans. H.C., dedicated to Henry Sidney (London, 1686), p. 167. An incisive discussion of the nature of politico-legal rhetoric is given in Peter Goodrich, *Legal Discourse: Studies in Linguistics, Rhetoric and Legal Analysis* (Basingstoke: Macmillan, 1987), pp. 89–90. Delarivier Manley, *The New Atalantis* (1709), ed. Rosalind Ballaster (London: Chatto, 1991), p. 13.

[2] Aphra Behn, *Love-Letters Between a Nobleman and his Sister*, in *The Works of Aphra Behn*, ed. Janet Todd (London: William Pickering, 1993), II, 174. Subsequent references are to page (not letter).

between political and sexual conduct in the writings of the late seventeenth century.[3] That Philander, sexual predator, is a conspirator *against* the Stuart monarchy hints at the complex adversarial politics of language in fiction in the same period. In order to explore these sexual-political issues, this chapter investigates the discursive importance of gender in the politicized writing of the 1670s and 1680s; it traces relationships amongst the apparently highly distinct politicized prose genres of memoirs, letters, and scandalous history. It analyses the claims to virtue made in the memoir of Lady Anne Halkett and the letters of Rachel Russell, and ends with a discussion of Behn's *Love-Letters* as a response to the politicized rhetoric of authenticity. If conspiracy is everywhere in the Restoration world and its writings, where are women in the plots?

Those involved in political conspiracy, asserting their position against official views, are tied to a use of language which is formed, maybe distorted, by its insistence on a representation of political relations opposed to those sanctioned by government. The language of opposition, lacking recourse to law, is constantly drawn towards the figurative. At the same time, oppositional Restoration texts—if we use the term 'oppositional' broadly—anticipated being, as they were, understood as conspiracy, even as treason. Against governmental and often legal assertions of treason, the words of those opposing Cromwell, Charles, or James were guaranteed only by honour and virtue of a kind best described as personal; they relied upon ethos without institutional support. Against the accusation of conspiracy or disloyalty personal virtue was asserted as having political currency. Indeed, assertions of such personal virtue by men and women show just how complicated was the status of the 'private' in the public web of honour, virtue, and political necessity. However, even as political discussions asserted that it was virtue that fitted men for high office, assertions of virtue which lacked institutional force were subject to a supplementary logic such that they tended to exceed or fall short of political decorum. Thus claims to oppositional virtue tend to inflate, become bombast, boasting, promises, excessive oaths, lies. Or such claims deflate to become pathetic, hyper-personalized; they are vulnerable to parody.

---

[3] On prose fiction see Paul Salzman, *English Prose Fiction* (Oxford: Clarendon Press, 1985), pp. 307–21.

The uneasy and unstable relationship of the language of conspiracy to political decorum was bound up with the status of conspiracy itself. The legal status of conspiracy registered some of the category's shadowy power. It was always a specific crime, distinct from treason because of its collective nature and, significantly, it was also distinct from the actual end at which it aimed. Besides the public dimension under common law, conspiracy was significant in the areas of commercial and sexual dealings. Seen as a public and collective crime against all, so powerful was the idea of conspiracy in English law that the penalties exacted for it were at times greater than the maximum penalties for the offence the accused had conspired to commit. The seventeenth century saw Coke's judgment on the Poulterer's case, where he wrote, 'a false conspiracy betwixt divers persons shall be punished, although nothing be put in execution'.[4] Conspiracy itself, regardless of its end, rendered the participant suspect. Moreover, while Habermas situates the emergence of a public sphere committed to the ideal (if not the practice) of free communication in 1688, many contemporaries saw the opposite image—of a society operating through covert networks. The ideal of an explicitly *public* sphere within which free communication is an ideal indeed implies an opposite understanding of political events.

The issue concerns whose language is to pass current, to be believed as authentic, virtuous, and (consequently) an accurate register of political truth, a 'demonstration' rather than inauthentic, inaccurate, lying. At the same time, those who had lived through the reversals of the Civil War and Restoration would see that the huddled conspirators might become the governors, treason might become truth as the world reversed itself once more.[5] As John Barrell indicates in his discussion of the way in which treason—defined with notorious vagueness as imagining the king's death—was bound up with conflicts over the meanings of words in the 1790s, the place of writing in such a world was fraught and genres associated with history and the recent past were highly politicized.[6] In 1677 Gilbert Burnet noticed, 'Every year we get new

---

[4] Alan Harding, 'The Origins of the Crime of Conspiracy', *Transactions of the Royal Historical Society* (1983), pp. 89–108: 90.

[5] See Alan Marshall, *Intelligence and Espionage in the Reign of Charles II, 1660–1685* (Cambridge: Cambridge University Press, 1994), p. 117.

[6] John Barrell, *Imagining the King's Death: Figurative Treason, Fantasies of Regicide* (Oxford: Oxford University Press, 2000), pp. 1–5.

Memoires of some one Great Person or another. And though there are great Indiscretions committed, in publishing many Secrets and Papers, not fit for Publick View: Yet this way of Writing takes now more in the World than any sort of History ever did.'[7] Relying on the truth-claims of the narrator, the memoir—as secret history, fiction, and history—was central to the construction of the Restoration political world, and especially to the shaping of that world's understanding of the English Civil War.

That the highly hybridized generic qualities and extraordinary paranoia of Restoration memoir pass without comment by historians is an indication of the extent to which such narrative makes up the very material with which such scholarship works. One duality of such material, as is clear from the memoirs of Burnet, Margaret Cavendish, Lucy Hutchinson amongst many, is an attitude to past and present in which, while the past is to be faithfully recuperated and recorded by the lights of the memoirist, it is also to be reshaped as a history for the present. Restoration memoir both articulates the political crimes of the past and recasts them according to the religious and political exigencies of the present. As memoir, taken broadly, was one of the dominant genres in which history of the Civil War was made in the period from 1660 to the publication of Catherine Macaulay's pioneering *History* in the late eighteenth century, the test to which such writing was subjected by its readers was that of political commitment. Was it true? Whose side was it on? Moreover, while such manuscripts circulated and were known (Lucy Hutchinson's memoir of her husband is a case in point), publication was bound up with the question of the appropriate political moment, and both Burnet and Clarendon delayed publication of their memoirs by a generation, arguably to allow their writings to emerge into a public debate in which their assertions were less contentious, though with the simultaneous intention of imposing their view of English history on the next generation. That the reader is prompted to remember a past just slipping from mind and to recall its centrality to the present is one of the main strategies of memoir in this period; offering an aide-memoire,

---

[7] Gilbert Burnet, *Memoirs of the Lives and Action of James and William, Dukes of Hamilton and Castleherald* (1677), preface, as quoted in Margaret Bottrall, *Every Man a Phoenix: Studies in Seventeenth-Century Autobiography* (London: John Murray, 1958), p. 160.

genres such as the memoir set up a reading dynamic of discovery and disclosure in which the reader is prompted to see the lineaments of the characters' present morality suggested in the prophetic shapes of their past conduct.

What was the place of gender and sexuality in this discursive world? While it is obvious that not only men wrote their memoirs and, concomitantly, that sexual relations were used to figure political betrayals, how these two can be seen as connected is less clear. Arguably it was the way conspiracy, like adultery, duplicated the structure of that which it betrayed which invited its figuration as sexual in texts such as Otway's *Venice Preserv'd*, Behn's *Love-Letters*, and Manley's later *New Atalantis*. The feminocentric focus of the last two texts indicates that they, at least, acknowledge the appearance of women in the political sphere—as political as well as sexual agents. Clearly, women did participate in political conspiracy throughout the Civil War and after (Lady Stanhope, Diana Gennings, and various unnamed but observed conspirators), and though obviously there is no direct correlation, literary representations of women conspirators might covertly or openly register political roles.[8] Both contemporaries and later scholars have acknowledged the figural connection between women and conspiracy, but less attention has been paid to writings connected to and by women in the Restoration struggles for political legitimacy.[9] Gender has a particular place in the accusations and counter-accusations of the 1670s and 1680s. The feminine voice in the mode of sacred, political, or sexual complaint functions discursively in the debates over conspiracy. We find the feminine voice contradictorily used and interpreted as *both* an authenticating ground for political truth because located *outside* the political sphere, and as figuring a falling away from, or corruption of, political virtue by telling of desire, seduction, and deceit.

Accordingly, taking a limited timespan from 1677 to 1688 this chapter explores the reconfiguring of conspiracy and the way political

---

[8] On female spies see e.g. David Underdown, *Royalist Conspiracy in England 1649–1660* (New Haven: Yale University Press, 1960), pp. 171–2.

[9] See Rachel Weil, ' "If I Did Say So, I Lyed": Elizabeth Cellier and the Construction of Credibility in the Popish Plot Crisis', in *Political Culture and Cultural Politics in Early Modern England*, ed. Susan D. Amussen and Mark A. Kishlansky (Manchester: Manchester University Press, 1995), pp. 189–213.

claims are made in the writings of Anne Halkett and Rachel Russell. It also examines the way in which the transmission of the texts by these writers—writing from very different political positions—has tended to bleed away the political content, or implication, present in their writings.

Once we see the way in which each uses personal virtue to underwrite political virtue, it is also possible to trace some of the ways in which my third example, Behn's *Love-Letters Between a Nobleman and his Sister*, responds debunkingly to such legitimizing writing strategies.

Responding not directly to Halkett and Russell but to the writing strategies used by those who were disenfranchised under the Stuart settlements, Behn's fiction seeks to reinforce that such writing is morally dubious. Seeking to expose Whig duplicity, *Love-Letters* parallels sexual and political treason.[10]

Thus, in asking how the writing of conspiracy represents those opposed to government, or who find themselves marginalized by it, the chapter traces interrelationships between discontented Stuart writing, justifications of republican and anti-Stuart action, and Tory prose satire. Female first-person narration of political scandal has been recognized as an important aspect of the Restoration fictions exposing conspiracy; and that writers of satirical and semi-pornographic fictions should be Tories (like Behn and Manley) rather than nonconformists seems obvious.[11] We hardly need to search deeply the works of John Bunyan and Elizabeth Singer Rowe to see why nonconformist and republican literary culture did not usually parallel Tory achievements in porno-political fiction. However, although Tory and nonconformist *fictional* modes might exist in separate aesthetic worlds, fictions such as *Love-Letters* comment precisely on the authenticating genres and literary strategies often used by those variously excluded by the shifting politics of the 1670s and 1680s. What follows examines the making, but also the reception, of the claims to truth of confession, history, letter, memoir, diary.

---

10 Manley, *New Atalantis*, p. 13.
11 On romance see Helen Hackett, *Women and Romance Fiction in the English Renaissance* (Cambridge: Cambridge University Press, 2001), pp. 10–19, 159–93; Rosalind Ballaster, *Seductive Forms, Women's Amatory Fiction, 1684–1740* (Oxford: Clarendon Press, 1992); Jane Spencer, *The Rise of the Woman Novelist* (Oxford: Blackwell, 1986).

ANNE HALKETT: 'MEMOIR', MEDITATION, AND THE WRITING OF CIVIL WAR CONSPIRACY

First I want to examine the use of memoir to assert female political virtue. Anne Halkett, whose manuscript memoir of the Civil War was written in the 1670s, was hardly an enthusiastic opponent of the Stuarts, whom her family had long served. Indeed, her main political connections came from her assistance to James, Duke of York, when he escaped custody in London in 1648, to fly to France. After the Restoration Halkett remained attached to the Stuarts, particularly Charles I and James VII and II, and these loyalties were part of increasingly fraught complex personal, religious and political positions that she sustained through her long life as a widow in Scotland. Halkett wrote two kinds of texts in which she is obliquely and fairly directly critical of some aspects of the very monarchy on which her significance as a political actor depended. And, as we find in her final manuscript notebook, these texts were explicitly intended for posthumous circulation.[12] Halkett's marriage, from 1656 to 1670, divides what can loosely be seen as three periods of religious and political involvement. These periods roughly coincide with the life stages of maid, wife, and widow, though, as we shall see, Halkett experienced each transition as problematic. During the Civil War she aided the Duke of York's escape and acted as a royalist activist in London and then in Scotland; in the second period she wrote the narrative of her life which has come to be called her 'memoir' and began her daily meditations; and in the third part of her life—her widowhood in Dunfermline—this form seems to have constituted her writing life in which she expresses and structures complicated religious and political antipathies and sympathies.[13]

---

[12] See Margaret J. M. Ezell, 'Anne Halkett's Morning Devotions: Posthumous Publication and the Culture of Writing in Late Seventeenth-Century Britain', in *Print, Manuscript and Performance: The Changing Relationships of the Media in Early Modern England*, ed. Arthur F. Marotti and Michael D. Bristol (Columbus: Ohio State University Press, 2000), pp. 215–31.

[13] The present memoir may not be as Halkett wished. John Loftis, *The Memoirs of Anne, Lady Halkett and Ann, Lady Fanshawe* (Oxford: Clarendon Press, 1979), p. xi. I am very grateful to Dr Suzanne Trill, who generously allowed me to see her work and discussed Halkett. I am grateful too for discussion with Dr Faith Lanum whose work on Halkett is forthcoming. See Susan Wiseman, ' "The Most Considerable of My Troubles":

The best known of Halkett's texts is also the one amongst her surviving manuscripts that tells a story. By the time she writes her memoir Halkett is, as she may always have been, devout. However, religious observance is not the sole determinant of the way she considers her past. Her account of the Civil War was written in 1677–8 when James, Duke of York, her royal contact and a Roman Catholic since 1672, was increasingly under pressure from those who felt that a Catholic could not succeed Charles II. As a memoir, although Halkett's text is a defence of its protagonist, it is housed in terms of genre and readership, in the same discursive field where female conspiracy was sexualized and eroticized.[14] As I will argue, the memoir and her other texts show in action some of the literary practices which attempted to justify political conspiracy by grounding it in personal virtue and—in Halkett's text more importantly—seek to use political loyalty to underwrite sexual misconduct.

Halkett's manuscript memoir is a central text in assessing her political trajectory, her self-understanding as a political agent and, later, as a writer. Halkett wrote her memoir in 1677–8, after her husband's death but at the point when the Duke of York, in the period preceding the Popish Plot, was at the centre of political and religious controversy. Thus the memoir describes Halkett's past in a present which has changed the political and personal meanings of her Civil War affiliations.

Anne Halkett and the Writing of Civil War Conspiracy', in *Women Writing, 1550–1700*, ed. Jo Wallwork and Paul Salzman, *Meridian*, 18, No. 1 (2001), pp. 25–45. On Halkett see also N. H. Keeble, 'Obedient Subjects? The Loyal Self in Some Later Seventeenth-Century Royalist Women's Memoirs', in *Culture and Society in the Stuart Restoration: Literature, Drama, History*, ed. Gerald Maclean (Cambridge: Cambridge University Press, 1995), pp. 201–18; Sara A. Murphy, '"A Stranger in a Strange Land": Cultural Alienation in Lady Anne Halkett's *Meditations*', M.Phil., University of Edinburgh, 2005; Sheila Ottway, 'They Only Lived Twice: Public and Private Selfhood in the Autobiographies of Anne, Lady Halkett and Colonel Joseph Bampfield', in *Betraying Ourselves: Forms of Self-Representation in Early Modern English Texts*, ed. Henk Dragstra, Sheila Ottway, and Helen Wilcox (Basingstoke: Macmillan, 2000), pp. 136–47; Mary Beth Rose, 'Gender, Genre, and History: Seventeenth Century English Women and the Art of Autobiography', in *Women in the Middle Ages and the Renaissance*, ed. Mary Beth Rose (Syracuse: Syracuse University Press, 1986), pp. 245–78; Suzanne Trill, ' "Refreshment", "Intertainement" and "Imployment": Lady Anne Halkett's *Meditations* and the Practice of Daily Devotion' (forthcoming); *Lady Anne Halkett: Selected Self-Writing*, ed. Suzanne Trill (forthcoming, Ashgate).

14 See also Donna Landry, 'Eroticizing the Subject, or Royals in Drag: Reading the Memoirs of Anne, Lady Halkett', in *The Intersection of Public and Private Spheres in Early Modern England*, ed. Paula Backscheider and Timothy Dykstal (London: Edward Arnold, 1995), pp. 134–49.

As she writes, her main political contacts from the 1640s are suspect and she justly feels unrewarded for her service. As John Loftis points out, the memoir works by inference and implication, and this is especially so with regard to the courtship between the narrator's younger self and Colonel Joseph Bampfield (C.B. in the narrative), who lured the then Anne Murray towards a bigamous marriage by telling her that his wife was dead, or at least by failing to inform her that she was alive.[15] At Christopher Love's trial John Jekyll was interviewed about Bampfield's place in contacting the Scottish Presbyterian royalists, and he eventually became one of Thurloe's agents.[16] By the time Halkett was writing, Bampfield had long been an ambiguous figure and for some (Charles II particularly) was highly suspect. Halkett describes her past estimation of Bampfield: 'his discourse was serious and handsome, and tending to imprese the advantages of piety, loyalty, and vertue'; but she inserts a caveat:

I thought his own practise contradicted much of his proffession, for one acquaintance had told mee he had not seene his wife in a twelvemonth; and it was impossible, in my opinion, for a good man to bee an ill husband, and therefore hee must defend himselfe from one before I could beleeve the other of him. Hee said itt was nott nesesary to give everyone that might condemne him the reason of his being so long from her, yett to satisfy mee hee would tell mee the truth, which was that, hee being ingaged in the King's service, hee was oblieged to be att London, where it was not convenient for her to bee with him, his stay in any place being uncertaine. Besides, she lived amongst her friends, who though they were kind to her yett were not so to him, for most of that country had declared for the Parleament and were enemys to all that had, or did, serve the King[17]

Could someone who lacked personal virtue be a true royalist (and vice versa)? Halkett invites the reader to begin to question Bampfield's personal loyalty, but, as we will see, postpones the key revelation that he is married.[18] The narrative is managed so that Halkett's own political

<hr>

[15] Loftis, *Memoirs*, pp. ix, xi, xii. See also Loftis's revision of the accepted version of Bampfield in *Colonel Joseph Bampfield's Apology*, ed. John Loftis and Paul H. Hardacre (Lewisburg: Bucknell University Press, 1993), pp. 245–50.

[16] *Bampfield's Apology*, ed. Loftis, pp. 158–60.

[17] Loftis, *Memoirs*, p. 23.

[18] For discussion of when Anne Murray's suspicions must have been confirmed in life, see, as before, Loftis's chapter in *Bampfield's Apology* (pp. 245–50). As one of Loftis's great virtues as an editor is his enthusiasm for each subject, probably the best account of possible events is formed by reading Halkett's memoir and meditations and Loftis's accounts of each player in *Memoirs* and *Bampfield's Apology.*

loyalty and virtue contrast with Bampfield's; the critical stance attributed to the young Anne Murray implies that she could tell virtuous conduct from its opposite. Personal virtue, here, is a litmus test for political virtue. As we will learn, a true royalist will have both. And, in the circumstances Murray is in—those of conspiracy—personal virtue is the sole basis for trust. The testing of personal qualities is also tied up to the quality of conspiracy as collective, yet desiring privacy until enacted. Political conspiracies are guaranteed solely by the vows and qualities of the conspirators—by their word given in secret, yet in relation to the public world. Murray recognizes, even emphasizes, a correspondence between personal honour and her loyalty to the king. The discussion of Bampfield's honour establishes the importance of personal virtue in Halkett's text. While critical discussion has focused on Halkett's sexual and marital conduct (used as key to her character by the first writer of her life), the memoir implies a broader understanding of virtue than the solely sexual.[19] Personal virtue operates explicitly as the guarantee of Murray/Halkett's *political* loyalty and vice versa. 'Virtue' is the password used to open doors to the sphere of political action, and in her memoir Halkett's political loyalty is used to underwrite her sexual honour.

Thus, the scene of her main political contact and evidence of her loyalty to the troubled Stuarts serves also as evidence of her virtue. The key political action of her life was her participation in the 1648 plot to liberate James, Duke of York. Halkett's task was to 'get the Duke's cloaths made and to drese him in his disguise':

I had desired him [C.B.] to take a ribban with him and bring mee the bignese of the Duke's wast and his length to have cloaths made fitt for him. In the meanetime C.B was to provide mony for all nesesary expence, which was furnished by an honest cittisen. When I gave the measure to my tailor to inquire how much mohaire would serve to make a petticoate and wastcoate to a young gentlewoman of that bignese and stature, hee considered it a long time and said hee had made many gownes and suites, but hee had never made any to such a person in his life. I thought hee was in the right; butt his meaning was, hee had never seene any woman of so low a stature have so big a wast. However, hee made it as exactly fitt as if hee had taken the measure himselfe.

---

[19] See also Sarah Findley and Elaine Hobby, 'Seventeenth Century Women's Autobiography', in *1642: Literature and Power in the Seventeenth Century* (London: Routledge, 1981), pp. 11–36.

It was a mixt mohaire of a light haire couler and blacke, and the under petticoate was scarlett.[20]

There is no doubt that Halkett regarded the chance to help the Duke of York as the proof of her loyalty and the foundation of her political career. To royalist circles it proved her loyalty, courage, and ingenuity. She was trusted, she knew the body of the Duke intimately, she served as perhaps only a woman could in organizing the making of the clothes. The account of the Duke's actual getaway is heavily freighted with detail corroborating the narrator's claim to have been there. The young Duke escapes St James's during a game of hide-and-seek, and is brought to Murray by water. Though they are late, C.B. having told her to leave if they had not arrived by ten o'clock, she waits and:

while I was fortifying my selfe against what might arive to mee, I heard a great noise of many as I thought comming up staires, which I expected to bee soldiers to take mee; butt it was a pleasing disapointmentt, for the first that came in was the Duke, who with much joy I tooke in my armes and gave God thankes for his safe arrival. His Highnese called 'Quickely, quickely, drese mee', and putting off his cloaths I dresed him in the wemen's habitt that was prepared, which fitted His Highnese very well and was very pretty in itt.

Halkett tells us she fed him 'a Woodstreet cake (which I knew hee loved)', and C.B. led him across the bridge 'to the staires where the barge lay'. They 'were soone out of sight'.[21] Circumstantial details verify her own participation in the rescue, and, therefore, in Stuart politics. She also conveys that she is right to disobey Bampfield, and that her desire to serve the Stuarts leads her into danger. Although in danger she serves the King. The detailed description is designed to verify both her presence and her loyalty.

However, Halkett's testimony also has to negotiate the relationship between past and present. The telling of the story in the late 1670s was to an extent complicated by James's Catholicism. As important, though, her connection to James was through Bampfield, and this passage has to negotiate the fact that in the incident on which her personal and political credit is founded, Halkett's aid to the Stuarts was bound up with the very circumstance which threatened to undermine it—her involvement with Bampfield. While the details of the Duke's flight

[20] Loftis, *Memoirs*, p. 24.   [21] Ibid., p. 25.

may seem comic, each one is also proof of Halkett's political virtue. Although she was a woman, to be caught assisting the escape of a Stuart would have been a disaster. The escape and the detail she gives prove the intimate basis and strength of her loyalty to the Stuarts; that loyalty acts as an insurance policy for her closely connected sexual honour. Writing in the 1670s Halkett had to grapple with the complex relationship between past royalist conspiracy and an arguably degenerated Stuart present. In doing so her narration is sophisticated, using implication and irony to nuance past loyalty.[22] While Halkett's narrative is, certainly, one of sexual adventure or misadventure, it is not so much that—as Bottrall and Loftis suggest—she ignores the great world as that in shaping a narrating persona the memoir uses her political loyalty to recuperate tarnished reputation:

The earnest desire I had to serve the King made mee omitt noe opertunity wherin I could bee usefull, and the zeale I had for His Majesty made mee not see what inconveniencys I exposed myself to; for my intentions being just and inocentt made mee not reflect what conclusions might bee made for the private visitts which I could not butt nesesarily make to C.B. in order to the King's service.[23]

Far from neglecting events in the world, Halkett uses the part she played in such events to justify dubious sexual conduct: the narrative implicitly answers sexual slurs on political, rather than sexual, terrain.[24]

One strategy the narrative employs to anticipate and counter the reader's doubts about her sexual honour is the assertion of the narrator's virtue as ensured by her political loyalty. Thus, much of the memoir splits Murray (the narrated, past, self) and Anne Halkett, with the effect of maintaining each as virtuous. As I have said, the text only gives away that Bampfield's wife lives, at the moment when the young Murray herself confronts it. Thus, when Sir James Halkett tells her that he has been reliably informed that 'undouptedly CB's wife was living and was now att London, where shee came cheefely to undeceave those who beleeved her dead', a significant unification of narrative perspective takes place so that protagonist and narrator now have the same knowledge.[25] The innocent Anne Murray who had, she claimed, concealed

---

22 Compare e.g. Bottrall, *Every Man a Phoenix*, p. 151.
23 Loftis, *Memoirs*, p. 27.
24 Marshall, *Intelligence and Espionage*, p. 170.
25 Loftis, *Memoirs*, p. 72.

her engagement because C.B. 'durst nott without hazard of his life avowedly apeare' and so she had kept secret 'what might have beene (in those times) ruine to us both' becomes one who hates to appear in public because 'I apprehended every one that saw me censured mee' and with 'too just grounds'. The way Halkett manages the revelation, while leaving some details in doubt, enables the reader to engage empathetically with the protagonist's horror. Simultaneously, Halkett reminds us that she, too, was a royalist plotter sufficiently important to have misgivings about appearing in public. The contents of two mysteriously missing pages torn out at the height of the Bampfield drama have engaged scholarly curiosity about Halkett's exact relationship to Bampfield (a passage in Simon Couper's life of Halkett also suggests that she might have travelled with him to Holland). However, Anne Murray's 'misfortune' signals that, from this point, the reader is to consider the narrator as knowing and repentant. She continues with her services to the royalist cause (ironically her aid to the Earl of Belcarres might have been made necessary by another Bampfield betrayal) and is eventually able to marry the true royalist, James Halkett.[26]

That the 'personal' events and issues in Halkett's text—her sexual relationships and possible misconduct, her attention to virtue and honour, her relationship to the Stuarts—are shot through with political implications invites some reconsideration of the way the memoir might be read, and might have been read. To interpret this text as a 'personal' confession is to limit the significance of marital and sexual detail by seeing marital, familial, and sexual alliances in a way more modern than early modern. Such alliances are not 'private'—separate from rather than woven into—the fabric of the explicitly political world. While some critics have been keen to confine the memoir to the boudoir, others have been alert to Halkett's strategy of implication and the literary techniques which are used to enhance her status and to ensure her virtue by giving it a politicized, adventurous, scene of action. Halkett uses models from romance plotting and drama to shape significant events in her life and text; such uses of generic convention, most significantly, recast potentially squalid personal misadventures as part of a dramatic and romantic adventure—and this is very clear in her

---

[26] Ibid., pp. 72, 204.

description of the central political episode of her life.[27] When she wrote, readers understood the memoir as a staple form of politicized history, and other men and women were writing their own accounts.

I am arguing, then, that the memoir concerns itself with justifying its protagonist on the terrain of her political (rather than sexual) honour and is written with the politics of 1677–8 in mind; Halkett is not writing solely a confessional memoir but, by implication, something which is at least in part a *political* life. Her life is exemplary in Bacon's sense of a 'lively representation' which can be taken 'for example in another case'.[28] The memoir's repeated return to politics, and its insistence on private and political virtue as mutually guaranteeing, stylistically and generically link it to other Restoration memoirs. That this particular discursive link has not been fully acknowledged in the way the text has been read returns us to the wider question of how women's writing on politics, particularly on conspiracy, has been shaped by the nature of its transmission. Halkett's memoir takes the threads, or shreds, of Stuart credibility, primarily their Civil War past, and weaves them together to support carefully made assertions of her own virtue. The memoir establishes a legitimate political past which validates the past actor and the present writer. Halkett's emphasis on piety—like that of Lucy Hutchinson, and Rachel Russell—is closely linked to her political involvement and provides such involvement with a basis in personal virtue.

Halkett did imagine an audience for this complex text, but not as an isolated fragment.[29] The memoir is not, as it is sometimes treated, her only work but related to a large number of manuscripts, some of which were posthumously printed.[30] These texts, particularly her daily 'Meditations',

---

[27] See Kim Walker, 'The Lives of Lady Anne Halkett', in *Women Writing*, ed. Wallwork and Salzman, pp. 133–49: 139–41.

[28] Francis Bacon, *The Advancement of Learning* (Oxford, 1640; repr. Aldburgh: Archival Facsimiles, 1987), pp. 92–3.

[29] See Lois Potter, *Secret Rites and Secret Writing: Royalist Literature, 1641–1660* (Cambridge: Cambridge University Press, 1989), p. 108.

[30] See e.g. S.C. [Simon Couper], *The Life of the Lady Halket* (Edinburgh: Symson & Knox, 1701); 'Books Written by the Lady Halket', H2^r–H4^v. *Meditations on the Twentieth and fifth Psalm* (Edinburgh, 1701); *Meditations and Prayers, Upon the First Week; with Observations on each Day's Creation: and Considerations on all the seven Capital Vices, to be oppos'd: and their opposit Vertues to be Studied and Practised* (Edinburgh, 1701); *Instructions for Youth* (Edinburgh, 1701). On the Scottish book trade see Alastair J. Mann, *The Scottish Book Trade 1500–1720* (East Linton: Tuckwell Press, 2000).

broadly shaped on the English church year, and her personal memorials express her complex political and religious ideas. They also comment on political and religious life in 1680s and 1690s Scotland as experienced by a would-be proselytizing, but guarded, angry and anxious—yet assertive—Church of England believer. In the religious complexities of Scotland her English religious observance, her loyalty to the Stuarts and, perhaps, the fact that James II finally paid her a pension are mutually reinforcing; Halkett supported episcopacy in Restoration Scotland where Charles II had scarcely been enthroned before he was petitioned to remember to use the Covenant.[31]

If Halkett was increasingly pushed aside because of her financial and political vulnerability, then these texts talk back to the world that at least partially rejected Halkett and in which she felt only partially lodged. The meditations, then, are important for any longer study of Halkett. Fourteen volumes of manuscripts survive from an original total of twenty-one.[32] Unlike the memoir, these meditations include a range of different genres—meditations, extended biblical analyses, poetry, dated entries 'recording' significant events. They tend to be grounded in a present of writing, with Halkett sometimes seeming to store up rage for a day before unleashing an analytical, often self-critical, but also politicized account of quite recent events. Written between the 1650s and her death in 1698, the manuscripts thus register loyalty to Stuarts and her dead husband but also mark quotidian reality and an annually cyclical spiritual journey constantly adapted and revised. Their various forms contrast with the memoir's summative and analytical narrative. Yet, like the memoir, surviving texts show Halkett—often obsessively—linking her life to political events throughout the 1660s and 1680s. Thus, the manuscript books both offer a context for the writing moment of the memoir and elucidate her response to the events of Charles II's and James II's reigns. While these texts deserve expansive treatment, here I want to make only a few points about them.

[31] On the Covenant in Scotland see e.g. Raymond Campbell Patterson, *A Land Afflicted* (Edinburgh: John Donald, 1998), pp. 226–93.

[32] It seems that, according to the numbering in Simon Couper's *Life*, the manuscripts now extant are: v–vii, ix–x, xii–xiii, xv–xxi. Seven volumes were already missing in 1870 when John Gough Nichols was editing his autobiography. *National Library of Scotland Catalogue of Manuscripts* (Edinburgh: HMSO, 1986), V, 1–10.

Politically a Jacobite but deeply attached to Church of England observances, Halkett's life in Scotland was, as Suzanne Trill has argued, one of isolation and estrangement as well as assertion of cultural identity and power.[33] The manuscripts tell us about Halkett's feelings about politics and particularly the Stuarts. The focus of her loyalty is Charles I. Halkett describes her thoughts at his death, meditating on the Psalms, and recalls 'the prayers I dayly ofred for the present King in his exile & all the Royall family' after his death, noting God's favourable response.[34] She often articulates her loyalty by summoning up the increasingly distant scene of Charles I, 'murdered publickly before his owne gates by a handfull of people'.[35] In an undated observation she addresses the vexed question of Charles II's reformation, and anticipates God 'bringing him at his owne apointed time to be a true reformer both of himselfe & people'.[36] A large section from 1660–1 canvasses 'the many disappointments I mett with in my busynese at Court'—her attempt to claim her promised pension.[37] Only her faith in 'an over-rulling providence' prevents her from allowing herself to 'repine att the many disappointments that I meet with'. The court, 'next heaven' is 'the greatest place for all beggars to resort to'. There, 'all I receave is Civilittys'; '& yett I see others, of as litle merit as my selfe gett all they seeke & more then they could expect'.[38] The 'handsome' refusal of the court again contrasts with her own continued virtue.[39] Yet, even as she

---

33 See Trill, forthcoming (Ashgate). See also Murphy, ' "Stranger in a Strange Land" ', *passim.*

34 NLS MS 6493, fo. 5.

35 NLS MS 6491, fo. 20. She was ecstatic to have had 'the first kiss of his Ma[ties] hand' after Charles II's coronation: NLS MS 6493, fo. 28. She regularly expressed her veneration for Charles the martyr: 'This is a day on which the greatest murder was committed that ever story mentioned except the crucifying of our Saviour, and many hath lain under the guilt of itt these many yeares who perhaps hath never ofred up to God a Sigh or teare for pardon of itt': NLS MS 6491, fo. 30.

36 She marks the notebook as begun in June 1673. Meditating on the king she expects 'the Lord' will make him 'an instrument of much Glory to himselfe by bringing him at his owne apointed time to be a true reformer': NLS MS 6493, fo. 9; 'I will dayly pray for the hastening of it': NLS MS 6493, fo. 25.

37 NLS MS 6491, fo. 43.

38 The passage ends, 'I envy no mans hapinese but have a share in the sattisfaction any person hath in obtaining there desire yett I cannot but secretly say why cannot I arrive to this degree as to have something while others want nothing they desire. But are wee nott all as clay in the hand of the potter & may hee nott doe wth us as he pleases.' NLS MS 6491, fos. 43–4.

39 Halkett vows 'to forbeare nothing thats rationall in pursuance of this end' but also fears that 'these delays & disappointments are to make triall how I would make good

unsuccessfully petitions Charles, she remembers a vow that, should God permit his coronation to take place she 'would for ever after during my life make that day a day of praise'.[40] Loyalty and discontent are in tension.

The accession of James II brought her some limited financial relief, but she remained isolated from English politico-religious practices such as the celebration of Charles I's execution. On 30 January 1687/8 she suddenly recalls the festival meaning of the day—and with it a startling feeling of her own attenuated connection to English politics:

> Had I nott had occation to be up early this morning to write letters And by dating them came to remember the horid & never enough to be detested Regicide committed this day upon the best of Kings perhaps I might have forgott itt And so wanted that great remorse & greife & sorrow that the act of this day calls for ... [41]

Halkett neither wants to forget, nor to be forgotten and if the memoir struggles to make her past properly understood the meditations strive to retain good practice in the present and shape a self for posterity. Politics is one theme of these writings, but another is the question of the survival of her texts. The late manuscripts reveal Halkett's plans to ensure the survival, and if possible publication and circulation, of her writings. Her example would invite 'others of greater capacity [to] imploy them to the honor of God when they see what an unworthy person like my selfe hath indeaured'.[42] Never intending her writings 'should be seene to any as long as I lived':

> But fearing when I was dead if undisposed of, they might fall into such hands as might make ill use of them. Therefore I writt ^{ye} Contents of every one of them & inclosed them in a sheet of paper sealed up & derected them to Mr Cooper & Mr Grene with a letter aquainting them; that as I had formerly aquainted them with the Account of my life and the occations ^{yt} made me put it in writting.

She offers to send 'the Trunck' of her writings, 'the greatest treasure of my Soule' to Mr Couper with 'as many of them as itt would hold'.[43]

---

what I have often said, To see the king brought in, in peace & established in his just prerogatives I would bee Content to beg all my life after': NLS MS 6491, fos. 45, 46.

[40] NLS MS 6491, fo. 50; see also ibid., fos. 63–4.   [41] NLS MS 6497, fo. 345.
[42] NLS MS 6502, fo. 226.   [43] NLS MS 6502, fos. 226–7.

When he asks to have 'one Booke at a time', 'promising secrecy', she continues:

I delivered him the Parchment booke with the Pincke ... riban wherein the most considerable of my troubles are registered. The desorder I was in att the given itt. And what disquiet of mind I had aboutt it for severall hours after itt; had any knowne, They would have freed me from thinking that Vanity had any prevelancy in itt. For I hate vaine thoughts.[44]

We may never know, exactly, what Halkett found so disturbing to reveal in the parchment book. However, it is evident that she sees her writings as potentially exemplary and of lasting significance. Although she is anxious about passing on 'the most considerable' of her troubles, perhaps the memoir, she wants to deliver everything—her diaries, prayers, meditations, list of good women from the Bible—to readers whom she both feared and avidly desired.[45] At least at this late point, she understands her writing activity as exemplary and her identity as built in that writing as properly a part of historical—that is, inevitably, political—thought. If she can reach the right readers it is they who can understand her life and make it productive.

How can Halkett's relationship to the conspiracy of the 1640s and the politics of the 1670s and after be understood? Rachel Weil, writing about the account given by the midwife in the mealtub plot, Elizabeth Cellier, notes that Cellier worries about 'modesty' rather than 'the fact that she is a woman with political conviction'; Cellier's 'persuasiveness' is 'oddly bound up with Cellier's representation of herself in the text'.[46] Weil's focus on the legitimating techniques used by Cellier to make herself a credible witness despite her social status has some resonance in Halkett's very different case. Halkett is, certainly, highly aware of potential readers and of how they might question her text, and therefore her virtue. Her writing is marked by a dynamic of confession and withholding which is characteristic of writing about conspiracy at the Restoration, perhaps more generally. Thus, the political as well as confessional persuasiveness of Halkett's memoir rests on our acceptance of her carefully nuanced self-representations. This self-representation

---

[44] NLS MS 6502, fos. 228–9.
[45] 'Women mentioned in Scripture' (Eve, Rebecca, Miriam, Ruth, Hannah, Bathsheba, Deborah, Blessed Virgin, etc.): NLS MS 6499, fos. 254–370; MS 6502, fo. 228.
[46] Weil, ' "If I Did Say So, I Lyed" ', pp. 198, 201.

includes as a foundational building block the trauma or scandal which her later life repairs and to which her writing repeatedly returns. That she develops moral, political, religious, and writerly relationships to this event or events presumably involving Bampfield makes those events, perhaps paradoxically, central to her claim to posthumous exemplarity. In the memoir, although the subject is a woman, virtue is taken as having a wider meaning than simply chastity. The young Murray's political and personal virtue are bound up together in such a way that the disclosure of her political actions (her part in James's escape, her plotting in Scotland) justifies her possibly serious lapse in sexual morality with Bampfield. Moreover, Halkett's other texts and her apparently clear decision that they should all be made available, at least to the right sort of reader, invite us to see her output not only in terms of piety. Piety is a foundational strain in the texts, particularly the 'Meditations', and its written expressions (such as obsessive memorialization) and other expressions (such as the charity discussed by Sara Murphy) articulate amongst other things a complicated historically, theologically, and locally grounded sense of honour. We can also trace her changing relationship to her past political world.

More generally, Halkett's texts tell us something of wider application about women's relationship to the political world through the writing about conspiracy. As I have argued, the structures of conspiracy mimicked the official political world while, simultaneously, creating a situation in which conspirators could offer only private virtue as a guarantee of future public goodness. In her memoir, Halkett asserts her virtue in contrast to those who betray her. Private virtue is the credit underwriting her political loyalty, and vice versa. Repeatedly, and most significantly in the cases of Bampfield, and of the traitor William Howard, sexual and ostensibly 'private' misconduct implies public wrongs. The question of legitimate or illegitimate political activity is weighed and nuanced according to the private and public virtue of protagonists. Personal and political betrayal are paired in Halkett's enemies, who also turn out to be enemies of the Stuarts, and contrast with her loyal royalism. It is her loyalty, she tells us, which leads her to put her reputation at risk. In offering hers as an exemplary history she attempts to separate herself from Bampfield and other traitors. Yet Halkett's text is ambiguous not only because of the 'key' missing pages but because this exercise of discrimination is both essential and cannot be fully completed—her past, her virtuous conduct, and her hope of reward are tied to these figures. The memoir's overdetermined connecting of personal and political virtue would have been evident to any reader who knew something of events; that is, to most seventeenth- or eighteenth-century readers.

Published after the Glorious Revolution, the *Life of the Lady Halket* (Edinburgh, 1701) is probably by Simon Couper, the Edinburgh defender of episcopacy to whom Halkett gave her manuscripts. Changing the complex patterning I have traced here, this first published account of Halkett isolated the theme of struggle for personal virtue and turned it to distinct political ends.[47] For whatever reason, the vital connection between personal and public virtue which characterizes other writing on conspiracy besides Halkett's and which certainly points to the political impetus underlying her memoir, is broken. Utterly changing the narrative strategies of the memoir which it takes as its 'raw' material (excerpting it with other texts), S.C.'s *Life* uses excision, indirection and redesignation to make an 'account of her *exemplary life*'.[48] Removing Halkett's first-person, present-tense narration, removing the initials of those with whom she conspired, and removing the fictionalizing generic markers (apparently drawn from experience of romance, secret history, and memoir) in the *Life* S.C. makes feminine virtue drive, and dominate, Halkett's politics. S.C. might well have feared responses to Halkett's sexual misconduct, but his own religio-political position—as a supporter of bishops—was perhaps as important.[49] Thus, 'Our Vertuous Lady was too Generous and ingenuous' not to assist the Stuarts; both 'Loyall principles which education and Religion had fixed in her Heart' and 'obligations, which the Royall bounty had put on her Fathers Family' justify her political action.[50] While S.C. presents the inescapable link between Halkett's political loyalty and personal misfortunes, he keeps religion and virtue to the fore. Halkett had:

---

[47] For example, Couper remakes Halkett, as 'fully satisfied of the Legitimacy' of Prince William (*Life of the Lady Halket*, p. 24). I am very grateful to Dr Suzanne Trill for discussion of this point.

[48] See S.C., *Life of the Lady Halket*.

[49] See Simon Couper, *Three Essays Concerning Church Government* (Edinburgh: Andrew Symson, 1704); Robert Whyte, *The Fable of the Sacred Phenix, or, Of Prelacy revived from the Ashes of its Funerals* (1704); Simon Couper replies in *The Moral of the Phoenix Justified* (Edinburgh: Andrew Symson, 1705).

[50] S.C., *Life of the Lady Halket*, p. 15.

scarce well appeared on the Stage of the World, in a publick Place, and Critical Age when she found exercise enough for her Vertue; & almost all sorts of Tryals, to prove the constancy of her Mind: Being tossed, as it were between waves and pursued with a constant series of difficulties and incumbrances for the space of fourteen Years, both in *England* and *Holland*;

She is as 'one Shipwrack'd & bereaved of all Comforts (Except her Vertue and Integrity)'.[51] After her death Couper is making or remaking Halkett for the beleaguered Episcopalians. Halkett's writing was undoubtedly pious, but her piety was politicized. For all that Halkett chose Simon Couper to receive her writings, and so perhaps shared his priorities, his 'notable Passages of Eminent *Piety & Virtue*' occlude the memoir's allusive, implicatory qualities: piety isolated is turned to his politicized ends.

For subsequent editors, feminine virtue, though sexualized and placed in the context of the confessional, eclipses politics as the theme of Halkett's writing. The very dynamic of writing about conspiracy, involving drives to both concealment and revelation, has assisted in obscuring the significance of Halkett's text as a political as much as a sexual memoir. The processes of transmission to which her texts were subject tend to use the personal virtue she asserts to separate her from a political world, yet clearly part of the narrative and even diaristic function of piety was to recuperate Halkett's past (and her present meditations on it) as *political* activity in the best sense—virtuous, unavoidable, and, if open to the charge of unchastity, then open to that charge precisely because of the risks she took for her virtue.

If men found it hard to place themselves in relation to the appropriate dividing line between public and private action and writing, it was even more complicated for women. Conspiracy intensified pre-existing tensions. Editors responded to her texts' attempt to deal with the question of feminine as well as other virtue by understanding female virtue solely in the senses of sexuality and piety; Halkett's writings on conspiracy indicate that female virtue, though crucially expressed through the care of the body, is also an index of the soul. Understood thus, female virtue, though grounded in chastity, encompasses and is guaranteed by virtues such as constancy, loyalty, and prudence which inhabit the borderland of public and private conduct.

[51] Ibid., p. 13.

RACHEL RUSSELL'S LETTERS, WILLIAM RUSSELL'S REPUTATION: WRITING AND RESISTANCE

Virtue and authenticity are of crucial importance in the writings generated by Lady Rachel Russell. Texts from William Russell's trial and execution for his part in the Rye House plot serve as my second example of women and the writing of conspiracy. The texts written by and associated with Rachel Russell, in some ways an absolutely exemplary pious widow, again show the interconnection of personal and political virtue. Rachel Russell attempted to counter the tarnishing effect of accusations of conspiracy—indeed, treason—on the reputations of the dead and the living. Aptly described by her recent biographer as having a 'conventional' though also 'ambiguous' attitude to women's political engagement, Russell was also the preserver (to an extent the creator) of the posthumous political reputation of her husband.[52] The letters she wrote after his death were saved and circulated. They were published much later, in response to Sir John Dalrymple's memoirs, which questioned William's conduct.[53] How did Rachel Russell put the idea of virtue to work in writing?

On 28 June 1683 John Evelyn wrote, 'After the *Popish*-plot &c there was now a new (& as they call'd it) *Protestant-Plot* discover'd that certain

---

[52] Lois G. Schwoerer, *Lady Rachel Russell* (Baltimore: Johns Hopkins University Press, 1988), p. 70.

[53] Sir John Dalrymple, *Memoirs of Great Britain and Ireland* (Edinburgh: W. Strachan and T. Caddell, 1771). Dalrymple exposed the financial connection between Charles II and France. Dalrymple's sin with regard to Russell was to perpetuate the image of Russell as indecisive, tainted by the moral and rhetorical ambiguity attendant upon his desire to tell the truth at his trial, but without incriminating himself or others. Thus he wrote: 'When brought before the council, he refused to answer any thing that might affect others: With regard to himself, he confessed some things with candour; and in denying others, shewed what difficulty a man of strict honour finds, to distinguish between concealing truth and expressing falsehood.' Dalrymple could not really be said to be hostile to Russell. He wrote of the dignity of his death and takes up the image of Russell as a young paterfamilias, valorizing his pious widow (Dalrymple, *Memoirs*, pp. 31–2). He even commented in a footnote, 'What a picture might the parting of Lord Russel with his family and friends make in the hands of a Hamilton!' (ibid., p. 32). In all this he recirculates and even extends the pro-Russell propaganda in such texts as *The Last Legacy Or affectionate and Pious Exhortations and Admonitions Of the Late William Lord Russel, to his Vertuous Lady, and dear Children* (1683), in which Russell's portrait sits above those of three rather alarmingly beheaded youngsters as a tribute to his virtuous family status.

Lords, & others should design the Assacination of his *Majestie* &
Duke.'[54] The uncertain status of this conspiracy, known as the Rye
House plot, and the bloody sufferings of those associated with it, made
it and its participants the enduring objects of debate and speculation.
And after the arrival of William of Orange in 1688, this moment had
renewed significance in the making and marring of political reputations.
One of the plot's casualties, Lord William Russell, was executed, with
'few believing' he had 'any evil Intention against Majestie or the
Church'.[55] Although few felt Russell deserved to die, his status as a
political martyr was unclear, clouded by questions about what he did—
and, more significantly, about what he believed. Yet by the mid-nine-
teenth century, the stain of treason retrospectively removed, Russell's
image came to inhabit the corridor between the Lords and the Commons. How did an acknowledged political featherweight come to have
his image installed in the very passages of democratic process?[56] From
the time of his trial and the moment of his death Rachel Russell was at
work, modelling William Russell's reputation as a martyr—using words
to memorialize her husband and to attribute to him a thoroughgoing
political philosophy. In Rachel Russell's shaping of her husband's martyrdom, two connected issues are at stake. First, there is the significance
of conspiracy as shadowing legitimate political activity, a status particularly important for the Rye House plot and plotters (of which William
Russell was one) because of the reversal of their fortunes at the so-called
Glorious Revolution of 1688. Secondly, there is the significance of the
political career and writings of Rachel Russell, William's wife.

Named after an awkward corner in the road where Charles and James
might have been assassinated as they returned from the races in New-
market, the Rye House plot remains a shadowy set of possible plans,
conspiratorial links. There is little doubt that Lord William Russell had
had seditious conversations with William Howard. As Richard Greaves
points out, Russell admitted that at Shaftesbury's house he had discussed
the seizure of the King's guards—though he said that he had objected to
it. An unsent letter to James, Duke of York, also seems to confirm guilt.

[54] *Diary of John Evelyn*, ed. E. S. de Beer (Oxford: Clarendon Press, 1955), IV, 321.
[55] Ibid., p. 323.
[56] See Blair Worden, *Roundhead Reputations: The English Civil Wars and the Passions
of Posterity* (London: Allen Lane, 2001), pp. 298–9.

In a detailed discussion of January to June 1683, Jonathan Scott notes that the period in which William Russell was conspiring involved at least two 'plots' which the government, it seems, sought to link using witnesses who turned state's evidence. Howard's testimony alone gives evidence of the first two meetings of the 'Council of Six' (Howard, Essex, Russell, Hampden, Monmouth, Sidney).[57] The meaning of such evidence was disputable and was contested. But William Russell was an ambiguous witness. At the time of his trial two questions were central: was Russell a traitor, and what were the (theoretical) grounds for his behaviour? William Howard's evidence helped to seal his fate as a conspirator, though defenders have pointed to the fact that he appeared to be doomed before the start of the trial. The trial's outcome would seem to have been preordained. Certainly, many felt so at the time despite its nine judges and a performance of fairness.

William Russell's defence in effect returned to the question of conspiracy. He argued that to imagine the levying of war against the King was not equivalent to a design to kill him; on technical grounds, he argued that no two witnesses had sworn to the same act proving him to have sought Charles II's death by seizing his guards. The chief witness was the traitor Lord William Howard of Escrick. In summing up, the question of witnesses was ignored. However, the ambiguous nature of William Russell's participation in the various 'consults', and the number and nature of the various plots, remained a burning question for contemporaries. So, after the Glorious Revolution, Sir Robert Atkyns wrote to defend Russell against the charge of treason. According to Atkyns, being present where '*others do consult and conspire to do some Treasonable Act*' does not make him guilty of treason as charged under the statute of Edward III. Treason, so defined, involved 'Compassing or imagining the Death of the King, Queen, Prince' or actually 'Levying War against the King'.[58] Attempting to rehabilitate Russell, Atkyns directly addresses the problem that the patriot might, really, have been a traitor.

On the evening preceding his execution, William Russell 'wound up his watch; and said, now he had done with time and was going to

[57] Jonathan Scott, *Algernon Sidney and the Restoration Crisis, 1677–1683* (Cambridge: Cambridge University Press, 1991), pp. 283–9.

[58] Sir Robert Atkyns, *A Defence of the Late Lord Russel's Innocency, confuting a libellous pamphlet called 'an Antidote Against Poison'* (1689), pp. 3, 11.

eternity'.[59] On the morning of the trial Russell's co-conspirator, Lord Essex, was found dead by his own hand. On 21 July the Earl of Ormond wrote from St James's Square:

> Whilst I am writing I think my Lord Russell is upon the scaffold making his last speech. He hath written a letter to the King which he hath ordered his wife to deliver or send when he is dead. This being, at least for the present, the last execution, I think the whole proceeding will be printed and a declaration will be made by his Majesty on the subject, and a day of thanksgiving will follow, which, in effect, will be a declaration to every parish.[60]

Russell was executed in Lincoln's Inn Fields, close to the city; on the scaffold he delivered his paper, looked once towards his home— nearby, beyond Holborn—and went to his death. At the moment he died, or even before, the struggle to constitute him as a political martyr began.[61] In this fashioning of someone executed for treason as a political martyr personal virtue was Rachel Russell's premium political capital.

Russell was widely regarded as wrongly targeted and harshly punished. But this alone cannot account for the cult that developed around him, or his presence as an heroic patriot in the nineteenth century, when his image, with that of his wife, found a place inside the houses of Parliament. The paper he delivered on the scaffold was the only political tract he wrote, and several commentators thought even this was not his. The scaffold speech was immediately at the centre of controversy. Was it, as Rachel Russell and Burnet asserted, made in consultation with the Revd Gilbert Burnet or had Burnet simply written it? Contemporaries, including Charles II, thought that it was not of Russell's composition. As one put it:

> There is come over by the last post a printed speech of my Lord Russell's, part of it pretended to have been spoken by him, and the other part of it to have been writ by him; but I am very much mistaken in him for he made either of them

[59] William Russell on the morning of execution: 'He drank a little tea and some sherry.' Burnet, *Memoirs*, p. xvi.

[60] Ormond to the earl of Arran, 21 July 1683, HMC 36 (1912), p. 79.

[61] See Rachel Weil, *Political Passions* (Manchester: Manchester University Press, 1999), p. 101.

himself; but I guess who was the author, though they were not so well penned as I thought that Reverend Doctor [Burnet] would have done them.[62]

Who wrote the speech? Rachel Russell was with William throughout the trial. She and Burnet were in consultation with him as he composed his scaffold speech for distribution. With regard to composition, Burnet gave Rachel Russell 'An Account of all that passed between ye late Lord Russell, & me, concerning his last Speech, and Papers'.[63] Burnet, suspected of penning the speech, writes:

We also had great Discourse about ye Unlawfulnesse of Resistance, & I thought that, by the ground I gained at first, it would be easy to persuade him, that it was absolutely Unlawfull. But indeed he went no farther at last, than he did at first:[64]

Contradicting the rumour of his own implication, Burnet left a detailed account of Russell's composition of the speech. Again and again he spoke to Russell of the unlawfulness of resistance.[65] Yet, despite itself, this clarification further emphasized the ambiguity of Russell's position as both conspirator and theorist. It seems that Russell continued writing on Wednesday and Thursday, initially leaving, and then filling up, two 'void spaces' until, finally, it seems that his views on resistance had been clearly recorded:

In his Paper he writ these Words relating to the Matter of Resistance.—viz For my part I cannot deny but I have bin of Opinion, That a Free Nation like this might Defend their Religion, & Liberties, when Invaded, & taken from them, tho under pretence and Colour of Law. But some eminent and Worthy Divines who have had the charity to be often with me, have offered me Weighty Reasons to persuade me, that Faith and patience are ye proper wayes for ye Preservation of Religion; & that ye Method of the Gospell is to suffer Persecution, rather than to use Resistance. But if I have sin'd in that, I hope God will not lay it to my charge; since 'twas only a sin of Ignorance.[66]

However, in Lady Russell's copy of her husband's scaffold speech, described by the handlist as in her hand and endorsed—'A True Copy

---

[62] Arran to Ormond, 28 July 1683, HMC 36 (1912), p. 88.

[63] Gilbert Burnet, 'An Account of all that passed between ye late Lord Russell, & me, concerning his last Speech, and Papers', 'Papers relative to the Trial & Execution of the Lord Russell'. MSS Duke of Devonshire at Chatsworth.

[64] Burnet, 'An Account', and 'Papers'. MSS Devonshire, Chatsworth.

[65] Ibid.   [66] Ibid., fo. 1ᵛ.

attested soe by my Lords signing it'—a passage which is very likely this one is scored out.[67] This apparent indecisiveness, or ambiguity, is corroborated by Dalrymple's later assertion that: 'Lord Russel's examination is in the paper-office full of interlineations: Even the interlineations are interlined.'[68]

The writing and unwriting of Russell's resistance in this way gives significant textual expression to conspiracy and transgressive political thought and theory. The passage on the legality of resistance is triply displaced: it exists in a copy claiming to quote Russell's opinion and words; it seems to be implied as something the writer would commit himself to only after hesitation in the discussion; and, finally, in a 'true copy' the passage is absent, though also implicitly present—scored out. Later on the same sheet Russell repeats the equivocation made at his trial about the question of seizing the King's guards having murderous implications with regard to the King. In *practical* terms in this equivocation, and in *theoretical* terms in the scored out passage on resistance, conspiratorial thinking marks this text. It appears as an alternation of assertion and denial; a dynamic of presence and absence marks the text as conspiratorial. Disclosure vies with concealment as the insistence that it is a 'signed' 'true copy' of the scaffold speech as it was to be printed becomes only an assertion of resistance and obedience simultaneously. Does obedience perhaps triumph—in the scoring out? If so, resistance, like forbidden knowledge, remains in the very scratchings out that conceal it.

In what sense were the events called the Rye House plot truly a plot or conspiracy, and what were Russell's views and actions? The documents of

[67] See MSS Devonshire, Chatsworth: MS Correspondence I and II. MS Correspondence II, 'Papers relative to the Trial & Execution of the Lord Russell', item No. 4, 'A Paper in Lady Russell's handwriting thus endorsed—"A true Copy attested soe by my lords signing of his paper he ordered to be printed &, it was soe" '. The letters visible beneath the scoring out look very like the passage from Burnet and the printed version includes a gap at this point. William Russell has signed this text which the Chatsworth handlist says is in Rachel Russell's hand. There are also versions of Gilbert Burnet's accounts of his counselling of William Russell. See No. 5, 'A paper Endorsed "Dr Burnets relation what happened during Ld Russells confinement" '—'this relation was writ by me on Sunday morning at my Lady Russells desire & only for her private use'. See also *The Speech of the Late Lord Russell, To the Sherriffs Together with the Paper deliver'd by him to them, at the Place of Execution, on July 21 1683* (London, 1683), p. 3.

[68] Dalrymple, *Memoirs*, pp. 28–9; Thomas Birch, *Life of the Most Reverend Dr. John Tillotson* (London: J. and R. Tonson, 1752), pp. 122–3.

Lord William Russell's final days articulate very clearly the conspiratorial dynamic, moving between official and unofficial political forms, assertion and concealment, and so on. It was the accusation and trial of her husband but also, centrally, the poignant uncertainty of his position as a republican plotter or an 'innocent' patriot—the two positions between which Russell seems unable to decide in his final speech—that produced Lady Russell as the focus and later maker of political discourse in her attempts to resolve ambiguities. She helped her husband during his trial (following the famous example of the royalist conspirator's wife, Elizabeth Mordaunt) and then established herself as a player in the political debates of the years to come.[69] Not only is her 'true copy' of his confession marked by the ambiguity of his political and conspiratorial position, but her first act after her husband's death was to intervene in the making of him as a political figure by writing to the King:

'Tis a great addition to my sorrows, to hear your Majesty is prevailed upon to believe, that the paper he delivered to the Sheriffe at his death was not his own. I can truly say, and am ready in the solemnest manner to attest, that ~~during the imprisonment~~ I often heard him discourse the chiefest matters contained in that paper, in the same expressions he therein uses, as some of those few relations that were admitted to him, can likewise averr. And sure 'tis an argument of no great force, that there is a phrase or two in it another uses, when nothing is more common than to take up such words we like, or are accustomed to in our conversation.[70]

The 'chiefest matters' are, of course, his opinion concerning resistance, and Russell is here indicating that the printed paper properly represents her husband's sentiments in this regard—not simply during his imprisonment when he was pressed to articulate them (that is the point of the crossing out), but always. Russell here combines defences of Gilbert Burnet and her husband. It is also an initial attempt at the public shaping of his and her reputations: in attempting to take control of

---

[69] *The Private Diarie of Elizabeth, Viscountess Mordaunt* (Duncairn: privately printed, 1836), pp. 1–7, 16–21.

[70] *The Letters of Rachel Russell; From the Manuscript at Woburn Abbey* (London: Edward and Charles Dilly, 1773), Letter V, pp. 5–6. Unless otherwise indicated I have used the 1773 edition. From existing manuscript copies it is clear that the letters are not always complete. See e.g. *Letters of Lady Rachel Russell and . . . the Trial of Lord William Russell* (London, 1809).

her husband's one political text her assertion of its authorship and meaning signals the start of her creation of his posthumous standing.

In this letter Lady Rachel Russell puts to work her own political obedience. The equivocation about obedience and resistance that so significantly marked her husband's final writings and their interpretations is resolved by her in a way which carefully preserves her own position as outside the political realm. Piety and obedience in effect insure her bid to clear his name. In this way, as soon as he was dead, Rachel Russell laid the foundations by which William Russell became a Whig martyr and she herself the focus of political expectation and a symbol of political virtue. By apparently strictly limiting her intervention to posthumous reputation and familial virtue, Russell's wifely persona shifts the terrain of the debate to that of virtue. She invokes the affective potential of the events, inviting the reader—and the first reader presumably was Charles II—to understand political change through the suffering of a subaltern in terms of gender, if not of status. Yet this displacement lays the foundation for the mythologization of William Russell and for the emergent position of Rachel Russell as a figurehead of virtuous political activity.

Initially, the trial and death of her husband established Rachel Russell's place in the political world, giving her an opportunity to become a political agent. The haunting ambiguity of Russell's political opinions, as I have begun to suggest, played a crucial precipitating role in this emergence and in her retrospective attempts to stabilize his patriotic image. The 'confession' was one part of her attempt to recuperate her husband's reputation, but her most sustained effort was through letters. As soon as her husband was dead, Rachel Russell began writing letters, perhaps most significantly the one to Charles II, which asserts her husband's 'clearnesse and sincerity' as evidence that he would not,

at the point of death doe so disingenious and false a thing as to deliver for his own what was not properly and expressly so. And if after the losse, in such a manner, of the best husband in the world, I were capable of any consolation, your Majesty only could afford it by having better thoughts of him, which when I was so importunat to speak with your Majesty, I thought I had som reason to believe I should have inclined you to, not from the credit of my word, but upon the evidence of what I had to say. I hope I have writ nothing in this that wil displease your Majesty. If I have, I humbly beg you to consider it as coming from a woman amazed with grief; and that you will pardon the daughter of a prson who served your Majesty's father in his greatest extremityes ...[71]

Not surprisingly, bearing a highly charged message for her husband's public, this letter seems to have circulated in copies at the time.[72] Thus, when Rachel Russell began correspondence with her various spiritual advisers her actions and writings were already tied to the publicity surrounding her husband's death and attempts, managed primarily by her, to shape him as politically steadfast, meditative and—above all—having the kind of clear political conviction which would allow him to be made into a patriot-martyr. Rachel Russell, losing the happy, politicized sociability of her marriage, was also tied to political circumstances; the time of her memory and mourning was political time. On 25 July 1687 she wrote to Dr Fitzwilliam, a trusted clergyman who had been her father's chaplain, that 'There are three days I like best to give up to reflection; the day my Lord was parted from his family, that of his tryal, and the day he was released from all the evils of this perishing world.'[73] This letter is prompting its reader, too, to remember a sequence of anniversaries stretching from past to future. Most of the letters which were later published came from a correspondence between Rachel Russell and Fitzwilliam, built around the death of her husband—though she also corresponded with Burnet and Tillotson. The intense exchange of letters with Fitzwilliam immediately after her husband's death dramatizes her life in a desired submission to divine will, and her failure to do so: 'I need not tell you, good Doctor', she writes, 'how little capable I have been of such an exercise as this.'[74] By reply Fitzwilliam supplies an authority against which to define her own inability to be consoled, suggesting that her 'thoughts may dwell too long upon that disconsolate theme, and so prejudice both your body and your soul'. He reproves her for rendering her body 'so macerated as not only to be made unserviceable to the mind, but to render that so to

---

[71] Letter V, *Letters*, p. 6.
[72] *Letters* (p. 5) indicates that this has already been printed, and refers to the extracts in Birch, *Life of Tillotson*.
[73] Letter XLVIII, *Letters*, pp. 93–4. The misleading annotation in the 1773 edition is corrected in the 1809 edition to indicate Russell's arrest was 26 June, trial 23 July, execution 26 July.
[74] 30 Sept. 1683, Letter VI, *Letters*, p. 6.

herself'.[75] Fitzwilliam, unlike Burnet, seems able to respond to Russell's vehemence.[76]

Russell describes to Fitzwilliam her 'wild and sad thoughts'.[77] Yet these letters, claiming the legitimacy and intimacy implied by the chronicling of spiritual suffering, cannot be understood simply as 'private' letters between a woman and a spiritual adviser. Theirs was not a 'private', even domestic, correspondence which later made its way into print. Russell, though she writes that she fears 'punishment in both states'—living and dead—clearly has much to gain for refusing to relinquish her focus on the event which has deprived her of happiness. She has also been discussing the publication of her letters with Fitzwilliam since the early days after her husband's death. A year later, in late May 1685, Russell alludes to an understanding with Fitzwilliam that the letters might be published, 'you are writing for my good, and advantage in particular, and perhaps for all that can read in general, if you please to give them opportunity, by making publick what you first, I believe, designed for private use'.[78]

By 1685 a shift is perceptible in the letters; without relinquishing her grief, Rachel Russell incorporates political affairs, 'news' (mainly political affairs), and questions. Thus, on 20 May discussion of the publication of the letters was immediately followed by news: 'The parliament met and chose Sir John Trevor as speaker, and so adjourn'd till Friday, then 'tis expected the King will speak.' The postscript returns directly to political questions, discussing Ireton's escape from prison, and saying that others have been imprisoned. Two years after her husband's death Russell is once again involved in the political world, albeit as a commentator and correspondent and not, as before, as the focus of political action though, as I will show, that role was to return. From Southampton House in London, on 21 July 1685, the anniversary of her husband's execution and just after Monmouth's rebellion, Russell sent Fitzwilliam the following letter:

---

[75] n.d. Letter VII, ibid., pp. 8–9.
[76] e.g. Burnet to RR, 2 Feb. 1683, Letter VIII, ibid., pp. 10–12.
[77] 20 Apr. 1684, Letter XI, ibid., pp. 16–17.
[78] RR to Fitzwilliam, 20 May 1685, Letter XXI, ibid., p. 35.

You imagine that these late confusions have afforded matter of tumultuous devouring thoughts, and tho' not so well digested, as they are in your letter, yet every clause in it I have tossed up and down.

And now, Doctor, I take this late wild attempt to be a new project not depending on, or being linkt in the least to any former design, if there was then any real one, which I am satisfied was not no more than (my own Lord confessed) talk. And 'tis possible that talk going so far as to consider, if a remedy to supposed evils might be sought, how it could be formed? but as I was saying, if all this late attempt was entirely new, yet the suspicion my Lord must have lain under would have been great; and some other circumstances I do confess must have made his part an hard one. So that from the deceitfulness of the heart, or want of true sight in the directive faculty, what would have followed God only knows. From the frailty of the will I should have fear'd but little evil; for he had so just a soul, so firm, so good, he could not warp from such principles that were so, unless misguided by his understanding, and that his own, not another's; for I dare say, as he could discern, he never went into anything considerable, upon the mere submission to any one's particular judgement. Now his own, I know, he could never have framed to have thought well of the late actings, and therefore most probably must have sate loose from them. But I am afraid his excellent heart, had he liv'd, would have been often pierced from the time his life was taken away to this. On the other hand, having I trust, a reasonable ground of hope, he has found those mercies, he died with a chearful persuasion he should, there is no reason to mourn my loss, when that soul I loved so well, lives in felicitys, and shall do so to all eternity. This I know in reason should be my cure; but flesh and blood in this mixed state is such a slave to sense, the memory how I have lived, and how (as I think) I must ever do for the time to come, does so prevail and weaken my most christian resolves, that I cannot act the part, that mere philosophy as you set down many instances, enabled many to an appearance of easiness, for I verily believe they had no more than we, but vainly affected it.

Southampton-house 21 July, 1685[79]

Spiritual and political concerns open on to one another, with thoughts in one realm prompting address to the other. The 'tumultuous devouring thoughts' eating her up signal responses to Monmouth's rebellion in which personal memory, political conviction and concern with her own and her dead husband's political and spiritual condition, well up together. What part would William Russell have played in the 'late confusions'? What would his reaction have been to this rebellion, as

[79] Letter XXI, ibid., pp. 38–40: 39–40. See also Birch, *Life of Tillotson*, p. 122.

one who, in the run up to the Rye House plot, counselled moderation yet acknowledged the Duke of Monmouth as a political leader? Russell pointedly remembers her husband's place in the former design as 'no more than (my own Lord confessed) talk'. And although that talk might have canvassed 'a remedy' it was not conspiracy. Talk is not thought, she implies, and takes the opportunity to reiterate that he reached his own opinions on politics (that is on the legitimacy of resistance to the monarch) rather than copying those of others (such as Burnet or Tillotson). She attempts to imagine his decision in 1685; between his heart and his 'directive faculty', she finds 'his part an hard one'. Implicit in the letter is a question: had he lived on, would it have been only to be lost after this rebellion, as so many others were? Ultimately, she does return to her spiritual condition, only to diagnose herself as a 'slave to sense'—to memory, political excitement, the imagination of what might have happened had her husband lived. The letter ends with spiritual discipline acknowledged, though under the sign of a kind of rejection 'that mere philosophy' she finds nothing but a sham. Political events are registered in a spiritual language, yes, but memory, religious thought, and present political events are bound together.

Mixing political and spiritual writing, Russell's letters invite a re-appraisal of the meaning of their publication. Fitzwilliam saved her letters and continued with the plan for publication although it was clear that they were not solely pious in their concerns; if he began with the model of an exchange of letters between the martyr's widow and her spiritual counsellor to be used as an index of Whig piety, he and Russell were soon heavily involved in a correspondence in which spiritual questions ran into political, and memory was mixed with meditation, with the present, and with analysis of political action.[80] It seems that Russell's and Fitzwilliam's plan for publication must have acknowledged that, far from being the apotheosis of Rachel as an index of William Russell's virtue, the letters offered vivid explorations of the question of conspiracy. Consistent in that they always approach politics from a carefully situated point of view which allows her husband's conduct to be presented as legitimate resistance, the letters as we have them engage the reader with the political agency of the widow, putting before us the reactions and actions of a woman whose husband was part martyr, part

---

[80] Schwoerer, *Rachel Russell*, *passim*.

political icon for the future. Although we do not have them in a form edited by Russell and Fitzwilliam for publication, it is hard to imagine an editorial process which would completely remove Rachel Russell's powerful evocations of the political implications of her situation. In writing as she did to Fitzwilliam, increasingly canvassing political affairs in the form of news which sometimes led to political speculation, Rachel Russell was quite consciously building up a corpus of letters in which her writing persona is poised between the spirit and the world.

The correspondence of the early years of Russell's widowhood (as her response to Monmouth's rebellion indicates) circles her husband. It is here that we can see the myth of the patriot beginning to be woven from events subsequent to his death; he becomes the phantom actor of Russell's speculations. The object of Rachel Russell's mourning also permits her to canvass political events and causes by referring back to her husband's role and re-imagining him reacting to current events. He is the pretext of her canvassing of the right course of political action, the imagined actor substituting for herself, whose fantasized choices render vivid both his memory and the contemporary maze of ethical problems presented to the living who meditated on Monmouth's acts. The point is not that Russell's vivid re-animation of her husband is cynical, but rather that she has preserved him as a significant figure in events. As this letter testifies, he is both a political figure whose reactions might be imagined by both writer and reader and, inevitably, a figure through whom Russell can present her own views.

There is no doubt that, in these letters as in her—ostensibly—more 'public' publication of her husband's speech, endorsements of texts as 'his', and letters to Charles II, Russell is putting her piety and grief to work in the world. Producing herself explicitly in relation to Fitzwilliam's disciplinary demands, Russell also usurps authority through her very inability to achieve spiritual submission. Many, even most, of the letters written after William Russell's execution are linked by their reference back to that point, and this is Russell's consistent point of recourse in the opening sequence of letters to Fitzwilliam. These are, accordingly, marked by a dynamics of power over Russell's struggle for spiritual submission.[81] If, as Lois Schwoerer suggests, the letters record

---

[81] The correspondents dance back and forth between the superiority of the claims of the spirit and the urgency of the world, as Russell meets Fitzwilliam's advocacy of submission to

a life of piety it is also a life of striving for Christian comfort rather than its achievement: she is God's 'murmering servant'; she doubts providence, writing to Fitzwilliam, 'I will imitate you and not call it chance.'[82] As late as Christmas 1692 Russell measured herself as wanting against the ten commandments; in relation to the first commandment she finds herself 'highly discontented, or murmuring at his dispensations of afliction to solicitous for help from men not hartily enof blessing & thanking my god for either blessings or pleasures of life, or his fatherly chastisemants'. She finds it hard, too, to 'keep my self intent' in religious observance.[83] Such assertions, while not to be taken at face value, are indicative of her opinion of her spiritual state.

By 1687 Russell's letters to Fitzwilliam seem to have fallen into the pattern of an account of her spiritual state either blending into or more abruptly followed by a final, vivid, section on political news with which the letters end—a familiar pattern in letters of the period but in this case made significant by the persons involved and events as they unfolded.[84] Fitzwilliam shared her passion for news; she tells him 'your curiosity, Doctor, is sure blameless' and promises to send him the Gazette.[85] Correspondence from the Princess of Orange, discussing 'the sad misfortunes you have had', signals that under the political climate of intrigue and political pressure of summer 1687 the meaning of Russell's tragic loss was, once again, a live political issue. The latter months of 1688 see her agog for news and clearly deeply involved in the circulation of political material. In October 1688 she writes to Fitzwilliam that 'things are coming about ... above any expectation you or I had when we last met'; she also tells him that 'The *Anatomy of an Equivalent* is the newest good paper I know; I have been lent it only to read, and have it not any more.'[86]

God's will with agreement and reminders of the specific causes of her worldly suffering. See e.g. RR to Fitzwilliam, 1 Apr. 1687, Letter XLV, *Letters*, pp. 76–8: 77.

[82] 13 June 1687, Letter XLVII, ibid., p. 79; 21 July 1687, Letter L, ibid., pp. 82–3: 82.

[83] See Uncatalogued Box 2, MSS Duke of Devonshire at Chatsworth; 'confessions', or lists of faults, made on paper folded into strips, shaped like folded bookmarks.

[84] RR promises to 'wait with a quiet submission', but ends with a political round-up. 1 Apr. 1687, Letter XLV, *Letters*, pp. 77–8: 77.

[85] See e.g. Oct. 1687, Letter LI, ibid., pp. 84–5; 22 Oct. 1687, Letter LII, ibid., p. 87.

[86] 7 Oct. 1688, Letter LXXI, ibid., pp. 108–9: 109.

On 16 November 1688 Russell writes, 'I have rambled the more, because one is in prudence confined not to talk of matters one is strangely bent to be talking of.' A note to the printed letter here adds: 'The Prince of Orange now being landed; his declaration; the King's answering it; the association; desertion of the King's troops; some of the Prince's friends taken; petitions for a parliament, with other circumstances at that time, must fill all minds with apprehensions and anxiety.'[87]

The collected volume of Russell's letters, first published in 1773, traces a path from a time before the crisis when her children were born, to a present, after the Glorious Revolution, in which conspiracy has been reshaped as legitimate political activity. The issue of how Rachel Russell's letters came to take this shape and her reputation and that of her husband are linked. We have seen the highly successful way Russell used her status as pious widow to shape her own reputation and that of her husband so that, in 1688, they were both ready for recuperation by Williamite society. To an extent the very blankness of William Russell was an aid, as well as a problem, in retrospective recuperation. What Rachel Russell's own claims to sincerity, personal spiritual struggles, and wifely obedience enabled her to do was to fashion her husband as not treasonable, not a conspirator, but a believer in resistance theory—the perfect Protestant martyr to be taken up by the Prince of Orange. The patriot-martyr of the nineteenth century was the result of further adumbrations of this idea, but Rachel Russell's work in making and maintaining the effigy allowed this to happen. Her claims to sincerity, her own status as noble martyr, paradoxically both endorse and exceed those of her husband. But the thing which made his creation and invention possible was the success—hardly private—of her persona of pious privacy.

Although Russell's letters were understood as politicized both at the time of writing and when they were published a century later, her status as a pious widow is habitually isolated from her acquisition of political power. For all his promises of an exemplary volume in which he would administer to her 'spiritual estate', Fitzwilliam did not edit the correspondence, though her letters to him were 'by him returned in one packet to her Ladyship, with his desire they might be printed for the

[87] 16 Nov. 1688, Letter LXXV, ibid., pp. 111–12.

benefit of the public'.[88] They were amongst her papers at her death, forty years after her husband's execution, and found by her estate manager, who added others. When they were printed in 1773 piety and politics were still bound together, as Rachel Russell's virtue was to counter the slurs in Dalrymple's *Memoirs*. Yet she is seen as the pious, not the political, widow.

Rachel Russell's excursion into the domain of publicity rested on a virtue much less assailable or ambiguous than that of Anne Halkett. It was very successful. Time—in the guise of the Glorious Revolution of 1688—turned out to be on Russell's side in making William the traitor into William the patriot. Yet without the groundwork of the 1680s and her tireless textual efforts there would have been no carefully prepared martyr ready for his niche. However, oppositional claims to personal and political virtue were always open to dispute. It is evident in the way Halkett structures her memoir and in Russell's use and circulation of material associated with her husband that they anticipated that their accounts might be questioned. Both writers evidently imagined hostile readers and knew that the very assertion of virtue might lead to a sceptical reception. The hostility anticipated by such self-justifying and self-authenticating writing was, of course, ready to hand, articulated in the scandalous fictions which sought to expose political and personal virtue—fictions like Aphra Behn's *Love Letters Between a Nobleman and his Sister*. How can we trace the responsive relationship between claims of virtue and authenticity and their exposure?

TRUE RELATIONS: CONSPIRACY, FEMININITY, AND DISCLOSURE IN APHRA BEHN'S *LOVE-LETTERS BETWEEN A NOBLEMAN AND HIS SISTER*

That a reader might not believe their version of events was a hazard of which Anne Halkett and Rachel Russell were painfully aware. The very strategies they used to underwrite their own virtue and that of their subjects were likely to invite the reader to find deceit where honesty was asserted and apparently guaranteed by the use of an intimate testimony

---

[88] Fitzwilliam to RR, 12 Aug. 1686, Letter XXXVIII, ibid., pp. 65–7: 65; John Sellwood to John, Duke of Bedford, dated 1748: ibid., p. lxv.

and genre. *Love-Letters Between a Nobleman and his Sister*, a text which evidently attacks those disputing the Stuart succession and their rhetoric, offers a commentary on such texts and their persuasive mixture of assertions of virtue, pathos, witness, and memory. Taking the events of summer 1683 and the Rye House plot as its starting point, Behn's fiction famously developed with events. For Behn, the fact that the reader might, in Ros Ballaster's words, 'wilfully misinterpret' was a powerful part of political representation.[89] Accordingly, *Love-Letters* figures anti-Stuart politics in complex correspondences between sexual and political disloyalty. How does *Love-Letters* engage the Whig rhetoric of authenticity?

Reproaching her lover-to-be and brother-in-law, Philander, Sylvia complains that in his mind she is 'huddled up confusedly with your graver business of State, and almost lost in the ambitious crowd?'[90] She continues:

> Is it not enough, oh *Philander*, for my eternal unquiet, and undoing, to know that you are Married and cannot therefore be intirely mine; is not this enough, oh cruel *Philander*? but you must espouse a fatal cause, too, more pernicious than that of Matrimony, and more destructive to my repose: oh give me leave to reason with you ... what is it, oh my Charming Brother then, that you set up for, is it Glory? oh mistaken lovely Youth, that Glory is but a glittering light that flashes for a moment, and then it disappears; 'tis a false Bravery, that will bring an eternal blemish upon your honest fame and house; render your honourable name, hated, detested, and abominable in story to after Ages; a Traytor! the worst of Titles, the most inglorious and shameful; what has the King, our good, our Gracious Monarch, done to *Philander*?[91]

Sylvia goes on: 'oh! what a pity 'tis, unhappy young man, thy education was not near the King'.[92] Had it been so, she implies, he would have himself been touched by the glances from the 'royal forgiving sufferer' whose 'piercing, wondrous eyes' would beget 'a trembling Adoration'. That Sylvia is at this point still a virgin insures the sincerity of her political sentiments but, even though she later becomes sexually professionalized, a seducer of 'prey', her political opinions remain constant.

Using Sylvia as an as yet relatively politically healthy mouthpiece, the letter redescribes 'loyalty' to Monmouth and the republican cause in

---

[89] Ballaster, *Seductive Forms*, p. 69.   [90] *Love-Letters*, p. 38.
[91] Ibid., pp. 39–40.   [92] Ibid., p. 40.

terms which—even though they appear to be sympathetic because spoken by the lover and political intimate of one of the conspirators—nevertheless systematically describe motivation in pro-Stuart terms. Thus, as Sylvia enquires about Philander's possible motivation she offers to him, and to the reader, words which relentlessly shape Philander's politics in Tory terms as self-interest, ambition, desire for money and glory. Philander himself is given the same terms to use when he writes back with a strange politico-sexual fantasy of Sylvia as an erotic Venus paraded through the conquered streets. Simultaneously, the rhetoric Sylvia uses to describe Charles II is significant. Pro-Stuart rhetoric is grounded in the king's body, and enlists the power of Charles I the martyr to buttress his son's dubious virtue. The often priapically satirized Charles II is here presented in terms of suffering justified by his exile. The way in which Behn is challenging the values encoded in political rhetoric becomes a little clearer when we contrast the victimized body of Charles II with the appearance of Philander as Tarquin with which I began this chapter.

'[J]ust such I fancy'd fam'd *Lucretia* was, when *Tarquin* first beheld her': so Philander describes a newly desired love in Book II, and in so doing casts himself as the rapacious Tarquin. As we have seen, the story of the founding the Roman republic was a violently contested example throughout the seventeenth century. Making Philander describe himself as Tarquin, Behn ascribes to the republican supporters of Monmouth the political and sexual slurs associated with the Roman tyrants. In doing so she challenges the political rhetoric which saw Charles's sceptre and 'prick' as 'of a length' (like tyrannical Tarquin, ruled by lust), and annexes for that king the suffering status claimed in Whig martyrologies. If the method Behn uses to transvalue political vocabulary reminds us sharply of Lucy Hutchinson's opposition to Restoration rhetoric, it also alerts us to Behn's engagement of classical myths in a porno-political discrediting of anti-Stuart conspiracy. Thus, Behn not only challenges the fraternal rhetoric of republicanism by focusing on a case of a republican brother committing incest with his wife's sister while, as the fiction is at pains to remind us, his own wife Myrtilla is said to be committing adultery with Cesario (the narrative's version of the Duke of Monmouth); she also uses the sexual charge of classical myth to attack the sexual and political morals of Cesario's supporters.

Telling his friend 'I love!—I languish, and am dying—for a new Beauty' for 'a new affair of Gallantry', Philander describes to Octavio his first sight of the new beauty he desires, vulnerable in sinisterly 'gloomy' shade:[93]

> Thus she lay! A smiling melancholy drest her Eyes, which she had fixt upon the Rivulet, near which I found her lying: just such I fancy'd fam'd *Lucretia* was, when *Tarquin* first beheld her, nor was the Royal Ravisher more inflam'd than I! or readier for th'incounter. Alone she was … [94]

In sexual terms Philander's self-identification with Tarquin makes explicit the rapacious current of his libertine identity. The political work of the analogue is more complex. By identifying Tarquin and Philander Behn recalls the Lucretia myth from what might seem like its obvious place in republican ideology to make the opposer of the Stuarts the tyrant-rapist. Behn's observation of Philander anatomizes the seducer's 'easie' (and faithless) 'heart'.[95] Yet her close attention to Philander's faults as a Whig, a libertine, and a traitor engages the reader closely to his seducer's specular, spying, shifting perspective. In Books I and II Philander's letters dualistically both immerse us in a conspiratorial world of seducer and traitor and provide us with the tools to know him as false and build a distance between the reading self and the seducer. The reader is offered the pleasure of intimate and affecting narrative *and* the pleasure of political condemnation.

Philander's desire for the nymph he characterizes as Lucretia continues *Love-Letters'* use of classical myth in porno-political satire. The name of the nymph is, in fact, Calista. Calisto was one of Diana's nymphs, raped by Jove in female dress (we recall, I think, the episode of Philander's cross-dressing in Book I).[96] And once again the girl is a wife and a sister: she is the sister of Octavio to whom Philander writes so excitedly of his 'new affair'.[97] Why might Behn select the name Calista?

---

[93] Ibid., pp. 171–2.   [94] Ibid., p. 174.   [95] Ibid., p. 174 n.

[96] Harriette Andreadis, *Sappho in Early Modern England: Female Same-Sex Literary Erotics 1550–1714* (Chicago: University of Chicago Press, 2001), pp. 154–76; Valerie Traub, *The Renaissance of Lesbianism in Early Modern England* (Cambridge: Cambridge University Press, 2002), pp. 254–7; Ros Ballaster, ' "The Vices of Old Rome Revived": Representations of Female Same-Sex Desire in Seventeenth and Eighteenth Century England', in *Volcanoes and Pearl Divers: Essays in Lesbian Feminist Studies*, ed. Suzanne Raitt (Binghamton: Harrington Park Press, 1995), pp. 13–36.

[97] *Love-Letters*, p. 175.

In 1674 John Crowne's *Calisto: or, The Chaste Nimph* was a masque at court. The story of Calisto was that she was a nymph of Diana who was made pregnant by Jove while he was disguised as a woman. All the performers in Crowne's *Calisto* were female, though there were male dancers, foremost among whom was the Duke of Monmouth. So Calisto was played by Princess Mary, and Henrietta Wentworth played Jove, who attempts to rape her. Even if Crowne was, as he claimed, truly trying to 'write a clean, decent and inoffensive Play, on the story of a Rape' and same-sex disguise, by 1683 the masque seemed to allude prophetically to the subsequent lives of its actors and dancers—and this seems to be its appeal for Behn.[98] By the time Behn was writing, Henrietta Wentworth (Jove) had long been the Duke of Monmouth's mistress so Behn was able to use the myth and the memory of the masque in several ways. Thus, Cesario's mistress is called Hermione and the name of Calista given to this chaste and loyal nymph seduced by Philander.

Behn used the names Tarquin and Lucretia to wrest control of a political exemplar, but the name Calista would have spoken scandal and politics simultaneously to contemporary readers, and Behn uses its scandalous power. That she does so alerts us to the fact that the real-life counterparts of her story, in so far as *Love-Letters* truly follows their role in anti-Stuart conspiracy and sexual adventure, were all newsworthy and had public exposure as sexual-political agents. Let us look, briefly, at the tangled sexual and political affairs of the figures on which Behn's fiction focuses. Myrtilla, the wife of Lord Grey, was said to have been having an affair with the Duke of Monmouth. In *A True Relation of a Strange Apparition* the apparition appears to Lady Grey when her husband—Lord Grey of Werke—is not around. The apparition insists that Monmouth is not of the royal blood, and the reader is reminded that when it appears she is alone with Monmouth at 'about 11'; as Lady Grey says, '*We are alone*.'[99] As early as 1681 Samuel Pepys copied this out, and Behn probably knew it, but this was one satire among many.[100]

---

[98] John Crowne, *Calisto: or, The Chaste Nimph. The Late Masque at Court* (London, 1673), A1ᵛ; Andreadis, *Sappho*, p. 169; Ballaster, ' "The Vices of Old Rome" '.

[99] *A True Relation of a Strange Apparition which Appear'd to ye Lady Grey Commanding Her to Deliver a Message to His Grace the Duke of Monmouth* (London, 1681), pp. 1, 2.

[100] Ibid.; BL MS Add. 38849, fo. 108.

While Myrtilla's infidelity clearly has political resonance in *Love-Letters*, the treatment of the twin figures of Cesario (keyed to the Duke of Monmouth) and Hermione, his mistress, is more significant. In December 1684 one correspondent wrote, shocked, that Henrietta Wentworth had gone back with Monmouth to Brussels, '& consequently bid farewell to all modesty'; now 'noe Woman of quality or Credit will converse with them'.[101] Behn follows the lovers abroad and back, to the rebellion. In Book III of *Love-Letters* the first-person counterpoint of Philander and Sylvia is dissolved, and we are in the hands of the narrator—or various narrators. Throughout *Love-Letters* we attend to the gendered and sexualized voices of the intra-diegetic lovers. The sex of the narrator in *Love-Letters*, though, is not disclosed.[102] Yet we can notice that narrator's emphasis on knowledge, reason, and control as opposed to pathos and empathy. The denouement of the story of Cesario, Hermione, and the rebellion begins by, our narrator tells us, being told to Sylvia by Brilljard.[103] In this section we find a powerful parody of rhetorics and modes of political authentication.[104] Exemplarity is significant here. Enigmatically, Monmouth is compared to Elizabeth I while Henrietta Wentworth is compared to the sorcerers Medea and Circe, and she herself describes a box as magically worked by the Sybils. Later, Roman honour is invoked to indicate Cesario's failure and Philander's cowardice. Every paragraph flaunts its relationship to other authenticatory texts or discourses—Roman history, *Gerusalemme liberata*, even, perhaps, the Bible. However, crucial to this section is an explicitly theatrical scene in which Cesario's future is prophesied.

Ferguson takes Cesario, faltering in political purpose and distracted by love, to be 'shown' his future. As Cesario watches a semi-allegorical vision, a rock splits in two to reveal a 'magnificent Apartment'. This in turn gives way to a bower or garden which then reveals a world of political business. All this is revealed to Cesario in the vault under some decayed waterworks—the very scene in which the supposed revelations take place is a decayed example of artifice. Parodying the

---

[101] Bernard Skelton to Sir Richard Bulstrode, BL MS Add. 38847, fos. 122, 123.

[102] Compare first-person narrative in *A New Vision of the Kady Gr—S, Concerning her Sister, the Lady Henrietta Berkeley, In a Letter to Madam Fan*— [1682(?)] in *The Works of Aphra Behn*, ed. Todd, II, 462–4.

[103] *Love-Letters*, p. 396.   [104] Ibid., pp. 397–405.

prophetic visions of *Macbeth* and the troubling bowers of Spenserian romance, this scene uses the stage vocabulary of the court masque combined with the potentially authenticating but more often comically disclosing theatrical use of 'openings' on to spaces. The reader recognizes black magic as theatre and rhetoric—visions, *coups de théâtre*, stereotypical scenes persuading away from love and towards honour—as motivated rather than true language. Perhaps we even remember the masque *Calisto*. Certainly, this material, related by Brilljard, leaves almost no kind of truth claim unquestioned, no kind of speech or writing unparodied. The truth claims of Cesario are as false as his visions; he lacks even the ability to reason.

At the end of *Love-Letters* some figures are returned to history and some continue to live in fiction. Thus, Monmouth's astrological leanings and superstition (amply attested in his pocket book, found on him after he fled Sedgmoor) are uncannily close to Behn's representations in Book III.[105] Lady Henrietta Wentworth was apparently said to have 'sacrificed her life to her beauty', 'painting so beyond measure that the mercury got into her nerves and killed her'.[106] The harshness of her attack notwithstanding, Behn spares her Hermione this indignity. But, where in life Lady Henrietta Berkeley returned to England, Behn's Sylvia, never a conspirator, exits from history into picaresque. Satirizing Monmouth and his followers by exposing the rhetoric and genres they use, Behn leaves *Love-Letters* without political, sexual, or moral closure; the forensic power of her sexual-political anatomy overrides the pleasures of comedic resolution.

Where, if anywhere, are political truth, trust, and authenticity at the end of *Love-Letters?* In the enigmatic final sentence we find Philander at court 'in as much Splendour as ever, being very well understood by all good men'.[107] If what is described here is in part the falsity of court life

[105] 'Pocket Book of the Duke of Monmouth', BL MS Egerton 1527. See fo. 45, 'pour scavoir si une person sera fidele et sil tendra paroles'; fo. 56ᵛ songs including a pastoral song: 'how blest how innocent | and happy is a country life', reworking Katherine Philips; fo. 70ᵛ notes on war and politics. There are also recipes, prayers, and directions from London to Lady Henrietta Wentworth's home.

[106] Given as from the Savile correspondence as quoted from Elizabeth D'Oyley, and cited in Harold Armitage, *Toddington Tragedy: The Love Story of the Baroness Wentworth and the Duke of Monmouth* (Letchworth: Letchworth Printers, 1940), p. 143.

[107] *Love-Letters*, p. 439.

which permits such strange recuperations it is also, as significantly, the complete dissolution of Whig truth claims. Our narrator knows that Philander kisses the King's hand and is understood: implicit in this knowledge is that besides being a coward he is, as is known, an informer. If there is anything we can trust it seems to be rational language and what is *not* said. The continuing circuits of deceit are known—he is 'very well understood by all good Men'—but that knowledge cannot be redeemed, 'cashed', or made into language which will pass current.

'A TRICK IN EVERY THING'

That *Love-Letters* so systematically undermines the claims to virtue made by the prose supporting counter-Stuart politics, suggests its place in a wider crisis in language and truth. Finished in 1687, *Love-Letters* might be said to have been produced during a deepening crisis in political rhetoric which had continued through the 1670s and 1680s as conspiracies and counterclaims escalated. Reminding us that the 1680s saw rule without Parliament, James Grantham Turner says that at this point 'political *pornographia* entered its terminal condition'; the condition of porno-political rhetoric was, though, imbricated in contemporary understandings of truth and trust in politics.[108] In 1694 William Wotton wrote:

Men apprehend or suspect a Trick in every Thing that is said to move the Passions of the Auditory in Courts of Judicature or in the *Parliament-House*: They think themselves affronted when such Methods are used in Speaking, as if the Orator could suppose within himself, that they were to be catched by such Baits.[109]

Although critical writing is no doubt right to locate scepticism about eloquence and rhetoric in the drive towards an empirical language of expression, it is evident that the various plots from the mid-1670s to 1688 and—more to the point—plot talk in its highly variegated written and spoken forms of intelligence, information, scandal, rumour,

---

[108] James Grantham Turner, *Libertines and Radicals in Early Modern London: Sexuality, Politics and Literary Culture* (Cambridge: Cambridge University Press, 2002), p. 252.

[109] William Wotton, 'Of Ancient and Modern Eloquence and Poesie', in *Reflections Upon Ancient and Modern Learning* (London, 1694), p. 38.

self-justification, confession, scaffold speech, letter, memoir, scandalous history—had played a specific part in undermining and debasing the rhetoric of truth claims. Certainly, *Love-Letters* makes any crisis of linguistic credibility politically and narratively productive while itself offering only the *body* of the king as a functioning guarantee of truth.

As Todd points out, several of the models Behn might have used were epistolary (*Five Love-letters Written by a Cavalier*, translated by Roger l'Estrange in 1678, or *The Familiar Epistles of Colonel Henry Martin*, published in 1662 and reprinted in 1680), and others were scandalous memoirs. While *Love-Letters* takes up these models of scandalous writing, it also addresses the very genres in which political claims were made in the political world she inhabited. It is clearly true that epistolary fictions offer models both formally and in terms of their exploration of the affective potential of sexual betrayal; yet it is also the case that the very political circles Behn moved in, and the political sphere more generally, was one of circulated manuscripts and print. The political sphere was full of letters, memoirs, and affidavits attesting to political truths and experiences. Thus, the insertion of *Love-Letters* into a literary tradition of the novel can coexist with knowledge that it cohabited with and—importantly—addressed itself to texts like the circulated letters of Rachel Russell, and many other texts asserting political virtue in opposition to the Stuarts. In participating in the drive to represent conspiracy, *Love-Letters* 'exposes' the truth claims of authenticatory political narratives in several ways, but two are important here. First, it trains the reader to be sceptical of the linking of passion and politics in republican rhetoric by repeatedly disclosing that these apparently sincere lovers and conspirators are mere deceivers in love and politics. Secondly, it re-genericizes the confessional letter and memoir as fictional forms: the letters are part of a fiction even as they refer, by key, back to the world. Its attack on the genres it characterizes as belonging to those which oppose the Stuarts both allow the reader the pleasures of responding to an authenticating voice and gives them the pleasure of finding it to be false. It is a consummate critique.

It is hardly surprising that the material written in opposition to Charles II should be in a complex and knowing *generic*, as well as political, relation to that which, like *Love-Letters*, seeks to justify his conduct. Nor is it surprising that a partly disillusioned supporter of the Stuarts, such as Halkett, should also write texts which she intended for circulation, albeit after her death. A writer—and reader—of epistolary political fiction might well be in a position to set the French romances alongside the circulated and printed memoirs of the Restoration. It is here, in Behn's use of sexual and political betrayal as figuring each other, that we can see the connection between authenticatory writing asserting personal virtue and scandalous fiction. We can see, too, the claims to political legitimacy made by those variously excluded from the Stuart settlements (in different ways Halkett and Russell) and the interpretation of such claims to virtue as fraud. Moreover, as we set Russell's claims to virtue against Behn's disclosures, we can see the literary forms used to set positions against one another and—therefore—the oppositional connection of the two positions orchestrated by aesthetic means—by narrative style and form.

Why, then, is Behn's fiction in its current critical configuration so sharply separated from the writings it opposes and ingests? Readers are keenly aware of the political contexts of Behn's *Love-Letters*. Nevertheless, this fiction has been disengaged from a large part of the political and politicized epistolary, memoiristic, 'historical', and even confessional writing which contemporaries must have understood it as responding to, re-genericizing, fictionalizing—and attacking.[110] Part of an answer lies in the depoliticization of female virtue and particularly piety in the processes of textual transmission to which texts such as those of Halkett (as women's memoirs) and Russell's letters (as women's letters) have been subject by earlier editors and by the assumptions about private and public spheres and women's relationship to manuscript, print, politics, and virtue found in some more recent critics. Simultaneously, the potentially isolating taxonomies of the early novel, illuminatingly criticized by Michael McKeon, have penned up *Love-Letters* in a realm of fiction to which it does belong, but which only partly represents the world it inhabited and the texts and ideas to which it responded.[111]

Thus, Behn's *Love-Letters*, Halkett's memoir, and Russell's letters now exist in a condition of separation by critical taxonomy. This separation, even as it does justice to some of their aspects, tends to obscure the way

[110] See Jane Spencer, *Aphra Behn's Afterlife* (Oxford: Oxford University Press, 2000), pp. 3–4.
[111] Michael McKeon, *The Origins of the English Novel* (London: Century Hutchinson, 1987) pp. 1–64 and *passim*.

such texts were locked into combative, yet intimate, critical relations. The separation itself is the effect of other assumptions which have isolated female virtue as a concept and the practice of female piety from the political issues to which these qualities and practices, and the writings they generated, were bound in the mid-seventeenth century. The recontextualization of the writings of Halkett and Russell offered here gives some sense, I hope, of the discursive significance of gender in the writing of conspiracy in the Restoration. Not only do sexual relations figure politics, but the claims of women specifically to virtue—at times personal, at times political—participate in the striving for legitimacy and dominance in the political sphere that was conducted in letters, memoirs, fiction, and all the other literary genres in the 1670s and 1680s. More significantly, the gendered claims to virtue in the texts I have chosen illuminate the way that conspiracy, already bound to a hyper-personalized sense of virtue, precipitates women's virtue in the public sphere as important capital. The letters of Russell and the writings of Halkett are hardly wholly private but are rather part of what Delarivier Manley describes as the 'hieroglyphics' of fame, where fame is rumour, feminine good fame, and political reputation. It is not simply that letters and memoirs by women as well as men participate in the battle to possess political 'truth', but that an acknowledgement of this allows us to begin to qualify and reinterpret the political and porno-political genres and vocabularies of the Restoration.

Epochs Revisited

This has been a study of the specific locations of women in the political languages of the early modern period. It has argued that attention to the uses of language in this period—theoretical, satirical, forensic, imaginative—can tell us more than we knew before about women's relationship to politics in early modern England. Part of this claim is, and remains, that the political formations of the seventeenth century repay study outside the teleological paradigms implied by contract theory or the 'rise of the bourgeois individual'. But consider this—a newspaper commentary on delegates at a political conference in the UK (the Liberal Democrats, as it happens) in 2004:

Many of them had in their possession the Orange Book, a work of Lib Dem rethinking so controversial that its launch meeting here was cancelled. People hissed when it was mentioned. I noticed that people reading it had hidden their copies inside Richard Desmond's *Hot Asian Babes* Magazine.[1]

If Simon Hoggart's use of colonial desire and 'race' to supply comedy is only partly familiar from the political attacks we have discussed, his mixing of politics, gender, and sexuality sound clearer echoes. And the use of innuendo is strikingly similar to the material we have examined. We might think of Thomas Edwards striving to render Milton's *Doctrine and Discipline of Divorce* a blueprint for scandal; or Bargrave's use of Christina of Sweden as sexualized evidence of religious and political conspiracy; or Aphra Behn's attack on conspiracy in *Love-Letters*.

Clearly, then, it would also be possible to consider seventeenth-century political rhetoric diachronically, even teleologically, as feeding into the scandalous political rhetoric of the present. Certainly, old vocabularies die hard, or linger on—in the great repositories of news

[1] Simon Hoggart, 'A clear message, carefully amended', *Guardian*, 21 Sept. 2004, p. 2.

and political satire. Equally certainly, there might be as much to gain from connecting Hoggart's political rhetoric to the social and political formations from which it can be understood as in some attenuated sense derived, as by separating the two periods as this study has done. In teasing out the patterns of language and thought in a particular period, rather than tracing a teleology, I have been trying to locate and explore the specific ways in which early modern English writing articulated women's relationship to politics. In order to respond to the overdetermined historiographical stories of the Renaissance, and sometimes equally overdetermined narratives of women's lot, in which the past is used mainly to point towards the present, the project has framed or reframed its object of study broadly epochally. It has also expanded the textual materials considered to crucially illuminate (if not always necessarily to constitute) political thought beyond those of the canon of political theory. There are, as I have argued, limits to the illuminating power of narratives of progress or regress, improvement or decline, in women's fortunes. The allegorical and mythic power and so also the problems of teleological thinking are evident—whether about the past, the Civil War, women, or politics. However, as Hoggart's exhausted tropes remind us, epochal thinking presents its own problems; is the division between epochs distinct enough to give a generalization a reasonable chance of expressing some qualified kind of truth?

For the purposes of this study, as should be clear, the early modern political sphere, though possessed of specific characteristics, can as a timespan be only roughly demarcated. Such a measure is only partly productive. Mary Wollestonecraft's political thinking is clarified as that of modernity when it set against Brilliana Harley's. At the same time, it is also the case that Catherine Macaulay's historical writing of the mid-eighteenth century offered both an innovatively 'objective' (modern?) history of the Civil War and used examples in ways familiar from our period. The situation is not clear-cut. Simon Hoggart's metaphors, too, alert us to the rising power, pervasiveness, and currency of colonial language from the earliest encounters, and the intersection of gender and colonial writing supplies another—epochally distinct?—terrain of politicized expression. Moreover, though the epochs offered are inconsistent and overlapping, explicitly and implicitly epochal thinking permeates literary and historical writing on the period I have been discussing. A Big Bang Enlightenment can be understood as starting with Descartes's discussion of thought in 1649; Habermas and others following him track a transformation in those inherently elusive concepts and states of being, public and private, beginning with the Glorious Revolution. And as any reader will know, another kind of modernity can be said to begin with 1492.

In the long run, modernity is constituted by changes in economic, political, and literary culture which mean that, amongst other things, women are widely, though not universally, understood to be political subjects. The mid-seventeenth century, or, roughly 1620 to 1685 (the short run) shows conflicting, contradictory and uneven tendencies. Even so, in researching women's relationship to politics, early modern ways of thinking about, expressing, understanding and imagining women's place and lack of it in a political world can, if not unequivocally, be traced. While this might in part be a product of the critical eye (of, as it were, reading for difference), the wealth of material constitutes substantial supporting data. The claim this book makes, then, is that rich textual evidence suggests that there were, in mid-seventeenth-century England, traceable and distinct ways in which women were put in relation to the political. Certainly, the political contours and texture of such writing and thinking become clear in broad comparison with later writing. Yet it is also the case that some shifting determinants of social and political being were important in the later, distinct, constitution of women as political participants. It is striking how often the memory of the Civil War, particularly, or seventeenth-century political writing, is invoked as important to nineteenth-century and late modern political narratives—of feminism, political theory, freedom. The role of women in the Civil War and the place of seventeenth-century political theorists in marking out the contractual terrain of the modern are important to historians, literary critics, and political theorists delineating the problematics of a modernity which, though different, can be understood as having roots in the period covered here.

To return to the question of epochs, specifically the epochal status of the early modern political imaginary. This book's central premise is that we need to look again at the ways in which politics, writing, and women are related in seventeenth-century England; its central argument is that we can trace out more about those relationships by looking at a wide range of genres and kinds of writing. The stakes of such a study must be both what it can tell us about its objects, narrowly conceived, and how attention to differences can illuminate the modern itself, certainly how such attention can contribute to clarifying the way the past presents itself to us. For the Civil War period, particularly, myths are bound up with how we come to 'primary' materials. Indeed, certain moments, transformations in the movement of capital and the understanding of self and state in the mid-seventeenth century, have status as constitutive of changes leading to modernity in ways that are simultaneously, intertwinedly, mythic and historical. For example, the meanings of the regicide, the Levellers, of Civil War women prophets are constituted by a web of mythic and historicist thinking where that pair can appear to the reader as opposed, or mutually undermining, or mutually reinforcing. In the terrain this book covers myths and histories are neither separate nor, always, distinctly motivated. Accordingly, this study has attempted to respond to the mythic as well as the specific contours of seventeenth-century women's relationship to politics. It has responded to the questions of how to approach the textual the articulation of political relationships, and the later uses of those texts, in two ways. In method, this study attempts to trace out the circumstances of specific groups of texts and, at times, to rethink the movements by which they have found (or lost) a place in literary, political, and historical study. In the analysis of the textual evidence offered by a range of genres it teases out the language (implicit, evident, discreet, overt, literal and figurative) which put those exemplary subjects—women—in relation to politics. *Conspiracy and Virtue* is a study of writing in an epoch when language both articulates and produces particular, yet fluid, formations of thought about women and politics—but also a study of a period whose writings, because of paradoxical relationships to modernity, remain a terrain where the modern is disputed.

Index